Jordan Lee Harding

American House
Domestic Architecture in the USA

American House
Domestic Architecture in the USA
General Editor: Jeffery W. Howe

Batsford

Produced by

PRC Publishing Ltd
64 Brewery Road
London N7 9NT

A member of **Chrysalis** Books plc

Published in 2002 by

B T Batsford
64 Brewery Road
London N7 9NT
www.batsford.com

A member of **Chrysalis** Books plc

© 2002 PRC Publishing Ltd.

ISBN 0 7134 8796 8

A CIP catalogue record for this book is available from the British Library.

Printed and bound in China for the publishers

The general editor and publisher would like to thank the authors for their contributions to this book.

Tom O'Gorman is a Chicago writer and editor at *The World of Hibernia Magazine*. He is the author of *Park Life, the Summer of 1977 at Comiskey Park, A History of the Irish Fellowship Club of Chicago*, and, most recently, *New Spaces From Salvage*. He also writes for *Town and Country* magazine and is a member of the Irish Georgian Society.

Doreen Ehrlich is a professional writer and lecturer with over twenty-five years experience. Her many previously published works include a range of books on art and architecture including *Frank Lloyd Wright Glass, The Bauhaus, Henry Moore*, and titles in the *Frank Lloyd Wright at a Glance* series.

Abby Moor is currently working toward her Ph.D in the History of Design. She has previously published several books on Frank Lloyd Wright and two monographs on topical issues in the history of architecture, as well as several articles for journals. She also works as an editor and lecturer.

Following a career as a magazine journalist **Sandra Forty** has published books on the history of art and has contributed to books on architecture.

CONTENTS

"Mid pleasures and palaces though we may roam,
Be it ever so humble there's no place like home!"

From the 1823 opera *Clari, the Maid of Milan*
by John Howard Payne (1791–1852)

Americans have long had a profound attachment to their homes, which is not surprising for a nation of immigrants. Symbols of security and identity, the connotations of home and house, have evolved with the history of the country, reflecting changes in society and technology. "Home Sweet Home" was one of the most popular songs ever written, and the boyhood home of John Howard Payne, the author, has been made into a museum. Whether castle or log cabin, houses provide shelter and define our private spaces, but also offer a public face to the world and represent our values. The outer clothing of style is very distinctive, and provides a rich index to the values of individuals and broadly held cultural ideals. Homes fulfill and embody our psychological and spiritual needs as well as our physical requirements.

As a survey of American domestic architecture, this book is intended to serve several purposes: firstly, a history of the development of American hous-

Right: Rowan estate, Federal Hill, KY, 1818. After visiting his cousins here, Stephen Foster was inspired to write the song "My Old Kentucky Home."

es and, by implication, American social history and building technology; secondly, a guidebook to assist in the identification of the style of individual buildings, based on historical examples of typical houses; thirdly, a travel guide to regional monuments of interesting architecture; and finally, a guide to the possibilities of architecture. By showing what has been created before, these houses may inspire new builders to construct their own dream houses.

This book contains over 600 photographs, the majority of which were taken by the general editor over a twenty-year period, enhanced by a similar number of drawings. Ground plans are provided for many houses to show the layout of interior spaces. This extraordinary wealth of images, illustrating different periods and varieties of American houses, is intended to give a detailed portrayal of American building, from mansions to ordinary houses. Clusters of drawings illustrate key features which help to identify the different housing styles and construction. An illustrated glossary at the end explains technical terms, and there are brief biographies of many of the important figures in the history of American building.

Below: "Home Sweet Home" historical site; this is the reputed childhood home of John Howard Payne, author of the song (1822). It is a seventeenth century house at 14 James Lane, Easthampton, NY.

Organization of the Book

A general introduction sketches the overall history of American houses, and the forces that shaped them. Subsequent chapters examine the development of American domestic architecture in greater detail, from the earliest dwellings of native American peoples *(Chapter 1)*, to the most recent contemporary experiments *(Chapter 6)*. Ordinary, or vernacular, housing is presented as well as "high-style" architect-designed buildings, to present as complete a picture of the range of housing as possible.

In addition to surveying Native American housing, the first chapter defines the nature of pre-industrial, vernacular architecture, and contrasts it with developments after the coming of the railroads. The development of colonial housing in the seventeenth and eighteenth centuries is presented in Chapter 2, including English, Dutch, Scandinavian, German, and Spanish traditions. The third chapter investigates the first European Revival styles of the early nineteenth century, from Classicism to medieval revivals. The panoply of Victorian revivalism is the subject of Chapter 4, represented by such extraordinary houses as Olana, the Frederick Church home in the Hudson River valley. Chapter 5 explores the new range of eclectic revivals in the late nineteenth and early twentieth centuries. This was the period of pioneering Modernist experiments in the work of Frank Lloyd Wright and Gustav Stickley. Wright and Stickley grew out of the Arts and Crafts tradition, which stressed artistic creation. This was also the era of the first mass-produced, mail-order homes, such as those made by the Aladdin company, which promised that they would be "built in a day." The final chapter surveys the range of houses created in the modern age, from mass-housing developments such as Levittown to the bold experiments of Postmodernism and beyond.

The Significance of Style

Architectural style is the primary focus of this book, since it is one of the most visible signs of historical and cultural values. The term "style" refers to the consistent qualities and features that link different works together into groups. The history of style in American housing is as complex and rich as the history of the nation and its people. There is no single American style of architecture, nor has there ever been. Different immigrant groups and individuals have adapted their own national traditions,

Left: Parson Capen House, 1 Howlett Street, Topsfield, MA, 1683. This is one of the original prototypes for the so-called garrison colonial house.

Above: Calvert Vaux (1824–1895) and Frederic E. Church (1826–1900): Church home, "Olana," Olana, NY, 1870. Olana reflects Church's love of the picturesque and exoticism.

and many have borrowed or combined stylistic traditions to create hybrid designs that may confound the architectural historian. In the heyday of eclecticism, about 1865–1930, the entire gamut of historical styles was revived at one point or another. In many cases, the style chosen was meant to signify the allegiances or aspirations of the homeowner. The castle built for Potter and Berthe Palmer in Chicago in 1885 was clearly intended to identify them as part of the new mercantile nobility. In some cases, however, styles were freely combined, and it can be very challenging to identify which style a particular house represents.

Stylistic labels are frequently associated with value judgments. When making a conscious choice, Americans have tended to pick revival styles on the basis of moral values attributed to them. Thomas Jefferson felt that Classical architecture promoted clear thinking and civic virtues, and so was the style most suited for the new republic. Exotic styles appealed to a spirit of adventure and discovery, reminding world travelers such as Frederick Church of favorite places and stimulating the imaginations of those who had not been to these far-off lands. However, borrowing styles from European sources was increasingly viewed

Above: William Levitt (1907–1994) and Alfred Levitt (1894–1991): Levittown, Long Island, NY, c. 1947. General view of a typical street.

Above: Garrison colonial developer house, with aluminum siding, Waltham, MA, c. 1960s.

as inauthentic by more avant-garde architects and clients. Champions of twentieth century Modernism argued that the new style marked a complete break with the past, and signified a return to fundamental principles of architecture. The very concept of style was thought to be obsolete, since the method of Modernism was thought to be as true and as inescapable as the scientific method. In the latter part of the twentieth century, Postmodernism challenged that idea, and the various forms of Modernism have taken their place among the historical development of styles.

Visiting Historic Homes

Visiting historic homes can be the highlight of a trip, or even the occasion for one. Numerous historic homes included in this book are open to the public. Some are only open during special seasons, however, so be sure to check ahead. For visiting very special houses, such as Fallingwater or Taliesin, it is advisable to make advance reservations. There are also many examples of private homes in this book, and while it is perfectly permissible to gaze with admiration upon them from a public street, it is only courteous to respect the homeowner's privacy.

How to Research an Old Home

This book should be useful to homeowners or prospective buyers who may want to research the history of a house. Exploring the history of one's house can be a fascinating and fulfilling project. Houses touch many areas of history, including the history of crafts, immigration and ethnic history, local and national history, and the social aspirations of the builders and later owners. Understanding your house and its history can give you a glimpse into the simplicity of the colonial past, the understated elegance of the Federalist era of the early republic, the inventiveness of the Victorian era, or the Post-War era of mass housing such as Levittown.

As you begin to explore your home's history, you may want to consider these questions:

Left: Gustav Stickley (1858–1942): Craftsman Farms, 2352 Rte. 10, Parsippany (Morris Plains), NJ, 1911. This log home was intended as the community center for Craftsman Farms, but Stickley moved in when the project did not grow as fast as planned.

- What style is it? Knowing the style will help you place it in its historical period.
- When was the house built? Are there any clues in the materials or techniques that connect it to a specific era?
- Who was the architect, if any? The builder?
- What did the house originally look like? How has it changed over time?
- Who was the original owner or occupant?
- How does the house fit into the history of the neighborhood or location?

To find answers to these questions, your public library and local historical society are tremendously useful resources. There you can find valuable sources such as:

- local histories and guidebooks
- local newspapers and magazines
- maps and atlases—fire insurance maps are especially useful
- photographs
- Historic American Buildings Survey publications

You should also consider looking for official records at local government offices such as the City or Town Hall and County Clerk's office, and the office of the Tax Assessor. Increasingly, the Internet is a useful tool for research on historic houses, but you will probably still need to consult the specialized records found in archives and libraries. Previous owners and neighbors might be able to give you information for an oral history of the house. This book will give you an understanding of the historical context of American houses, and where the styles originated and how they changed over time. The illustrations will provide a wide range of examples for comparison. But be forewarned: as with genealogical research, digging up information on historic houses can become addictive!

Left: Advertisement for Aladdin Homes, 1917. Prefabricated homes were promised to be "built in a day," as if by a genie.

Above: Modernist beach house, shed roof, Dune Road, West Hampton, Long Island, NY.

The History Of Domestic Architecture In The United States

Jeffery Howe

Architecture is the only essential art, from a strictly practical point of view. Shelter is a basic necessity. Accordingly, architecture is the art form most deeply integrated with society—it affects the most people, can last for centuries, and literally defines the public domain. But despite being the most universal form of art, it is also the one most frequently ignored. We take our houses for granted, seldom reflecting on what they reveal about us as tokens of our material culture, when in fact they embody not only the current assumptions of what is necessary for the good life, but also the technological and economic possibilities available to an individual, a society, and an era.

What makes successful architecture? In particular, what makes a good home? There is no shortage of opinions on this matter. The ancient Roman architect Vitruvius identified the three necessary qualities of architecture as "commoditie, firmeness and delight," according to Sir Henry Wooten's 1624 translation of the Latin text. This is still a useful formula. In modern terms, we might say that architecture must provide a useful function, with shelter being the most universal (commodity). Architecture must be structurally sound (firmness)—it has to stand up, and bear up under wind and weather to keep its occupants safe. A building must also have an element of beauty in its design to make it appeal to current and future generations (delight). Great architecture is an expressive art and not merely functional; it touches our lives in many ways, and conveys meanings through both physical and psychological effects. The definitions of all three of these qualities have changed dramatically during the history of housing in America. The techniques and tools available have spanned the range from stone-age to space-age technologies. Definitions of and attitudes toward beauty have undergone equally radical changes. Concepts of comfort and privacy have also changed dramatically, from the stark

Below: Alexander Jackson Davis: design for an American cottage, Rural Residences, 1837. An attempt to create a rustic classicism appropriate for the new American culture.

Left: Abbé Marc-Antoine Laugier (1713–1769): the origins of architecture, illustration from *Essai sur l'architecture*, 1753. The first temple is shown here to be a sacred grove of trees, with primitive gables added. The origin of architecture is thus attributed to the dual influences of nature and religion.

simplicity of the earliest shelters to the latest "smart homes," with computer-controlled heating, lighting, communications, and security. With new materials and technologies have come the possibilities of new shapes; after centuries of building in traditional wood, brick, and stone, strikingly new expressive shapes are being created by architects such as Frank Gehry and Bart Prince, to name only two.

Architecture brings order out of chaos; geometry and natural irregularity are the two poles which frame architectural design. Both have their virtues, and architects and builders frequently combine them. The simplest huts are typically geometric in shape, and some of the most sophisticated buildings, either Victorian or Postmodern, tend toward a picturesque irregularity. The tension between geometry and nature, or order and disorder, was symbolized in the frontispiece to *Essai sur l'architecture* of 1755 by the Jesuit Abbé Marc-Antoine Laugier. The quest for the primitive origins of architecture was a preoccupation for architects and philosophers during the eighteenth century Enlightenment. The image of the early temple formed from living trees is a mythic explanation of the origin of architecture, as recreated by an eighteenth century Classicist. The synthesis of natural forms and abstract design is depicted as the foundation of architecture. Many different combinations of these two principles exist in the history of American architecture. In 1837, Alexander Jackson Davis proposed a design for an American cottage which recalls Laugier's tree-trunk columns. The cottage is a rustic version of a Greek temple, and the porch columns are crudely dressed logs, with the ends of branches left at the top. This house invokes both the Classical tradition and the power of nature as the fitting framework for the American family. The home has traditionally been identified as the center of moral and spiritual values for American society; the vision of a life in a pure natural setting was to have enduring appeal.

Symmetry vs. Asymmetry

Symmetry is a fundamental principle of nature, and is the basis of much architecture and design. Symmetry, which creates balance and harmony, was one of the defining characteristics of Classicism, and is embedded deeply in the design practices of American builders. However, there has also been an ongoing tension caused by the desire for organic, if asymmetric growth. Asymmetry can create more dynamic rhythms in space, and permits plans based on functional needs.

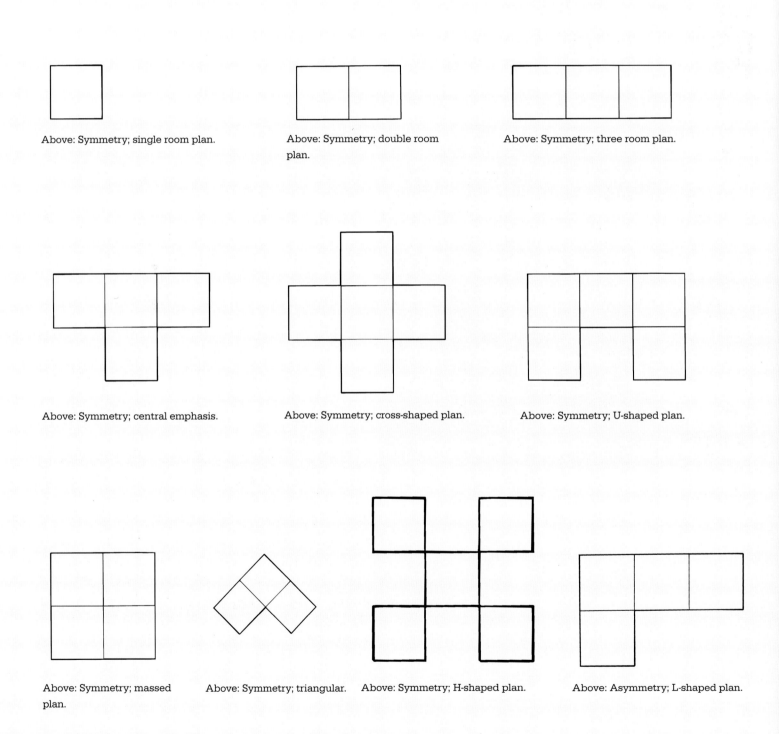

Above: Symmetry; single room plan.

Above: Symmetry; double room plan.

Above: Symmetry; three room plan.

Above: Symmetry; central emphasis.

Above: Symmetry; cross-shaped plan.

Above: Symmetry; U-shaped plan.

Above: Symmetry; massed plan.

Above: Symmetry; triangular.

Above: Symmetry; H-shaped plan.

Above: Asymmetry; L-shaped plan.

Above: Symmetry—single block. Charles Bulfinch: first Harrison Gray Otis House, Boston, MA, 1796.

Above: Symmetry—central building with two identical flanking buildings. The tripartite design scheme is typical of classical architecture.

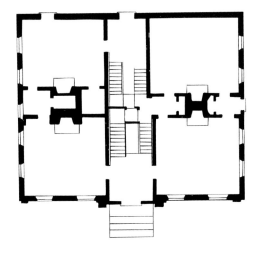

Above: Symmetry—plan of the John Vassall (Longfellow) House, Cambridge, MA, 1759. Geometric symmetry outweighs functional requirements here.

Above: Symmetry—central plan octagon house. The octagon was thought to be a perfect geometric shape, and conducive to mental and physical health.

Left: Symmetry—Purcell and Elmslie: Airplane House, Woods Hole, MA, 1911–1912.

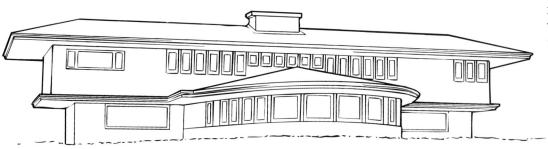

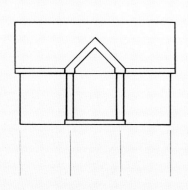

Above: Symmetry vs. asymmetry in façade masses.

Above: Asymmetry—House of Seven Gables, Salem, MA. Medieval architecture is not tied to the simple geometry of classicism.

Above: Asymmetry—Henry Austin: Victoria Mansion, Portland, ME, 1859. Italianate mansions such as this combined Renaissance forms and picturesque asymmetry.

Above: Asymmetry—Greene and Greene: Gamble House, Pasadena, CA, 1908. In the twentieth century, a dynamic asymmetry became more pronounced.

Left: Asymmetry—Wallace Neff: concrete balloon house.

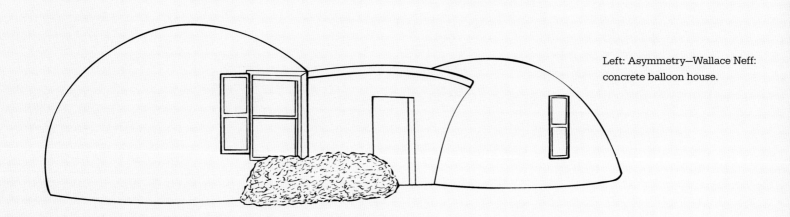

Early Architecture in the U.S.

The changing relationship of people to the environment is also inscribed in the history of American housing. The earliest settlers, the Native Americans who inhabited the Southwestern pueblos and Western plains, and the Northern and Eastern woodlands, utilized natural materials and pre-industrial techniques which had a minimal impact on nature. Despite limitations of materials and tools, many of these traditions are quite complex and well adapted to the environment. Pueblos possessed remarkable thermal qualities, providing a consistent internal temperature despite the extremes of climate. The rapidly demountable tipis provided efficient shelter for the plains peoples. Spiritual and social ideals shaped the structures also; the corbelled dome of the Navaho hogans echoed the shape of the dome of Heaven, and the kiva, a sacred ritual chamber, was an essential part of the pueblo. The plank houses of the Northwest tribes were decorated with sacred symbols, generally of natural totems, and the functional layout of their interiors was based on the clan structures of the social group. When the European colonists arrived, there were many thriving Native American cultures, with a rich variety of home building traditions; these were soon severely diminished by disease and conquest, however.

The first European settlers in America were not trained architects, and in many cases their early houses were far inferior to the Native American dwellings. The so-called "English wigwams" and crude dugouts of the

Above: Pioneer Village, Salem, MA. The first shelters created by the colonists were far from the elegant white colonial villages that some have imagined.

Salem and Plymouth settlements provided only the barest necessary shelter, with little comfort and no privacy. The reality was far removed from later romanticized visions of the colonial settlements.

Style was not a high priority for these early Europeans, nor was there any thought of creating a new

Above: Whipple house, 1 South Village Green, Ipswich, MA, 1639.

Above: Henry Whitfield House, Old Whitfield Street, Guilford, CT, 1639. The oldest house in Connecticut, and the oldest stone house in New England.

Above: Boone Hall Plantation, 235 Long Point Road, Mt. Pleasant, SC, early 1700s. This Palladian villa was at the center of a plantation of over 17,000 acres.

architecture for the new world. They were simply transplanted Europeans, and sought to reproduce the kinds of houses they had known in their homelands as quickly as possible. Since there were no trained architects among them, and both labor and capital were in short supply, the early dwellings tended to be simple and rather small. Even wealthy men like Adam Thoroughgood in Virginia or prominent clergy, such as Parson Capen in Topsfield, Massachusetts, lived in houses with only two rooms on the ground floor. Ceilings were low and the original windows were small. Massive fireplaces provided heat and were also used for cooking. Houses were seldom painted in the early years, and glass was precious. Windows were small and made of tiny panes of glass in lead frames. Their frames were solidly built, however, as proven by their continuing existence. Cultural differences between New England and the Tidewater region are

reflected in these buildings as well. The Thoroughgood House was the center of an estate of 5,250 acres, as the plantation system was already being established in the South. Such small houses would be more elaborate mansions in later years.

The earliest colonial houses were essentially folk-style buildings, made to fulfill functional requirements in the manner of the simple vernacular housing traditions the settlers had known in Britain and continental Europe. Vernacular architecture is driven by practical needs and shaped by craft traditions, which tend to be conservative. Unlike court-based architecture, which changes style rapidly according to the developments of knowledge or patterns of taste in the court, vernacular architecture changes very slowly. The post-medieval houses built in New England in the seventeenth century were very much like those built centuries earlier in form and layout.

Above: Beauregard House, 8606 Street Bernard Highway, Chalmette, LA, 1833. A country residence with an octastyle (eight column) portico at front and rear of the house, built near the site of the Battle of New Orleans.

Above: Ward Hall, Georgetown, KY, 1853.

Above: Orton Plantation, 9149 Orton Road, S.E., Winnabow, NC, 1725; columns 1840; wings 1910.

Right: Shotgun House, (double house), New Orleans, LA, 1892. The shotgun house is a distinct housing type, of African-American origin. Houses are only one room wide.

Although it is usually the most common kind of building, vernacular architecture is also the least likely to be preserved, and therefore is much less familiar to us than mansions or government buildings. The simplicity and depth of tradition reflected in these houses, however, made them appealing to later architects such as Frank Lloyd Wright, who sought the roots of American architecture in the first houses built here. Study of vernacular architecture leads one to consider regional building types such as the Southern "shotgun house," which brings to light the contributions of otherwise neglected groups such as African-Americans.

The eighteenth century brought economic growth and cultural consolidation, and stronger ties to the European courts, with a resulting transformation of the dominant architectural styles. This set a pattern for frontier settlement which persisted through the nineteenth century, as successive waves of settlers built simple homes of wood or even sod, in the Western prairies, replacing them with more elaborate houses as quickly as they could. Regional differences and the different traditions of the national groups who settled these regions were very important. The coming of the railroad led to a more homogeneous architecture, as materials and designs were more easily transported. By the end of the nineteenth century, entire homes were available as mail-order kits which were shipped all over the country.

Colonial

The seventeenth century in America was marked by strong regional differences. There was no unity among the colonies founded by rival nations. They were competing ventures, seeking to establish themselves and to gain primacy over the native inhabitants and each other. Nor did the multicultural settlements of the time lead to mutual cooperation. Each rival group sought a foothold: the Spanish in Florida and the Southwest, the British along the Eastern Seaboard in New England and Virginia, the Dutch in New Amsterdam (now New York) and the Hudson River valley, the French in Canada and Louisiana, and Swedes and Germans in the Delaware valley. Each colonial group had to adapt its national building traditions to the American environment, which was frequently much more extreme than the European climate. In the Northeast, winters were much colder, and the summers much hotter than in England. In the South and Southwest, the range of temperatures was also much more extreme. The life of the colonists was hard; the importance of home as a source of security and shelter cannot be overestimated. There was little energy for or interest in stylistic innovation, and American building lagged considerably behind the fashions of European architecture.

Central vs. Open Plan

Centralized plans are the simplest to build, and can create symmetrical, harmonious designs, and are typical of Classicism. The central "box" plan can be restrictive, however, limiting both the functional use of spaces in the house and the expressiveness of the exterior. Gothic Revival styles in the nineteenth century allowed more open plans, and architects such as Frank Lloyd Wright made a complete break with the restrictions of the box plan. Contemporary house plans can be extraordinarily free in design.

Above: Breaking out of the Box—plan of simple box (left), and the same with a central porch entrance added.

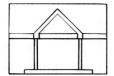
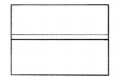

Above: Breaking out of the box—elevation of simple box (left), and the same with a central porch entrance added.

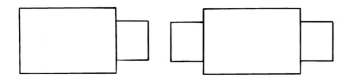

Above: Breaking out of the Box—plan of two box house (house and garage, at left), compared with a similar house, with a third box added for symmetry.

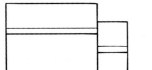

Above: Breaking out of the Box—elevation of two box house (house and garage, at left), compared with a similar house, with a third box added for symmetry.

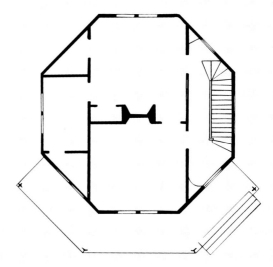

Above: Centralized plan—octagon house, 1853.

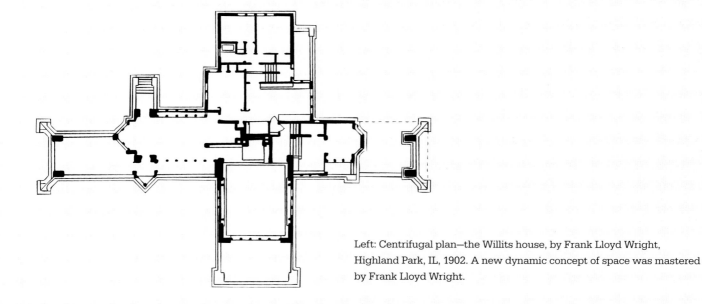

Left: Centrifugal plan—the Willits house, by Frank Lloyd Wright, Highland Park, IL, 1902. A new dynamic concept of space was mastered by Frank Lloyd Wright.

The timber-framed houses in New England, for instance, were basically rural farm houses or village houses—a far cry from the elegant Baroque homes built for the wealthy in England at the same time; these would not be matched until the late nineteenth century. Early New England homes had steep pitched roofs, like the medieval architecture of centuries earlier. The steep pitch was extremely practical for shedding rain and snow in the new land. Rural farm houses were frequently shared with animals; they were sheltered in a shed joined to the living quarters, and under the same roof. This conserved building materials and the humans may have benefited from the body heat of the animals in the winter. On the interior, there was very little differentiated space for specific functions. Rooms served multiple purposes, depending on the time of day. Generally, there would be one or two rooms on the ground floor for people, with sleeping chambers and sometimes grain-storage space in the floor above. A central fireplace served for both heat and cooking.

The typical colonial home in the seventeenth century was not a log cabin; that building type was introduced by the Swedish colonists at New Sweden in Delaware in 1638, but that colony did not last, and the log cabin did not spread until later. It only became a symbol of American life during the presidential election of 1840.

The eighteenth century brought a greater homo-geneity of style on the east coast, as the Classically-inspired Georgian style spread across the region. The

Above: McPhedris-Warner House, corner of Daniel and Chapel streets, Portsmouth, NH, 1716–1723.

Right: Jeremiah Lee Mansion, 161
Washington Street, Marblehead, MA,
1768.

Above: Wentworth-Gardner House, 50 Mechanic Street, Portsmouth, NH, 1760.

time lag between the appearance of new European styles and their introduction in America began to shorten, as trained builders and carpenters came to the New World, and books on architecture began to be imported. In the absence of trained architects, these books were invaluable to the gentleman builders of the era. They were scarce, however; even one of the largest libraries, the collection of 4,000 books amassed by William Byrd II in Virginia, had only twenty-three books specifically on architecture. Thomas Jefferson's great library of nearly 7,000 volumes which he sold to the Congress in 1815 to form the core of the Library of Congress included forty-three books on architecture. Skills in drawing and architectural design were considered important parts of a gentleman's education, and some of the most notable American houses were built by such enthusiastic amateurs as George Washington and Thomas Jefferson. Until 1797, when Asher Benjamin published *The Country Builder's Assistant* in Greenfield, Massachusetts, all books on architecture were imported from Europe.

The colonies on the East Coast became more unified in the eighteenth century, with a more homogeneous style of housing based on British Classicism. The period is called Georgian, after the ruling English monarchs. After the reign of Queen Anne (1702–1714), George I ascended the throne (ruled 1714–1727), followed by George II (1727–1760) and George III (1760–1820), who ruled during the American Revolution. American homes began to imitate British country houses and estates, as New England merchants and Southern planters became more self-conscious about the style of their residences. Classical details such as columns, pediments, and porticos began to appear, and there was a greater emphasis on symmetry. Hipped roofs replaced the steep medieval gables of earlier homes. Houses were now larger, with higher ceilings and much bigger windows. Even in New England, houses were no longer built around a massive central fireplace and chimney; pairs of chimneys moved to the outer walls instead. Although they could not match the elegance and stone building materials of

Left: Captain John MacPherson house, "Mount Pleasant," Fairmont Park, Philadelphia, PA, 1761–1762. Mount Pleasant is a beautiful Georgian house with two separate dependencies. It was built by a Scottish privateer, and later sold to Benedict Arnold, who never occupied it.

English houses, northern homes like the Jeremiah Lee Mansion in Marblehead, Massachusetts, and Westover, the Byrd estate in Virginia, were much more stylish.

The new urbanity of American housing can be seen in the Mcphedris-Warner House in Portsmouth, New Hampshire, of 1716–1723. Built of brick with a gambrel roof, it is much more sophisticated than the simple wooden saltboxes that came before it. Stone was still a rarity in American building, but a theatrical illusion could be created by cutting wide wooden boards to imi-

tate stone; sometimes sand would be mixed with the paint to give a more complete stone effect, as in the Robert "King" Hooper House in Marblehead, or the Wentworth-Gardner House in Portsmouth. The elegant mansion built in 1759 for Capt. John MacPherson in Fairmount Park in Philadelphia, called Mount Pleasant, is a fine example of a Georgian country house built of stone. There are many Classical features here: the overall symmetry, emphasized by the central pedimented pavilion and two identical flanking outbuildings, the

Above: Dwight House, c. 1725, remodeled 1755, Springfield, MA, moved to Deerfield, MA, in 1954.

Palladian window, the use of quoins, belt course, and the balustrade on the rooftop.

Some of the more rural adaptations of European design were creative in their own way. William Pierson has described the language of Classicism at Deerfield, Massachusetts, as being spoken with "a thick Yankee accent." Contrary to earlier beliefs, most houses in the eighteenth century were not painted white—a wide variety of colors has been discovered by modern preservationists. Even in rural Deerfield, some houses were painted in pink and blue; others were left unpainted.

National traditions were reflected in the architecture of different settlements; Dutch and Flemish settlers continued to build impressive homes in the New York region and along the Hudson river valley. New Paltz, New York, contains a very well preserved street of Huguenot homes, built amidst the surrounding Dutch

towns. In the French territories, distinctive building techniques are preserved in such houses as the Cahokia Courthouse, in Cahokia, Illinois, which was built as a private house in 1737.

The second half of the eighteenth century saw increasing sophistication in terms of style and craftsmanship. The Georgian style was succeeded by a Classical style strongly influenced by the British architect Robert Adam (1728–1792). It is often called either the Adam Style or the Federalist Style, after the Federalist period of American government. This period also saw the rise of more professional architects, such as Charles Bulfinch (1763–1844) in Boston and Samuel McIntyre (1757–1804) in Salem, Massachusetts. Their houses are marked by elegant Classicism, and a continuing influence from British precedents. Bulfinch was the first American to attempt to make a living as a professional

Above: Bevier House, Huguenot Street, New Paltz, NY, 1698. Dutch colonial house built by Huguenot settlers in the Hudson River valley.

architect, although he still needed salaries from positions he held with the city government. Despite bankruptcies in 1796 and 1811, he profoundly changed the appearance of Boston with his many brick town houses.

At this time, imitation of historical precedents was valued more than innovation; it was the era of Classical revivals in painting and sculpture as well as architecture. Independence in architecture was to be found not in creating a new style, but in a new choice of models.

In the late eighteenth and early nineteenth centuries, a new form of Classical architecture arose and quickly spread around the world. Inspired by Enlightenment studies of ancient history and archeological excavations at Pompeii and Herculaneum, Neoclassic architects strove for a higher degree of accuracy in their recreation of ancient forms. The many newly established academies in Europe encouraged artists and architects in this study of history. One of the most influential proponents of Classical art, Johann Joachim Winckelmann, summarized the academic attitude: "There is but one way for the moderns to become great, and perhaps unequalled; I mean, by imitating the ancients." This did not mean that they were dispassionate; Thomas Jefferson (1743–1826), the most important Neoclassicist in America, described his feelings about a Roman temple he had seen in France as like those of a lover staring at his mistress. This was a Romantic Classicism, motivated by high ideals and a yearning for a new and better era.

Some were impatient with the progress of architecture in America; Thomas Jefferson wrote a scathing dismissal of the buildings of Virginia in 1785: "The private buildings are very rarely constructed of stone or brick, much the greater portion being of

Above: Cahokia Courthouse, First and Elm streets, Cahokia, IL, 1737. Originally a private house, this French colonial house was used as a courthouse from 1793 to 1814. The house was disassembled and exhibited at the World's Fair in Chicago in 1933.

scantling and boards, plaster with lime. It is impossible to devise things more ugly, uncomfortable, and happily more perishable."

The new republic needed good examples in architecture as well as in politics, and Jefferson sought to create buildings which would improve the public taste and sense of design, and perhaps also create better citizens.

Although designs were frequently merely copied from ancient Greek and Roman prototypes, another important factor, the rationalist admiration for geometry, inspired architects to a style of simplicity and purity of form. Compared to Baroque or eighteenth century architecture, Neoclassical buildings are more severe, with simple colonnades and more planar wall surfaces. Classical architecture was associated with the foundation of learning and law, and hence was frequently used in library and government buildings. The Enlightenment confidence in the rational design of social and political institutions was reflected in the choice of the best examples of Classical architecture for their institutions.

The end of the eighteenth century witnessed the first Neoclassical buildings in America, created by Thomas Jefferson. The initial designs for Jefferson's own house, Monticello, were first closely modeled on the villas of Andrea Palladio, but it became increasingly complex as Jefferson transformed the rigid symmetry of the original geometric plan into a series of rooms shaped by functional requirements and his own personal predilections. Its location on the top of a small mountain echoed the practice of ancient Roman villas, which provided an ideal escape from the city. Other Southern mansions were more typically located on lowlands near rivers to take advantage of the ease of transport. Building was a passion for Jefferson; as with many modern homeowners, he never stopped building his ideal house, and construction continued throughout his life.

Above: Samuel McIntyre (1757–1804): Gardner-Pingree House, 128 Essex Street, Salem, MA, 1804–1806. A fine example of Federalist architecture.

Above: Thomas Jefferson (1743–1826): Monticello, near Charlottesville, VA, 1769–1782; 1796–1809.
An early example of Roman classicism in America, Jefferson's mountaintop villa reflected his
experimental nature.

Construction Elements—Lintels and Arches

Structural elements such as post-and-beam construction and arches are fundamental to the art of building. Although rooted in age-old tradition, these simple structural devices provide powerful tools for creating expressive and inventive architecture.

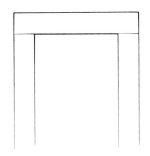

Above: Posts and lintel. Simple post and beam construction is the basis of much architecure.

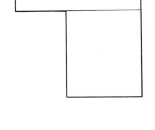

Above: Diagram of a cantilever. The cantilever allows more experimental forms.

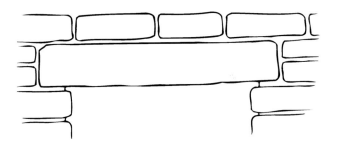

Above: Stone lintel.

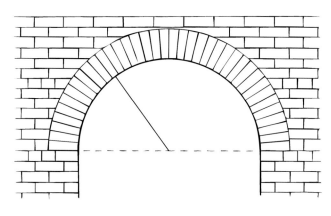

Above: Diagram of a semi-circular arch made of brick. The arch was the basis of Roman architecture, and offers more design possibilities than post and beam structures.

Above: Acute arch; also known as a lancet arch. This example is from a cottage in Connecticut.

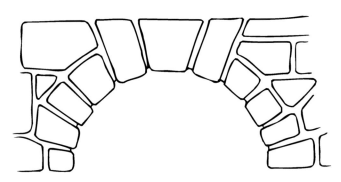

Above: Semi-circular stone arch. Vaulting with stone was beyond the capabilities of American architects for many years.

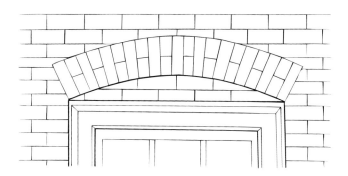

Above: Segmental arch, from Macphaedris-Warner House, Portsmouth, NH. Segmental arches were frequently found in eighteenth century architecture.

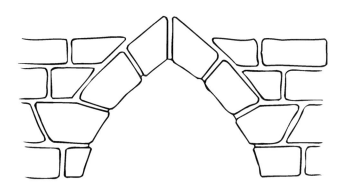

Above: The pointed Gothic arch was introduced in the middle ages, and became popular in the Gothic Revival of the nineteenth century.

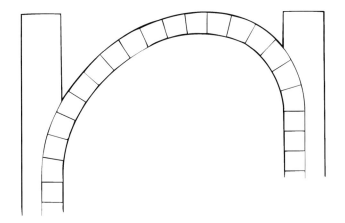

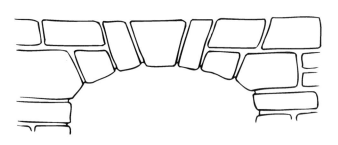

Above: Elliptical stone arch.

Above: Rampant arch. The springing of the arch is higher on one side; these unusual forms are found in late Victorian houses.

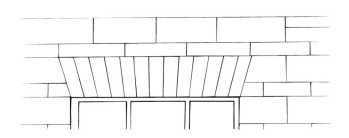

Above: The flat, or splayed arch, was commonly found in eighteenth century houses.

Above: Horseshoe-shaped arch, from a late Victorian house.

European Revivals

In the nineteenth century, the range of historical reference and stylistic expression expanded dramatically, with styles consciously chosen to reflect an emotional or ideological association. In this period, many cultural movements focused on memory. There was a great increase in historical knowledge, and an increasingly sophisticated awareness of the relationship between style and social values. Since there were no direct links to these historical traditions in America, styles were a matter of deliberate choice. In this eclectic century, nearly every historical style that had flourished in Europe was revived at some point.

The Greek Revival, which flourished from 1818 to 1850, was the first national style in the U.S., spreading across the continent, and being used in all levels of building, from high style to folk architecture. The Greek Revival was fostered by such books as *The Antiquities of Athens* by James Stuart and Nicholas Revett (London, 1762), which featured the first measured drawings of ancient Greek architecture. Not all Neoclassical buildings incorporated elaborate quotations from Classical models, however. Neoclassicism was a flexible style, which could be adapted to many different building types, from houses to commercial buildings. In its simplest manifestation, a Greek Revival home could be built by any carpenter; many are simply traditional gable-ended houses with the gable end turned toward the street. The entrance is placed at the narrow end, and the gable is designed to resemble a Classical pediment or cornice. Pilasters may be placed at the ends of walls. Good examples can be found in houses at Wickford, Rhode Island, and Haddam, Connecticut. Urban townhouses might also include distinctly Greek pedimented porticos and other ornament to ally them to the new style. For example, Louisburg Square in Boston, built from 1826 to 1840, includes several Greek porticos in the series of bow-fronted houses. This is one of the best adaptations of a British residential square, with rowhouses grouped around a commonly owned private park, found in an American city.

Above: Ithiel Town (1784–1844): Russell House, Wesleyan University, Middletown, CT, 1828–1830.

Above: S.P. Fuller, builder: Louisburg Square, Boston, 1826–1840. An early example of a planned development, following the precedent of British town squares with a commonly owned private park. The tradition of caroling on Christmas eve, and placing candles in windows, is said to have begun here in the late nineteenth century.

Above: Greek Revival house, Haddam, CT.

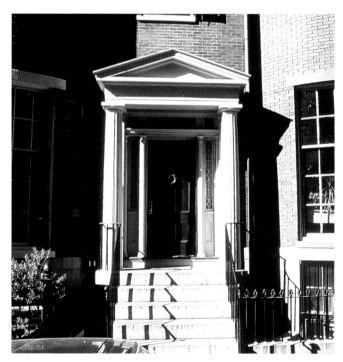

Above: S.P. Fuller, builder: Louisburg Square, Boston, 1826–1840. Detail of Greek portico.

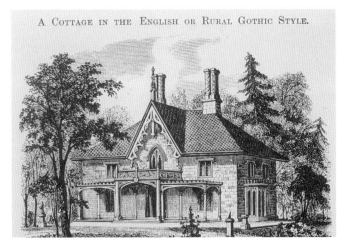

A Cottage in the English or Rural Gothic Style.

Above: Andrew Jackson Downing (1815–1852): Cottage, Design II, 1842, *Cottage Residences*, 1842. Featured in one of the most successful pattern books ever published, this design was frequently copied.

The chief rival to the Greek Revival in the early nineteenth century was the Gothic Revival, which flourished from about 1820 to 1860. This style was based on medieval precedents, encouraged by popular literary trends. The first Gothic novels in the eighteenth century presented an exotic and imaginative view of a romantic medieval past. An early example of Gothic Revival architecture is Sunnyside, the home of the writer Washington Irving, in Tarrytown, New York. This was a remodeled Dutch colonial house of the seventeenth century with its characteristic stepped gables, expanded with additions containing Gothic pointed windows and an expansive porch to allow contact with nature. This style appealed to a wide social spectrum, and was used in houses ranging from simple "Carpenter's Gothic" cottages to high style mansions, such as Lyndhurst, in Tarrytown, New York.

Above: "Sunnyside," Washington Irving House, West Sunnyside Lane, off Route 9, Tarrytown, NY, 1835–1847. This house is a seventeenth century Dutch colonial house, which was remodeled in the Gothic style by the famous author. Porches help bridge the gap between house and nature.

Connotations of individuality and freedom were felt to be implicit in Gothic architecture, and the style became extremely popular in American residential buildings. Pattern books such as A. J. Downing's *Cottage Residences* (1842) and *The Architecture of Country Houses* (1850) provided practical solutions for suburban homeowners seeking designs that would proclaim their individuality and sophistication. Downing observed that: "a beautiful house fully reflects a fine character."

A growing conviction that the irregular and picturesque Gothic architecture was more closely attuned to nature than the abstract Classical style also encouraged its popularity in the U.S. Gothic houses were built up and down the East Coast, and all across rural America. Good examples from the 1850s can be found today in Salem, Massachusetts, and many other towns. Even Frank Lloyd Wright identified the Gothic spirit with a true apprehension of natural principles and harmony with nature, which he calls Organic Architecture. Wright asserted in the introduction to the first German publication of his works (*Ausgeführte Bauten*, 1910) that the feeling for the organic quality of form was more perfectly realized in Gothic architecture than in any other style.

Nostalgia for the richness of European cultural life continued as a factor in the popularity of Gothic as well. The Wedding Cake House, built by George Bourne in Kennebunkport, Maine, in 1855 is an ornate refashioning of a plain Federalist box into a dazzling display of the carpenter's prowess with a scroll saw that was intended to suggest the style of Milan Cathedral.

The appeal of medieval architecture resonated powerfully in a society that believed one's home is one's castle. One of the grandest of nineteenth century houses was built for Potter and Berthe Palmer in Chicago, in

Above: Brooks House, Salem, MA, 1851. This house follows Downing's Design II very closely.

1883–1885. This castle provided an appro-private setting for Mr. and Mrs. Palmer's art collection, which would later form the core of the Impressionist paintings at the Chicago Art Institute. This palatial home provided a symbolic link between the new mercantile royalty of Chicago and the aristocratic traditions of the old world. Medieval castles for urban merchants and suburban squires were built fairly frequently between 1840 and 1940. Fonthill, the home of the Shakespearean actor Edwin Forrest, was a dramatic example built in the Bronx in 1848.

By mid century, other style options appeared. The lure of Italian villas was very strong, and the Italianate style flourished from about 1850 to 1870. This was another style with broad appeal which was easily adapted to both wood-frame structures and stone villas. Pattern books such as those by A.J. Davis and Samuel Sloan played an important role in popularizing this style. Form variants included nearly cubic villas, with wide overhanging eaves, as seen in Henry Austin's Dana house of 1849 in New Haven and a house in Guilford, Connecticut, from the 1850s. The other popular form was an L-shaped plan with an asymmetrically placed tower. The Italianate mode could be more flexible than the Greek Revival, but was less fussy than the Gothic Revival. It was particularly recommended for those with artistic tastes. The Norton House in New Haven by A.J. Davis (1848), and the Morse-Libby House in Portland, Maine by Henry Austin (1859) are good examples.

The nineteenth century was a period of individualism, with a number of experimental revivals of styles

Above: George Bourne, builder, "Wedding Cake House," Kennebunkport, ME, 1826/1855. Note the gingerbread ornament.

remote in history or geography. While exotic styles such as the Egyptian Revival were more commonly used for cemeteries and public memorials, such as the Washington Monument, there were also a number of houses built with Egyptian columns and other devices reminiscent of the ancient culture.

Swiss chalets were revived for those with a taste for the picturesque and nostalgia for Europe. Downing's books and Sloan's *Homestead Architecture* (1867) offered designs for these. In 1858, Samuel Colt built a whole neighborhood of Swiss style cottages for workers in his wicker factory in Hartford, Connecticut. In the second half of the twentieth century, the Swiss villa was revived as a favorite style for housing near ski resorts in Vermont and elsewhere.

There is an enduring propensity in American culture for experiments in utopian or idealistic social communities. Some of these had quite interesting architectural possibilities, although only the religious groups such as the Shakers actually developed long lasting communities. Robert Owen was a British industrialist with progressive ideals influenced by the French socialist Charles Fourier. Owen proposed building a European-style communal development at New Harmony, Indiana. The communal center for work and social activities was designed by Steadman Whitwell in 1825, but was never built. The desire to create a new and reformed mode of living had motivated the early Puritans, as well as such worldly idealists as Thomas Jefferson.

Above: Alexander Jackson Davis (1803–1892): Lyndhurst, 635 South Broadway (Route 9), Tarrytown, NY, 1838/1865. This house was built in two stages for two different owners, twenty-seven years apart, but by the same architect.

Left: "A Man's home is his Castle"— Henry Ives Cobb (1859–1931) and Charles Sumner Frost (1856–1931): Potter Palmer Mansion, formerly at 1350 N. Lake Shore Drive, Chicago, 1882–1885. A fanciful castle in the midst of what came to be Chicago's "Gold Coast," the mansion included a three-story picture gallery for the owners' art collection. The house was demolished in 1951.

Reformers paid attention to the individual family home as well. Catharine Beecher and her sister, Harriet Beecher Stowe, attempted to reform domestic architecture, paying particular attention to the actual patterns of work done within the household. Catharine Beecher published her *Treatise on Domestic Economy* in 1841, and she published *The American Woman's Home* with her sister in 1869. The external form of the house in these books remained conventional; the innovations were inside. Catharine Beecher's designs incorporated improved technology in heating and plumbing to enhance health and ease the burden of the women who

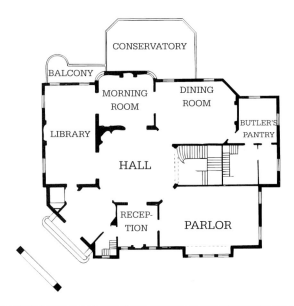

Left: Cobb and Frost: plan of Potter Palmer Mansion, Chicago, IL, 1882–1885. This enormous mansion had no exterior doorknobs; entrance was granted by the twenty-seven servants who were on duty.

Above: Thomas L. Smith: Edwin Forrest House, "Fonthill," W. 261st Street and Palisade Avenue, (now part of college of Mount Saint Vincent), Bronx, NY, 1848. This medieval castle was built by one of the most famous actors of the nineteenth century, known for his Shakespearean roles.

Above: Andrew Jackson Downing: Design VI, Italian Villa, *Cottage Residences*, 1842.

Above: Andrew Jackson Downing: Design VIII, Italian Villa, *Cottage Residences*, 1842.

Left: Henry Austin (1804–1891): James Dwight Dana House, 24 Hillhouse Avenue, New Haven, 1849. The cubic form was very popular for villas in the mid-nineteenth century. The L-shaped addition breaks the symmetry.

Above: Italianate villa, Guilford, CT, c. 1850s. This house has a pronounced cubic form, one of the most common forms of the Italianate style.

Above: Henry Austin (1804–1891): John P. Norton House, 52 Hillhouse Avenue. New Haven, CT, 1848–1849.

Above: Alexander Jackson Davis (1803–1892): Apthorpe House, Hillhouse Avenue, New Haven, 1837. The Egyptian Revival is one of the rarest styles for houses in America.

did most of the work. Laundry and kitchen areas were reorganized for convenience. Servants were commonly employed at this time; in 1850 A. J. Downing defined a cottage as any house with less than three servants. However, Downing and Catharine Beecher agreed that servants would become less common as other economic opportunities arose, and that houses would have to become more efficient, to save domestic labor.

Health and self-improvement were the focus of Orson Squire Fowler's octagon houses, which grew out of the context of his overall attempt to improve health along phrenological lines. Phrenology was the study of mental faculties and moral character, as revealed by the external bumps on the skull. Extremely popular in the nineteenth century, largely because of Fowler's publications, American phrenology had a focus on self-

Left: Henry Austin (1804–1891): Morse-Libby House (also known as the Victoria Mansion), 109 Danforth Street, Portland, ME, 1859. One of the most luxurious houses to follow Downing's Italianate designs.

Above: Swiss-style houses built by Samuel Colt,
Hendricxsen Avenue, Hartford, CT, 1858.

improvement, based on the conviction that specific apti-
tudes could be developed through exercise. Besides
touting the efficiency of the octagonal plan, his books
urged the use of concrete for solid foundations and
healthful basements. This was one of the earliest uses of
concrete in American architecture.

Even such idiosyncratic examples as Henry David
Thoreau's self-built cabin of 1847 at Walden Pond reflect
a philosophical return to simplicity, recreating the
essence of frontier life within walking distance of downtown Concord, Massachusetts.

The pragmatic counterpart to these idealist developments was the low-cost housing built for workers after
the Industrial Revolution. These ranged from boarding

Above: A modern Swiss chalet, Pico, VT.

Left: The Cloisters, 632 W. Main Street, Ephrata, PA, 1741/1743. Residences for an idealistic and celibate religious community. The men's and women's dormitories were in seperate structures.

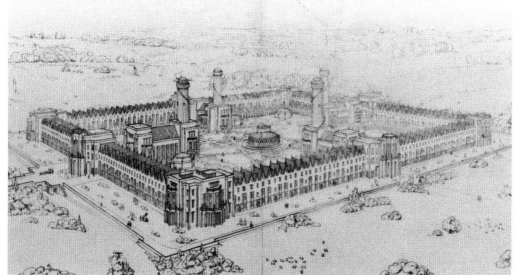

Left: Stedman Whitwell (d. 1840) and Robert Owen: New Harmony, Indiana, 1826. Seeking a new utopian community, Robert Owen had Stedman Whitwell draw up designs for a communitarian structure, with individual living spaces grouped around communal centers. It was never built.

Left and inset: Fairbanks House, Dedham, MA, 1636. Frame reconstructed for the Boston 350 celebration, 1980. Spaces between the timber posts and beams were filled in with woven sticks ("wattle"), and covered with clay ("daub").

Above: Worker housing, at Lowell, MA, Boott Mill Complex, c. 1830s.

Above: Triple decker, Jamaica Plain, MA, late nineteenth century.

houses and corporate rowhouses in Lowell, Massachusetts, to corporate developments of single-family houses as in Harrisville, New Hampshire, and some mill towns in Connecticut. The rise of capitalism and urban factories made the problem of housing workers particularly urgent in the nineteenth century. Examples of worker housing still survive in the New England area. The Boott Mill Complex in Lowell (begun 1821) included dormitories and rowhouses for workers. These mills tapped a new labor source for the first time: large numbers of single women left farms to work in the mills. Some surviving examples of mill towns, such as Harrisville (built in 1820–1860) provide examples of smaller-scale worker housing, with rows of identical small houses. In urban areas, such as the streetcar suburbs of Dorchester and Jamaica Plain, Massachusetts, large triple deckers—houses with homes on three floors for separate families—were built.

Construction Elements—Walls

Walls are one of the basic structural elements of a house, and the materials and techniques used reflect different building traditions and the evolution of building technology. Every building technology used by humans appears in American houses, from post-medieval timber framing to masonry walls of brick and stone and even walls of glass and steel, derived from skyscraper construction.

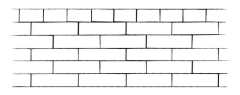

Above: English brick bonds. The English pattern was of alternating rows of headers (bricks laid with the short end facing the front) and stretchers (bricks laid lengthwise).

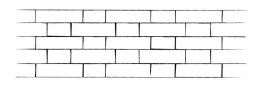

Above: Flemish brick bonds. The Flemish bond alternated headers and stretchers in the same row.

Mortar joints

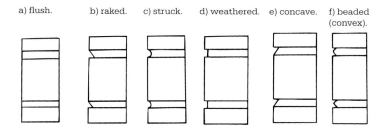

a) flush.   b) raked.   c) struck.   d) weathered.   e) concave.   f) beaded (convex).

There were also different traditions of treating the mortar joints.

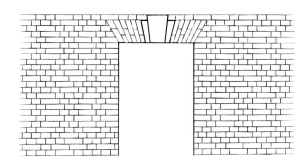

Above: Flemish brick bond. Diagonal brick pattern.

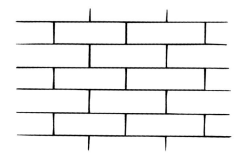

Above: Ashlar masonry. In ashlar masonry, all stones are rectangular, and of the same size, and are laid in continuous courses.

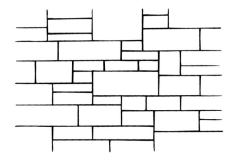

Above: Random ashlar masonry. Stones are rectangular, but not of the same size, and not laid in continuous courses.

Above: Coursed rubble masonry.

Left: Irregular polygonal masonry. This is used in early stonework traditions, and revived for a primitive effect in the late nineteenth century and after.

Right: Brick and wood wall construction diagram from a nineteenth century book. A = foundation, B = sill, C = brick wall, D = plaster, E = studs.

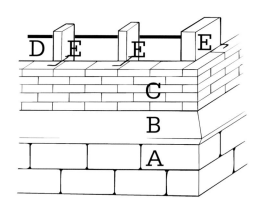

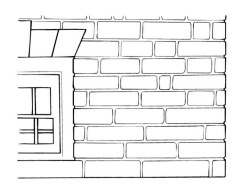

Above: Ashlar masonry, from Mount Pleasant, Philadelphia, 1761–1762.

Above: Brick quoins, from Mount Pleasant, Philadelphia, 1761–1762. Quoins were used to reinforce the corners structurally as well as visually.

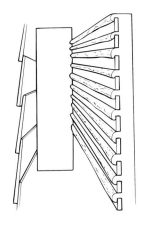

Above: Plaster wall construction; section of early plastered wall.

Above: Diagram of post and beam frame. This heavy beam construction was typical of American architecture of the seventeenth and eighteenth centuries, and continued well into the nineteenth for barns.

Above: The pattern of the half-timber frame shows clearly against the white plastered infilling in this farmhouse.

Above: Brown House, Watertown, MA. With the clapboards removed, the basic half-timber structure of the post and beam frame is revealed.

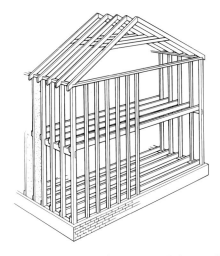

Above: The balloon frame was a lighter weight framing structure of standardized two-by-fours, created in Chicago in 1833. It soon replaced the more complicated post and beam framing technique.

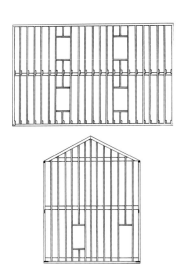

Above: Diagram of balloon framing, from William Bell, *Carpentry Made Easy*, 1859.

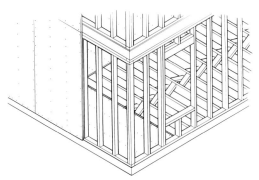

Above: Diagram of wall framing with plywood sheathing. The twentieth century introduced new materials, such as plywood.

Victorian Styles

The Civil War marked a transition in American building; after the conflict, a rich variety of highly decorated styles from wider ranges of historical and geographic sources flourished. This was an age of economic and geographic expansion in the United States, which Leland Roth has aptly called an era of energy and enterprise. Although styles were still derived from European precedent, increasing signs of innovation appeared. A new professionalism emerged in architecture at this time, with the first school of architecture founded at the Massachusetts Institute of Technology in 1868. Illustrated journals of architecture also appeared in the 1880s.

One of the most vibrant styles to appear at this time was the British-inspired High Victorian Gothic. This modern Gothic style was inspired by the writings of John Ruskin, and included an emphasis on polychromy and irregular patterns derived from Venetian and French Gothic buildings. This was one of the dominant styles for public buildings during the period of 1860–1880, but the style was flexible enough for houses. This rather showy mode was less used in America for residences, but examples can be found, such as the house in Newton, Massachusetts, or Olana, the richly eclectic house built for the painter Frederick Church by Church and Calvert Vaux in 1870 near Hudson, New York (see page 9). Olana, which incorporates Islamic arches and Chinese tiles, tokens of Church's passion for travel, in a dramatically picturesque towered mansion near the Hudson River, is in a class by itself. Mark Twain's remarkable house in Hartford, Connecticut, designed by Edward Potter in 1874, is equally striking. A large, rambling structure with many gables, porches, and sculptural chimneys, Twain's house uses combinations of colored bricks to create a vibrant polychromatic effect.

The main competitor for stylistic dominance in this third quarter of the century was another richly ornate

Above: Edward Potter (1831–1904): Mark Twain House, 351 Farmington Avenue, Hartford, CT, 1874. One of the most elaborate High Victorian houses in America.

Above: George Lord Little House, Kennebunkport, ME, 1875.

style derived from French examples. It is called the Second Empire Baroque because it was a Baroque revival style that appeared during the reign of Napoleon III in France, which was known as the Second Empire (1851–1870). The expansion of the Louvre in Paris at this time contributed enormously to the prestige of this style. One of the hallmark features of this style in housing is the use of mansard roofs, with their distinctive profile. The Second Empire, or Mansard Style, was flexible, and could be built on a very large and ornate scale in stone, or on a much smaller cottage-like scale using wood, making it possible for different classes to utilize it.

The passion for ornament and individualism combined with the thriving lumber industry was to lead to the creation of a less common, but highly decorated style of wooden architecture, known as the Stick Style. Not named until Vincent Scully called attention to it in the 1950s, the Stick Style flourished from about 1860 to 1890, and featured angular and rectilinear patterns of boards used as ornament on the exterior of the house. Excellent examples include the Carson House in Eureka, California, and the Villa Vista in Stony Brook, Connecticut.

One of the most popular styles ever used in American houses was the Queen Anne style of about 1880–1910. This was a highly elaborate style, with only the loosest connection to the historical Queen Anne, who reigned just before George I. These houses typify the term "Victorian" to the average person, and include many of the so-called "Painted Ladies." The first example of a Queen Anne house in America is generally considered to be the Watts-Sherman House in Newport, Rhode Island, by H. H. Richardson in 1874. The appearance of half-timbered British buildings at the Philadelphia Centennial Exposition in 1876 helped encourage the spread of this style.

Houses built in these richly decorated styles were large, and typically had a variety of rooms dedicated to special purposes: parlor, library, nursery, sewing room, dining room, breakfast room, and more could be found. Rooms, if not form, followed function in these Victorian houses. The proliferation of specialized spaces represented a dramatic departure from the seventeenth century and even eighteenth century houses, where multi-purpose rooms were the norm. New concepts of private life flourished at this time as well; cultural

parallels include the novels of Henry James and the development of psychoanalysis at the turn of the century, which found such an enthusiastic response in America. These houses, with their picturesque irregularity and their many inner spaces, literally reflect a more complex view of the self. Perhaps this is why psychological thrillers such as the films of Alfred Hitchcock so frequently use Victorian houses as the setting; Norman Bates' Second Empire Baroque house in *Psycho* (1960) is a good example.

Delightfully odd houses were also built during these late Victorian years. One of the most unusual was "Lucy," the house built in the shape of an elephant in Margate, New Jersey. Patented by James Lafferty in 1881, this house was made of a wooden frame covered with tin, and painted to look like a real elephant, had two floors of living space inside the body of the elephant, and a belvedere for viewing the seascape built in the shape of a howdah (riding platform) on the elephant's back. The staircase was in a rear leg. Although built for publicity purposes, this structure perhaps carried the metaphor of natural shapes for houses a bit too far; only three of these houses were built, and only Lucy remains. After serving as a house, tavern, and hotel, it is now a museum.

The second half of the nineteenth century saw a marked increase in leisure time for the middle class, and new resorts created for them. The seaside resort town of Cape May, New Jersey, was one of the first of these. After a series of devastating fires, it was rebuilt about 1870, and is a showcase of ornate Victorian homes. The wealthiest individuals also built conspicuously magnificent summer mansions near the sea. The eclectic Lockwood-Mathews Mansion in Norwalk, Connecticut of 1864–1869 set the pattern for these. The highest concentration of these gilded-era mansions, many of which rival European palaces, was built in Newport, Rhode Island.

For those seeking an alternative to the busy variety of materials and forms in the Queen Anne and other Victorian styles, the Shingle Style offered a greater simplicity. A distinguishing feature is a continuous skin of wooden shingles for the roof (now generally replaced by composition roofing) and wall surfaces. The Shingle Style appeared in the last quarter of the nineteenth century, and was one of the first styles to tap into American building history for its sources. Partly inspired

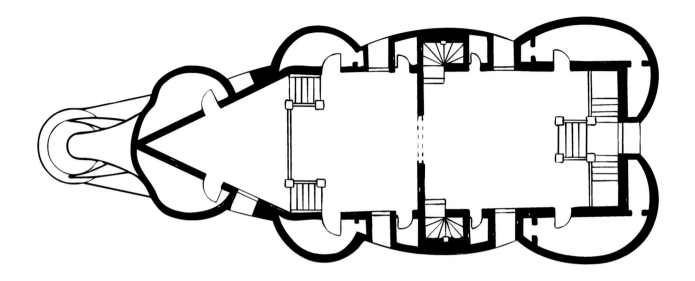

Above: Plan of main floor of "Lucy," house in the shape of an elephant, built by James Lafferty, Margate, NJ, 1881. The second floor contained bedrooms. The trunk was used as a laundry chute.

Above: "Lucy," house in the shape of an elephant, built by James Lafferty, Margate, NJ, 1881. Built as a publicity stunt, and modeled after P.T. Barnum's Jumbo, this odd structure of wood covered with tin was nonetheless used as a house, and later as a tavern and hotel.

by seventeenth century colonial architecture, when many houses were covered with shingles instead of clapboards, this style also included design elements from Japan and from Britain. The centennial exhibition of 1876, commemorating the Declaration of Independence, helped encourage interest in American design precedents. Architects such as Stanford White and Charles McKim made sketching tours of New England villages, and published some of their drawings. Their house for Isaac Bell of 1881–1883 in Newport, Rhode Island, is one of the most impressive Shingle Style houses. Henry Hobson Richardson also used this style to great effect, and the earliest work of Frank Lloyd Wright, including his own house in Oak Park in 1889, was built in the Shingle Style.

One of the most original architects of the late nineteenth century was Henry Hobson Richardson, who introduced a new style based on European Romanesque architecture. Although it was another historical revival, the new style was distinctive enough that it came to be called the Richardsonian Romanesque. Richardson adapted the heavy stone construction of French and Spanish Romanesque architecture to new purposes and modernized forms.

As the Industrial Revolution progressed, urban populations began to explode, with many cities experiencing enormous growth. Boston went from a population of about 15,000 at the time of the revolution to over a half million by 1900; Chicago grew from a population of less than 30,000 in 1850 to nearly 1.7 million by the end of the century. Suburbs also grew at a tremendous pace, made possible by the development of streetcars and, later, subways.

In response to this sudden industrialization and urban growth, there was a reconsideration of

Above: Peter Schmidt: Haas-Lilienthal House, 2007 Franklin Street, (between Washington and Jackson), San Francisco, CA, 1886. A richly ornamented Queen Anne house.

Above: Detlef Lienau: Lockwood-Mathews Mansion, 295 West Avenue, Norwalk, CT, 1864–1869.

Above: Charles F. McKim, William Mead and Stanford White: Isaac Bell House, 70 Perry Street, Newport, RI, 1881–1883.

Above: Henry Hobson Richardson (1838–1886): Robert Treat Paine House, Waltham, MA, 1884–1886. Richardson updated a Second Empire Mansard house by adding large additions with a sweeping porch and a continuous skin of shingles, combined with a rough masonry base.

pre-industrial society and its values. In particular, the religious and social values of the middle ages received new appreciation for the centrality of religion, and the direct connection between the lives of people and the arts and crafts which provided their goods. William Morris and John Ruskin in England promoted the idea that a return to medieval practice could provide an antidote to the alienation of modern industrial society. The Arts and Crafts movement that they inspired was enthusiastically received in the United States. During the period from about 1880 through the 1920s a large number of homes were designed by American followers of this movement. Gustav Stickley, a noted furniture maker, published a magazine called *The Craftsman* from 1901 to 1916, which contained photographs and plans of homes and furniture embodying the principles of the Arts and Crafts movement. Frank Lloyd Wright shared many of these values; in 1901, he lectured at Hull House in Chicago on

"The Art and Craft of the Machine." In this lecture he defined some of the principles of his new Prairie Style homes, and argued for the artistic use of machinery and mass production, rather than a fall back to strict medieval craftsmanship. The Craftsman homes of Gustav Stickley (see page 11) and California bungalows also reflected this trend.

In addition to the high style, architect-designed buildings, a great deal of creativity was manifested by folk builders in this period. These houses are typically built with a balloon frame, and adapt some aspects of the Gothic Revival or perhaps blend it with Italianate or other eclectic styles. The term "Folk Victorian" has been used to describe these homes, and the style was most prevalent during the period of about 1870–1910, or after the coming of the railroad up to just before World War I. Examples can be found all across the U.S.

Above: Henry Hobson Richardson (1838–1886): F. L. Ames Gate Lodge, North Easton, MA, 1880–1881. Richardson's unique blend of Shingle Style and medieval masonry is shown here.

Construction Elements—Roofs

Roof types are one of the first indicators of architectural style. Different profiles are characteristic of different eras and national origins. The level of available technology at the time, and the climate needs also shape roof types.

Above: Steep pitched late medieval gable roof, from a seventeenth century house in Salem, MA. The steep pitch of the gable was related to Gothic design, and also helped northern roofs shed snow and rain efficiently.

Above: Thatched European farmhouse, sixteenth century, with clipped (or jerkin-head) gable. Thatch was also a common roofing material in America during the seventeenth century. By 1800, fire laws forbade both thatch and wooden shingles in urban settings.

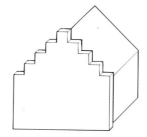

Above: Flemish stepped gable. The stepped gable, which is a false front before a regular steep gable, was characteristic of Dutch and Flemish settlements in the seventeenth and eighteenth centuries, and revived during the eclectic revivals of the nineteenth.

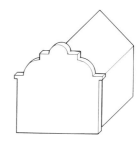

Above: Flemish Renaissance gable. Curving forms were introduced in the Netherlands during the sixteenth century, and also used in America.

Above: Gambrel roof—English seventeenth century type. The gambrel roof was more complicated to build, but offered more usable space on the second floor.

Above: Gambrel roof —North Carolina and Connecticut. Different regions utilized characteristic roof profiles.

Above: Gambrel roof—English seventeenth century, North Carolina and Maryland.

Above: Gambrel roof—New England and South Carolina.

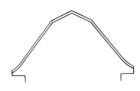

Above: Gambrel roof—Dutch or Flemish.

Above: Gambrel roof— Swedish.

Above: Hipped roof. The hipped roof gave a lower and more unified profile, and was typically used in classical houses in the eighteenth century.

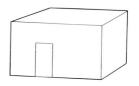

Above: Flat roofs are common in early architecture, such as adobe houses and pueblos of the American Southwest, as well as Mediterranean building. They are also a hallmark of the International Style in the 1920s and 1930s.

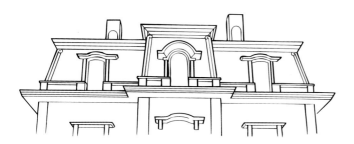

Above: Mansard roof (from a house in Portsmouth, NH). The Mansard roof was an invention of the seventeenth century French architect Jules-Hardouin Mansart.

Above: Flat roof, with overhanging eaves.

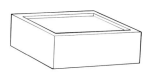

Above: Flat roof, with parapet.

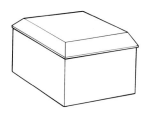

Above: Deck, hipped with flat top.

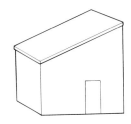

Above: Shed roofs were frequently used in late twentieth century modernist homes.

Right: Clipped (or jerkin-head) gable roof.

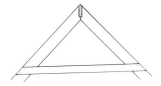

Above: Postmodern roof; organic shape. Bart Prince, house in Corona del Mar. Postmodern design concepts, and new materials, have opened a wide range of design possibilities.

Above: Postmodern roof; pyramid shape. Anthony Predock, Fuller House, Phoenix, AZ, 1986–1987. The lure of archetypal forms remains strong.

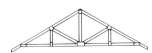

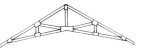

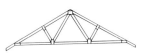

Above: Collar beam, tying rafters together. The collar beam counteracts the natural tendency of the rafters to spread apart, adding strength to the roof.

Above: Diagram of a king post truss. There are several commonly used truss forms used to frame roofs.

Above: Diagram of a scissors truss.

Above: Diagram of a W–truss.

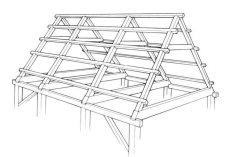

Above: Diagram of a purlin roof frame

Above: Diagram of a gambrel roof frame.

Above: Corner of roof and wall section, showing soffit.

Pre-WWII—Eclectic Revivals

The period 1880–1940 saw a wide variety of historical styles utilized for home designs. Many architects now had extensive academic training, and the revivals were frequently more historically accurate than in the preceding decades. These historical revivals provided a counterpoint to the Modernism which was to develop in this period. New standards of comfort were attained, with central heating, plumbing, and electricity now common.

There was a revival of American eighteenth century house forms, the first revival of American buildings. Some impetus for this was given by the renewed interest in American history occasioned by the Centennial Exhibition in 1876 in Philadelphia. Many examples of the Colonial Revival were built across the United States between about 1880 to 1955. Some are nearly perfect copies of Georgian houses, while others are more eclectic.

European revivals were still very important; among the most prominent of these eclectic revivals were:

Neoclassical—c. 1895–1950: this style was inspired by Roman and Italian Renaissance architecture and was characterized by large entrance porticos with monumental columns. This style was used only for expensive homes.

Tudor—c. 1890–1940: inspired by English Tudor and late medieval architecture this style was characterized by steep pitched roofs, and often had half-timbered façades. Homes in this style could be lavish mansions built of stone, or simple cottages.

Chateauesque—c. 1880–1910; inspired by French chateaux of the Loire region, the first examples were produced by Richard Morris Hunt, the first American to graduate from the Ecole des Beaux-Arts in Paris. Houses in this style were typically of masonry construction, and expensive; some wood-frame houses were occasionally built in this style.

Beaux-Arts—c. 1885–1930; this was a Renaissance-inspired style made popular by the training of the Ecole des Beaux-Arts. Generally reserved for high style, architect-designed homes, the Beaux-Arts style is characterized by formality, symmetry, and lavish ornament. The success of the Classical 1893 World's Columbian Exposition in Chicago contributed to the popularity of this style.

Right: Tudor house, Andover, MA, 1920s. This smaller house used a simplified English Tudor style, popularized by many mail-order house companies such as Sears.

Above: French eclectic house, Chestnut Hill, MA. This chateauesque house represents an ideal of suburban living popularized in the 1920s.

French Eclectic—c. 1915–1945; a style inspired by French country houses, especially in Normandy and Brittany. Frequently of stone or brick, with high, steeply pitched hipped roofs.

Italian Renaissance—c. 1890–1935; modeled on Italian Renaissance villas, these houses are frequently of stone or brick, featuring symmetrical designs and low hipped roofs, often tiled. Although similar to Spanish Mission Style homes, the overhangs are not as broad. The first example may have been the Villard Houses by McKim, Mead, and White in New York, 1883. San Simeon, the Hearst Mansion designed by Julia De Morgan in 1937, is an unusually elaborate composition.

These eclectic styles represented the vast majority of homes built in the early twentieth century, despite the critical enthusiasm for Modernist building. Most people preferred the traditional styles with their European roots. Despite the unifying force of the railroad, regional patterns remained strong. The Spanish colonial tradition continued to be reflected in several revival styles in California and the Southwest, including:

Mission Style—c. 1890–1920; this style originated in California, and recreates the earlier Spanish colonial architecture. Houses feature stucco walls and red tile roofs, with Spanish-inspired detailing.

Spanish Eclectic—c. 1915–1940; a more historically accurate style, incorporating aspects of the entire history of Spanish building. The style was given a major boost from the 1915 Pan-American exhibition in San Francisco, and the contemporary studies of Spanish architecture by Bertram Grosvenor Goodhue, designer of the exhibition. It is most common in the Southwestern states, and Florida.

Monterey—c. 1925–1955; an eclectic mixture of Spanish Eclectic and Eastern Colonial Revival styles. This style is most frequently, but not exclusively found in California and Texas.

Pueblo Revival—c. 1910–present; a mixture of elements from Spanish adobe flat-roofed construction and Native American pueblos. Most common in Arizona and New Mexico.

Above: Julia De Morgan (1872–1957): Hearst Mansion, 750 Hearst Castle Road, San Simeon, CA, 1937. A richly romantic Classical fantasy palace.

Left: Walter Burley Griffin (1876–1937): Carter House, Evanston, IL, 1910. Griffin had worked as an assistant to Frank Lloyd Wright, and this is a very accomplished example of a Prairie School house.

Regionalism was not absolute, however; examples of Mission Style and Spanish homes can be found across the country, including Cape May, New Jersey, and Massachusetts. The wide-ranging eclecticism of this era offered many choices of imported styles, with modifications for modern plumbing and heating.

The question of a truly American style was more urgently raised in the early twentieth century. The most important effort in this regard was the Prairie Style; an indigenous American style created by Frank Lloyd Wright and his Midwestern counterparts which

Above: Frank Lloyd Wright (1867–1959): Ward Willits House, Highland Park, IL, 1902. The Willits House has an extremely open plan, as Wright fulfilled his goal of breaking out of the box.

flourished from about 1893 to 1920. The style includes aspects of the Shingle Style, fused with elements from Japanese architecture and a rejection of European historicism. Wright's later Organic Architecture and Usonian houses build on the principles of the Prairie School. Both Wright and Louis Sullivan strongly condemned American architects' continued borrowing of European forms. In his introduction to the edition of his works published in 1910 in Germany, Wright declared that the use of forms borrowed from other stylistic periods and cultures will inevitably lead to an architecture divorced from the inner life of the people. Wright noted that American culture was particularly susceptible to this alienation, since we had no traditional architecture.

In an interview with William MacDonald in 1958, quoted by P. J. Meehan, Wright explained that he borrowed the term "Usonia" from Samuel Butler, who used it to replace the more long-winded "United States of America. " The word Usonia was also linked to the concept of freedom, and the term Usonian architecture thus meant free architecture, an architecture for democracy.

Wright felt that a new architecture based on modern living patterns, technologies, and concepts of space had to be created. Rather than seeing the house as a box containing various rooms, he wanted to create the

Right: Frank Lloyd Wright (1867–1959): Edgar Kaufmann house, "Fallingwater," Mill Run, PA, 1934–1937. Still the most famous private house in America, Fallingwater is a perfect union of architecture and nature.

interiors first, and then shape the house around them. His concept of space was strikingly dynamic, and almost mystical, as he explained in *The Future of Architecture* in 1953:

"Space. The continual becoming: invisible fountain from which all rhythms flow and to which they must pass. Beyond time or infinity."

By emphasizing the flow of space in his houses, Wright helped shift American architecture from an architecture of solid mass to one of volume and transparency. With windows treated as banks of light screens, walls became more dynamic as well.

Another very original American style was that of the Craftsman Style bungalows; between 1905 and 1930 this was one of the most popular building formats in the nation. The style originated in California, based on the

Right: Ho-o-den, Japanese pavilion at 1893 World's Columbian Exposition, Chicago. The Ho-o-den was a half-scale replica of a Japanese temple built by Japanese workmen for the 1893 fair. It was the first chance Frank Lloyd Wright and many others had to see an example of Japanese architecture.

Right: Walter Gropius (1883–1969): Gropius House, 68 Baker Ridge Road, Lincoln, MA, 1938. Gropius built this house for himself near Walden Pond. He was teaching at Harvard University, after fleeing Nazi Germany.

Arts and Crafts-inspired designs of Charles Sumner Greene and Henry Mather Greene. Masterpieces such as the Gamble House in Pasadena reflect the highest level of craftsmanship.

After World War I, homes built in the colonial revival and other traditional styles still dominated the housing market, but new Modernist experiments emerged, especially in California. Architects in Europe embraced modern materials such as metal and glass, and firmly rejected historical ornament. Many of them admired and were influenced by Frank Lloyd Wright, but they went even further in creating a new style for the new age. These Modernist styles at first appealed only to a small elite seeking a new mode of life, but eventually were embraced by a broader segment of American society. At first, as Michael Webb has observed, the American public was as "shocked by nudity in buildings as in people." However, the focus on the modern resonated with the longstanding American desire to create a new world, beyond Europe's borders, owing nothing to the past.

The most important current of the new architecture was the International Style, which began about 1925 and continues to the present day. A Modernist style which rejects historical ornament, the International Style was named for a 1932 exhibition of the works of Le Corbusier, Ludwig Mies van der Rohe, and Walter

Left: Ludwig Mies van der Rohe (1886–1969): Dr. Edith Farnsworth House, 14520 River Road, Plano, IL, 1945–1951.

Above: Ludwig Mies van der Rohe: 860–880 Lake Shore Drive, Chicago, 1948–1951. The first skyscraper high-rise apartment building in the U.S.

Gropius at the Museum of Modern Art in New York. Modern building technology is revealed by the frequent use of curtain walls, ribbon windows, and cantilevered floors. European-born architects such as Rudolph Schindler and Richard Neutra brought first-hand knowledge of these new directions to America. Significantly, both men came to the United States to work with Frank Lloyd Wright in the early 1920s. Two of the main creators of the International Style, Walter Gropius and Ludwig Mies van der Rohe, immigrated to America in the late 1930s to escape Nazi Germany, which rejected the tenets of Modernism. Both Gropius and Mies had a tremendous effect on American architecture, through their buildings

as well as their teaching; Gropius headed the Harvard School of Design from 1938, and Mies directed the Illinois Institute of Technology in Chicago. Gropius' own home in Lincoln, Massachusetts (1938), is a masterpiece of the new style. Mies's Farnsworth House in Plano, Illinois (1945–1950) was a near perfect example of a house as a pure volume of space enclosed by glass. Stunning in its beauty and simplicity, this stark home is not for everyone, but it exemplified the ideals of a purist and ascetic Modernism. Mies influenced another area of modern housing; he pioneered the use of skyscraper apartments in his 860–880 Lake Shore Drive towers in Chicago (1948–1950).

Walter Gropius and Mies van der Rohe had both been associated with the most famous design school in Europe, the Bauhaus in Germany. Gropius created it in 1919 in Weimar, and designed its new headquarters in Dessau in 1926. The new Bauhaus included houses for the master teachers, which were demonstrations of the new aesthetic. Mies directed the school from 1930–1933. The Bauhaus replaced an earlier school of arts and crafts, and although it embraced mechanical production, it too was intended to break down barriers between the so-called fine arts and design arts, and to stress the collaborative nature of construction. Art was to reclaim its central role in modern life, even if it was not all handcrafted. The Bauhaus became almost synonymous with International Style design; the use of flat roofs and glass walls became a trademark.

Left: Walter Gropius (1883–1969): Master's House, Bauhaus, Dessau, Germany, 1926. As head of the famed Bauhaus school in Germany, Gropius had been one of the creators of the International Style, characterized by simple abstract geometric shapes, functional design, and lack of ornament.

Walter Gropius' classroom building at the Bauhaus showcased a paradigmatic curtain wall of glass; the transparency and infinite variety of viewpoints expressed a Utopian program for the future. Modernist transparency dissolved the restrictions and barriers of the old order. The quasi-mystical belief in the healthfulness and morality of glass architecture was only partly rationalized in the architecture of the International Style. The Health House built for Dr. Lovell in Los Angeles by Richard Neutra in 1927–1929 embodied the belief that glass and sunlight led to improved health.

Ironically, the glass architecture of the International Style, which grew from utopian hopes of a transformed society and health concerns, eventually became the favorite style of modern corporate architecture. Despite many criticisms, glass boxes are still highly regarded; in April 1999 the *New York Times* architecture critic Herbert Muschamp named the Seagram Building the most significant building of the millennium.

One serious flaw in the International Style, according to many, was the abandonment of all ornament; there were architects who admired the sleekness and modernity of the International Style, but felt it could be combined with Modernistic ornament. A style which is somewhat generically called Modernistic evolved between 1920 and 1940; variants of it are also called Art Deco or Arte Moderne. These houses reject historicist ornamental features in favor of streamlined simple geometry, planar walls, and often flat roofs. Traditional construction methods are generally used, instead of the steel frames or concrete slabs of International Style designs.

Surpassing even the architects of the International Style with his experimental Modernism, R. Buckminster

Above: Richard Neutra (1892–1970): Philip Lovell House, Los Angeles, CA, 1927–1929.

Fuller created a visionary design called the Dymaxion House in 1927–1929. A hexagonal-plan house, suspended from a central mast, it was far ahead of its time, and was too expensive to be built during the depression. Some of the key ideas were reused in Fuller's Dymaxion Deployment Units, "dwelling machines" designed to address the great housing shortage at the end of the war. During the war, some examples were built using circular core units from silo factories. In 1945, an aluminum prototype was produced by Beech Aircraft of Wichita, but it never went into mass production.

Other innovative architects who demonstrated experimental homes at the Century of Progress exposition in Chicago in 1933 included George Fred Keck, who showed an all-glass house. Keck and his brother William developed a successful practice in the Midwest, which designed the first modern solar houses.

Paradoxically, the same age that saw the energetic abandonment of historicist ornament in the new Modernist styles, also brought a renewed respect for the past, and the development of the historic preservation movement. During the nineteenth century, despite the plethora of historic revivals, many old houses were torn down, even those belonging to such historic figures as John Hancock, whose house in Boston was demolished in 1863. Even Monticello itself was in some danger. Paul Revere's house was saved in 1909, and the preservation movement began with the restoration of significant early homes such as that of Parson Capen (1913). Some needed extensive rebuilding—Revere's house had been used for commercial purposes, and had been drastically altered with an additional floor, eliminating the steep pitched roof. Photographs taken of the Old Corner Bookstore in Boston, before and after restoration, show

Above: Paul Revere House, 19 North Square, Boston, MA, 1676; 2001 photo.

Left: Paul Revere House, Boston, MA, 1676. This 1905 postcard shows the condition of the house before its restoration in 1913. It was being used for commercial purposes, and a third-story dormer had been added. The restoration of the Revere house was an early example of historic preservation.

what damage has frequently been done to old houses. Fortunately, there are others such as the Jeremiah Lee House (purchased by the Marblehead Historic Society in 1909) which had been left basically unchanged since they were constructed. There was a strong sense that these relics of the past could offer connection to traditions and values that were being challenged by the modern age. In addition to individual houses, entire communities were rebuilt or restored, not always with

archeological accuracy, such as Colonial Williamsburg, Virginia, begun in 1926. The William Penn House, known as Pennsbury Manor, was originally built in about 1683–1699 in Morrisville, PA. It was destroyed at the end of the eighteenth century, but recreated in 1933–1942. In keeping with the prevailing attitudes of the times, the focus in these restorations was on the homes of the wealthier classes. Only recently have the homes of working class residents of the nineteenth century industrial

Right: Thomas Crease: "Old Corner Bookstore," corner of School and Washington streets, Boston, MA, 1711. This was built as a private home, and later used as a bookstore. This old postcard shows the building before restoration in the twentieth century.

areas and the earlier slave quarters been deemed worthy of historic preservation. As the focus of preservation expands, even the artifacts of the early modern period are now considered historic monuments; Walter Gropius' 1938 house is now protected by the Society for the Preservation of New England Antiquities.

Above: Pennsbury Manor, William Penn House, 400 Pennsbury Memorial Road, Morrisville, PA, built c. 1683–1999, destroyed at the end of the eighteenth century, and recreated in 1933–1942.

Construction Elements—Heating

The technologies of comfort have evolved tremendously in American houses. The colonial houses of the first period relied on massive and inefficient fireplaces for heat and cooking. Benjamin Franklin designed a significantly improved stove in the eighteenth century, and in the nineteenth century architects such as Andrew Jackson Downing studied the design of fireplaces and furnaces according to scientific principles. Catherine Beecher and her sister, Harriet Beecher Stowe reformed house design with an early form of scientific management based on functional patterns of household work, and the use of technology.

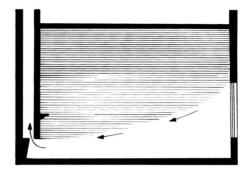

Left: Room heated by fireplace, with poor ventilation (A.J. Downing). Nineteenth century architects and engineers became more concerned with the impact of house design on health as well as comfort.

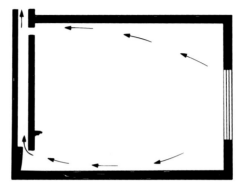

Left: Room heated by fireplace, with good ventilation (A.J. Downing).

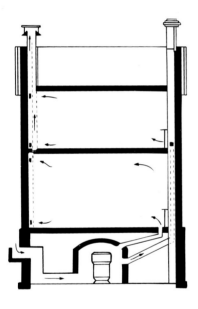

Left: Room heated by furnace, with good ventilation (A.J. Downing). New technologies in the eighteenth and nineteenth centuries provided more options for heating.

Right: Diagram of faulty vs. correct chimney flue construction, in *The House, a Pocket Manual of Rural Architecture*, New York: Fowler and Wells, 1859. Pattern books such as this were used by builders to guide them in the construction of houses.

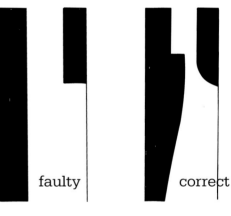

faulty | correct

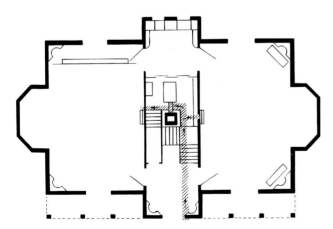

Above: Design for an efficient house, by Harriet Beecher Stowe and Catherine Beecher; first floor. The relationship of design and social patterns were the concern of reformers such as the sisters.

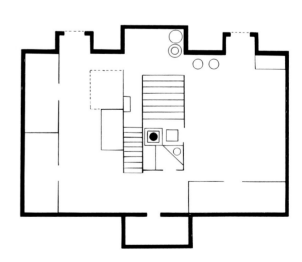

Above: Design for an efficient house, by Harriet Beecher Stowe and Catherine Beecher; basement.

The Modern Age

The Post-War era saw a huge growth of housing in the decades of prosperity which followed the war. Mass housing in simplified traditional styles dominated the market during the baby-boom era, although a small number of very experimental houses has dominated the field of architectural criticism. The tensions between high culture and mass culture have never been more intense, or led to more interesting results.

In the design of small houses, a simplified modern style predominated. Even houses that included some traditional elements eliminated the ornamental features which had been so distinctive in the pre-modern styles, in the name of efficiency and cost-savings. A wide spectrum of basically a-historical houses was produced during this period, including such sub-types as:

Minimal Traditional—c. 1935–1950; simple boxy houses with some minimal reference to traditional building styles, but little ornamental detail.

Ranch—c. 1935–1975; small horizontal one-story houses based on California ranch houses, with some influence from the Prairie School.

Split Level—c. 1955–1975; a variant of the ranch house, with a two- or three-story section added to allow greater separation of living spaces.

Contemporary—c. 1940–1980; frequently used for architect-designed homes, with two main sub-types. Flat-roof houses show a continuing tie to the International Style; gable-roof houses reveal the influence of Frank Lloyd Wright and the Prairie School.

Shed—c. 1960–present; Modernist houses with simple geometric shapes and shed roofs, frequently sliced at different angles. Gables may be combined. The style was primarily inspired by the works of Charles Moore and Robert Venturi.

Above: Quonset Hut, Abingdon, MA, 1940s. These pre-fabricated huts were produced in great numbers (over 170,000) at the naval base at Quonset, RI, providing cheap housing after WWII.

These house types have been widely built by individuals, and also by developers creating suburban communities.

One of the most successful examples of a planned community was the development of the suburb of Levittown on Long Island, New York. Built by William and Alfred Levitt between 1946 and 1951, Levittown used a small number of basic house styles and standardized construction to provide housing for nearly 18,000 households, including many soldiers returning after World War II (see page 10). The affordability of these small houses, combined with financing for G.I.s, made them very popular. Although Levittown was frequently characterized as a symbol of featureless uniformity in the modern world, it is clear that the community answered a real need. In subsequent decades, many of the houses have been expanded or altered to make them more individualized. The original development in New York was followed in the 1950s by Levittown, Pennsylvania, and Levittown, New Jersey.

The success of Henry Ford in making the automobile available to the majority of people through the economies of mass production has led to a number of efforts to adapt assembly-line techniques to homebuilding. In the early decades of the twentieth century, the Aladdin Homes company advertised prefabricated houses that were "built in a day," as if by a genie. This was a slight exaggeration, since it did not include the site preparation or building the foundation. During WWII, over 170,000 Quonset huts with prefabricated steel arched rib frames were produced for inexpensive housing. Others attempted to build houses almost completely out of metal; the Motohome was an experimental metal house built on Long Island in the late 1930s. From 1947 to 1950, the Lustron company sold 2,500 largely metal houses which needed almost no maintenance, since the metal walls were covered with permanent enamel, and the roofs were made of durable tile. The houses contained many built-in conveniences, but were more expensive than the average house, and could not easily

Above: Colonial Re-revival house, Andover, MA. The lure of tradition and historical context is strong in historic communities.

be expanded or altered, so the company was unable to sell enough to stay in business. Seven percent of American housing is represented by mobile homes, which in reality are not very mobile, but are prefabricated and transported complete to the home site. Two units can be joined together to make a "double-wide" home. Truly mobile living has been achieved by some retirees who live in R.V.s (recreational vehicles) or trailers which are moved from northern climates to warmer southern regions during the winter.

The last decades of the twentieth century saw a proliferation of stylistic options, including:

Late Modern—1970–present; an important group of high style, architect-designed homes in this era that continue the research of Modernist architects into non-historical, efficient yet dramatic housing, often with highly theoretical underpinnings. Examples include the designs of Richard Meier and Peter Eisenman.

Neo-eclectic—c. 1965–present; very popular with developers, who populate whole neighborhoods with variants of this style. Substyles include Mansard, Neocolonial, Neo-French, Neo-Tudor, Neo-Mediterranean, Neoclassical Revival, and Neo-Victorian.

Contemporary Folk—1940–present; inexpensive housing in this era includes mass-production mobile homes and Quonset huts, which were utilized during and immediately after WWII. Handmade houses of this period include very geometric geodesic domes, A-frames, free-form houses made up of scrap materials, and even yurts (Mongolian tents).

Recycled Housing—c. 1970–present; a by-product of the historical preservation movement which gained strength in the 1970s was the conversion of older building types into housing.

Above: Robert Venturi (b. 1925): Vanna Venturi's House, Chestnut Hill, PA, 1963.

Examples of structures that have been successfully converted include: nineteenth century mill buildings, urban industrial lofts, churches, barns, train cars, firehouses, and even lighthouses. The sweeping spaces and historic framework of these houses, combined with the sense of being in direct contact with history, appeals to many.

Green Architecture—1970–present; since the first Earth Day in 1970 and the energy crisis of the 1970s, a growing awareness of environmental concerns has shaped the construction of new homes. Even conventional homes are now fitted with more insulation and more efficient heating systems; a number of homeowners have built homes that rely only on renewable energy sources. Solar heating, which actually dates back to the turn of the century, has been improved. Some homes, called "Earth Ships," are made from recycled materials and use only solar power or wind power. Reviving a frontier technique, houses have even been built using straw bales for the wall construction.

Above: Steven Izenour (1946–2001): George and Hildegard Izenour house, Stony Creek, CT, 1985–1986.

INTRODUCTION

Postmodern—c. 1963–present; rejecting the ascetic geometry and stylistic absolutes of Modernist architecture, Robert Venturi and other architects sought to reintroduce complexity and rich human experience into their architecture. Historical ornament and contextual allusions were no longer taboo, although frequently used with irony. Venturi's house for his mother, Vanna Venturi, in Chestnut Hill of 1963 was one of the first of these Postmodern houses. Tucked away in a leafy suburban neighborhood near Philadelphia, the broken pediment form of the main gable and arcane allusions to Classical orders are still surprising. The seaside home built by Steven Izenour in Stony Brook, Connecticut in 1985–1986 draws on the local traditions of shingle cottages, but adds Postmodern variants of Classical columns to the façade, unusual patterns and shaped windows reminiscent of nautical wheels.

Striking challenges to the purism and exclusivity of Modernism are also found in Frank Gehry's own house of 1978 in Santa Monica, California, which uses banal materials such as corrugated steel and chain link fencing in surprising combinations for domestic architecture; the use of these industrial materials in a house owed something to the precedent of the Bauhaus, but the everyday quality of the materials created a completely different effect than the precious perfectionism of Mies van der Rohe's architecture. The strongly individual expressionist shapes of Bart Prince's houses in New Mexico and California evoke associations with biological and geological shapes, and even overtones of science fiction.

New Urbanism—c. 1980–present. A recent development is the creation of entire planned communities, such as Seaside, Florida, begun in 1982, and Celebration, near Orlando (1996), which seek to restore not only pre-modern architectural forms, but also pre-modern community structures. Modeled on an idealized vision of small-town life, the scale of the houses was kept deliberately small and the role of front porches as gathering points is prominently emphasized. The styles are based on eighteenth century Classicism and sometimes the Gothic Revival. The public has responded positively to these centrally planned developments, although they also have been featured as symbols of excessive societal surveillance in recent satirical films.

Homes are the primary stage upon which we live our lives. Originality and the search for authenticity have frequently competed with the appeal of tradition and historical continuity in American home building. One aspect of the American dream is to be a self-made millionaire, yet many prefer to live as if they were descended from European royalty. Although contemporary critics such as Ada Louis Huxtable, Jean Baudrillard, and Umberto Eco have shone a powerful spotlight on the prevalence of surrogate experience and synthetic settings in American life, the lure of such theatrical settings shows no sign of diminishing. The search for the perfect home is as important as the search for a perfect mate in contemporary American culture.

Chapter 1

Early Architecture in the U.S.—
Folk Architecture

Tom O'Gorman

Early architecture in America is intensely related to the twin pillars of geography and culture. This was as true for Native American peoples who populated the wide reaches of the continent for thousands of years as it was for newly transplanted European colonists who first arrived almost four hundred years ago. The evolution of an American style has its roots in this strangely evocative design imperative of geography and culture. Where you lived was as important as how you lived. Domestic architecture was primitive for each group, defined by the special limitations of materials and technolo-

Above: Earth-wall lodges, Pawnee tribe, Loup Fork, Nebraska; photo 1871.

Left: John White: watercolor of Secoton, NC, Algonquian village, 1585. This watercolor drawing is an important early record of Native American architecture and settlement patterns.

Left: An engraving of an Algonquian doctor or shaman concocting medicine in a simple wigwam of skins over a frame of poles lashed together.

Above: Tlingit chief's house, Cape Fox Village, Alaska, photo 1899. (National Anthropological Archives)

Left: British Columbia, Kwakiutl tribe. Gabled, plank-walled houses. Photograph c. 1889. Northwest coast tribes made use of abundant wood to make unique plank-walled houses.

gies, as well as pragmatic, concerned with the essentials of preserving family life amid the testing rigors of every-day subsistence. With a radical climate, more expansive and extreme than they had known in England, the first colonists in what came to be known as "New England" encountered changes in climatic conditions more challenging than they had know in their European homes. Ironically, the primitive design of peasant homes in rural England, formed of "clay and wattle" (wattle and daub), a throwback to medieval times, was far more similar in its design to that of Native American peoples than it was to the homes of their more aristocratic countrymen back in England.

Long before any contact with the peoples of Europe, the American continent was home to a vast population. From ocean to ocean they lived amid the far reaches of

forest, arid planes, grasslands, the tropical coastal reaches of the Southeast and the ever-changing climatic environments of the Great Lakes, Mississippi River valley, and deserts of the Southwest. In many ways native peoples were shaped by the continent's natural resources and they lived close to the earth in their every-day life. Their domestic architecture reflected spiritual values and a common-sense application of the land's natural resources. Their husbandry of nature reflects a pre-European American dependant on the bounty of the earth. Such influence was never far from their design motifs in the construction of both permanent and nomadic lodging. Three unique traditions emerge in what remains America's most truly definitive architectural folk style.

Northern Woodlands

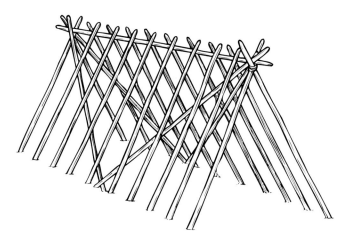

Above: Drawing of the frame of a Chippewa peaked lodge, northern Minnesota, c. 1900.

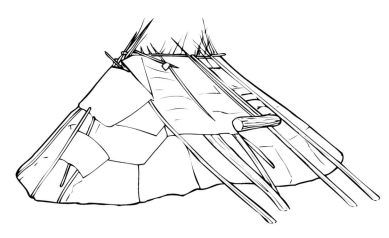

Above: Chippewa peaked lodge covered with birch bark, northern Minnesota, c. 1900. Birch bark lodges were used for temporary accomodation.

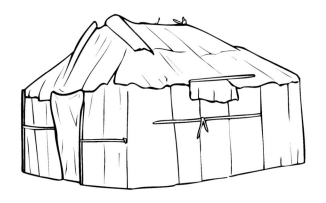

Left: Chippewa lodge covered with elm bark, northern Minnesota, c. 1900. Heavier bark was used for longer-term accomodation; in winter, insulation was provided by pine branches piled against the walls and covered with snow.

Northwest Coastal

Above: Tlingit plank house, deserted Cape Fox village, from 1899 photograph by Edward Curtis. Northwest coast houses used the abundant timber to create distinctive plank houses. This one is decorated with images of the sacred bear.

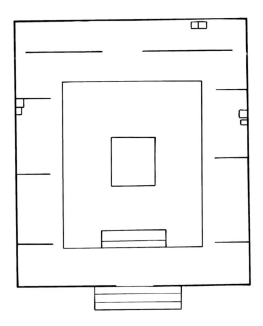

Right: Plan of a Tlingit clan house, Alaska. Various families were separated by cedar mats in these community houses.

The Longhouse

In the eastern portion of the American continent, a woodland of abundant vegetation, a wood-frame structure called a longhouse developed. It was constructed on a rectangular plan and was dominant among Native Americans. These great, arched-roofed houses reflected both their woodland geography, incorporating a wooden-frame construction with woven mat or tree-bark walls; and their sense of extended family creating expansive and spacious structures capable of housing multiple families. This architectural format relates a defining social characteristic about the tribes who fashioned these essentially permanent structures. The tribes along the Atlantic coast, those whom the colonizing Europeans would first encounter, were settled peoples, occupying familiar territory and villages on a permanent basis. Their domestic architecture reflected this sense of tribal settlement and their agrarian way of life.

The rectangular longhouse was a familiar home to such tribal people as the Iroquois, the Algonquin, and the Mohawk. Such lodges were the center of tribal family life and denote a cohesion among such woodland peoples who populated the reaches of what today are New York State, Massachusetts, and Canada. Long before the arrival of the English Pilgrims, and later British and French troops, the longhouse homes of these complex tribal organizations filled the most scenic and productive acreage in North America. Today, examples of such handsome architecture are available in centers like the New York State Museum in Albany. They are remarkable dwellings reflecting both the social imperatives and structural necessities brought on by their particular sense of non-transient living.

Above: Seminole tribe longhouse, Fort Lauderdale, Florida, photo c. 1917. This open-sided longhouse is covered with a thatched roof.

Eastern Coastal

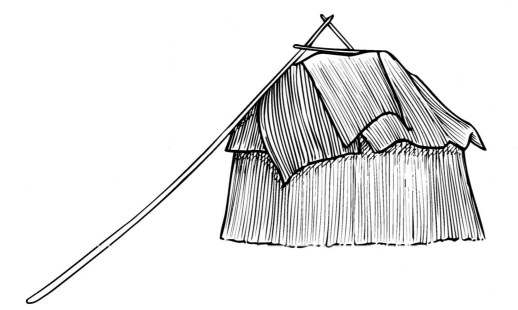

Left: Wigwam, covered with reed mats, Massachusetts coast.

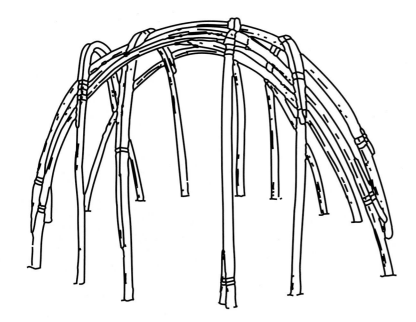

Left: Wigwam frame, Massachusetts coast. The poles of the frame are anchored in the earth, and lashed together. A smokehole at the top served as a chimney.

Left: Iroquois longhouse. Iroquois and other eastern groups constructed long buildings which housed several families.

The Pueblos

With a very different sense of geography and culture, the peoples of the southwest portion of the North American continent developed an architecture more suited to the arid quality of the land and the intensity of the climate. Their pueblos were permanent villages of multi-tier, flat-roofed, baked-clay dwellings. Sun dried earth or mud bricks called adobe were the essential building element. These structures follow a concept of rectilinear design not unlike multi-family habitations created by the woodland peoples of the East. Pueblos, however, were built in a series of rising dwelling units or terraces, assembled one atop another. In design, they appear remarkably modern. Their inherent practicality is what made living in the desert regions of the continent both bearable and efficient.

The adobe earth pueblos, their elevated layers replete with tall ladders for reaching the high tiers of loft-dwellings, are literally fashioned from the soil of the desert and provide naturally protective fortress-like heights. Employed by such tribes as the Navaho, the Zuni, the Apache, the Acoma, and the Hopi, the practicality and architectural simplicity of the pueblos impacted on the Spanish colonists who first encountered them and thus influenced the future of architectural development in the scorching barren landscape. The inherent architectural wisdom contained in their design would go on to help civilize the region as Spanish settlers from California and Arizona to Mexico adopted aspects of their balanced utilitarian design. The basic simplicity of the pueblos' structure can be seen as a dominant theme to this day. While interiors may have changed, the concept of exterior baked clay cooling the many tiers of the family dwelling remains a strong design element.

Above: Cliff houses, Mesa Verde, CO, 1100–1300. The earliest stone architecture in America is found in the Southwest.

Above: Pueblo Bonito, Chaco Canyon, NM, c. 1070. Complex living units for large settlements, pueblo architecture was well adapted to the environment. The thick mass of adobe walls kept the houses cool in the summer, and warm in the winter.

Above: Taos Pueblo, Taos, NM, sixteenth century.

Above: Zuni Pueblo, NM, photo 1879.

Southwest

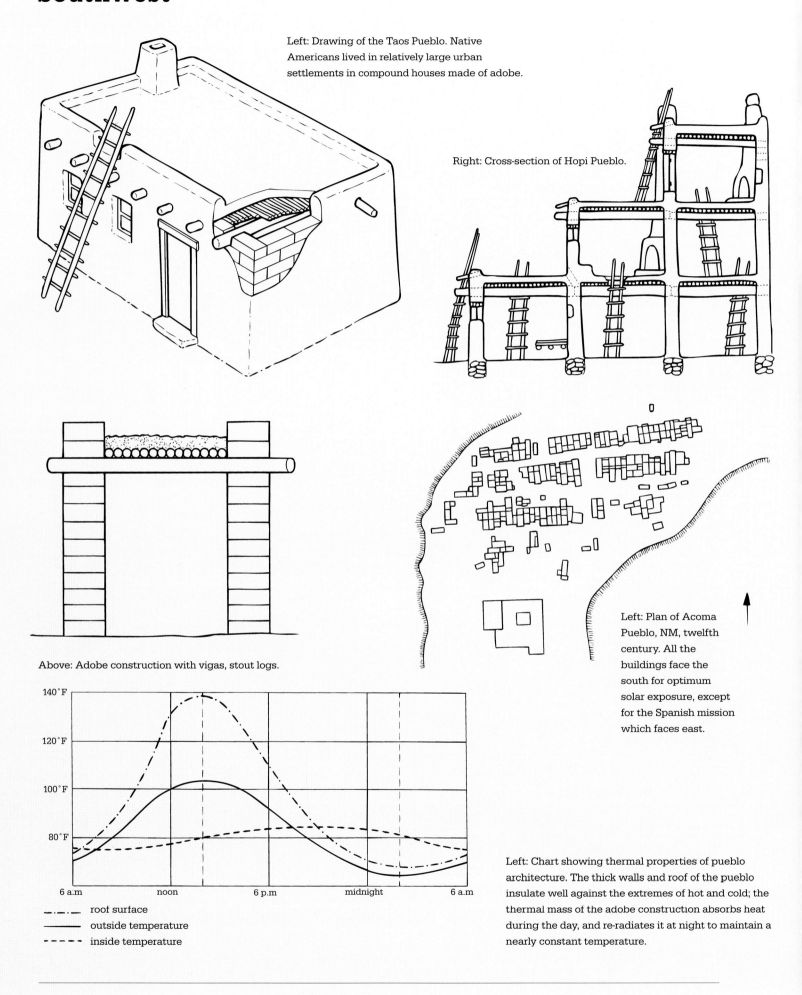

Left: Drawing of the Taos Pueblo. Native Americans lived in relatively large urban settlements in compound houses made of adobe.

Right: Cross-section of Hopi Pueblo.

Above: Adobe construction with vigas, stout logs.

Left: Plan of Acoma Pueblo, NM, twelfth century. All the buildings face the south for optimum solar exposure, except for the Spanish mission which faces east.

140°F

120°F

100°F

80°F

6 a.m   noon   6 p.m   midnight   6 a.m

—·—·— roof surface
——— outside temperature
----- inside temperature

Left: Chart showing thermal properties of pueblo architecture. The thick walls and roof of the pueblo insulate well against the extremes of hot and cold; the thermal mass of the adobe construction absorbs heat during the day, and re-radiates it at night to maintain a nearly constant temperature.

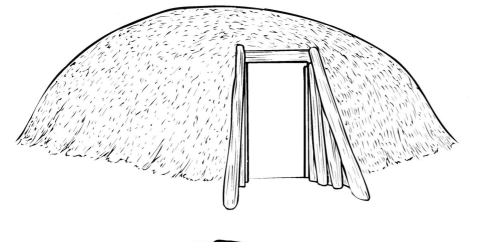

Left: Navaho Hogan; wooden frame is covered with earth. The hemispherical shape of the Hogan recreates the sacred dome of Heaven.

Left: Hogan frame; the heavy timbers will be covered with earth. The roof shape is not a true dome (based on an arch), but a corbelled dome, created by successive layers overlapping.

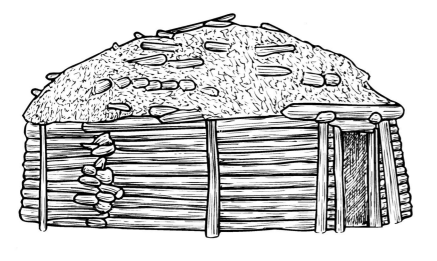

Left: Hogan, exterior view. After 1800, six-sided wooden hogans became more common.

Left: Chumash lodge built of logs and reeds, reconstructed in Satwiwa Native American Indian Culture Center, Point Mugu State Park, near Los Angeles, CA.

Tipis

For many, the conical-shaped tipi will always be the most familiar design of Native American architectural life, due mostly to the narrow exposure given to it in films about the American West. In reality these non-permanent tent-like structures were the shelter of the nomadic dwellers of the American plains. Architecturally simple, being the marriage of a frame-work of tall poles and animal-skin covering, the tipi permitted native peoples like the Sioux, the Arapahoe, the Cherokee, the Blackfoot, and the Crow easy geographical movement. The tribes of the American plains, roughly the area that stretches west of the Mississippi River to the Rocky Mountains, followed their main source of food—the buffalo. Their ability to gather up their dwellings and move on to more abundant areas for hunting and gathering was the central construct of their pattern of life. The natural architectural flexibility of the tipi enhanced their ability to move large numbers of hunters, warriors, and tribal peoples swiftly when necessity demanded.

The tipi was the tribal architectural design that white, mid-nineteenth century settlers in the decades just before and after the American Civil War encountered in their push to cultivate and populate the whole continent. This endeavor eventually unleashed fierce wars across the plains, which, in turn, brought a new strategic imperative to the tribes' need for mobility.

The design of the tipi had an extraordinary adaptability, providing its nomadic dweller with the ability to live comfortably in a wide range of climatic conditions on the sweep of the plains. In the winter months, the opening at the top of the tent poles could be maneuvered to permit smoke from internal fires to escape. In summer months, the skin flaps around those same poles could be manipulated to permit the winds of summer to circulate inside. A further arrangement of poles and skin flaps could be controlled during rainy weather to permit those within to remain dry. Through the passage of the seasons, the tipi's unique flexibility permitted tribal peoples the necessary movement to support their way of life.

Right: Chippewa wigwam, a round-frame, bark-covered house, from Wisconsin. (Photo, Field Museum, Chicago)

Right: Apache wickiup. Built on a frame of lashed poles, this wickiup is covered with organic materials such as grass to keep out the elements.

Right: Plains tipi; Kansas, Kiowa tribe, photo c. 1870. An extremely portable shelter for nomadic tribes.

Plains

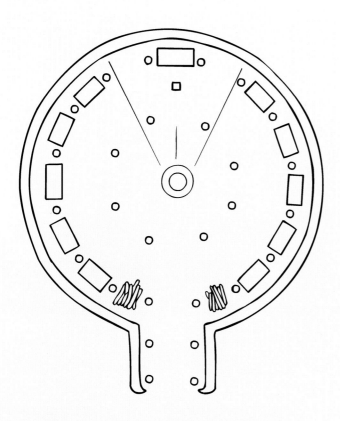

Above: Plan of a Pawnee earth lodge. The circular plan and axis toward the altar have spiritual significance. The entrance is oriented toward the east.

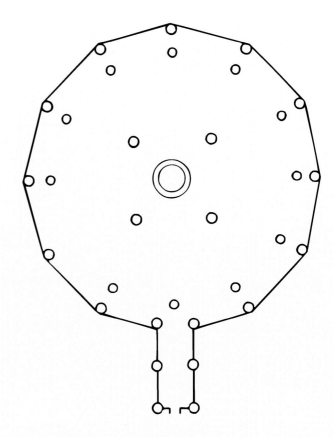

Above: Mandan earth lodge plan, showing the location of poles and fire pit.

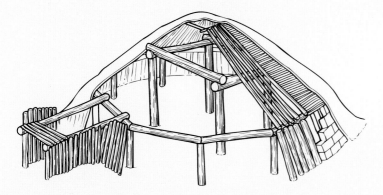

Above: Mandan earth lodge frame. Post-and-lintel frames carry the wall poles, which are covered with earth blocks and sod. The roof is made of sod put down over a grass mat laid on sticks.

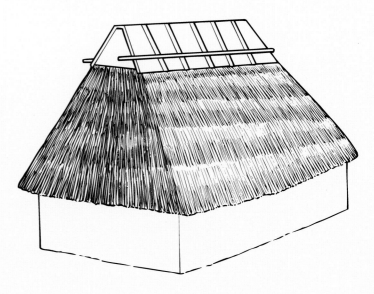

Above: Thatched house, Cahokia mound culture.

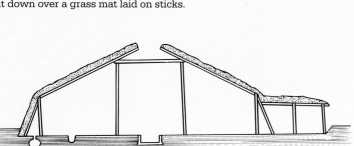

Above: Mandan earth lodge section.

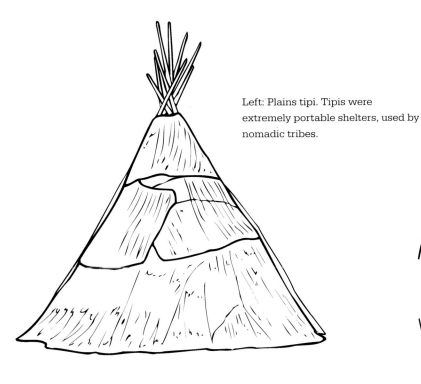

Left: Plains tipi. Tipis were extremely portable shelters, used by nomadic tribes.

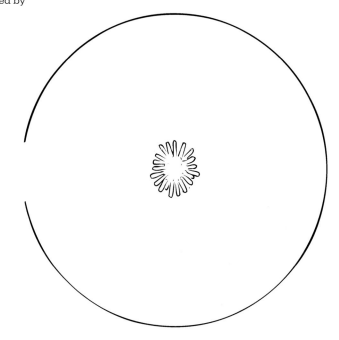

Above: Diagram showing typical arrangement of the hearth inside a Chippewa family tipi.

Above: Plains tipi frame. Frames of slender poles were lashed together and then covered with animal hides or bark.

Above: Apache wickiup. A wickiup is a domical structure of lashed poles, covered with grass or plant materials.

English Wigwams

When English colonists first set foot on the soil of the American continent in New England in 1620, they did so as fleeing exiles for whom religious independence had a primal urgency. The Puritans were religious separatists who had rejected the traditions of the established Church. They were neither landed aristocrats nor adventurers, but rather fervent yeoman dissenters freeing themselves from the excesses of their native culture. Removal to America for them was about the continued following of the simple, uncluttered life of a fundamentalist faith. The significance of this point is critical in understanding the architectural traditions that emerged among them in America.

The first colonists in American New England were country folk from the shires, people familiar with the primitive folk architecture of their native countryside, which still bore the rough imprint of medieval England for the poor. England's officially sanctioned colony of Jamestown, in Virginia, had been settled for more than a decade when the religious dissenters reached Plymouth Rock. Their tradition of simple, utilitarian living was sorely tested with their winter arrival and their most pressing need for adequate shelter. Architecture at its most pragmatic proved to be the order of the day.

The earliest and most primitive dwellings fashioned by the first English settlers of Massachusetts by their very nature did not stand the test of time, though historic depictions survive in the annals that were methodically kept by the first generations of colonists. From them we learn of the settlers' resourcefulness in adapting elements of native folk design to their own purposes. Nothing demonstrates this better than the so-called "English wigwam."

From their contact with native neighbors, the colonists recognized the utility of indigenous dwellings, and among the inhabitants of the woodlands, the English discovered a design form that suited their own needs admirably. For the Native Americans, from Canada to the Carolinas, the "wigwam" was an important traditional architectural structure. This oblong, dome-like dwelling was formed first of a pliable framework fashioned from supple tree limbs. The bottom ends of these poles were anchored by staking them into the ground. At intersecting junctures across the framework, the limbs were fastened with strips of animal skin or bark twine. The exterior walls and roof covering consisted of shingles of bark, woven mats or animal skins. The interior walls and roof could be insulated, thus providing a high degree of shelter and protection.

The practicality of this Native American design was well suited for the purposes of the colonists who readily adapted it for their own use. Indeed, the techniques

Above: English wigwam, Salem, MA, c. 1627 (reconstruction). English settlers used simple dugout shelters, and also copied Native American structures, adding crude fireplaces of wood, covering them with clay, thatch, or shingled roofs, and adding doors and windows from the English architectural tradition.

Above: English wigwam, Salem, MA, c. 1627 (reconstruction). The frames of the originals were poorly made, and none has survived.

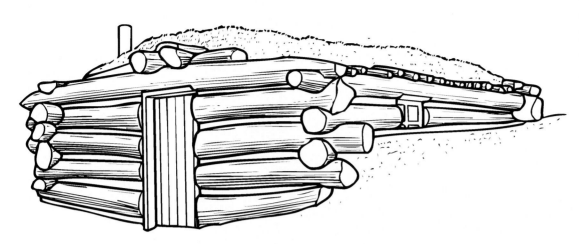

Left: Dugout house from Custer County, Montana. Frontier settlers recreated the earliest forms of shelter made by humans.

employed were not dissimilar to the kind of simple wattle-and-daub thatched medieval dwellings that they knew from their roots in rural England. While adapting this folk design the English transformed the native structures with a wide range of improvements. For instance, the introduction of wooden hinged entrance doors and rough-hewn frames gave a peculiar English look to the dwellings. With the placement of a fireplace and crude wooden chimney, the wigwam could provide added warmth and improved shelter against harsh New England winters. These structures were easy to build and more reliable than any other dwelling constructed by the colonists in their initial phase of settlement. Materials were always near at hand and the low level of technology and tools needed to build them enhanced their attraction. The familiar use of thatch on the external walls, also a common element of their English tradition, helped further to anchor the adapted dwelling against the severe conditions of their new climate.

Today, modern reconstructions of both Native American wigwams and English wigwams demonstrate their similarities and the peculiar shape and finish that the English added in adapting this particular folk tradition for their own use. The Native American wigwam by comparison is more rounded in the shape of its frame and has a roofline that creates a domelike effect. The English achieved a taller, more graceful shape in their construction with a highly tapered roofline, almost peaked. Traditional native construction often used animal skins in the fabrication of exterior walls, while the English utilized thatch or tree bark that gave a shingled façade that was handsome in appearance.

Modern replicas of the English wigwam can be seen at the Salem Pioneer Village, a historic collection of colonial dwellings located on an eleven-acre site in Salem, Massachusetts. Fabricating the appearance of Salem in 1630, this museum of early American history and culture provides an important look at the life and challenges of early settlement in America. Historic structures like the English wigwam have been recreated there within a woodland setting like that which existed more than three centuries ago. In the creation of the Salem Pioneer Village, in 1930 for the Tercentennial of the Massachusetts Bay settlement, the noted antiquarian-architect George Francis Dow insured that traditional methods of construction, and materials used in Salem's original 1630 creation, were used wherever possible.

In taking to themselves the design form of the Native American wigwam, the colonists demonstrated a shrewd appreciation of the their neighbors' intuitive ability to utilize the materials at hand for survival. In adapting this architectural form with elements of those they were familiar with from home, a fusion of cultures is revealed, the first budding of a characteristic that would become quintessentially American. In this architectural adaptation the colonists helped to accommodate themselves in a new environment and more fully found themselves at home.

Sod Houses of the Great Plains, 1890s

While more than two centuries separate the colonists of New England from the settlers of the Great Plains, the "sod-busters" of that vast endeavor faced similar hardships and deprivations in securing a new home in another wilderness. Like the Pilgrims of 1620, the settler of the flat lands west of the Mississippi had to look to nature and the prairie environment for the building blocks of survival. Far away from the rich forests of the east that made timber and logs readily available, those who traveled out to the far reaches of the Great Plains found meager materials to provide for shelter and settled living. Out of this peculiar set of circumstances another unique American folk style would emerge, the sod house of the plains.

New regions of the American continent opened up for settlement at the end of the nineteenth century, driven by the twin engines of history and technology. In North Dakota, an area west of the Missouri River, the 1880s saw the settlement of fresh lands formerly reserved for native peoples. Land was cheap and colonization was pushed ever westward by the advance of the railroad. As North Dakota was admitted to the Union as the thirty-ninth State in 1889, land, in abundance, was now available for homesteaders with the spirit and the tenacity to carve out a home.

Though arrayed with its own geographical grandeur and mineral resources, the Northern Plains' landscape was bereft of the natural supply of lumber and stone that shaped American architecture of the period elsewhere. On the plains, the settlers had literally to look to the earth for their source of building materials. Taking a cue from native peoples, like the Pawnee whose earth lodges often measured up to forty-five feet in diameter, these adventurous pioneers utilized the soil itself for their shelter. The sod of the prairie became their chief building material and proved to make a sturdy and practical dwelling, well suited to the rigors of pioneer living.

Sod was harvested for use as a building block by digging it up or cutting it with a special tool, known as a "grasshopper" plow, because the tines resembled the wings of grasshoppers. The plow lifted the top layer of dirt intact with the grass. These earth and grass bricks were taken from the ground in long, uniformly cut pieces—strips would generally be four inches thick and twelve inches wide—which would then be trimmed into a brick thirty-six inches long. The sod bricks, with the grass

Left: In the absence of trees for lumber, early settlers of the prairies would cut blocks of sod ("Nebraska marble") to construct houses.

side placed down, were arranged in layers alternating in a lengthwise and widthwise pattern that permitted a wall to be erected that was solid and uniform. Quite often, walls grew to a width of three feet, as two or three layers of sod were added. This provided added sturdiness to the structure, as well as giving a well-insulated barrier against the extremes of weather and temperature.

Wooden doorframes were added and window frames were set in place as the construction grew. The strategic arrangement of wooden planks around the top of the frames permitted the weight of the roof to be shifted off the windows and spread across the wall. Frames were finally secured into the sod wall by a series of wooden pegs.

A variety of roof designs could be utilized, due to the uniformity of the sod walls. Among the more common were the shed roof that sloped from front to back, the gable roof that sloped front and back from a raised center, and the more elevated hip roof that sloped from a central elevation in four sections. The gable roof was, by far, the most popular for traditional sod houses.

Inside, structural support for the roof was obtained with the introduction of a ridgepole, a large wooden beam that could be further strengthened by the use of forked poles. Wooden rafters gave strength and definition to the roofline. Beneath the final layer of roof sod was usually a layer of insulating prairie grass that further secured the weatherproofing of the roof. Inside the house a special canvas tarp or muslin drop cloth was stretched beneath the earthen ceiling to serve as a catchall for the insects, rodents, dirt, and other detritus that dropped from the mud and grass. Twice

Above: Sod house, McKenzie County, ND, 1903.

a year, cautious homemakers would launder the ceiling drop cloth.

The popularity of the sod house was largely due to the ease with which it could be built from an abundant local material in difficult circumstances, among people for whom quick, dependable domestic dwellings were a necessity. With their roots in the traditions of Native American folk design, sod houses became a highly adaptable architectural form. When seen against the limited resources of the geography of the Great Plains, sod houses stand as a sophisticated form and an inventive response that helped greatly in the settlement of the American plains.

Above: Sod house, Custer County, MT.

Above: Sod house, Newell, SD, c. 1911.

Pre-Railroad

Construction materials used in American homes varied greatly, depending on the period and location. In the seventeenth century, wooden pegs were used to join heavy timber frames, replaced by hand-wrought iron nails, and machine-cut nails after 1800. In the Great Plains, thick walls were made of sod in the late nineteenth century.

Above: Wrought nails, used before 1800.

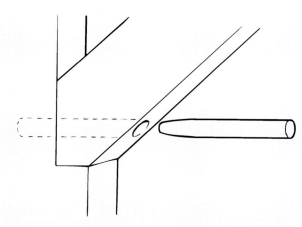

Above: Treenails (trunnels), wooden pegs used for early timber frames. Typically made of oak, these anchored the heavy beams.

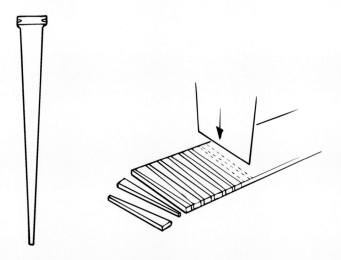

Above: Cut nails, used after 1800. Cut from a sheet of iron, they are tapered only on one side. Later in the nineteenth century, inexpensive wire-cut nails replaced them.

Above: Sod house, Loup County, NE, 1886. In areas without many trees, the thick sod of the prairie was used as a building material.

Above: Sod house, Minnesota, nineteenth century.

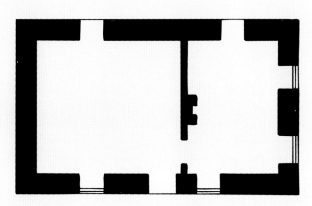

Above: Plan of sod house; rooms were small, and walls were very thick.

Vernacular Architecture

For more than 200 years, from the mid-seventeenth century to the mid-nineteenth century, architectural design in America was dependent on the local geographical realities. The evolution of domestic design was largely dependent on the availability of locally produced materials and the abilities of the area's craftsmen. Settlements placed near plentiful woodlands enjoyed the luxury of a wide variety of local wood and lumber products. Those along the great inland waterways or at the emerging coastal ports enjoyed a strategic accessibility of location in which they could receive and transport important building supplies from other waterway-accessible regions. Many communities, however, endured a natural geographical isolation that precluded variety in both materials and design styles. Isolation was the price to be paid for living amid the vastness of the ever-enlarging American nation. During this period, architecture was decidedly regional in its expressions and forms. Thus

Above: Log house in either Duchesne County, UT or Boundary County, ID.

ordinary, everyday architectural forms reflected not only the tastes of local people, but more critically, the limited availability of adequate building materials, tools, and sup-

Above: Log cabin, Abraham Lincoln's birthplace, 1933 World's Fair, Chicago, IL.

Above: Log cabin, on the grounds of Farmington Plantation, Louisville, KY, c. 1790.

plies. In this regional isolation, common or local styles of architecture evolved in the era before the advent of the railroad and industrialization.

The architecture of this broad period fitted the lives of ordinary people attempting to survive the rigors of ordinary life. Largely folk-inspired, it is known as vernacular design, stretches from the earliest days of colonization to the mid-Victorian era, and is reflected chiefly in the design and construction of domestic dwellings. Very often, these modest homes were fashioned and fabricated, not by established architects, but rather by the very people who inhabited them. In the process, a number of stylistic traditions emerged, each heavily influenced by pragmatic necessities and the patterns of folk artistry.

Over the long period of settlement on the American continent five particularly significant regional forms of vernacular architecture developed. The coastal northeast region of New England; the mid-Atlantic region anchored in Maryland; the Tidewater region of the Carolinas; the Spanish territories of the arid southwest; and the flat expanses of the Great Plains of the central west—each produced a mode of vernacular architecture that reflected both the needs and the resources of the settlers of each area.

The first vernacular architecture to take shape evolved out of the experience of colonization in New England. Domestic dwellings here relied on the abundance of good wood that was available from the forests that filled this portion of the Northeast. Among the first areas of America to receive permanent settlement, homes here were formed of heavy timber frames with exterior walls covered by wood boards or shingles with steep pitched roofs. Such homes populate New England still. The colonists created many dwellings that were very reminiscent of common timber homes in England. From the seventeenth century on, these practical but handsome one- and two-story linear plan houses grew more substantial, expanding to accommodate increasing prosperity and endowed with further refinements of comfort and technology. The well-known "salt box" and "Cape Cod" homes of the region have gone on to become icons of the New England tradition. Design plans later became more elaborate in the late eighteenth and early nineteenth centuries, adding distinctive expressions of local tastes with the development of roomy, gable-fronted and mass-plan dwellings. Such houses would become a signature design type that many New Englanders were to carry with them to the West.

Another vernacular tradition comes from the middle colonies of Maryland, Pennsylvania, Delaware, and New Jersey. It is again a timber tradition, but heavily influenced by colonists outside the cultural traditions of England. This region received immigrants from Northern Europe, particularly German and Central European settlers whose tradition for split-log construction and design introduced a new folk style. This was the tradition spread by the frontiersmen whose movements across the region of Appalachia and the Smokey Mountains transferred this architectural design deep into the culture of America for many generations to come. The log cabin and its larger counterpart, the longhouse, remain emblematic of frontier America. Indeed, the influence of this design form on the settlement of the middle region of America is without precedent. It enjoys a noble heritage, bringing to life characters of both myth and history—from Paul Bunyan to Daniel Boone, and from Davy Crockett and Abraham Lincoln to Lil' Abner and Mammy Yokum.

The house itself was fashioned of logs cut from the abundant nearby forests. These were hewn and stacked one on top of another in a horizontal pattern. The entire structure was stabilized by a series of interlocking notched groves. By the addition of clay, moss, mud, and other organic materials, the open spaces and gaps between the logs could be sealed and made weathertight.

The Tidewater tradition is another vernacular mode with its roots in the early English colonies of Virginia and the Carolinas. The term "Tidewater" refers to that strange mixture of coastal water produced at the confluence of the saltwater ocean and freshwater inland rivers. This area enjoys a milder climate than that encountered by the English of New England and this can be seen to have influenced the design and materials utilized in domestic dwellings.

Timber-frame construction was a common, popular form in early homes here, though dwellings frequently remained single-story. An example of the impact of the climate on design is found in the popularity of the shed-roofed full porch across the front of a house, demonstrating interest in providing a defined outdoor area connected to the house, but sheltered from both the sun and the southern rains.

As seen previously, the building tradition of the Great Plains was a vernacular style that was very expressive of the region and influential in the settling of the West. Without the luxury of timber, lumber, and logs found in abundance in other regions of the continent, the more barren area of the Great Plains pushed the early settlers to rely on using the sod of the plains to fashion a unique grass and clay brick that could be used to construct domestic dwellings. From Nebraska to the Dakotas, the abundance of earthen materials permitted adventurous pioneers the opportunity to stake their claim on the soil of the plains.

The desert regions of the Southwest offered the most radical climatic and geographical influence on the early evolution of American vernacular architecture. Amid the dry, sun-baked conditions of this land first settled by the Spanish, domestic architecture reflected the parched environment. Unlike all the other early vernacular traditions in America, the design forms that developed in the Southwest were of masonry construction. The plentiful resource of adobe clay provided a seemingly unlimited supply of hard baked bricks for the construction of simple dwellings that were often covered in a layer of stucco. Roofs of these structures were either flat or pitched, but replicated the familiar overlapping shingles popular in Spain. Wooden shutters were frequently used, as were iron window grills and grates that fit the desert conditions and the common need for interiors with adequate ventilation.

The style was very expressive of Spanish architectural traditions. As it evolved, long, wide, wooden balconies and porches were added—an indication of the lifestyles of the region. Such simple designs would become a lasting architectural expression in villages, towns, and cattle ranches across the vast reaches of the desert. From California to Texas, the influence and development of this evocative vernacular tradition remains strong. Its sturdy design form could be utilized in both the simplest peasant home and the grandest hacienda. Even in contemporary architecture, the influence of this Spanish folk tradition wedded to American practicality remains popular. In Arizona and New Mexico, for instance, this tradition continues to be refined and utilized, not only in domestic architecture, but also in public buildings, such as hotels, shopping malls, universities, churches, and schools. The practical elements of the style still fit the shape and flow of life in the Southwest.

The patterns of design that are found in these five essential regional modes were just the beginning of the enormously fluid architectural variety grounded in the practical folk traditions of first settlement that evolved in the age before the development of the railroads. With the arrival of that remarkable technological advance, the patterns of national life and architecture in America were altered forever. The rapid changes that ensued began a process that would begin to erase regional isolationism. The lasting influence, however, of these design traditions continue to effect the tastes and houses of America.

Farmhouses

Farmhouses embody the vernacular tradition of American architecture at its simplest and most self-sufficient. Typically stressing functionality over style, such houses nevertheless embody a considerable level of comfort and inventiveness.

Left: Rebecca Nurse House, 149 Pine Street, Danvers, MA, 1678ff. Rebecca Nurse was one of the women accused in the Salem witch trials; this saltbox house and farm remained in her family for centuries.

Left: Connected farmhouse ("big house, back house, little house, barn" all joined together); Hartland, VT. The harsh northern New England climate led to unified designs which provided more shelter in bad weather.

Left: Chester A. Arthur House, North Fairfield, VT, replica. The twenty-first president of the United States was born in the original of this small house in rural Vermont in 1829.

Above: Gable and
wing house, Greek Revival
house, Weathersfield, VT.

Right: Andrew Jackson
House, Nashville, TN, 1819.
The Hermitage, the
elegantly restored home of
the seventh president of
the United States, is a
plantation home with a
large Classical colonnade.
Although Jackson was
from humble origins, this
house takes the farmhouse
to new heights of style.

Pre-Railroad

Left: Diagram of an early one-room log cabin, c. 1840s. Log cabins were introduced by Swedish settlers in Delaware in the seventeenth century, and later built by settlers as they moved across the country.

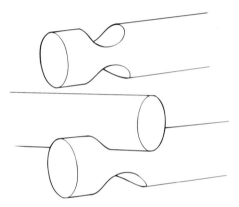

Above: Log construction techniques—saddle notch joint.

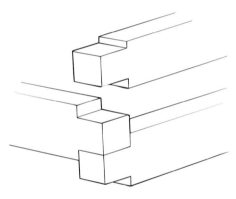

Above: Log construction techniques—square notch joint.

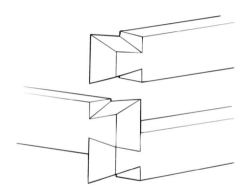

Above: Log construction techniques—dovetail joint.

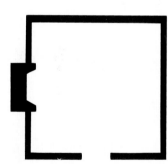

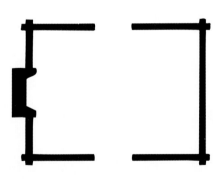

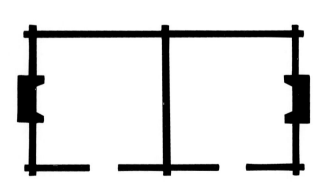

Above: Plan of early single-room (English style) log cabin. At its simplest, the log cabin was a one-room structure, with a door and fireplace.

Above: Plan of Scotch-Irish log cabin. Scotch-Irish colonists, descendents of Scots who had emigrated to Dublin before coming to America, typically built cabins with a door at the rear as well as at the front.

Above: Plan of "double-pen" log cabin. Two-room, or "double-pen" cabins were larger and more complex, frequently with chimneys at both ends of the house.

Left: Diagram of a saddlebag log cabin. A saddlebag cabin is one with two rooms built around a common chimney.

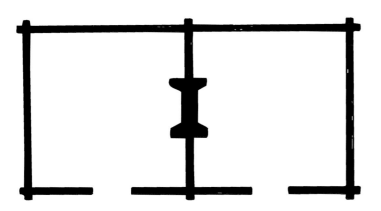

Above: Plan of simple saddlebag log cabin. The central chimney and common wall between the rooms anchor the house.

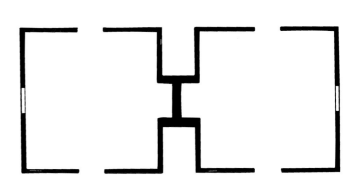

Above: Plan of notched saddlebag-style log cabin. In this variant design, the chimney alone connects the rooms of the house.

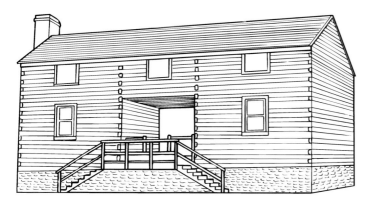

Above: Drawing of dogtrot cabin, with open passage between rooms; Dogtrot House, Jessamine County, KY, 1785.

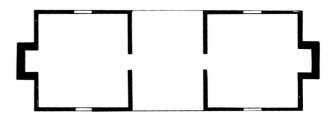

Above: Plan of typical dogtrot-style log cabin. The so-called "dogtrot"-style log cabin leaves a central passageway open on the first floor, large enough for dogs (and people) to walk through the house.

Left: Diagram of a shotgun house. Shotgun houses are derived from African and Haitian building traditions, and are found in the southern United States.

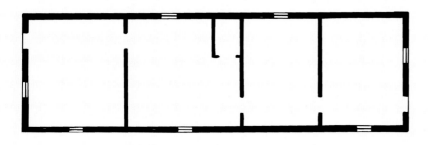

Left: Plan of shotgun house. The shotgun house, with its series of sequentially connected rooms, is typically one-room wide. The name comes from the legend that a shotgun could be fired straight through all the doors of the house.

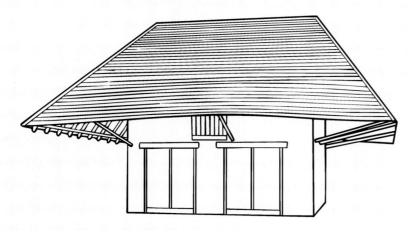

Above: The African House, part of Melrose Plantation, Melrose, LA., c. 1820s. This house is thought to have African origins.

Above: Drawing of camelback house. The camelback was a shotgun house with a second-story addition at the rear.

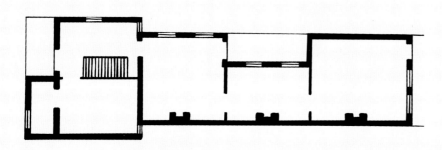

Left: Plan of camelback house.

Regional and National Trends

While the introduction of the railroad during the last half of the nineteenth century altered the mercantile terrain of America forever, its influence was equally substantial architecturally. The ever-growing network of railroads traversing the nation telescoped the distances between regions of the country, connecting them to centers of abundant material supply. The result was a lessening of dependence on traditional vernacular design. The very nature of architecture changed as railroads carried materials and technologies across the nation. It is worth mentioning, however, that though new trends in fashionable styles of architectural construction begin to spread, for a large portion of the nation, modest, simple homes linked to the traditions of the past continued to remain the norm. Nevertheless, the railroads freed people from the restrictions that regional isolationism had enforced. An innovative and imaginative era in domestic design rooted in the pragmatic designs of the nation's folk style was launched.

As a tremendous period of development began in fast-growing cities and rural towns, many design patterns deeply tied to the simple styles of the past were refreshed. These architectural forms became highly popular in the boom of expanding national development. Although grand architectural undertakings were also occurring at this time, introducing elaborate style into the domestic dwellings of the elite, the reworked vernacular styles of the past fit the needs of ordinary American people. These styles would influence the traditions of American home construction up to the first decades of the twentieth century, and formed the basis of many of the designs used for mass-produced homes which were available through mail-order companies such as Sears.

Long ignored, the shotgun house is a distinct housing type of African-American origin found in the southern states. Houses are long and narrow, only one-room wide and most often one-story high; the name is derived from the legend that one could fire a gun through the entire house.

The gable-front design reflected the Classical influence of a Greek temple façade, on a modest scale. Its slender two-story construction, with steep pitched roof, proliferated within the period's developing urban landscapes in the New England states. Its popularity was due in no small part due to its unpretentious scale, which was well suited for the physical dimensions of northern city lots. The success of this style is born out in its enduring presence in neighborhoods to which it was exported across the country. The design has given America millions of front porches from which homeowners preside over family and neighborhood life.

Above: Shotgun house, (double house), New Orleans, LA, 1892. The shotgun house is a distinct housing type, of African-American origin. Houses are only one room wide.

Above: Shotgun house, New Orleans, LA.

The gable-front and wing combination is a design that became highly popular in the nation's more rural environs. The addition of a side "wing," once again on a very modest scale, enlarged the size of the familiar gable-front house and gave an "L" shape to the plan of the dwelling. Shed roofed porches, steep and slanted, were a common accompaniment. This is the enduring architectural design of small-town America from New York state to Iowa. As large portions of the American interior grew and developed in the late nineteenth and early twentieth centuries, supported by the railroad, this style reached its peak. It is a heartland design that fit the stability and modest pride of middle America.

The hall-and-parlor plan, two rooms wide and one room deep, is yet another deeply influential house design that is evocative of rural America—the South in particular. It is an expression of folk housing that linked the small towns south of the Mason-Dixon line. Essentially this design evolved from the ordinary English folk style with the addition of a simple side gable. Its construction fit the climate and lifestyle of the South. This type is still seen in many small sleepy towns. With some exterior variances in porch forms, roof shape, or over-hang, from North and South Carolina, Kentucky and Tennessee to Alabama, hall-and-parlor style embodies a piece of the national character.

Above: Nixon home, Yorba Linda, CA, 1912. This simple house may have been a mail-ordered from Sears.

The I-House design is another format highly popular in the eastern United States with roots again entwined in the traditions of English folk architecture. Originally common in the Tidewater region of the South, before the advent of the railroad, these houses enjoyed renewed popularity in other areas of the country well into the twentieth century. These handsome two-story structures, like the hall-and-parlor style, are basically two rooms wide and one room deep. The comparatively roomy domestic proportions were to make this modest style an important part of life in the emerging Midwest where their larger size made them a welcome place in which to endure the more severe heartland winters.

The mass-planned, side-gabled design marks the enlarging of another popular American folk type, originally used in the Northeast. This initiated an important development in the proportions of modest domestic architecture, enlarging very simple homes to depths greater than one room—a significant expansion. Evolving from the folk traditions of early New England, the origins of this style necessitated a technical development in the construction of the roof. Its success demonstrated early builders were correctly able to master the framing techniques needed to cover the expanded proportions of multi-room design. With the coming of the railroad, this technology advanced further with the availability of lighter woods used in roof framing. Such materials were now easily transported to greater areas of the country. With enlarged interiors in more common use in domestic dwellings, the side-gabled form proved very popular and went on to replace the one-room-deep style of the hall-and-parlor and I-house styles in the South, the Midwest, and the Great Plains.

The pyramidal type takes its name from the generous roofing design known as the equilateral hipped roof—a high-pitched, four-sided peak. Its intriguing shape lends itself well to the square format of the house it encloses. Although such a specialized roof design required a more innovative technique in roof framing, early New England builders were able to master the complexity needed. In the process they utilized fewer rafters, thus making the roof less costly and hence more popular. The railroad again took this two-story home to the urban communities of the North and Midwest. In the more rural South, the design was more frequently built in single-story houses, but the pyramidal type became a popular substitute for hall-and-parlor there also. This is an enduring and simple American tradition that doesn't feature the application of any fancy details.

The evolution and use of these particular vernacular design forms is responsible for helping to evolve a unique American folk style. During the era of great national expansion, interior settlement, and urban development, these styles became important in the lives of countless Americans. Not only were they the key to creating a new sense of national cohesion, they were also responsible for helping to civilize the architecture of the nation. Beyond the luxurious architectural styles that were built for the families of great American fortunes and pedigrees, these practical and formidable developing folk styles had a deep affect on the larger soul of the nation. The vernacular style arose primarily out of necessity and in the process created a sense of national dignity that reflected the dominant cultural ideals of America.

Above: Ronald Reagan boyhood home, 816 South Hennepin Street, Dixon, IL.

Above: Stow House, 304 North Los Carneros Rd, Goleta, CA, 1872.

Above: One-story, mass-plan house, Waltham, MA.

Above: One-story, mass-plan, side-gable house, Waltham, MA.

Above: Two-story, mass-plan house.

Above: Two-story I-shaped house, Newton, MA, nineteenth century.

Post-Railroad

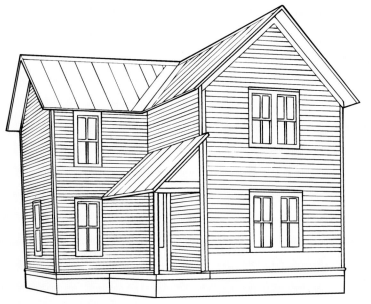

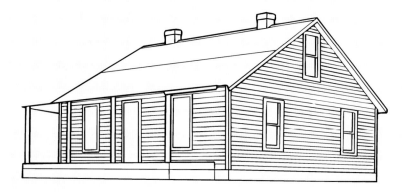

Left: An I-house, so called because the tall, narrow house looks like a capital "I" when seen from the side.

Above: Post-railroad national house type: gable-front and wing house.

Above: Post-railroad national house type: pyramidal roof, with massed plan.

Left: Post-railroad national house type: massed plan, with end gable.

Chapter 2

Colonial Architecture

Tom O'Gorman

Architectural variety in North America began with the arrival of the first colonists—the Spanish in Florida, the English in Virginia and Massachusetts, the Dutch along the Hudson River in New York, and the French in Louisiana. Their settlement of the American continent saw a wide array of architectural styles dramatically showcased. As we have seen in the previous chapter, most early designs were the result of the pragmatic need for shelter, protection, and a place to begin. Here the colonists relied on the simple, the ordinary, the tried and true. These modest "first period" styles flowed from the largely folk traditions of the colonists' own peculiar cultural and architectural sensibilities. In adapting them to the contours and necessities of New World living, America's own architectural history was begun.

Above: Pioneer Village, Salem, MA. Driven by necessity, the early colonists initially made do with very primitive shelters.

Left: Pioneer Village, Salem, MA. As soon as possible, more substantial houses replaced the early dugouts and lean-tos.

Post-Medieval English

This style is characterized by austere timber-framed houses with steep roofs. Made from clapboard, with two stories, and one room deep, such dwellings also have a central hearth and chimney. Built in New England, they were adapted by colonists from a style of English folk architecture—a tradition that went back to a post-medieval era of timber and frame house design. In contemporary America, a surprising number of such houses still exist. They serve as living examples of the "first period" English style, fashioned by the first generation of New England residents. Many good examples of these homes still remain as unbroken tethers from the Old World to the New.

The Fairbanks House in Dedham, Massachusetts, is America's oldest timber-frame house. Built in 1636, it represents an important link with the colonial past, as well as being a singular expression in the evolution of American design. It demonstrates the achievements that followed the colonists' initial struggle for adequate, temporary shelter. This substantial, permanent timber-framed house followed the era of the wigwam and rough cabin. Because the Fairbanks House remained a residential dwelling for the Fairbanks family well into the twentieth century, it was well maintained for more than

Above: Fairbanks House, 511 East Street, Dedham, MA, 1636. The Fairbanks House is one of the oldest houses in America, and the oldest in New England. The original part of the house is the steep gabled portion in the center; the gambrel roof and other elements were later additions.

three and a half centuries. The central portion of the house represents the earliest part of the building and the unusual and varied additions are an indication of the on-going development in the Fairbanks family's economic success.

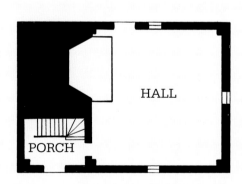

Above: Typical plan of New England colonial houses—one room. The massive fireplace is on one side. The large mass of the chimney helped store heat, which was re-radiated back into the house to help maintain a more even temperature.

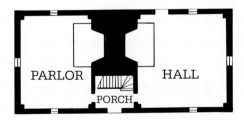

Above: Typical plan of New England colonial houses—two rooms. The massive fireplace is in the center. A small staircase leads up to a sleeping loft.

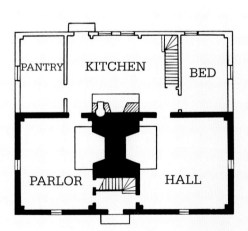

Above: Typical plan of New England colonial houses—two rooms, plus lean to. The lean-to provides space for a separate kitchen and pantry and an additional bedroom.

Above: Fairbanks House, Dedham, MA, 1636. View of the rear of the house.

Above: Fairbanks House, Dedham, MA, 1636. Frame reconstruction created for the Boston 350 celebration, 1980. It was assembled on Boston Common using authentic tools and techniques.

This page: Fairbanks House frame reconstructed for the Boston 350 celebration, 1980. Built before the age of mechanization and standardized lumber, large timbers were hand hewn. Each timber was custom fitted in skilled carpentry joints, using pegs ("treenails") instead of nails. Spaces between the timber posts and beams was filled in with woven stick filling ("wattle"), and covered with clay ("daub").

Its original construction reflected the building techniques of the English post-medieval tradition. The steep-roofed dwelling was essentially formed by the fabrication of a structure of beams and rafters joined with mortise and tenon joints. In this simple process, two pieces of wood are secured when the mortise, a hole made in a wooden beam, receives the tenon, a projecting wooden peg, and the two interlock in a secure fashion. Craftsmen employing this technique could pre-fabricate materials for assemblage later at a particular site. The walls of the house were filled with wattle and daub, a clay and moss mixture applied to oak laths (another distinctive feature of post-medieval construction). This gave the house insulation against the extremes of the New England winter. The exteriors of these walls were covered in a distinctive brown-stained clapboard siding.

The Fairbanks House as it now stands underwent a series of seventeenth century expansions. Originally fashioned in the familiar hall-and-parlor design of two rooms wide and one room deep, the parlor was later lengthened by six feet and the modest upstairs rooms also enlarged. Perhaps the most distinctive design feature of this home, and others like it, is the massive central hearth and brick chimney whose proportions (eight feet by ten feet) commanded attention for both their size and practical utility.

The Scotch-Boardman House, in Saugus, Massachusetts, was originally built in 1651 as a home for indentured Scots who had participated in political rebellion at home and found themselves sentenced to service in the colonies. In 1687, the house was purchased by the Boardman family, hence its hyphenated name. The saltbox form of the house, however, is a flawless

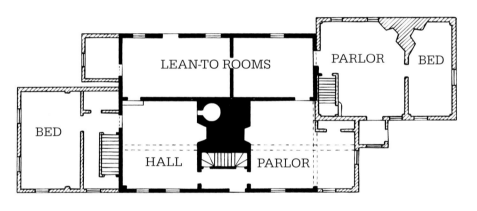

LEAN-TO ROOMS

PARLOR   BED

BED

HALL   PARLOR

Left: Plan of the Fairbanks House, Dedham, MA, of 1636. The oldest part of the house, consisting of the hall, parlor, and central fireplace, dates from around 1636. The other rooms were subsequent additions, expanding the house in an organic manner.

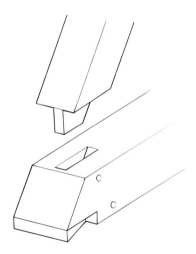

Above: Mortise and tenon joint.

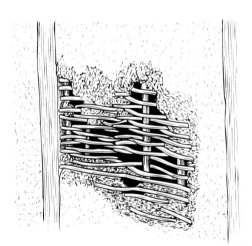

Above: With the outer surface removed, the woven sticks of the wattle (sticks) and daub (clay or plaster) infilling show between the posts.

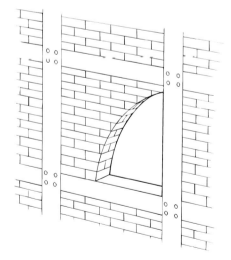

Above: Infilling between posts and beams in a half-timber frame is called brick fill, or "nogging."

Above: Jackson House, 76 Northwest Street, Portsmouth, NH, 1664. This big house with a dramatically long roof which extends over a lean-to, was home to the large Jackson family; over twenty people lived in the house at some times.

Above: Jackson House, Portsmouth, NH, 1664. Rear view, showing the long slope of the roof.

product of the period's modest, but refined, sensibilities. A simple symmetrical façade and an elegantly slopping roofline demonstrate a familiar external modesty. The handsome timber framing, exterior wooden cladding, and shingled, steep pitched roof are complemented by an unusually elegant central chimney, replete with brick pilasters. Many original interior features, such as batten doors, wainscoting, and a garret stairway, are typical in such "first period" dwellings.

The evolving style of New England's signature timber-frame design is represented in Farmington, Connecticut, in the Whitman House, built in circa 1720. Its most distinguishing characteristics are the six-inch gable overhangs at each end of the house and the expansive overhang that juts out more than eighteen inches across the front of the house. Projecting from this front overhang are four carved post ends from the second story. These pendants add a decorative touch to the exterior design. The windows are diamond-pane with vertical mullions. Interior rafters were altered in a 1700 expansion that reset the pitch of the steep rear roof. Red sandstone bricks were employed in the construction of the central chimney above the roofline, but the interior

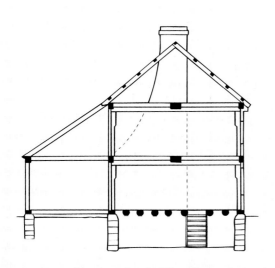

Above: Diagram of typical New England saltbox frame.

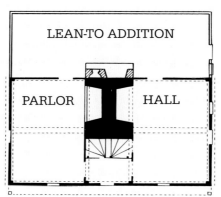

Above: Plan of the Whitman House, Farmington, CT, c. 1660/1720.

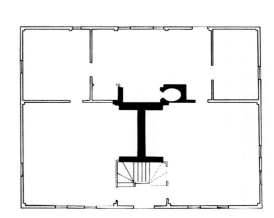

Above: Plan of the Scotch-Boardman House, Saugus, 1686.

Above: Scotch-Boardman House, Saugus, MA, 1686. A typical "saltbox" house, with a continuous roofline over the house and the lean-to which added space at the rear.

Above: Scotch-Boardman House, 17 Howard Street, Saugus, MA, 1686. Rear view.

Above: Stanley-Whitman House, 37 High Street, Farmington, CT, c. 1720. A typical saltbox shape; the mass of the central chimney helped keep the heat in the house. As with most early colonial houses, it faces to the south to maximize solar heat as well.

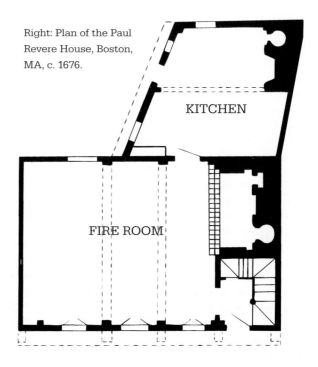

Right: Plan of the Paul Revere House, Boston, MA, c. 1676.

KITCHEN

FIRE ROOM

Left: Stanley-Whitman House, Farmington, CT c. 1720. Detail.

Below: Saugus Ironworks House, Saugus Ironworks National Park, Saugus, MA, c. 1664. A reconstruction of a first period house with multiple gables.

chimney is fashioned from fieldstones and a mixture of clay and wattle.

The City of Boston's oldest and most historic home is the "first period" timber framed, two-story, hall-and-parlor dwelling of one of America's most well known revolutionary patriots. The Paul Revere House, constructed between 1676 and 1682, is an enduring part of the landscape of Boston's North End, an area that was once the very heart of the city's maritime industry. The house was originally built by a Mr. John Jeff and only came into Revere's possession around 1770. It had expanded to three stories by then and was only restored to its original design in 1908, after many decades of neglect. Today, the façade, with overhang, and the exterior pendants, windows, and shutters, roofing shingles and front door are restored to their seventeenth century origins. The second story, however, with plaster and paneling, has been

Above: Paul Revere House, Boston, MA, 1676. Side view.

Above: Paul Revere House, 19 North Square, Boston, MA, 1676. Now a museum, the Revere House went through many alterations before being restored in 1907–1908. Paul Revere owned it from 1770–1800.

restored as it would have been in Revere's late-eighteenth century era.

The heavy oak-frame two-story design of the Parson Capen House, in Topsfield, Massachusetts, built in 1683 and restored to a high state of authentic seventeenth century splendor in the early decades of the twentieth century, stands as one of New England's most remarkable architectural sites. Built in the popular hall-and-parlor tradition, its textured dark brown cladding, weathered roofing shingles, strong central brick pilaster chimney with Tudor lines, deep front overhang with carved pendant embellishment, and second-floor gable-end overhangs, express this structure's remarkable pedigree and superb horizontal lines.

Above: Parson Capen House, 1 Howlett Street, Topsfield, MA, 1683. The date June 8, 1683, is carved in the summer beam in the hall.

Above: Parson Capen House. The overhang of the second floor is the rsult of period framing techniques and the habits of English architecture. The pendills or "drops" are almost the only ornament.

Above: Jabez Wilder House, 557 Main Street, Hingham, MA, c. 1690. This house has an unusual curved gable, based on late-medieval cruck frames.

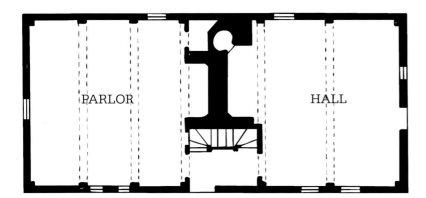

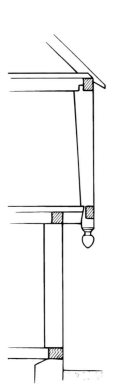

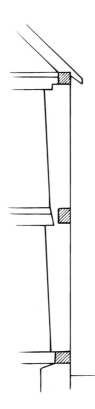

Left: Plan of the Parson Capen House, Topsfield, MA, 1683. The dotted lines indicate the position of main beams. The largest is known as the "summer" beam.

Right: Parson Capen House, side elevation.

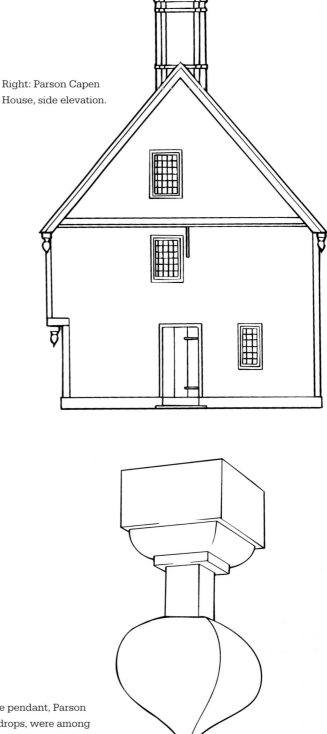

Above: Diagram of colonial frame with second-story overhang.

Above: Diagram of colonial frame with no overhang.

Right: Pendill, or decorative pendant, Parson Capen House. Pendills, or drops, were among the few ornamental features of first-period (seventeenth century) colonial houses.

Small, square-paned, lead casement windows add to the perfection of this modest, but rich Pilgrim dwelling.

The town of Ipswich, Massachusetts, northeast of Boston, boasts a number fine timber-framed, first-period houses. None is more handsome or evocative of the refinements of the times than the Whipple House, built in 1639. It is a house that expanded with the size and fortunes of a family. Captain John Whipple, by whose name this house has been known for more than three and a half centuries, was actually the second owner. He acquired the house shortly after it was built by a Mr. John Fawn. Originally, the house was constructed on the familiar one-room plan, but Whipple initiated a sizable enlargement in 1670, doubling its size. From this point on, the familiar proportions we see today took shape. The large brick chimney, once at the side of the old house, was centered within the structure during the expansion. The house's asymmetrical façade is emboldened by the horizontal lines of its cladding. Though built without a central overhang, two hewn overhangs were added to the gable-ends of the second story. Fashionable

Above: Whipple House, 1 South Village Green, Ipswich, MA, 1639. An early frame house with multiple gables, and a long saltbox profile over the rear lean-to.

Above: Whipple House, Ipswich, MA, 1639.

Left: Henry Whitfield House, Old Whitfield Street, Guilford, CT, 1639. Side view.

Above: Henry Whitfield House, Guilford, CT, 1639. An early stone house in Connecticut.

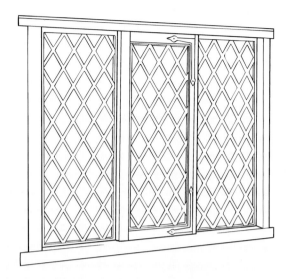

Above: Diamond-paned casement windows, Whipple House, Ipswich, MA. Glass was expensive, and difficult to obtain in large panes, so windows were made of small diamond-shaped pieces, held by leaded strips.

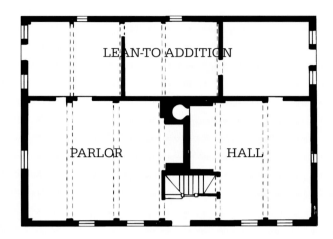

Above: Plan of the Ward House, Salem, MA.

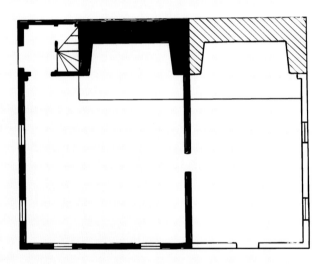

Above: Plan of a typical Rhode Island stone ender.

Above: Drawing of a typical Rhode Island stone ender. The chimney covers one entire end wall of the house.

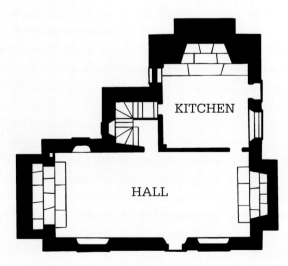

Above: Plan of the Whitfield House, Guilford, CT.

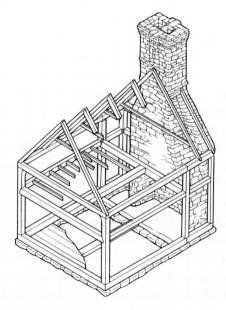

Above: Diagram of Clemence-Irons House frame, Rhode Island.

diamond-paned, triple-paneled, vertical, mullioned windows were also added. Within the interior of the house heavy summer beams were crossed at right angles, introducing an unusual but strengthening device to the construction. The third owner, the captain's son, Major John Whipple, built the sweeping and sizable rear addition that gave the house its present form.

The John Ward House of Salem, Massachusetts, built in 1684, began life, more typically, as a much smaller dwelling—the section that stands today as the western portion of the house. Though modest in its proportions, even then it displayed one of Salem's most extravagant overhangs, featured at both its front and west ends. In the course of its expansion, John Ward transformed the structure with the addition of a handsome fireplace of excessive size and a hall of massive beams. He also reset the pitch of the roof. What is most significant is the remarkable manner in which this house has become an icon of the period because of its irregular lines.

There is a highly imaginative "off-centeredness" to Ward's extensions. Windows are off-center to the axis of the house. Gables are of different dimensions. The front middle window is not above the front entrance. The front door and the chimney are just off-center. What is so remarkable is that this variations in the balance of the façade demonstrates the colonial lack of interest in symmetry, which was of far more interest to a later generation of Georgian aesthetes. Nowhere does the distinction between the two periods find more clarity than here in John Ward's Salem home. It has been suggested that this first generation of colonial settlers had more in common with the Gothic spirit of medieval England than with the tastes of the Georgian England of the future.

No first-period house is more fixed in the cultural imagination of America than the Turner House of Salem, built in 1668. Its fame is as much literary as it is architectural, thanks to the mid-nineteenth century American writer Nathaniel Hawthorne who sets his novel *The House of the Seven Gables* there. Ironically, if Hawthorne had a more developed sense of his town's architectural history, he might have more accurately named it "The House of the Eight Gables," for that is what John Turner actually had designed.

Above: John Ward House, 132 Essex Street, Salem, MA, 1684.

Above: Turner House (the "House of the Seven Gables"), 54 Turner Street, Salem, MA, 1668. Built for Captain John Turner, this house is more well known for its connection with Nathaniel Hawthorne's novel.

Left: Turner House, Salem, MA, 1668.

Like much in Salem, the Turner House had its own distinct Gothic personality that seems to haunt its external façade. Few houses have endured more change and renovation that this one. Originally, the house was built on a simpler two-room plan that held two gables in the front. The size of the house would after this parallel the growing Turner maritime fortune. First came the addition of a south wing, as well as a two-story porch. This obscured the original façade, resulting in a third gable and the addition of new double-casement windows throughout the house. The exterior was then richly accented with carved pediments. Turner died quite young in 1680 and left a large family.

When his son, John Turner II, came of age in 1692, Salem residents were living through the infamous witch trials, a dangerous time for young women. Further additions to the house at this time included the building of a massive new kitchen. Young John Turner then had a secret stairway built inside the old kitchen chimney, which permitted access to a second-floor garret. Presumably, such a passage was wanted should the need suddenly arise for quickly hiding his four sisters.

Renovation in 1720 saw a change as the small casement windows were improved with still larger sliding-sash windows. At this time, exposed beams were encased and Georgian paneling was added to the parlor. At its height, the house boasted fourteen rooms and eight gables, standing as an odd assortment of wings, gables, and curious rooms that looked out to the source of the family's fortune, Salem Harbor. Later, in the nineteenth century, one of the gables was removed and the overhangs were encased. This would have been the house that Nathaniel Hawthorne knew as a young man. Like many first-period homes, by the end of the nineteenth century it had fallen into disuse and shabbiness. But in 1908, in an era of renewed interest in the importance of period American architecture, Turner's house was rescue and restored. Today it is a major point of interest in Salem.

No first-period dwelling is more haunted by the sad events of Salem's witch hunts than the saltbox classic known as the Rebecca Nurse Home (see page 96). Built in 1678, in what was then Salem Village, today the town has come to be known as Danvers, Massachusetts. The Nurse Home is one of the earliest surviving framed houses in Salem of the one-room plan design. Over the years, it has been enlarged many times. But what the ill-fated Rebecca Nurse would have known was the house and its original great hall, an expansive seventeen by seventeen feet in size. Huge chamfered summer beams, running front-to-back, give the house a look of textured strength, while the seven-foot-wide fireplace with two ovens, big by local standards, added its own enlarged personality to the house. Casement windows, fitted with glass, set the handsome face of the house and a lean-to at the rear runs the full length. The sweep of the roof design provides it with a deep profile.

Right: Hancock-Clarke House, 36 Hancock Street, Lexington, MA, 1698/1734.

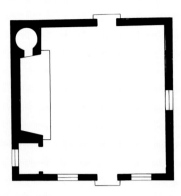

Above: Plan of small Southern colonial house, seventeenth and early eighteenth centuries. One room, one-story house.

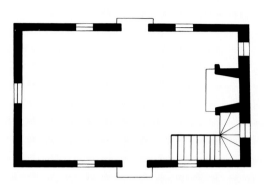

Above: Plan of small Southern colonial house, seventeenth and early eighteenth centuries. One room, two-story house, with two entrances.

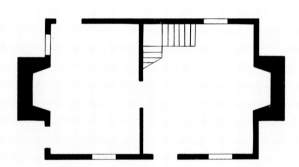

Above: Plan of smaller Southern colonial house, seventeenth and early eighteenth centuries. Two room, two-story house.

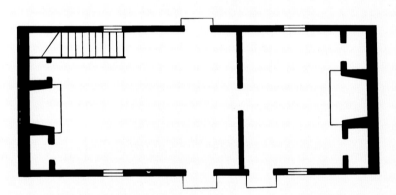

Above: Plan of Southern colonial house, seventeenth and early eighteenth centuries. Two room, two-story, larger house.

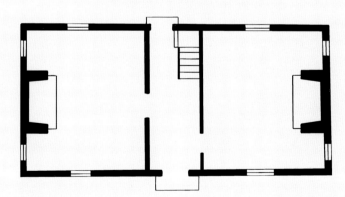

Above: Plan of Southern colonial house, seventeenth and early eighteenth centuries. Two room, two-story house with central hall.

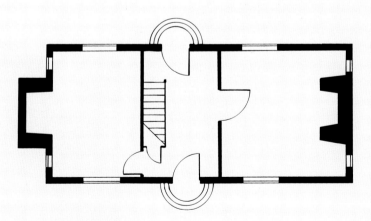

Above: Plan of the Adam Thoroughood House, c. 1636.

In 1692, the seventy-one-year-old Rebecca Nurse was accused of witchcraft by some distraught young girls in Salem. Following a questionable trial, she was hanged. The house remains a memorial to her place in local history. Like similar historic dwellings, the Nurse homestead was restored in 1908, in what became a golden period of respect for the architecture of America's colonial past.

During the same period in which settlement was under way in the area of New England, a similar pattern of colonial growth was underway among England's other colony further south in Virginia. A rich expression of post-medieval design developed there as well, creating its own unique architectural traditions. The southern colonial style, too, reflected its English roots.

Nothing demonstrates that connection more than one of the oldest houses in the English-speaking colonies, the Adam Thoroughgood House, in Princess County, Virginia, not far from Norfolk. Built in 1636–1640, the house reflects the masonry construction that was popular in the southern colonies. Its signature features—solid brick construction with one and a half stories and a steep gable roof—became a familiar format for Virginia farmhouses. The central front door was fashioned in double layers, with horizontal boards on the interior and vertical boards on the exterior. Doubled chimneys, one on each end of the house, were another significant feature of this design. One chimney was usually set into the wall of the house, while the other was set into the external wall. Medieval cross-mullion windows with leaded, diamond panes, were also important features. The house is a simple, hall-and-parlor layout, a plan that denotes both strength and simplicity; its roots in the ordinary architecture of medieval England are easy to identify. The Thoroughgood House employs a remarkable brick-laying style. Three sides are executed in the English tradition, while the front is done in the Flemish style. Although many of the features of this Southern colonial house are different from those built in New England, the traditions share a fervent desire for simplicity of design and modesty in ornamentation.

Bacon's Castle in Surrey County, Virginia, built in 1655, is a great house of high Southern colonial style. It, too, is an important example of early masonry design. A two-story house built originally for a Mr. Arthur Allen, it stands as the earliest example of a cross, or cruciform, plan house in Virginia. Bacon's Castle rises two-stories

Above: Adam Thoroughood House, 1636 Parish Road, Virginia Beach, Princess Anne County, VA, 1636–1640; side view. The Thoroughood House is one of the oldest houses on the Eastern Seaboard. As is typical with Southern houses, the chimneys are moved to the exterior walls, to keep the inside cooler.

and its remarkable molded brickwork includes some unusual ornamental features not seen before in the colonies. For instance, over the central door there is battlement motif with a triangular pediment of molded brick. Elsewhere, there is a projecting band of molded brick that forms a line separating the first and second stories. Over the first-floor windows there are segmental arches, while over the windows on the second level are brick frames. The decorative work at the end of the gables is truly unique in the colonies—Flemish gables, corbelled parapets, and a rectilinear finial each create a particular sense of highly decorative design. The triple chimney, or clustered chimney, adds an intense sense of artistry to the proportions and lines of the house. Many of these elements are found in examples of the Tudor Gothic style back in England. In the colonies, this style proved to be a dramatic architectural influence.

Early colonial architecture among the settlers of English origins demonstrates a remarkable reverence for the traditions of their roots, while at the same time connoting a respect for the fresh contours of life in America. This tradition would have a long influence on the design of domestic dwellings in the new land.

Above: Bacon's Castle (Arthur Allen House), Route 617, Surry County, VA, 1655. Side view. Although built by Arthur Allen, this house is known for its historical association with Bacon's rebellion in the seventeenth century.

Above: Bacon's Castle; side view. The clustered chimney stacks reflect English architecture, while the curved gables reflect Flemish design.

Above: Bacon's Castle in its seventeenth century state. Front view.

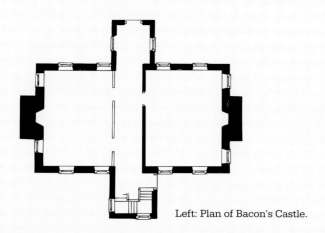

Left: Plan of Bacon's Castle.

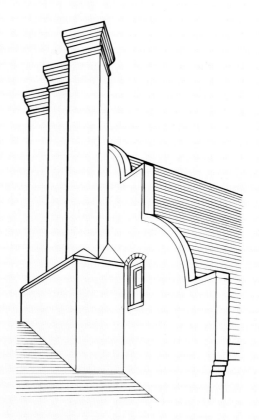

Above: Bacon's Castle. Detail of chimneys and Flemish gable.

Stone and Brick Houses

Above: Eleazer Arnold House, 487 Great Road, Lincoln, RI, c. 1687. An early "stone ender" in Rhode Island. Only the left end is built of stone, around the massive chimney.

Above: Eleazer Arnold House, side view.

Above: Clemence-Irons House, 38 George Waterman Road, Johnston, RI, c. 1680. Another "stone ender."

Above right: Clemence-Irons House, end view.

Right: Peter Tufts House (Craddock House), 350 Riverside Avenue, Medford, MA, c. 1680. A rather elegant early brick house built by a governor of the Massachusetts Bay colony. The brick masonry includes segmental arches over the windows; the pedimented porch is a later addition.

Wood Framed Houses—Late Versions

Left: Smith's Castle, 55 Richard Smith Road, Warwick, RI, 1678; remodeled 1740. In the 1740 remodeling, the façade gables were removed, and the house was expanded and unified. The house was the center of a large plantation of over 3,000 acres.

Above: Thankful Arnold House, Walkley Hill Road, Haddam, CT, c.1794–1810. First built as a small house with a shop below, it was expanded in 1800, and again in 1810 with the addition of a two-story ell.

Colonial Town Houses

Above: Colonial house, 139 Elfreth's Alley, Philadelphia, PA, 1703. Elfreth's Alley is a well-preserved block of original rowhouses, built between 1703 and 1839.

Above: Josiah Elfreth House, 132 Elfreth's Alley, Philadelphia, PA, 1789. Josiah Elfreth was a blacksmith who lived on this street.

Dutch Colonial

Steep pitched roof, one-story, side-gable, brick or stone construction with traditional half-door entrance, small-paned windows with shutters are the hallmarks. The footfall of the Dutch colonists in America is contemporary with that of the British. They first sailed into the harbor of what became New Amsterdam (later New York) in the early 1600s. The Hudson River was their central avenue for settlement and gave them access to what is now heartland New York and New Jersey. Manhattan, Long Island, and the area up state around Albany became the central region of their colonial enterprise. But the dramatically expanding dominance of the British cut short the colonial experience of the Dutch after little more than half a century. Their influence, however, endures through the domestic architecture that survives almost four centuries later.

The civility of their domestic design, reflecting a Netherlandish heritage from the Old World, coupled with social restraint and simple fervor, has left an important architectural footprint. A number of remarkable examples of their imaginative style still survive.

The Schenck House, Brooklyn, New York, built about 1676 (now partially reassembled at the Brooklyn Museum of Art), is a unique example of Dutch design in that its wood-frame construction is unusual. This early farmhouse in the Flatbush community had a sweeping steep roof, single chimney, and a flared front eave that was a signature device of Dutch design. Some of the exterior wall siding up to the roofline can be seen, as well as some intact small-paned windows. The interior, a rich harvest of early Dutch-influenced farmhouse-ware, can also be seen in its original setting. This is an important expression of Dutch rural domestic design.

The Bevier-Elting House, New Paltz, New York, near Poughkeepsie, just west of the Hudson River, was built between 1694 and 1696. It is a handsome, yet simple, stone house deeply evocative of the Dutch aesthetics of the time. Originally built by Louis Bevier on a smaller scale, it was extended in what has come to be known as the Netherlands Townhouse style. An unusual gable-front entrance sets the façade of the house, as do the small-paned, large Dutch windows with external shutters. With such large-scale windows, convenient side porch, and long well-sweep, this has

always been considered a house designed for the feelings and the work of women. A strong, sweeping roof adds a definitive Dutch character to the design, as does the double chimney. It is said that some of the beams of this house were brought from a barn in Holland. In the 1740s, the ownership of the house transferred to the Elting family, hence the compound name. The Bevier-Elting House is located on Huguenot Street, which has the distinction of being the oldest street in America on which the original houses can be seen. A National Historic Landmark, it is maintained today by the Huguenot Historical Society.

The Abraham Yates House, in Schenectady, New York, just northwest of Albany, is one of the town's earliest homes, having been built sometime between 1710 and 1730. The house's urban nature is underscored by its construction close to the street and sidewalk. It incorporates the familiar steep, sloping roof and small-paned windows with external shutters and double chimneys. A small porch, known in Dutch as a "stoep," frames the traditional entrance. A series of decorative dagger-shaped, black, wrought-iron fixtures set across the façade are actually supportive devices for strengthening the roof and wall beams. The sidewalls of the house have wood frames. Bricks across the upper area of the house are laid at right angles to the roof. The Yates House is a significant piece of early urban architecture and remains the only extant piece of Dutch urban construction in which the entrance to the home is in the narrow gable-end of the house.

Perhaps the most emphatically designed rural Dutch house of the period is the Luykas Van Alen House (see page 134) in Kinderhook, New York, a Hudson River region that was a heartland of early Dutch settlement. Built in 1737, this is a substantial farmhouse with little variation from those known back in Holland. The interior boasts massive smooth-planed joists and exceptionally tall casement windows that fill the house with intense light, considered a necessity by the Dutch. Such windows are a product of the high ceilings that owe their stability to the brick reinforcement of the timber frame. The exterior of the house includes windows framed by traditional shutters, three half-doors in the Dutch style and three chimneys, one on either end and one in the center. The steep roof adds to the grandeur of the farmhouse design, as well as indicating the addition of an extension to the house that is faithful to the same Dutch design aesthetics. The house's interior contains a remarkable collection of period Dutch kitchen items and other mid-eighteenth century furnishings.

The legacy of the Dutch in the evolving architectural design of America was substantial despite their short ascendancy in the affairs of the colonies. They have imparted a rich and robust domestic influence that continues to interest and inspire architects of the present.

Above: Schenck House, Brooklyn, NY, c. 1676. Built by Jan Schenck in the seventeenth century, this house was moved to the Brooklyn Museum in the 1960s.

Above: Bevier-Elting House, Huguenot Street, New Paltz, NY, 1698.

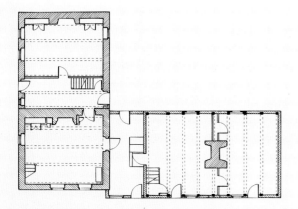

Above: Plan of the Pieter Bronck House, Coxsackie, NY, c. 1663 and 1738. The original house, built of local stone, is on the left side of the structure.

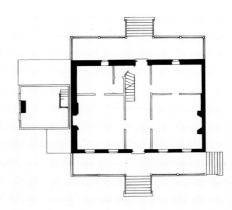

Above: Plan of the William Dyckman House, 4881 Broadway at 204th Street, Bronx, NY, 1783.

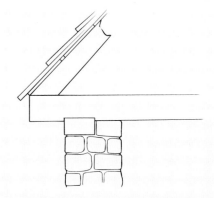

Above: Huguenot stone house construction; roof timbers rest on the stone wall.

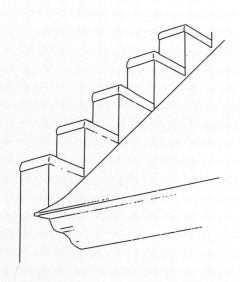

Above: Stepped gable, common in Flemish and Dutch architecture. Also called a crow-step gable.

Above: "Flemish" or "Dutch" gables; Hanseatic houses, Lübeck, Germany, seventeenth century. The so-called "Dutch" gable may have originated in north Germany.

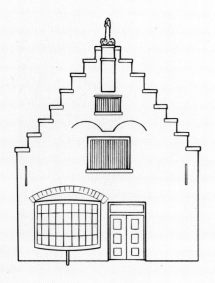

Left: Stepped gable urban house from New Amsterdam, c. 1648.

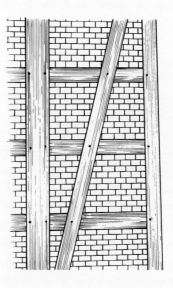

Left: Detail of German half-timbering, Dodge County, WI, c. 1850. The brick infilling shows clearly.

Above: Jean Hasbrouck House, Huguenot Street, New Paltz, NY, 1694. New Paltz was settled by French Huguenots who came to America after first sheltering in die Pfalz (the Palatinate) in Germany.

Above: Dubois Fort, Huguenot Street, New Paltz, NY, 1705.

Above: Freer-Low House, Huguenot Street, New Paltz, NY, 1720.

Above: Van Cortland Manor, South Riverside Avenue, Croton-on-Hudson, NY, eighteenth century.

Above: Luykas Van Alen House, Route 9H, Kinderhook, NY, 1737.

Above: Pieter Bronck House, Coxsackie, NY, c. 1663 and 1738. The diagonal zig-zag pattern in the brick gables is called "mousetooth."

Above: Pieter Bronck House, Route 9W, Coxsackie, NY, c. 1663 and 1738.

Left: William Dyckman House, 4881 Broadway at 204th Street, Bronx, NY, 1783.

Above: Single Brother's House, Old Salem, NC, 1769. An example of the German "fachwerk" (half-timber) tradition.

German and Moravian Colonial

German and other central European immigrants brought their own building traditions to America, including "fachwerk" construction (German half-timber style) and stone masonry. One of the most influential immigrant groups in the eighteenth century, German speakers were noted for their diverse religious identities. Their characteristic stonework and half-timber houses are found in Pennsylvania and the mid-Atlantic, as well as later in Wisconsin and the Midwest. The steeply pitched roofs and heavy wood frames reveal the origin in a northern climate, and were well suited to the American setting. Stone houses were extremely rare in the seventeenth century, but became more common with the arrival of skilled craftsmen in the eighteenth century. Some German-speaking groups settling in Pennsylvania became known as the Pennsylvania Dutch (from Deutsch, or German). The Amish and Mennonites were among these settlers.

Closely related houses by German-speaking Moravian immigrants are found in Pennsylvania, North Carolina and New Jersey. The Moravian church is a Protestant sect which originated in what were then Bohemia and Moravia, now part of the Czech Republic; the church traces its origin to the fifteenth century reformer John Hus (1369–1415). After moving to Germany to escape persecution in the eighteenth century, they arrived in America in 1735. Settlements were founded in Bethlehem, PA, Winston-Salem, NC, and Hope, NJ.

Above: Moravian house, Hope, NJ, 1775. Hope, New Jersey, was founded by a group of Moravian immigrants. Their architecture is very similar to German stonework traditions, and characterized by the distinctive use of masonry, with brick segmental arches over the windows.

Above: Moravian house, Hope, NJ, 1780.

French Colonial

Single-story, steep-pitched hipped or side-gabled roofs, multiple narrow doors and windows, wooden shutters, exterior walls of stucco applied to timber framing, in city settings cottages often flush with the street, in rural environs large covered porches frame the façade.

The French settled significant portions of the American interior in the seventeenth century, chiefly from the Gulf of St. Lawrence to the mouth of the Mississippi River. They plunged deep into the heartland from their base of New Orleans, which soon grew into a thriving center of commerce and culture in the region of the Gulf of Mexico. The French carried with them a unique architectural tradition that quickly made adaptations to the climate and raw materials of the American continent. Louisiana obviously still reflects in style, custom, and language traces of this important cultural influence, but other less well-known areas of the interior also remain touched by their presence. Architectural remnants that speak of French colonization are also to be found in what are today Missouri and Illinois.

The most distinctive expression of French colonial design in domestic architecture is found in the urban landscape of New Orleans and the rural areas that surround it. City homes still bear a French imprint. Single-story French urban cottages were the most popular dwellings built during its period of colonial ascendancy. Their proximity to the sidewalk and street along which they were built is an essential feature of their design—these homes did not have the more familiar porches of a later period of design. But they did incorporate the French penchant for multiple doors and entrances, often from each individual room to the outside. Roofs were usually hipped or side-gabled. French homes lacked the familiar hall or corridor of English tradition; rooms most often opened into other rooms or the outside.

Because New Orleans suffered two devastating fires in 1788 and 1791, few early colonial dwellings remain. In the rebuilding that ensued, the more familiar multi-storied residence "above the shop," with wrought-iron balcony, was created.

Rural French colonial architecture developed in the agricultural region surrounding the city. Here, following a more simple beginning of porches at ground

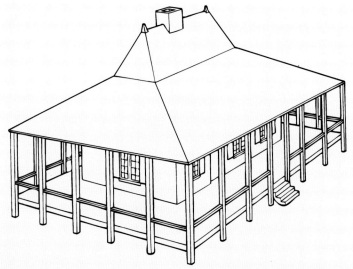

Above: Drawing of French colonial house in the Mississippi valley. The broken gable roof is characteristic, as is the construction based on poles set directly into the earth.

level, the French incorporated their unique design for the spacious, timbered second-story porches that became their signature feature. Houses in the country were generally built of masonry foundations with masonry columns supporting the generous veranda-style porch.

Arcadia House, circa 1765, built in St. Martinville, Louisiana, by the Chevalier D'Auterive, is a good example of the fashion for creating engaging outdoor space for use in the mild, but often tropical, weather. The steep roof pitch provided the necessary extensively protruding eave to canopy the porch, a practical feature against the heavy Delta rains. Rural homes also featured multiple entrance doors, that permitted each room a passage to the outside porch. These also provided a welcome source of ventilation in the humid countryside. Generous stairways gave outside access to the second-story porches.

Many remarkable rural examples of such French plantation houses grace the willow-laden countryside. At Parlange—a beautiful plantation constructed in 1750 by a French grandee, the Marquis Vincent de Terrant—the columned wrap-around porch echoes the refinements of another age. The exquisite lines of its hipped pyramidal roof remain in delicate symmetrical proportion to both the house and the landscape.

One hour south of the city of St. Louis, Missouri, stands the only original French colonial village in America, Ste. Genevieve. Here a remarkable remnant of French domestic architecture survives intact near the

Above: Bolduc house, Ste. Genevieve, MO, late eighteenth century.

banks of the Mississippi River. What is notable about the village is not only the number of dwellings, but also the range of styles that can be found there. This is a rare example of pure French Creole vernacular design. A construction technique known as "porteaux-en-terre," or post-in-ground fabrication, was used here. Of the five surviving examples of this type of design in the United States, three of them are found in Ste. Genevieve. No

house foundation was built in this process; instead logs, usually cedar, were set directly into the ground. A system of king-post trusses and wind braces, subsequ-ently, were employed in the roofing design. The Beauvais House, built in 1770, and the Amoureux House, built in 1792, are two good examples of this style, each built on a strategic agricultural site. Other homes were constructed with foundations in a style known as vertical log design. The Bolduc House, built in 1770, now a museum and a carefully restored example of this style, supports a distinctive hip roof, double chimney, and stockade fence. The influence of French colonial design can be seen here in a rare unobstructed setting.

Not far from this settlement, just across the Mississippi River's eastern bank, is another remarkable example of French influence, the Cahokia Courthouse, in Cahokia, Illinois. This is an even rarer example of domestic French Colonial design from 1737. Between 1793 and 1814, this building served as the local court-house, hence its name. Constructed in a half-timber design method, known as "colombage," with a limestone rock filling, known as "pierrotage," the courthouse is Illinois' only such domestic structure. The original timbering was of black walnut and was connected with mortise and tenon joints. Its steeply pitched pyramidal hip roof enveloped it. Such eighteenth century relics are rare here. In 1903, the entire structure was disassembled

Left: Cahokia Courthouse, First and Elm streets, Cahokia, IL, 1737. Originally a private house, this French colonial house was used as a courthouse from 1793–1814.

Left: Pierre Menard Home, Ellis Grove, IL, 1800

and rebuilt for display at the great World's Fair of 1904 in St. Louis, commemorating the bicentennial of the Louisiana Purchase. During the late 1930s, excavation was done in preparation for a future reconstruction of the building at its original site. Today, the Cahokia Courthouse remains a significant example of the enormous footprint of the French empire in America and its lasting influence on domestic design.

Although the presence of the French was longer lasting than that of the Dutch, their control of the interior territory of the continent ended largely with Thomas Jefferson's historic purchase of French lands in 1803. Nevertheless, while the Louisiana Purchase secured the American Republic's ownership of much of its central land mass, homes of French architectural influence remain national treasures.

Spanish Colonial

Single-story dwellings, low-pitched or flat-top roofs, thick baked earthen walls of adobe or stone, often covered with stucco, unglazed window apertures, heavy wood shutters, iron window grillwork, multiple door openings.

The Spanish came to the American continent and established settlements in the early sixteenth century, well before other Europeans. Their maritime abilities wedded to their buccaneer interest in gold moved them relentlessly over a wide swathe of the New World.

Encompassing important colonial settlements on both the southern Atlantic and far southwestern Pacific coasts, Spanish influence was both powerful and far-reaching. Unlike their Protestant fellow colonists, the Roman Catholic, Spanish post-Reformation conquistadors and settlers were bent on large scale religious conversion of the native population. This led to the early construction of missions and schools wherever they went. It is said that the real initiators of Spanish-influenced architectural design were the Franciscan and Dominican friars who accompanied the colonists in large numbers. Through their efforts, there was an immediate engagement with native peoples and quick development of ecclesiastical centers.

Most influential in the design of Spanish colonial domestic dwellings were the practical realities of settlement in the desert environment of the Southwest and the tropical conditions of coastal Florida. The design development that they espoused incorporated ways of dealing with such climatic extremes.

In Florida, the settlement at St. Augustine, in 1565, saw military and ecclesiastical considerations as paramount for the Spanish. Little remains of their early presence with the exception of the Cathedral of St. Augustine that enjoyed centuries of use until a fire in the late nineteenth century almost destroyed it. Today, only the limestone walls remain from the original building. Stone was also employed in the construction of the Fort

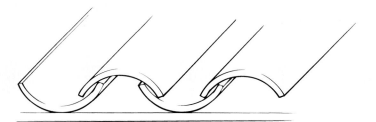

Above: Spanish, or Mission Style roof tiles.

of San Marco that guarded St. Augustine. Both the cathedral and the fort were built out of native coquina limestone, a soft gray-white stone that was readily available. The mortar used in the construction was a local blend of limestone mixed with crushed oyster shells. The fort remains the finest example of European-style fortification in the United States.

The oldest extant Spanish domestic architecture in Florida, at St. Augustine, is eighteenth century. The Gonzales-Alvarez House is a two-story clapboard structure whose lower walls were fashioned from local coquina limestone. At each end of this structure are second-story roofed veranda porches that are sheltered by a traditional hip roofs. Large fireplaces and cedar beams shape the interior of the house.

When Florida became part of the United States in 1821, the influence of the Spanish was already on the decline. Little remains of their architectural contributions on the South Atlantic coast.

A much more substantive Spanish look pervades the architecture of California. A long line of coastal mission stations staffed by Franciscan friars would later develop into the familiar cities of contemporary California. From San Diego to San Francisco, a durable, practical, and efficient architectural heritage developed. Churches and mission schools were established, built of traditional adobe bricks, baked clay, often covered in an earthen stucco. The use of adobe had roots back in Spain from the era of the Moors. Construction utilizing these mud bricks was a familiar technique and style, easily adapted to the conditions of colonial life. Interiors were fashioned of hewn wooden beams. Domestic dwellings followed a similar format. Traditional Spanish homes varied widely from other colonial styles—low-rise buildings of one- and two-room proportions were often built off central patios; additional rooms were often added as needed. Spanish custom incorporated entrances to individual rooms from off the common patio rather than off corridors or halls. A later period of colonial affluence saw the construction of larger dwellings, which retained the familiar modest simplicity of design.

Spanish architecture in New Mexico has its own flavor incorporating significant influence of local native peoples. The design and decorative techniques of the Pueblo people were readily incorporated in the early missions there. In New Mexico, Native Americans were settled agriculturalists rather than nomads.

Above: Larkin House, Calle Principal at Jefferson Street, Monterey, CA, 1835. Adobe.

Above: Stevenson House, Monterey State Park, Monterey, CA, 1830s. A good example of adobe building.

Above: Petaluma Adobe, Petaluma Adobe State Historic Park, Sonoma County, CA, 1836–1846.

Above: John Rains House, Rancho Cucamonga, Cucamonga, CA, 1860. An adobe house on a 13,000 acre ranch.

Above: Plaza Hall, the Zanetta House, San Juan Bautista, CA, 1868.

This fact is expressed in the permanency, efficiency, and protective nature of their dwellings. The native pueblos had a tradition of large, communal earth-brick dwellings and these terraced multi-tiered homes impacted deeply on the colonial style. One of the most remarkable structures is the mission church of 1772 at Ranchos de Taos. Fashioned of baked adobe bricks and stucco of a similar composition, its lines and proportions demonstrate the blend of Spanish and native traditions with notable grandeur. The pueblo of San Geronimo de Taos, built sometime in the early sixteenth century, also displays a highly technical design form.

Santa Fe, New Mexico, was established as a colonial capital in the early seventeenth century. Its earliest non-Indian building is the colonial Governor's Palace. Built in 1610, it still survives. This structure was constructed by native people and incorporates the best of their designs. It is an elongated, low structure of adobe brick with a prominent covered porch supported by a long series of wooden posts. The heavy door framing and the capitals at the main entrance are traditionally Spanish. An enclosed patio injects another central feature of Spanish design.

Spanish colonial architectural influence also deeply penetrated arid Texas. Its most famous architectural

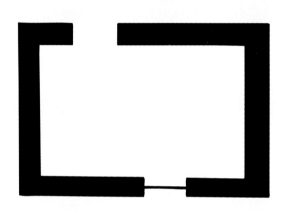

Above: Plan of adobe house; one room. Adobe construction typically involves very thick walls.

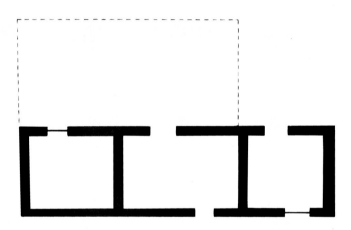

Above: Plan of adobe house; three rooms.

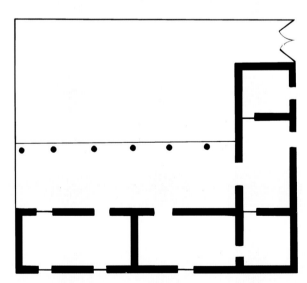

Above: Plan of adobe house; five rooms.

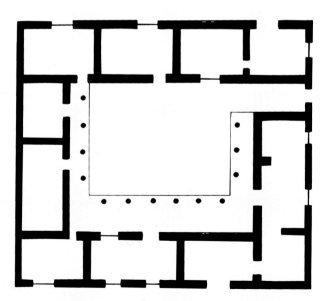

Above: Plan of adobe house; twelve rooms.

Above: Palace of the Governors, Santa Fe, New Mexico; as restored to original condition.

Above: Palace of the Governors, 100 Palace Avenue, Santa Fe, NM, 1610.

landmark, built in the city of San Antonio between 1744 and 1757, is the Alamo. Originally a Spanish mission that collapsed in 1762, it entered the pantheon of Texas mythology during its war of independence from Mexico in 1836. Larger-than-life Americans Davy Crockett and Colonel Jim Bowie died with 150 other Texas patriots in a desperate siege. Its rich design, however, is almost as famous as its political significance. An elaborate stone carved front and intricate double pair of column pilasters are deeply European in their design. Though the dome and vaulted ceiling are long gone, the building has been restored and stands as a treasured part of Texas history.

San Antonio is also thick with other examples of Spanish political and religious power. The Church of San Jose y San Miguel de Aguayo, built between 1720 and 1731, was one of the most significant Spanish architectural structures north of Mexico. Fashioned of limestone covered in stucco, it is heavily encrusted with

sandstone detail. A great belfry and dome add to the rich design. A splendid circular window and elaborately carved stone frontal are highly textured Spanish motifs.

Midway through the nineteenth century, Spain's colonial influence in America quickly dissipated following America's move to claim the whole central portion of the continent. Still, Spanish artistic and architectural influence remains a valuable and practical part of design style in the region it once ruled. Rancheros and haciendas across the American Southwest still exude a spicy Old World grandeur shaped by the aesthetics of the Spanish grandees.

Above: Rancho de Taos, NM.

Above: Trevino House, San Ygnacio, TX, c.1851.

Left: Drawing of a Monterey Style house. The prominent balcony is typical of Monterey houses in California.

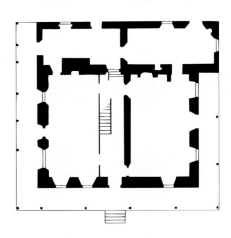

Above: Plan of Monterey house.

Left: Drawing of a larger Monterey Style house.

Georgian

Stately linear shapes, symmetry, door cases with broken pediments, distinctive Roman and Grecian Classical columns and pilasters, quoins, balconies and balustrades, florid ornamental detail, fanlights, sash windows, and glass chandeliers.

In the early decades of the eighteenth century, popular tastes were highly influenced by the rediscovery of the architecture and the Classical details of Greco-Roman design. In England, this corresponded to the reign of the Hanoverian kings—George I, George II, and George III. Georgian architecture took its name from the royals who would preside over this 126-year period. The popularity of this fresh, refined, and dignified style had its roots in the rejection of the Baroque, a style that was often criticized for its over-done opulence. In the colonies, the Georgian style was appealing for its simplicity. To the modest colonists, its refinements put distance, at last, between them and the rugged beginnings of colonial America. With few schooled architects to fashion this new style, most colonists had to make their way through the pattern books that helped in fabricating the proper designs.

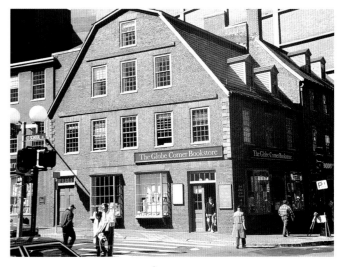

Above: "Old Corner Bookstore," the Thomas Crease House, 285 Washington Street, Boston, MA, 1712. This was built as a private home, with Crease's apothecary shop on the ground floor; in 1828 it became a bookstore.

One of the first buildings in Boston to be constructed in the new Georgian style was built in 1712 for a well-known apothecary, and is known as the Dr. Thomas Crease House. Through its later literary fame as one of America's earliest publishing houses, it came to be known as The Old Corner Bookstore. Designed in the

Above: Langley King House, 34 Pelham St, Newport, RI, c. 1711. Gambrel roofs become much more common in the eighteenth century.

Above: Harkness House, 38 Green St, Newport, RI, c. 1730. A one-story house, with dormers added to the attic in the gambrel roof.

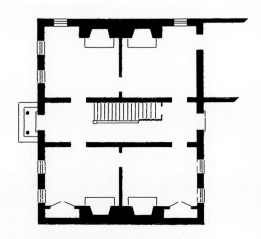

Above: Plan of typical Georgian house in New England. Georgian houses are larger than earlier colonial homes, and have higher ceilings and more windows, creating a more spacious and formal living area.

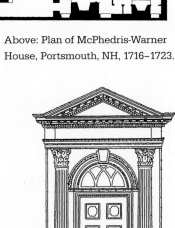

Above: Plan of McPhedris-Warner House, Portsmouth, NH, 1716–1723.

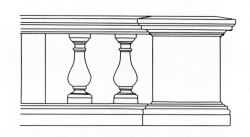

Above: A typical Georgian balustrade.

Above: Drawing of typical Georgian door with pilasters and triangular pediment. Eighteenth century architecture reflects a greater degree of wealth in the colonies, and a greater self-consciousness about Classical ornamental features.

Above: Drawing of typical Georgian door with pilasters and swan's neck pediment.

Above: Rounded pediment, doorway from McPhedris-Warner House.

Above: Thomas Griswold House, 171 Boston Street, Guilford, CT, 1774. A simple timber-framed saltbox, but with an elegant pedimented doorway.

Above: John Drew, builder: McPhedris-Warner House, 150 Daniel Street, Portsmouth, NH, 1718–1723. One of the earliest brick Georgian houses in New England.

Above: Pierce-Hichborn House, 29 North Square, Boston, MA, 1711. The eighteenth century saw an increasing number of brick houses being built in Boston. The house was built by Moses Pierce; Nathaniel Hichborn was a cousin of Paul Revere.

Above: Doorway of Georgian house, Montague, MA, eighteenth century.

Above: McPhedris-Warner House, Portsmouth, NH, 1718–1723. The door.

Anglo-Dutch style with a sweeping gambrel roof, its red brick exterior walls feature stone end quoins at the corners and sash windows that mark the influence of Georgian aesthetics.

Among the best examples of early Georgian domestic design is the McPhedris-Warner House, in Portsmouth, New Hampshire, built between 1718 and 1723. This handsome red-brick townhouse ostentatiously displayed the wealth of its prosperous owner, Captain Archibald McPhedris. The masonry walls are eighteen inches thick and help define the genteel symmetry of the structure. Generous windows have segmental arches on the first floor, while the pilasters and segmented arches over the entrance door are also emblematic of the new style. This is a central-hall type house designed with end chimneys.

Balustrade railings and a cupola top the structure and the dormer windows are each topped with an arch of Classical design.

The Thomas Hancock House, built between 1737 and 1740, may have been Boston's most elegant Georgian home. The uncle of patriot John Hancock was a man whose life embodied the Georgian ethos. A man of learning and high aesthetic tastes, his house set the tone for those that followed. This was a gracious three-story granite structure with end chimneys and quoin detailing around the generous windows which were made up of 480 panes of glass imported from London. A balcony with baluster railing, and double doors flanked by stone pilasters and topped by a great broken pediment were central to the façade. So too was the elegant entranceway beneath, with granite columns flanking both sides. Taking three years to complete, Hancock's residence on Beacon Hill became the talk of Boston. Gracious attention to the interior details matched the drama of the exterior. Bringing granite from Braintree and sandstone from Connecticut, Hancock set the standard for a new refinement in domestic architecture. Sadly, the house was torn down in 1863, a period of less enlightened interest in the Georgian style.

The Isaac Royall House, in Medford, Massachusetts, built between 1733 and 1737, like Hancock's great house, was an example of the interest in fashioning a dwelling using the proportions of the new aesthetic. Isaac Royall was intent on creating a structure of lavish architectural detail. He began by purchasing a brick house of two-and-a-half stories, then proceeded to enlarge it not in stone, but in wood, which lent itself more subtly to the degree of detailing he wanted. The brick was covered in wood cladding with wooden angle quoins added. So too were elaborate frame casings for the windows that were joined to spandrel panels to create a unified vertical panel down the façade. Also added were a mullioned cornice and a central entrance with pilasters against the treated wood of the façade. His son later added the double end chimneys and a further enlargement of the house. The interior was also executed in splendid Georgian detail. Epitomizing elegance were the staircase in the entrance hall and the pilaster paneling in the Great Chamber on the second floor.

The Lady Pepperrell House, built in 1760, in Kittery Point, Maine, just over the river from Portsmouth, New

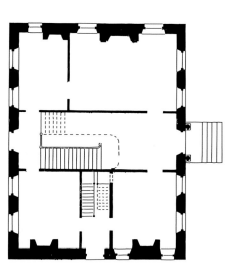

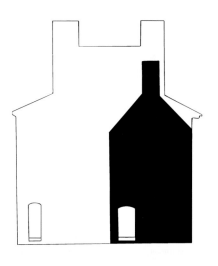

Above: The Thomas Hancock House, Boston, MA, 1737–1740. The first stone house in Boston, it was demolished in 1863. John Hancock lived here at the time of the revolution.

Above: Plan of the Thomas Hancock House, Boston, MA, 177–1740.

Above: Royall House, Medford, MA. Diagram showing the relationship of the original house to the later additions.

Above: Isaac Royall House, 15 George Street, Medford, MA, 1733–1737/1747–1750. East façade.

Isaac Royall, a wealthy merchant, significantly enlarged an earlier house in two phases, each time making it more Classical in the Georgian manner. This façade is covered with wooden clapboards, with wooden quoins at the ends. The end walls are brick.

Above: Isaac Royall House, Medford, MA, 1733–1737/ 1747–1750. West façade. This side is covered with boards cut to imitate stone, with full-length pilasters at each end.

Above: Isaac Royall House. This view shows the brick end walls of the Royall House; the simple clapboard building in front is the slave quarters, the only one remaining in New England.

Hampshire, is another house with lavish Georgian detailing that avails itself of wooden construction. Lady Pepperrell was the wife of America's only baronet, Sir William Pepperrell, the hero of the Battle of Louisburg.

The external walls of the house are fashioned entirely out of horizontal wood cladding. Generous sash windows, six panes over and under, provide all sides of the house with symmetrical balance. The main entranceway is set between a pair of two-story Doric pilasters, deeply grooved. Surrounding the entrance, clapboard panels run horizontally. The central door is also framed by a rich pediment and double cornice. Multiple brick

Above: Lady Pepperell House, Pepperell Road, Kittery Point, ME, 1760. An elegant Georgian house, built by the widow of a former governor of Maine.

chimneys are tall and themselves a feature of the symmetry of the house. A side porch continues the Classical detail with Doric columns supporting the roof. The corners of the house front and back are set with right-angle quoins. The craftsmanship of the wood cladding projects a sturdy elegance.

The 1760 Wentworth-Gardner House in Portsmouth, New Hampshire, is of similar vintage as the Pepperell House and is similarly clad in wood. The addition of a triple set of dormer windows to both the front and back of the hip roof distinguishes it. The Wentworth-Gardner House faces the waters of Portsmouth Harbor, nestled in a country neighborhood of rich period-built dwellings. Windows are six panes over and under sash, and on the first floor they are eye-browed with Classical arches. The entrance way of double Corinthian pilasters and swansneck pediment stretch only one-story but the richly fashioned door boasts fifteen panels. The cladding is cut to look like stone, with quoins at the edges.

The Robert "King" Hooper Mansion built in 1768, in the heart of Marblehead, Massachusetts, is a magnificent townhouse of three full stories. Surprisingly for its size, it enjoys an intimate connection to the environment around it, so balanced and proportioned is it in all its Classical detail. The façade gives the appearance of being made of large stones though it is actually made of wood. The front cladding contrasts with the horizontal

Above: Swan's neck pediment, Wentworth-Gardner House, Portsmouth, NH, 1760.

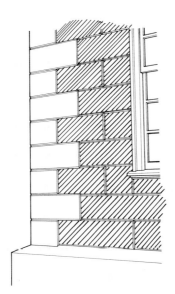

Above: Quoins, from Wentworth-Gardner House. These quoins are formed from boards cut to imitate stone.

Above: Palladian window. A symmetrical design invented by the Italian Renaissance architect Andrea Palladio, and disseminated in this country by books.

Above: Wentworth-Gardner House, 50 Mechanic Street, Portsmouth, NH, 1760. To enhance the impressiveness of this house, the wide boards covering the front façade were cut to look like stone; the side walls were left covered in clapboards.

Right: Wentworth-Gardner House, Portsmouth, NH, 1760. Detail of the door with swan's neck pediment.

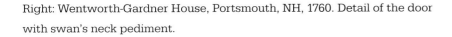

Above: Robert "King" Hooper House, Marblehead, MA, 1768.

Above: Robert "King" Hooper House, Marblehead, MA, 1768. Door with Doric columns and pediment.

side-cladding that is just half its width. The façade is balanced by the five windows that stretch across the front on the second and third floors. Four windows and the central door are street level on the first floor. The entrance, which is almost flush with the narrow side walk, is framed by simple pilasters and pediment. All fourteen front windows, six over and under, have double external shutters.

Another substantial Marblehead Georgian house is the Jeremiah Lee Mansion, also built in 1768. Three full stories, it is one of the largest among all of its contemporaries. Although also fashioned of rusticated wood, it again exaggerates its faux-masonry with right-angle quoins and keystone window lintels above all its windows—twenty in all, each a six under and over sash. A large fanlight makes a dormer light on the fourth floor and a cupola sits centrally on the hip roof that is dominated by two enormous brick chimneys. A pavilion of considerable size with double Doric columns, pilasters, and Classical canopy stands at the entrance. Rich, elaborately paneled interior rooms are also sturdy expressions of the Georgian aesthetic.

Above: Pedimented portico, from Jeremiah Lee House, Marblehead, MA, 1768.

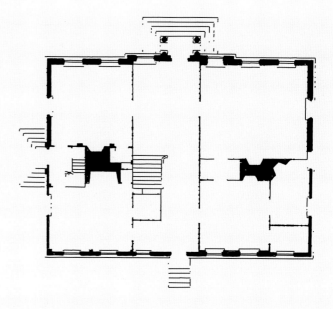

Above: Plan of the Jeremiah Lee House.

Above: Jeremiah Lee Mansion, 161 Washington Street, Marblehead, MA, 1768. The façade of this house also uses false stone. In some eighteenth century houses, sand was mixed with the paint to make it look more like stone.

Above: Jeremiah Lee Mansion, Marblehead, MA, 1768. Door with double Doric columns.

Within the rarified cultural heights of Harvard University, the Vassall-Longfellow House, in Cambridge, built in 1759, enjoys a privileged position, with a pedigree both historic and literary. Set on the high topography of Tory Row on famed Brattle Street, this dwelling once housed headquarters for General George Washington during the Revolution. It was later home to Henry Wadsworth Longfellow in the middle of the nineteenth century. The scale of the house is well

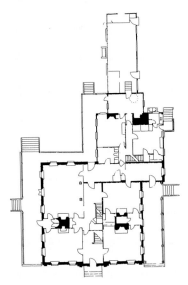

Above: Plan of the John Vassall-Longfellow House, Cambridge, MA, 1759. Includes later additions at the rear.

proportioned for the size of the generous property upon which it sits. Unlike other similar period homes, its sweeping lawns and long walkway provide wide dimensions to enhance the visual appreciation of the four two-story Doric pilasters and the balustrades that frame both the grounds in front and the hip roof above. Horizontal cladding richly defines a façade that holds a mullioned cornice with inset fanlight. The sash windows, six over six, are each framed with double exterior shutters. Two great chimneys sit atop the roof and add their own contribution to the visual scale. Two side porches extend the sight lines of the house that is set far from the traffic of the street. This is high late-Georgian design at its most ebullient.

The replication of the Georgian style in the western reaches of Massachusetts, far from the urbanity and resources of Boston, with its ready availability of materials, was most effectively practiced in historic Deerfield Village. In what were then frontier conditions, residents of this important outpost enjoyed considerable architectural success in adapting Georgian design. A kind of primitive chic developed, as pattern-book designs were executed in a more simplified and scaled splendor. Wide board cladding, abundantly available, created a more rustic appearance in Deerfield. Meticulous attention to architectural detail, married with the materials of western outpost living, created a hybrid of high rural

Left: John Vassall-Longfellow House, 105 Brattle Street, Cambridge, MA, 1759. John Vassall was a wealthy merchant with plantations in Jamaica. In the nineteenth century, the poet Henry Wadsworth Longfellow lived here.

Above: John Vassall-Longfellow House, Brattle Street, Cambridge, MA, 1759.

Above: Ropes Mansion, 318 Essex Street, Salem, MA, 1727.

Above: Capt. Gregory Purcell House (also known as the John Paul Jones House), 43 Middle Street, Portsmouth, NH, 1758.

Above: Metcalf Bowler House, 46 Clarke Street, Newport, RI, c. 1760. This house has the entrance in the gable side, to conform to a narrow urban lot.

Above: Thomas Cole House, Wickford, RI, 1786.

Above: Daniel Vaughn House, Pelham Street, Newport, RI, c. 1780.

Left: Sheldon-Hawks House, Old Main Street, Deerfield, MA, 1768–1772. Deerfield is a rich collection of early eighteenth century houses, most built after much of the town was burned during a raid in 1704.

Above: Dwight House, c. 1725, remodeled 1755, Springfield, MA, moved to Deerfield, MA, in 1954.

Above: Old Manse, Joseph Barnard House, Deerfield, MA, 1768.

Above: Dwight House, c. 1725, remodeled 1755, Springfield, MA, moved to Deerfield, MA, in 1954.

Left: Wells-Thorne House, southeast corner of Main and Memorial streets, Deerfield, MA, 1717/1751.

Below: Scaife dormitory, Deerfield, MA.

Left: John Barnard House, Deerfield, MA, 1768–1772.

Left: "Pink" House, Deerfield, MA, 1797. Modern scientific research has shown that colonial houses were not generally painted white during the seventeenth and eighteenth centuries. In the seventeenth century, they were seldom painted at all, and in the eighteenth century, a wide range of colors was used.

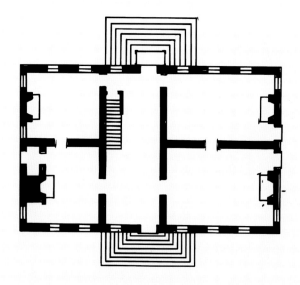

Above: William Byrd II and Richard Taliaferro: plan of Westover, the Byrd Mansion, Charles City Co., VA, c. 1730–1734.

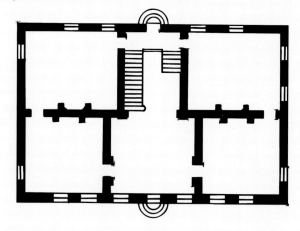

Above: Plan of Drayton Hall, Charleston, SC, 1742.

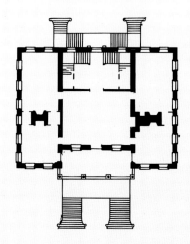

Above: Richard Taliaferro: plan of Carter's Grove, near Williamsburg, James City Co., VA, 1750–1753.

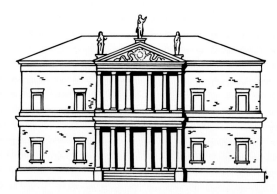

Above: This Palladian villa, with its central, double story portico, shows a marked similarity to the design of Drayton Hall and Jefferson's first design for Monticello.

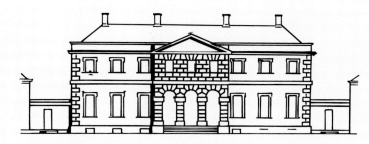

Above: James Gibbs: design for house, *Book of Architecture* (1728), plate 58. This house is extremely similar to Mount Airy, VA, 1748–1758.

Above: Hawks, Tryon's Palace, New Bern, NC, 1767.

Right: Hawks, plan for Tryon's Palace, New Bern, NC, 1767.

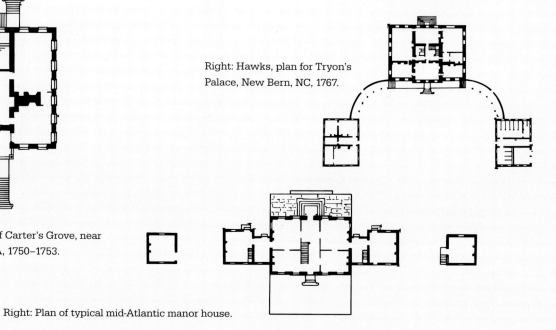

Right: Plan of typical mid-Atlantic manor house.

design. Splendid two-story houses, rich in the craftsmanship of window framing and replete with signature pediments and cornice treatments, created an architecturally refined wonderland far from the environs of Boston. Today, a surprising number of these remarkable homes have been preserved. They stand as museum houses, protected and in excellent condition.

Georgian—Palladian

Pavilions, porticos, pedimented front doors, entablatures, columns, pilasters, architrave, frieze, cornice, central Palladian window, brick masonry, central hall flanked by two rooms, proportionality, emphasis on the axis of symmetry.

An architectural transition took place in colonial domestic design with the introduction of Palladianism, a philosophical school of design based on the writings of the sixteenth century Italian Andrea Palladio. His attempt to introduce the style and symmetry of Roman design sparked a great movement in architecture. While much of Georgian architecture reflects the return to

Classical artistry, Palladianism is as much an intellectual movement as it an architectural one. Palladian design utilizes the constructs of Georgian design with a restrained, aristocratic elegance incorporating understated decorative detail, and faithfulness to the formalized system of proportions, or "orders," of Classical architecture. Remarkably, by the mid-eighteenth century, the Palladian ideal was being translated into domestic dwellings for the colonial elite. These houses exhibit an extraordinary sophistication and mark a coming of age in pre-Revolutionary War America.

Westover, the mansion built between 1730 and 1734 by William Byrd II and designed by architect Richard Taliaferro in Charles City County, Virginia, twenty-five miles from Williamsburg along the James River, is a good example of Palladian ideals. Byrd was a wealthy colonial gentleman who exercised great taste in building what many consider to be the best Georgian house in America. The brick, two-story, steep hip-roof house is beautifully symmetrical. Three tiers of windows, for instance, those on the first and second floors, and the dormer windows, all diminish in their height and width

Above: Tryon Palace, Gov. William Tryon House, 600 Block, Pollock Street, New Bern, NC, 1767–1770.

as they ascend. So too, does the size of the window panes and roof slates. All of this unusual detail adds to the perception of the size of the house, creating a magnificent façade that is only enhanced by the main north entrance door that, along with the south garden door, are said to have come directly from a manual for implementing Palladian design. Westover's interior is designed with a Classical central hall flanked by two great rooms on either side.

It is suspected that Richard Taliaferro contributed to another of America's great Palladian houses, Carter's Grove, built by Carter Burwell, in James City County, Virginia, between 1750 and 1753. There is a dramatic simplicity to Carter's Grove, but fewer windows and a roof employing a lower pitch distinguish it from Westover. The dark red brick masonry is also more modest. But a similar axis of symmetry running through its north and south entrances parallels the aesthetic grandeur of other Palladian manses. A belt of double brick separates the two stories of the house and all windows are nine panes over nine. The simplicity of the doorways also differ from other richer Palladian houses; here they are formed out of brick with a modest

crown pediment above. The placement of the two chimneys, a more central position in, rather than at the ends of the house, resets the placement of interior fireplaces.

The Palladian ideal is also reflected by architect William Buckland in the Hammond-Harwood House, built in Annapolis, Maryland in 1773. Though modest in its exterior appearance, it boasts one of the most beautiful doorways in colonial America. The red brickwork of the façade is enhanced by a door frieze richly executed with ornamental carved floral detail of laurel and roses that arch around a segmented fanlight. Ionic columns support a triangular pediment. Interior doors are equally well framed. Heavily carved interior shutters and pedimented windows display an academic symmetry and add to the rich carved design of the large first-floor dining room and second-floor ballroom. Even with these embellishments, this is reserved architecture without pretensions or vanity.

Palladianism achieved a republican personality when George Washington designed and built his Virginia villa, Mount Vernon, in Fairfax County, between 1757 and 1787. He transformed the modest farmhouse of his

Above: William Buckland (1734–1774): Hammond-Harwood House, 19 Maryland Avenue, Annapolis, MD, 1773–1774.

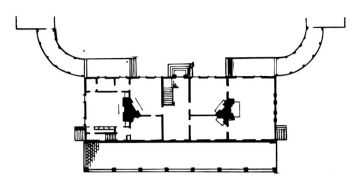

Above: George Washington: plan of Mount Vernon, VA, 1757–1787. Mount Vernon is also based on Palladian villas.

Above: George Washington: Mount Vernon, VA, 1757–1787. View of the south side.

father, fashioning it into one of America's most important domestic dwellings. The "Enlightenment" philosophies symbolized by Palladio's refinements were also a dynamic part of the agrarian pragmatism and republican idealism that Washington and his contemporaries shared.

The fine linear symmetry of Washington's home has become an American icon of refined ideals, a marriage of artistic excellence and noble purpose. The two-story structure with hip roof, cupola, and central pediment with bull's eye window creates a singular façade. While the exterior walls of Mount Vernon look as if made of stone, Washington actually employed rusticated pine with a sand finish to give the appearance of masonry con-

struction. Doors, windows, and pediments are all in proportion to one another and an arched colonnade, a signature Palladian detail, adds grandeur to the façade. A tripartite Palladian window—a triptych of glazed panes, pilasters, and broken pediment—is set within a two-story banquet room on the first floor at the north end of the house. The eastern two-story portico overlooking the Potomac River has an extended eave supported by eight pillars that extends the full length of the house, adding a refined dignity and proportion. The interior is also a reflection of Enlightenment sensibilities—not opulent, but with finely crafted plaster ceilings, Classical mantelpieces, and richly carved paneling. Washington himself oversaw the details of the plantings throughout

Left: George Washington: Mount Vernon, VA, 1757–1787. Mount Vernon is a country estate which uses many details inspired by Palladian design.

Above: John Kirk, master mason: Graeme Park, the Sir William Keith House, 895 County Line Road, Horsham, PA. 1721–1722. The exterior of this house is of powerful stone masonry; the interior features elegant and refined classical ornament skillfully carved from wood.

the grounds that he insisted be set in a natural, unstructured design. Mount Vernon very much reflects the character of America's first president.

Brice House, built in Annapolis, Maryland, in 1773, is an impressive house of brick masonry. Its distinctive grandeur derives from a steep roof design and the unusual tall, broad, thin double-chimneys. In addition to the central two-story structure, four other brick structures are inter-connected in a five-part plan. Though grand in its proportions, this house is bereft of the embellishments usually found in Palladian designs. The central doorway is purely rectangular without pediment or pilaster. Such simplicity of detail is often perceived as an indication that the builder was unfamiliar with the forms of Palladian style, Ironically, however, the house's impressive form echoes the character of the Palladian ideal.

The grand lines and exterior refinements of Graeme Park, in Horsham, Pennsylvania, built between 1721 and 1722, have little of the Palladian symbols of design. The house does, however, demonstrate a subdued simplicity. This two-story, gambrel-roofed, double-chimney house is highly textured in a rich stone masonry. Exceptionally tall doors and widows demonstrate an effective proportionality that adds to the sense of height. Designed by master mason John Kirk for Sir William Keith, the Colonial Governor of Pennsylvania, the house displays a

rich and highly Classical interior style. The drawing room is paneled floor to ceiling in gray-painted yellow pine that is sustained in the room's molded chair rail. A great winding staircase with turned balusters and square newel post has a simplicity of line and form. Original floorboards, like the painted panels, survive as fine examples of Georgian interior design.

The three-part Venetian windows that are so central to the façade of Mount Pleasant, at Fairmont Park, Philadelphia, built between 1762 and 1765 for John McPherson, a Scottish sea captain, are a dramatic component of the splendid external symmetry in what John Adams once called "the most elegant seat in Pennsylvania." An extraordinary Classical design can be seen at the main entrance way as well. The stucco exterior is fashioned to appear as stonework replete with corner quoins, while the hip roof is embellished with a four-sided balustrade. Windows are eight panes over eight sash. Two pavilions flank the central house; one was used as a summer kitchen and the other as the plantation office. The carved woodwork within the interior is among the finest in Philadelphia. Doric and Ionic Classical motifs decorate the entrance hall and acanthus foliage is a recurring design on chimney pieces in the parlor and main chamber. This late Georgian style was highly prized among the elite of Philadelphia. When Mount Pleasant was sold in 1779, it was bought by General Benedict Arnold.

The manorial splendor of Mount Pleasant and its compact architectural unity in many ways resemble Palladio's Villa Barbaro, built at Maser outside of Venice in 1554. The extraordinary designs of the façades of each demonstrate a Classical symmetry and imaginative fancy. The main block of Villa Barbaro centers all perspective on the enormous triangular pediment that spans the length of the structure. This design form is repeated at Mount Pleasant in the central pediment at roof level and above the main entrance. The shape of the central arched window at the Villa Barbaro is echoed in the Venetian window at Mount Pleasant.

Encouraging the building of such splendid country manors as Mount Pleasant, the English architect James Gibbs was highly influential among the grandees of the colonies. In his *Book of Architecture*, Gibbs expressed a hope that in even the farthest reaches of the colonies, gentlemen could use his book as a road map to design

Above: James Gibbs: design for house, *Book of Architecture* (1728), plate 63. This house is extremely similar to Tryon's Palace.

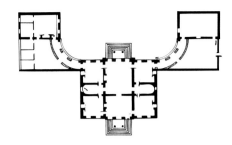

Right: James Gibbs: plan for house, *Book of Architecture* (1728), plate 63. This house is extremely similar to Tryon's Palace.

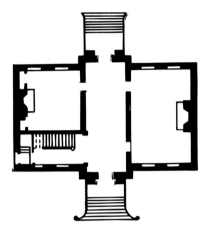

Above: Plan of Mount Pleasant, Fairmont Park, Philadelphia, 1761–1762.

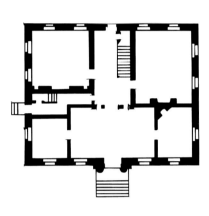

Above: Plan of Cliveden, Philadelphia, PA, c. 1767.

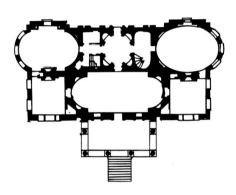

Above: Plan of Woodlands, Philadelphia, PA, 1788–1789. The oval rooms were a mark of distinction in highly refined eighteenth century architecture.

great houses in the tradition of Palladio. His book was a guide to Classical design, in much the same way as Palladio's was a guide to the ancient architecture of Rome as rediscovered in the writings and work of Vitruvius. Gibbs designed several buildings in Boston, not least of which is the historic Old North Church of Paul Revere fame.

The search for the perfect architecture was an abiding passion of colonial settlers who were influenced by the philosophy of the Enlightenment. Striving for intellectual perfection and aesthetic challenge, many men of intelligence went abroad to search out Classical design. William Hamilton of Philadelphia, a wealthy young man with a 250-acre site outside the city, possessed a passion for both botany and architecture. He set off on a two-year journey to England to familiarize himself with the architecture of the finest homes. On his return, he built Woodlands Mansion, fashioning a house that redefined Classical revival architecture in America. He devised a unique plan for the house that featured

large oval shaped rooms at the east and west ends of the house. The design used richly textured masonry, with a symmetrical façade, gently embellished with a central triangular pediment above six Ionic pilasters. Graceful fanlights arch above each of three entrance doors. Woodlands is a remarkably unified design in harmony with the great parkland that surrounds it. Its interior plan balances well-proportioned rooms that are well organized and in relationship to each other.

This was an enormous undertaking for a gentleman, but it expressed the aesthetic ideals for which Palladio strived. The unity and the harmonious organization here at Woodlands can be compared to Palladio's great Villa Foscari at Malcontenta near Venice, built between 1549 and 1563. Like Woodlands, this villa was designed as a suburban dwelling, a grand Classical house within easy reach of a city. Each are fashioned with temple-front porticos and, aesthetically, are temples for the builder.

Above: Richard Moncrieff, builder: Miles Brewton House, 27 King Street, Charleston, SC, 1769–1773.

Gore Place, in Waltham, Massachusetts, built in 1806, was fashioned with the same noble purpose. While traveling in Europe in 1799, the Gores, a family of considerable American nobility, received word that their Waltham home had burned. With a similar relish to that of William Hamilton, they set out to plan a new home of great architectural significance. They too investigated the houses of England and the Continent as well, finally choosing a design with restrained, neo-Classical ornamentation and that included oval parlors, not unlike those at Woodlands. The house was designed to be light and airy for use as a summer residence. A French architect, Jacques-Guillaume Legrand, is said to have assisted Mrs. Gore in the detail of design,

while the influence of Sir John Soane, the noted English architect, is also said to be seen in its refinements. The two-story house is built of brick masonry. A low-pitch hip roof and long windows permit the tall proportions of the central section of the house to appear to rise high above the single-story pedimented side wings. Gore Place was a house whose guests matched the nobility of its design. From James Madison and Daniel Webster to the Marquis de Lafayette, this most fashionable house exuded the philosophical rationale out of which Palladio worked and from which the appeal of Classical thought, art, and architecture evolved. It demonstrated not just the visual reality of ancient Rome, but its republican idealism.

Above: Captain John MacPherson House, "Mount Pleasant," Fairmont Park, Philadelphia, PA, 1761–1762.

Above: Mount Clare, Charles Carroll House, 1500 Washington Boulevard, Baltimore, MD, 1760.

Above: William Paca House, 186 Prince George Street, Annapolis, MD, 1765.

Left: Chatham Manor, near Fredericksburg, VA, 1768–1771.

Below: Gore Place, 52 Gore Street, Waltham, MA, 1801–1804. Gore was a governor of Massachusetts; the design of this country house has been attributed to his wife Rebecca Gore and the French architect Jacques-Guillaume Legrand.

Above: Kingsley Plantation, Fort George Island, Jacksonville, FL, early 1800s.

Above: Cedar Grove, Fairmont Park, Philadelphia, PA, c. 1750; significantly enlarged 1795.

Above: Montpelier, James Madison House, 11407 Constitution Highway, Montpelier Station, VA. First constructed in 1760, the house was altered by Madison in the nineteenth century, and doubled in size in the early twentieth century by the DuPont family.

Federal or Adam

Elliptical fanlights, two-story pilasters, double-hung sash windows, Palladian windows, Classical detail in door surrounds and entryway porches, porticos, and pavilions.

Following independence from Britain, a spirit of vitality and noble purpose emerged in the former American colonies. In the ensuing decades, the infant republic reinvented many customs, styles, and tastes. The Federal (or Federalist) architectural style, a refinement of the Georgian tradition, corresponds somewhat to the Regency style in England, 1780 to 1820. In America, however, this style was as much about national self-perception as it was a form of architecture. Federalism described the new cohesion among the independent American states. It also portrayed the bright, enlightened, American ideal that touched everything from architecture to citizenship in a land no longer a colony.

No-one demonstrated that refined self-perception more than American's first great architect, Charles Bulfinch (1763–1844). Born in Boston in the decade before independence, Bulfinch captured the national ideal in his commitment to the Neoclassical tradition. He was responsible for the design of some of Boston's most important public buildings, such as the Massachusetts State House. He also designed the central section and dome of the original Capitol Building in Washington, D.C., as well as making an important contribution to Boston's domestic architecture.

Tontine Crescent, on Franklin Place in Boston, built in 1794, marked Bulfinch's attempt to recreate the

Above: Charles Bulfinch: First Harrison Gray Otis House, 141 Cambridge Street, Boston, MA, 1796. The first of three houses built by Bulfinch for the Boston politician, it is very cubic in form, and features a low hipped roof to accentuate the compact unity of the design.

Right: Charles Bulfinch (1763–1844): plan of Third Harrison Gray Otis house, Beacon Street, Boston, MA, 1806. The oval room and its bay window originally looked out on to a garden; another house was later built in this space, encasing the room.

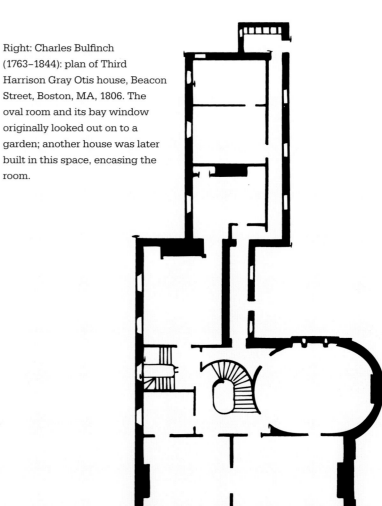

Above: Drawing of a typical Federalist row house. Town houses with bow fronts became very popular in the East, whether built singly or in groups.

Below: Plan of Gore Place, Waltham, 1801–1804. Design attributed to Rebecca Gore and French architect Jacques-Guillaume Legrand. This country house was designed for gracious living and high society.

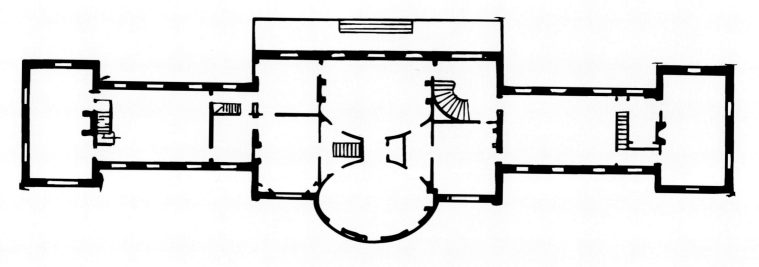

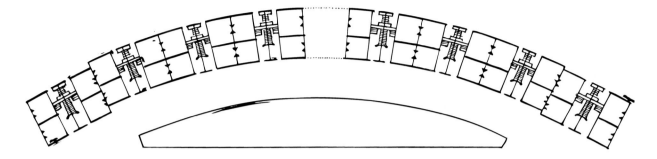

Above: Charles Bulfinch: plan of Tontine Crescent, Boston, MA, 1790.

Above: Charles Bulfinch: elevation of Tontine Crescent. This was an early venture in planned development in the United States. Although not a financial success, it was modeled on similar British constructions which shared a common garden. Destroyed during a great fire in Boston in 1872, only the curve of Franklin Street shows where the crescent was.

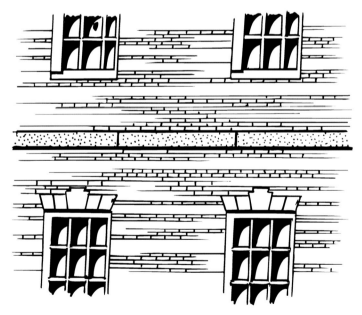

Above: Belt course, or string course used to mark the division between stories; Charles Bulfinch: First Harrison Gray Otis House, Boston, MA, 1796.

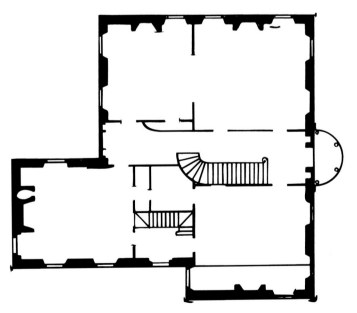

Above: Samuel McIntyre (1757–1804): plan of Gardner-Pingree House, Salem, MA, 1804.

well-planned urban townscape that he had seen in Bath and Paris. The designs of Robert Adam, at Portland Place in London, also strongly influenced his Boston designs. There, Bulfinch created a 400-foot-long curved row series of sixteen domestic townhouses of gray-painted brick that flowed from a central pavilion fashioned in the Palladian style. A great Palladian window and four Ionic pilasters rose above a vaulted arched lunette that created the central focus of the sweeping crescent. Secondary pavilions stood at either side of the crescent, adorned with six two-story pilasters that added decorative unity.

Each floor of the interior had two large rooms with a hallway containing stairways for both residents and servants. A second crescent was originally to be constructed on the other side of Franklin Place, but, sadly, the whole scheme proved to be too financially ambitious for Boston. Within fifty years of its construction, Tontine Crescent was razed by fire.

Bulfinch was eminently more successful in his endeavors to fashion a series of houses of refinement and fresh style that would last for Harrison Gray Otis, Boston's third mayor and a man of great wealth and

Above: Charles Bulfinch (1763–1844): doorway of First Harrison Gray Otis House, 141 Cambridge Street, Boston, MA, 1796.

influence. In 1796, Bulfinch built the First Harrison Gray Otis House on Cambridge Street, in what was then an emerging neighborhood of prosperous families—Bowdoin Square. This large, three-story brick residence had all the earmarks of the new Federalist style—a central second-story tripartite Palladian window, a third-floor segmented arched fanlight, first-floor entranceway fanlight and sidelights, and large six pane over six sash windows.

Though of considerable size and quality, the house was concise and modest in its external embellishments. It was inside that its true refinements were displayed,

becoming the talk of genteel Boston. Fine wallpapers, carpets, and furniture in a style influenced by Classical Greek design were fashioned in bold colors. Formal rooms were located on the first floor and family rooms were laid out on the second. Though the house was a comfortable fit for the Otis family, they only remained there for four years. Today, it has been restored and is open to the public as a museum.

At the turn of the century, around 1800, Otis and his business partners undertook one of the great building projects in Boston history, the development of Beacon Hill. As a leader in the construction of what would

Above: Charles Bulfinch (1763–1844): Second Harrison Gray Otis House, 85 Mount Vernon Street, Boston, MA, 1800–1802. Otis moved to the newly developed district on Beacon Hill in 1800, and asked Bulfinch for a second house. This one has large ornamental pilasters and an incomplete frieze.

become the city's most elegant residential neighborhood, Otis again sought the services of Bulfinch in creating the Second Harrison Gray Otis House on Mount Vernon Street on Beacon Hill. House number two is very much a living house in a great neighborhood. It is no museum. Nestled between other large urban manses, Bulfinch layered the residence with many more evocative elements of Federal embellishment.

The red brick, three-story structure is seen from the street with a façade unbroken by any entranceway. This has been placed along a drive at the east side of the house. The portico projects out at ground level and features Classical columns and detailed embellishments on the canopy. The sight lines of the house are rich in symmetry and architectural proportion. The windows, for instance, are elaborately long on the first floor and diminish as the floors ascend, enhancing the perception of height. Also strengthening that perspective are the four front upper-story Ionic pilasters that in pairs support an architrave section beneath the cornice. A cornice-line balustrade frames the roof and an octagonal glazed cupola sits atop the roof. Windows are six panes over six sashes and those on the front are double shuttered. Flat window lintels and a stone belt line between the first and second floors add a horizontal element across the façade. The design expresses a strength and grace that are the defining themes of the Federal Style.

Left: Charles Bulfinch: Third Harrison Gray Otis House, 45 Beacon Street, Boston, MA, 1805–1808. Otis once again asked Bulfinch for a design when he wished to move for a third time. This house is no longer free-standing; a neighboring house actually encases the projecting bay window, which protrudes into it. (The window has been bricked up.)

Right: Samuel McIntyre (1757–1804): Gardner-Pingree House, Salem, MA, 1804.

Above: Samuel McIntyre: Gardner-Pingree House, 128 Essex Street, Salem, MA, 1804–1806. A carpenter and self-trained architect, McIntyre made a number of distinguished Federalist houses.

doorway has wide sidelights but no fanlight. First-floor windows are simple six panes over six sash. But windows are elaborately heightened and embellished on the second floor, featuring six panes over six over six, creating tall floor-to-ceiling windows on the interior. Richly detailed entablatures frame the second-floor windows, while those on the third and fourth floors are reduced in size, marked only with granite keystones. The façade's height is further enhanced by a cornice-line balustrade.

In his design of the three Harrison Gary Otis homes, in a period of just over a decade, Bulfinch demonstrates a remarkable architectural evolution in high-quality, Federal-style residences. As both the fortunes and dwellings of the Otis family and the city of Boston expanded, the Federalist style permitted the development of a lasting, timeless architecture that was faithful to the ideals of both subdued Neoclassicism and the American republic.

In Salem, Massachusetts, the Gardner-Pingree House, designed by Samuel McIntyre for John Gardner in 1804, in the Federalist style, is another expression of a refined stately town home that reflects both the prosperity of the builder and the cautious artistic sensibilities of America's gentry. Though the house has an imposing presence within the townscape of Salem, its remarkable architectural balance and restrained proportions portray an integrity that evokes the nobility of Yankee aesthetics. The three-story masonry structure is

The Otis family remained only six years in this house. In 1806, Bulfinch was asked once again to design a more stately city mansion for them. The Third Harrison Gray Otis House sits along Boston's most prestigious cityscape, Beacon Street, overlooking Boston Common itself. During the building of this structure, sheep still grazed on this public land. This third house is a dramatic four-story Federal city mansion. Fashioned of red brick, the façade incorporates a portico with unadorned cornice supported by four full Ionic columns. A wrought-iron Greek-key motif balcony sits atop the portico roof. The

Above: Samuel McIntyre: The Vale, Lyman Estate, 185 Lyman Street, Waltham, MA, 1793.

Above: John Kimball: McClellan-Sweat House, 111 High Street, Portland, ME, 1801.

Left: Small Federalist house, 117 Elfreth's Alley, Philadelphia, PA, late 1700s.

Left: George Perot Macculloch House, Macculloch Avenue, Morristown, NJ, 1819. This brick mansion has a gambrel roof, and a monumental pedimented portico.

Above: Springwood, the Franklin D. Roosevelt Home, 4097 Albany Post Road, Hyde Park, NY, 1800, with additions in 1867 and later.

Above: Boscobel, the Morris Dyckman Mansion, Route 9D, Garrison-on-Hudson, NY, 1804.

Left: William Thornton (1759–1828): The Octagon, the Col. John Tayloe House, 1799 New York Avenue NW, Washington, DC, 1797–1800.

Above: James K. Polk House, 301 West 7th Street, Columbia, TN, 1816.

Above: Fort Hunter Mansion, the Capt. Archibald McAllister House, 5300 North Front Street, Harrisburg, PA, 1814.

Above: Homewood, the Charles Carroll, Jr. House, 3400 North Charles Street, Baltimore, MD, 1801–1803.

given a subdued perspective by the diminishing height of each floor. Two masonry belts divide each floor on all sides of the building and the windows also diminish in length on each floor. A cornice balustrade frames the roof, adding additional height and Classical beauty to the structure. The windows fill the face of the house on every side and are further enlarged by the placement of their keystone lintels. A portico with a rounded canopy is supported by side pilasters and front columns, centering the proportions of the house.

In Salem, as in countless other former colonial American cities, the Federalist style projects a stately grandeur that instilled pride not only in the builder, but also in the larger population of Americans for whom the style became emblematic of national ideals and identity.

Early Classical Revival

Symmetry and proportion in design, the forms and structures of ancient Rome, practicality, economy, harmony, geometric perfection, Classical columns, terraces, balustrades, loggias, and domes.

The revival and perfecting of architectural Classicism in the late Renaissance owes is dramatic second life to the genius and artistry of Andrea Palladio, the sixteenth century Venetian architect. His interest in the architecture of ancient Rome and his rediscovery of the writings and the work of its most prolific first century B.C. architect, Vitruvius (Marcus Vitruvius Pollio), became the catalyst to the development of a powerful reawakened architectural understanding.

Vitruvius wrote a ten-volume treatise, *De Architectura*, the only substantive architectural writing that survived from Rome through the centuries, but which influenced many subsequent architectural treatises more than fifteen centuries later. No-one was more interested and affected by Vitruvius than Palladio, who translated the principles discovered from him into an architectural system of harmony, balance, and revitalized Classical design that recalled the glory of ancient Rome. During the sixteenth century, Palladio revolutionized the architectural world of his native Venice by designing great public and private buildings that echoed the lost traditions of the ancient world. The publication of his treatise on Classical design, *Quattro Libri*, began a period of great architectural significance—his style fit the intellectual interests of the time perfectly. However, Palladio's genius was not just visual, but highly practical, as he sought to fashion dramatic architectural masterpieces that fit his

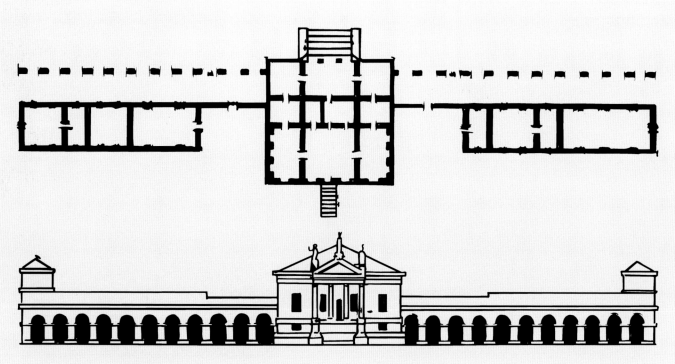

Above: Andrea Palladio: plan and elevation of the Villa Emo, Italy, sixteenth century.

Above: Thomas Jefferson (1743–1826): Monticello, near Charlottesville, VA, 1769–1782; 1796–1809. This country estate has an unusual location on top of a hill, in the manner of a Roman villa rather than a Southern plantation.

Left: Thomas Jefferson: Monticello. The first design and first groundplan for this house were strongly influenced by Palladio. When Jefferson returned to the house in the 1790s, the plan became more complex and governed by function rather than abstract symmetry.

Left: Thomas Jefferson: Monticello, Charlottesville, VA, 1769–1782.

theories of harmony and balance. He was commissioned to build many country villas for the wealthy elite of his day, finding frequent economic constraints an opportunity to experiment with and simplify his fabulous designs.

Two centuries after Palladio refashioned the hillsides and cityscapes of great Italian towns with monumental structures, his work, like that of Vitruvius before him, was rediscovered. People of gentle birth and artistic sensibilities touring the Continent at the beginning of the eighteenth century came face to face for the first time with the grandeur and simplicity of Classical style. Against the cluttered backdrop of the excesses of the Baroque era, the cool simplicity and mathematical balance of Classicism was a refreshing stimulus, both intellectually and artistically. No-one was more influential in helping to propagate the principles of this revival of Classical thought and design than the third Earl of Burlington, an English aesthete whose interest led him to have the writings of Palladio translated and published in England. Thus, with the earl's help, eighteenth century intellect-uals could reach back into the spirit and artistry of both the Renaissance and ancient Rome for a fresh simplicity and harmony in architectural design.

There were other encouragements published during the eighteenth century that further assisted the rediscovery of Classical design. In 1753, the Abbé Laugier published *Essai sur L'architecture* (Essay on Architecture) in which he raised the challenge for more architecture of refinement and simplicity. His abiding imagery was the "primitive hut" described by Vitruvius, the simplicity of which, he claimed, drew the line between man and beast. It became an architectural paradigm for a new "modern" architecture.

The English architect Sir William Chambers, a confidante of George III, spent his lifetime translating Palladian ideals into practical realities. He created some of London's greatest examples of Classical design, such as Somerset House, and went on to become a catalyst for the great movement of Palladian design in Ireland with his great Casino Marino and additions to Trinity College in Dublin. With his *Treatise on the Decorative Part of Civil Architecture*, published in 1759, he greatly influenced interest in and construction of buildings in the neo-Palladian tradition.

In America, Thomas Jefferson of Virginia was imbued with the spirit and the idealism of the Palladian aesthetic. As a Renaissance man of enormously genteel sensibilities and practical scientific learning, he found in the harmony and balance of Palladian symmetry an architectural expression of the great ideals of his age. When he set out to design his great Virginia country villa, Monticello, near Charlottesville, he looked to Palladio's *Quattro Libri* for inspiration and guidance.

The construction of Monticello, over a period of nearly forty years, 1770–1809, became one of Jefferson's great life's works. As an American patriot and aesthete, Jefferson lived the "Enlightenment" philosophy that was the underpinning of eighteenth century intellectual life. As a gentleman farmer of Virginia, he espoused the search for perfection and harmony that Classicism provided and Palladio had produced. In looking for an architectural archetype from which to fashion his beloved Monticello, Jefferson found in the Villa Rotonda, built in 1550 in the hills outside Venice, an artistic dwelling of unmatched magnitude and grace.

The Villa Rotonda, said to be inspired by the Pantheon in Rome, emphasized a unique symmetry for Jefferson. Its central two-story circular hall, low Classical dome, columns and pediments, terraces, and landscape were all echoed in the design of Monticello's similar temple-villa form. Most critical for Jefferson were the precise mathematical proportions of its interior rooms that demonstrated a higher order and harmony.

The same inspired design can be found in the third Earl of Burlington's Palladian masterpiece, Chiswick House, built in 1725, in the countryside outside of London. Chiswick is a domed temple-villa in the square plan style of the Villa Rotonda. In its scale and grandeur it is highly imitative. Burlington's loggias, columns, temple pediments, and terrace staircases brought the exuberance of the Renaissance to London.

With gardens and landscaping designed by William Kent, Chiswick, like the Villa Rotonda, demonstrated a harmonious relationship between house and nature.

Jefferson also looked to Palladio's Villa Cornaro, built between 1551 and 1552, near Padua, for inspiration at Monticello. It, too, portrayed the harmony of a temple set in nature. The colossal symmetry of its "loggia upon loggia," double-temple façade is monumental in its dramatic proportions and magnitude. But its design never loses its inherent harmony. Jefferson abstracted more of the spirit of Villa Cornaro than the design. This great temple marked a turning point for Palladio in domestic design. He had fused utility and recreation into a new concept in functional living and this would be Jefferson's intention at Monticello also.

The effect of Palladio on Jefferson is of great importance. It demonstrates not only the impact of the architect's work, but also, even more significantly, the impact of the philosophical harmony for which Jefferson searched. Jefferson, as perhaps America's most erudite, creative, and influential founding father, imbued the new American republic with that vision and hunger for higher order and harmonious perfection. Monticello demonstrates the uplifting impact of architecture and artistry on the larger national ethos. Savoring such idealism, the revival of Classical design connects the American republic to the nobility of Republican Rome.

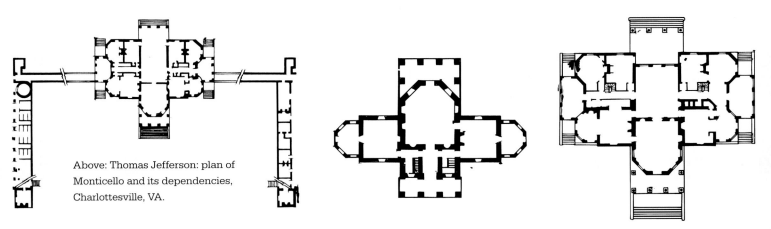

Above: Thomas Jefferson: plan of Monticello and its dependencies, Charlottesville, VA.

Above right: Thomas Jefferson: Monticello, first state plan. The earliest designs of Monticello followed the Palladian ideal of geometric design, with a simple layout of simple room shapes.

Above: Thomas Jefferson: final plan for Monticello. The final plan shows a complex relationship of rooms, based on functional requirements.

Chapter 3

European Revival

Doreen Ehrlich

The Greek Revival

The Greek Revival style reached its height in the two decades between 1820 and the middle of the nineteenth century, rather later in the Gulf Coast states. The zenith of the style was reached around 1830 when the Greek façade dominated architecture both public and private, with the most remarkable examples being found in the Washington and Philadelphia areas. There are various reasons for the dominance of the style, not least the fact that the spirit of the time identified the world of ancient Greece with democratic ideals in a similar fashion to that in which, at the turn of the century, ancient Rome had seemed to provide architectural models for Republican ideals. Greece was now perceived as the mother of Rome and both its architectural language and vocabulary were quickly adopted.

The style spread with the settlers across the states, and is found in the areas of the country with the largest population growth during the four decades from 1820, its prevalence becoming so great during the period that it became known as the National Style. The area of greatest population growth during the period was New York which garnered some two and half million extra citizens, while at the other end of the scale of population expansion, Louisiana, which saw some remarkable buildings in the style, still experienced a growth of about half a million.

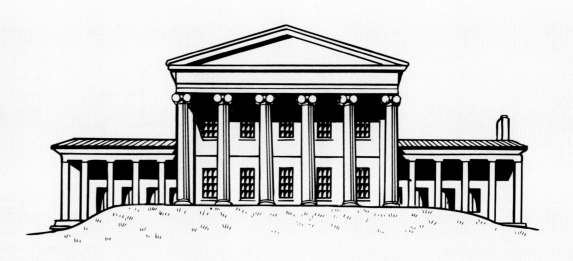

Right: Drawing of Greek Revival high-style estate house. The Greek Revival introduced a new archeological accuracy in the revival of antiquity. Classical principles of symmetry and geometric form were strongly emphasized.

Left: Ithiel Town and Alexander Jackson Davis: Russell House, Wesleyan University, Middletown, CT, 1828–1830. Detail of portico.

Below: Ithiel Town (1784–1844) and Alexander Jackson Davis (1803–1892): Russell House, Wesleyan University, High Street, Middletown, CT, 1828–1830. The monumental full-width portico of this Greek Revival house includes beautiful Corinthian columns.

At the beginning of the nineteenth century there was an increased interest in the architectural and cultural heritage of ancient Greece both in Western Europe and across the Atlantic in the United States. This was heightened by archeological excavations such as those at Bassae in 1812 and, in particular, by the transfer of Greek treasures to European museums, such as Lord Elgin's removal of the famous sculptures of the Parthenon to London's British Museum in 1801. This coincided with the political ferment of the War of Independence in Greece between 1821 and 1829, which aroused much support in other European countries such as France and England (the poet George Gordon, Lord Byron died fighting for the Greek cause at Missolonghi in 1824).

Hitherto the dominant Classical architectural style in the country had been the Adam style, based on the work of the Scottish architect, Robert Adam, and during and after the War of Independence, British models were supplanted by others felt to be more politically appropriate to the newly independent United States. It was felt that ancient Greece seemed synonymous with the ideals of democracy.

The style was used for both public and private buildings, and the entire period of the Greek Revival might be said to have spanned two well-known Philadelphia public buildings, the Second Bank of the United States of 1824 and the Ridgeway Branch of the Philadelphia Library of 1870. The Philadelphia-Washington area saw many of the best-known public buildings of the period: The Second

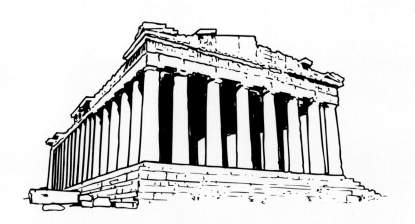

Above: The Parthenon, Athens, 447–432 B.C. Greek architectural models were avidly followed during the early nineteenth century Greek Revival. The first building in America to copy the Parthenon was a bank in Philadelphia in 1818.

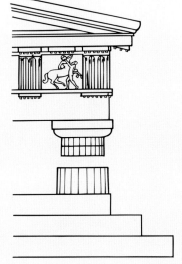

Right: Doric order. Classical architecture has characteristic sets of forms, called orders, which must be combined according to rules. The Doric is the oldest and most severe of these orders.

Above: A smaller Greek Revival house. The Greek Revival was the first truly national style in America, spreading from coast to coast, and from high-style mansions to simple buildings.

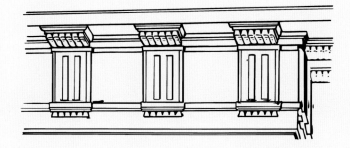

Above: Triglyphs and metopes; Doric frieze from the University of Virginia, designed by Thomas Jefferson, 1819–1826. The forms of Greek architecture are based on their origins in wooden building; the triglyphs represent the ends of wooden beams, and the metopes the blank spaces between them.

Above: Alexander Jackson Davis: Aaron Skinner House, 46 Hillhouse Avenue, New Haven, CT, 1832. This house has a central portico with Ionic columns.

Bank of the United States, more than almost any other structure of the period, established the characteristic Greek portico as a symbol of financial stability. It employs the Doric order of columns, the most severe of the Greek orders of architecture, which became the most popular because of its spartan character, which appealed to early nineteenth century taste. The lighter, more delicate Ionic order and the most elaborate of the orders, the Corinthian, appeared to suggest a luxury and sensuousness which were deemed less appropriate to the times.

The Doric order is also used in one of the best-known houses of the period, that built for the traveler, banker, ambassador, and dilettante, Nicholas Biddle, who had visited Greece as early as 1806 and commissioned the leading architect Thomas Ustick Walter to remodel in Classic dress the house on his estate Andalusia, Pennsylvania, with a Greek temple-style portico modeled on the Parthenon in Athens.

Above: Alexander Jackson Davis: Mary Prichard House, 35 Hillhouse Avenue, New Haven, CT, 1836. This nearly cubic house features a central Corinthian portico.

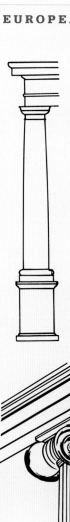

Left: The Tuscan order. Tuscan Doric was a simplified form of the Doric order, introduced by the Romans. Columns have no flutes, and are on bases.

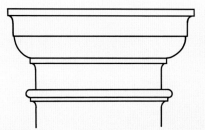

Above: Tuscan Doric capital.

Right: The Ionic order is similar to the Doric, but the columns are slimmer, are set on bases, and have scroll-like capitals.

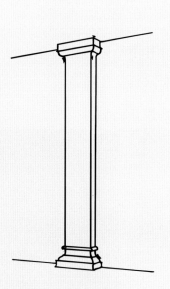

Left: Ionic capital, from the Skinner House, New Haven, CT.

Above: Corinthian capitals from the University of Virginia, designed by Thomas Jefferson, 1819–1826. The Corinthian order was much more complicated to carve than either the Doric or Ionic, and Jefferson had to forego them in his earlier designs due to the lack of skilled craftsmen.

Above: Pilaster, a flat column used for decorative purposes.

Left: Cross section of a Classical column, showing channels (flutes) and dividing ridges (arrises).

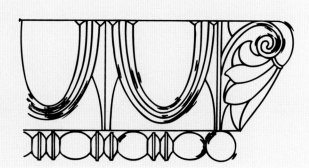

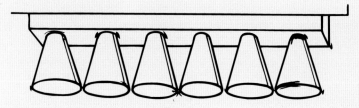

Above: Guttae, decorative pegs found below triglyphs on a Doric frieze.

Above: Egg and dart Classical ornamental detail, with bead and reel pattern below. These motifs are frequently used in Classical architecture.

Simplified Greek Revival—with Portico

Above left: Greek Revival house, Brunswick, ME.

Above: Greek Revival house, Coxsackie, NY.

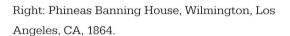

Left: Greek Revival house, Montague, MA, c. 1840.

The Classical portico, ultimately derived from Greek temples, is the most recognizable sign of the Greek Revival style, and is found in simplified form on many houses built in the nineteenth century. The Classical colonnade and pediment add a level of dignity to these otherwise nearly cubic gable-end houses.

Right: Phineas Banning House, Wilmington, Los Angeles, CA, 1864.

Simplified Greek Revival—Folk Style

Above: Folk Victorian with two-story porch, West Townsend, MA, c. 1845. The bulging columns of this house are very unusual, and not an accurate version of any Classical style. Classical Greek columns use a gentle swelling, called entasis, to break the strict vertical line of the columns, but it is much more subtle.

Above: Greek Revival house, Wickford, RI. One of the simplest forms of the Greek Revival, this is a typical gable house, with the entrance at the gable end rather than in the middle of the long façade. Vertical boards at the corners give the appearance of pilasters.

Above: Sanderson House II, Waltham, MA. A simplified Greek Revival farmhouse, with a broad gable and one-story colonnaded porch.

Above: Greek Revival house, folk style, Haddam, CT. In its simplest form, the Greek Revival could be seen in gable-end farmhouses in which the gable is made to resemble a Classical pediment by adding a cornice and pilasters at the end walls.

Left: Dunleith Plantation, 84 Homochitto Street, Natchez, MS, 1847. The plantation house is surrounded by a Greek colonnade.

In the Southern states, the Greek Revival reached a peak of popularity in the 1830s with such grand houses as Oak Valley Plantation, Vacherie, LA, built by Jacques Tellespore Roman, a Creole sugar planter from New Orleans. The house is surrounded by twenty-eight Classical columns and typifies the grandeur of the style in the Southern states, where it had to be adapted to the particular demands of plantation life.

Built nearly twenty years later, another Greek Revival house that also has a Greek colonnade, Dunleith Plantation, in Natchez, MS, shows the survival of the style in the South where it was to remain dominant for a longer period than in the rest of the United States, lasting at least until the period of the Civil War.

Elsewhere in the United States, the Greek Revival gradually became supplanted by other European-

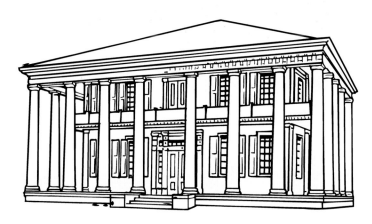

Above: Southern Greek Revival plantation house with peripteral Doric colonnade. A peripteral colonnade is one where the columns go completely around the house.

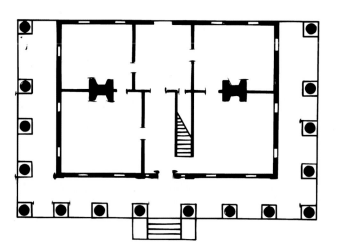

Above: Plan of Southern Greek Revival plantation house.

Southern Plantations

Above: Estevan Hall, 653 Biscoe Street, Helena, AR, 1826.

Left: Oak Alley Plantation, Vacherie, LA, 1836. Built by Jacques Telesphore Roman, a Creole sugar planter from New Orleans, the house is surrounded by twenty-eight Classical columns.

Above: Henry Howard: Madewood Plantation, Col. Thomas Pugh House, Napoleonville, LA, 1846.

Left: Ferguson Hall, Martin Cheairs House, Spring Hill, TN, 1854.

Above: San Francisco
Plantation, 2646 Highway 44
(River Road), St. John-the-
Baptist Parish, LA, 1856. Built
by Edmond Bozonier
Marmillion.

Left: Abner H. Cook
(1814–1884), builder:
Sweetbrush, Swisher-Scott
House, Austin, TX, 1852.

Right: Wilbur Cherry House, 1602 Church Street, Galveston, TX, 1852–1854.

Right: Abner H. Cook, builder: Woodlawn, 6 Niles Road, Austin, TX, 1853. The two-story Greek Revival mansion was designed for James B. Shaw, state comptroller.

Above: Charles Q. Clapp (1799–1868): Clapp House, now Maine College of Art, 97 Spring Street, Portland, ME, 1832.

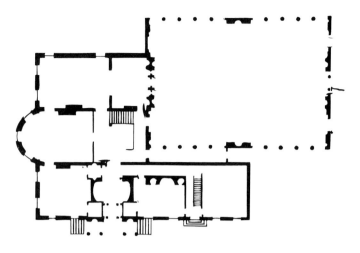

Above: Alexander Parris: plan of the David Sears House, Boston, 1818/1832.

inspired revivals, such as the Gothic and Italianate styles. This began first in East Coast urban centers in the fourth decade of the nineteenth century, while the Greek Revival style remained dominant in rural areas and in the interior states for at least another twenty years.

In other respects the legacy of the Greek Revival to domestic architecture in the United States had much greater staying power. The pediment and fine Corinthian columns of the façade of such an early Greek Revival house as the Russell House (see page 185), in Middletown, Connecticut (built between 1828 and 1830), designed by the architects Ithiel Town and

Alexander Jackson Davis, make it a quintessential example of the style. The Russell House, now part of Wesleyan University, is based on the typical "front-gabled" house though it is unusual in having a full-width colonnaded entrance portico. A more usual form of front gable has a steeply gabled façade with symmetrically placed windows. Variants on this form of façade were a dominant feature of detached houses in Northeastern and Midwestern cities until well into the modern period, that is until the second decade of the twentieth century, while in rural areas examples can still be found dating to the 1930s.

Left: Alexander Parris (1780–1852): David Sears House, 42–43 Beacon Street, Boston, MA, 1818/1832. This house was doubled in size with an addition at the left in 1832, and a third story was also added. The bow front helped set a fashion for Boston architecture. It is one of the earliest houses built of Quincy granite in the city. The simple geometry, white color, and Classical portico link it to the Greek Revival.

Above: S.P. Fuller, builder: Louisburg Square, Boston, MA, 1826–1840. A development of bow-fronted houses with Greek Revival features fronting a common park.

Above: Avery-Downer House, 221 East Broadway, Granville, OH, 1842. This twenty-seven room mansion was built for Alfred Avery, one of the founders of Granville.

Above: Francis Costigan: James Lanier House, 511 West First Street, Madison, IN, 1844. A two-story Corinthian portico with four columns dominates the riverside façade of this nearly cubic house. The pattern books of Minard Lafever were used for aspects of the design.

Gothic Revival

The Gothic Revival is a discernible trend in early nineteenth century architecture in both the United States and Western Europe even while Greece and Rome dominated the language of architectural style. The Gothic Revival—the revival of the style of the middle ages—had appeared first in England in the middle of the eighteenth century in the remodeling of Strawberry Hill. this was the country house, near London, of Horace Walpole, the wealthy arbiter of taste and author of one of the very first Gothic novels, *The Castle of Otranto* and grandson of the prime minister Robert Walpole. The house, with its battlements, mullioned stained-glass windows, and picturesque landscape setting, was in many respects a reaction against the logic and reason of the prevailing Classical revival styles and was widely copied. As an architectural movement, Gothic Revival is but a part of Romanticism, taking its place among the more famous literary, artistic, and musical exemplars such as the works of Byron, Shelley, and Keats, Goya, Turner, and Constable and Beethoven, Chopin, and Schubert. Gothic Revival architecture also embodies characteristics and tendencies which are opposed to Classicism.

In America, Gothic Revival buildings, both public and private, date in the main from the 1830s to around 1865. The invention of the so-called balloon frame in Chicago in 1833 greatly facilitated the growth of the style as the construction process (so-called because it was supposedly as simple as blowing up a balloon) dispensed

Above: Alexander Jackson Davis: Lyndhurst, 635 S. Broadway, Tarrytown, NY, 1838/1865. One of the most elaborate Gothic villas built in America, with a spectacular location overlooking the Hudson River.

with traditional building methods and houses could be built quickly and economically. Individual taste and feeling rather than the dictates of logic, reason, and tradition are the hallmarks of the Romantic movement. In architecture this can be readily noted in a taste for irregularity, rather than the symmetry so essential to the Classical style, informality rather than formality, and a tendency toward exuberant decoration rather than the restraints of Classicism. The taste for individual freedom in design and for visual picturesqueness led to a greater variety in domestic design, not only in the outward appearance of buildings, where irregular rooflines of

Above: A monumental example of Gothic picturesque irregularity, Lyndhurst has a dramatic natural setting on the banks of the Hudson.

Above: Detail of Lyndhurst. The large porch brings one closer to nature, an important theme of the Gothic Revival.

Above: Alexander Jackson Davis: Duane Barnes House, 327 High Street, Middletown, CT, c. 1847–1848.

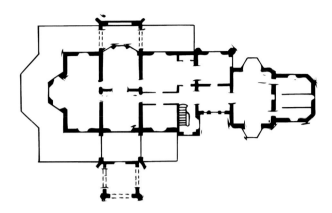

Above: A. J. Davis: plan of Lyndhurst, Tarrytown, NY.

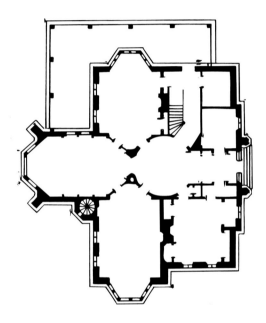

Above: A.J. Davis: plan of the original portion of Lyndhurst. The first phase of the house was only half the size of the final project.

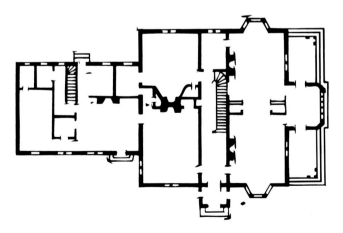

Above: Plan of the Bowen House, Woodstock, CT.

pinnacles, spires, turrets, and castlellation became the norm, but also in the greater freedom of interior design, with more flexible floor plans being adapted to the day-to-day requirements of family life.

It is significant that the first important spokesman for the Romantic style in America was the architect, writer, and landscape designer Alexander Jackson Davis (1803–1892). Davis termed himself an "architectural composer" and was well acquainted with the painters of the Hudson River School, notably Thomas Cole and Asher Durand, accompanying them to the scenes they made famous in their paintings. Davis's 1837 publication of *Rural Residences* was a key factor in establishing the Gothic style in America, being the first book to show not only house elevations and pattern details but also entire house plans and three-dimensional views.

While Davis may be regarded as the most successful builder of houses in the Gothic style in America for the greater part of the nineteenth century, before his untimely death, Andrew Jackson Downing (1815–1852) a close friend and collaborator, carried on and extended Davis' ideas, surpassing his influence and celebrity. Downing's first book, *Cottage Residences*, was an immediate success on its publication in 1842 and his next, *The Architecture of Country Houses*, published eight years later, went into nine printings and sold 16,000 copies. Designs from the book were extraordinarily influential and several examples survive in different states: the Brooks House, Salem, of 1851 closely mirrors "Cottage, Design II," for example.

Above: Gothic cottage, Newport, RI. A stone house influenced by pattern books.

Above: Joseph C. Wells: Roseland, the Abel Bowen House, Route 169, Woodstock, CT, 1846.

The book shows the influence of the ideas of the English architect and theorist Augustus Welby Northcote Pugin, the major proponent of the Gothic style in England, whose work *Contrasts* was a major influence on American architecture of the period. Like Pugin and the somewhat later English critic and theorist, John Ruskin, whose writings were to be a decisive influence on European and American ideas until the present day, Downing saw a moral imperative in the Gothic style, and believed in fine craftsmanship and the use of traditional building materials. The Greek Revival was anathema to both Davis and Downing, Downing wrote in the early 1850s when their collaboration came to an end, "The

Greek temple disease has passed its crisis. The people have survived it." Downing, through his best-selling books and his dynamic public manner, became a celebrity both at home and abroad.

Such surviving designs as the Gate House, Llewellyn Park, Orange, NJ, give a representative idea of Downing's importance. Llewellyn Park was an early planned community with the winding paths and picturesque vistas advocated in Downing's books, which included his earliest publication, written at the age of twenty-six, *A Treatise on the Theory and Practice of Landscape Gardening*. Downing believed that domestic buildings should be considered "conjointly with the beauty of the landscape," and that

Above: Joseph C. Wells: Roseland, the Abel Bowen House, Woodstock, CT, 1846.

Left: Joseph C. Wells: Roseland, the Abel Bowen House. Detail of window..

Above: Gothic Revival window, design by A.J. Downing.

Above: Gothic Revival window with hood molding.

Above: Gothic Revival oriel window.

Above: Gothic Revival lancet window.

Above:. Oriel window from the Bowen House, Woodstock, CT.

Above: The pinnacles of Lyndhurst.

Above: Crockets and finials.

Above: Decorated bargeboards (vergeboards), Bowen House, Woodstock, CT. Scroll saws made ornate patterns possible for even rural carpenters; this style is sometimes called "Carpenter's Gothic."

Above: A.J. Downing: Gothic Revival bargeboards (vergeboards). Downing's popular pattern books offered examples of detailed design and overall plans.

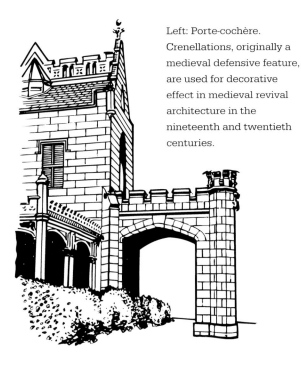

Left: Porte-cochère. Crenellations, originally a medieval defensive feature, are used for decorative effect in medieval revival architecture in the nineteenth and twentieth centuries.

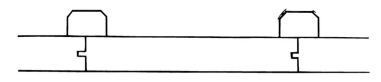

Right: Board-and-batten siding, Bowen House, Woodstock, CT.

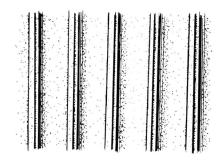

Above: Diagram of board-and-batten siding. The battens provided a vertical emphasis and an additional seal to the tongue-and-groove joints.

Above: Richard Upjohn (1802–1878): Kingscote, Bellevue Avenue, Newport, RI, 1839; addition by McKim, Mead, and White, 1881.

Above: Andrew Jackson Downing (1815–1852): gatehouse, Llewellyn Park, Orange, NJ, 1853. Llewellyn Park was an early planned community with winding, picturesque roads. The gatehouse is a fine example of Gothic Revival.

"the national taste is not a matter of little moment." He saw the gables, board-and-batten siding, and picturesque irregularity of the Gothic Revival style as particularly suitable for country cottages, homes, in Downing's terms, for "the cultivators of the soil," the "bone and sinew of the land."

While Davis and Downing stressed the essentially rural appropriateness of the Gothic Revival style and the importance of its relationship to the surrounding landscape, there were other uses to which the style might be

put, not least in the remodeling of existing buildings. The most famous of these is perhaps the "Wedding Cake House" in Kennebunkport, Maine, which is regarded as the quintessence of the style known as "Carpenter Gothic." A completely new façade was built over the existing brick Federal-style house by the owner and builder George Bourne between 1826 and 1855. The result is a fantastical and engaging exercise in popular taste, appearing in some lights to be covered in a filigree of lace, or perhaps icing sugar, and well served by its affectionate nickname.

By the middle of the eighteenth century the style had spread across the country, and so-called "gingerbread" Carpenter Gothic houses were particularly prevalent in areas as far apart as Martha's Vineyard, Massachusetts, and San Francisco where several houses survive as fine examples of craftsmanship. The whimsical forms the decoration took made the style especially attractive and this, together with the fact that new construction could be added to the original at any time without diminishing the whole ensured the wide-ranging popularity of the style.

Above: George Bourne, builder, "Wedding Cake House," Kennebunkport, ME, 1826/1853. Detail of the "gingerbread" woodwork.

Right: George Bourne, builder, "Wedding Cake House," 105 Summer Street, Kennebunkport, ME, 1826/1855.

Above: Pinnacles, "Wedding Cake House," Kennebunkport, ME.

Left: Ward's Castle, the William Evans Ward House, Port Chester, NY, 1875. This is apparently the first home built of poured concrete in America.

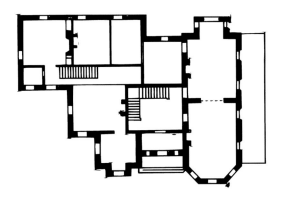

Above: Richard Upjohn: plan of Kingscote, Newport, RI.

Right: Gothic Revival chimneys, design by A.J. Downing. Elaborately decorated chimneys imitated British designs from the Tudor period and earlier.

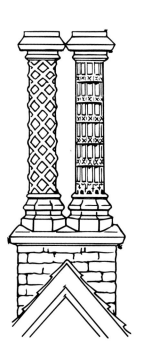

Above: Rest Cottage, the Frances Willard House, Evanston, IL, c. 1865. The home of the founder of the Women's Christian Temperance Union, this house has two large front gables, and a smaller one on the left extension. It is covered with board-and-batten vertical siding.

Above: Victorian house in Wellfleet, MA, with a tower and rich gingerbread ornament on the central gable.

Above: Gothic Revival house, Middletown, CT. This house has very elaborate bargeboards, wavy shingle patterns, and large clustered chimneys.

Above: Gothic Revival house, Hadlyme, CT. A very simple cross-gable Gothic cottage in the country.

Above: Glimmerstone, Route 131, Cavendish, VT, 1844–1847. A large stone house with fourteen gables in rural Vermont, built in the tradition of Scottish stone masonry, in a technique known as "snecked ashlar."

Above: E.B. White: Rose Hill Plantation, Bluffton, SC, 1858.

Above: Benjamin G. Lathrop House, 627 Hamilton Street, Redwood City, CA, 1863. A Gothic cottage in the West, which survived the 1906 earthquake.

Above: Ardoyne, the John P. Shaffer House, Terrebonne Parish, LA, 1897.

Above: Italianate house, with an octagonal lantern or cupola, and brackets, 85 Federal Street, Brunswick, ME.

Above: Italianate villa, Guilford, CT, c. 1850s.

Italianate Style

As the nineteenth century progressed, a number of other building styles took their place as alternatives to the Gothic and Greek revivals in different parts of the country. The first Italianate houses date from the late 1830s, although very few examples survive. The style, which was in its earlier manifestations a variant of the Picturesque, like the Gothic, was made popular—as was the Gothic—by means of the hugely popular pattern books of Andrew Jackson Downing.

The taste for the Gothic Revival was waning by the early 1860s and it was more or less supplanted by the Italianate Style, which had the distinct advantage that it could be employed in both urban and country architecture. The success of the Italianate Style may also be attributed to its solid, dignified appearance which relied on traditional methods of construction rather than the economical lightweight building so characteristic of the Gothic Revival, which was only made possible by the development of the balloon frame in Chicago in 1833. The balloon frame substituted the expensive traditional system of mortise and tenon joints with thin plates and

Above: Italianate Style villa. The Italianate Style combined asymmetrical informality and Classical design in houses recalling Tuscan villas.

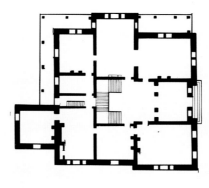

Above: Richard Upjohn: plan of the Edward King House, Newport, RI, 1847.

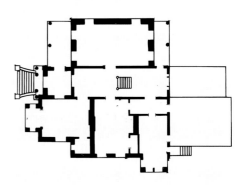

Above: Henry Austin: plan of the Victoria Mansion (Morse-Libby House), Portland, ME, 1859.

Above: Richard Upjohn (1802–1878): Edward King house, 35 King Street, Newport, RI, 1847.

studs held together with nails. This made for rapid construction, but on city sites in particular was susceptible to fire, and wood-frame construction was banned in several areas of the country in the later nineteenth century, most notably in Chicago after the disastrous fire of 1871. Balloon framing, a revolutionary mode of construction which soon became standard for the self-reliant builder, made possible the rapid development of the West in particular. Newly prosperous clients however, many of whom could employ architects rather than builders, wished to reflect their status in a different mode of architectural historicism, to which the Italianate Style could be adapted.

In its first appearances, the Italianate Style was practiced by well-known architects in the field of Gothic architecture, such as Richard Upjohn (1802–1878). Upjohn, who came to the United States from England in 1829, was the architect responsible for Trinity Church, New York, built between 1839 and 1846 and still a key New York City landmark. While building work was carried out on Trinity Church, Upjohn designed a Tuscan-style villa with towers for Edward King, in Newport, RI. However, it is the Morse-Libby House (Victoria Mansion) built in 1859 by Henry Austin (1804–1891) at Portland, Maine, which provides the best-known example of the style.

The Morse-Libby House takes as its prime influence Tuscan villas of the high Renaissance period. It is a grand, authoritative building with a tall tower, curved

Above: Henry Austin (1804–1891): Morse-Libby House (Victoria Mansion), 109 Danforth Street, Portland, ME, 1859.

and triangular pediments, Ionic columns, balustrades and richly textured quoins. The dignity and splendor of the Morse-Libby mansion was highly influential and several Italianate mansions of the period are close copies, including a version in Wethersfield Avenue, Hartford, CT, which is built in brick rather than stone.

While such rural models as Tuscan villas of the Renaissance served as prototypes to be adapted and modified for contemporary America, the Italian Renaissance urban style of domestic architecture was more rarely used as an inspiration. However, when architects did make use of it, the style was often more closely copied and its source more readily recognizable. An example by Henry Austin, which shows him adapting the Italianate villa style to different circumstances from that of the Morse-Libby House, is the mansion built for James Dwight Dana in New Haven in 1849. This is cubic in form with an L-shaped addition, which breaks the symmetry. Restrained and formal variants on the cubic Renaissance townhouse, employing a vocabulary of forms derived from the originals (which include the characteristic symmetrical façades, restrained entrance porches, and pedimented windows), may be seen throughout the country.

Variants on the Italianate style spread throughout the

Above: Henry Austin (1804–1891): John P. Norton house, 52 Hillhouse Avenue. New Haven, CT, 1848–1849.

Right: Italianate house, Wethersfield Avenue, Hartford, CT. A close copy of Austin's Morse-Libby House, in brick rather than stone.

Above: Henry Austin (1804–1891): James Dwight Dana House, 24 Hillhouse Avenue, New Haven, CT, 1849. The cubic form was very popular for villas in the mid nineteenth century. The L-shaped addition breaks the symmetry.

Above: Italianate villa, Wethersfield Avenue, Hartford, CT. This house adds a square lantern at the top.

Left: Hillforest, the Thomas Gaff House, Aurora, IN, 1856. Italianate; the rounded entrance portico was intended to resemble a steamboat, one of the sources of Gaff's fortune.

Above: Honolulu House, 107 N. Kalamazoo Avenue, Marshall, MI, 1860. This house was built for Judge Abner Pratt upon his return from the Hawaiian islands, where he served as U.S. Consul. It is Italianate, but with unusual columns and brackets and flattened arches, said to resemble his house in Honolulu.

details. For example, the unknown designer of the Honolulu House in Kalamazoo Avenue, Marshall, MI, of 1860, built for Judge Abner Pratt after he returned from serving as U.S. Consul in the Hawaiian islands incorporates into its Italianate styling unusual columns and brackets, together with distinctive flattened arches, which are said to recall the Judge's house in Honolulu. The adaptability of the style may also be seen in the Thomas Gaff House, in Aurora, IN, of 1856, where the curious rounded portico is said to have been intended to recall a steamboat, one of the sources of the client's fortune.

The Italianate-villa style, which took as its model grand historic villas with much land attached, can be seen to have been, in the main, the province of a wealthy middle class who desired their status to be reflected in their domestic space in a manner that looked back to an historic European past. By the 1860s the Italianate Style had completely overshadowed the Gothic Revival and exuberant or restrained variants may still be found throughout the United States, the great majority of surviving houses dating from about 1855 to 1880. Together with the related Second Empire style, it may be read as an appropriate reflection of a prosperous period in American history. With the changes in the financial situation in 1873 and the subsequent depression, it fell out of fashion. By the latter part of the decade when prosperity returned, the taste for the Italianate Style appeared outmoded and new fashions, particularly the eclectic Queen Anne, supplanted it.

United States from the 1840s onward. In fact, by the middle of the century the style, with its pronounced vertical emphasis, use of heavy cornices, and large brackets, had become the prevailing style for both private and public architecture in cities such as New York, where such decorative elements were even adapted to early brownstones. Where houses were commissioned it can be seen that even the cubic forms of the style could be adapted to suit a client's requirements in unexpected

Above: Brackets; the use of elaborate brackets was characteristic of the Italianate style.

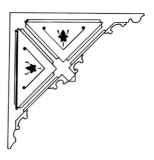

Above: Bracket design by G.E. Woodward, from *National Architect*, 1868.

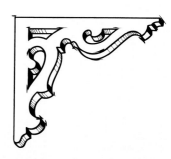

Above: Bracket design by G.E. Woodward, from *National Architect*, 1868.

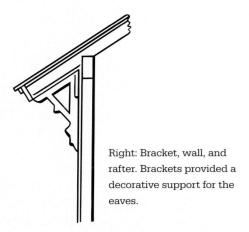

Right: Bracket, wall, and rafter. Brackets provided a decorative support for the eaves.

Above: Bracket, from design by Samuel Sloan, *Homestead Architecture*, 1867.

Above: Bracket design by G.E. Woodward, from *National Architect*, 1868. Pattern books offered many different design options.

With Towers

Above: Italianate house, Portsmouth, NH.

Above: Italianate villa, Haddam, CT.

Right: Italianate villa, Jamaica Plain, MA.

Below: Italianate house, 32 Route 35, Kennebunk, ME. The central gable is less common than the asymmetrical designs of the other Italianate villas with towers

Cubic Forms

Left: The Belvedere Mansion, J. Russell Jones House, 1008 Park Avenue, Galena, IL, 1857. Built for a former ambassador to Belgium.

Below: Samuel Sloan (1815–1884): George Allen House (the "Southern Mansion"), 720 Washington Street, Cape May, NJ, 1863.

Left: William Dennison: General U.S. Grant House, 500 Bouthillier Street, Galena, IL, 1860. An L-shaped Italianate house with wide eaves and large brackets.

Above: Ashton Villa, 2328 Broadway, Galveston, TX, 1859. An Italianate house built for hardware wholesaler, banking, and railroad tycoon J.M. Brown.

Above: House of the Seasons, 409 South Alley Street, Jefferson, TX, 1872.

Egyptian Revival

Napoleon's Egyptian campaigns lasted some ten years from 1789 to 1799 and Egyptian influence was at its height in Europe during this time, primarily due to the large numbers of antiquities brought back from there and put on public display, and the resulting scholarly interest in all things ancient Egyptian. In architecture, in both America and Europe, this style was most often used for the design of public buildings, although during the 1830s when interest in exotic foreign styles was at its height, a small number of domestic buildings showing Egyptian influence were erected, and Egyptian motifs were incorporated into houses built in such currently fashionable styles as Italianate or Greek Revival. By 1845, Alexander Jackson Davis, one of America's most influential architects, could state that he had designed buildings in fourteen different historical styles, including Etruscan and Egyptian.

The style is easily identified, particularly by its columns. One of very few surviving Egyptian Revival houses from the earliest period is the Apthorpe House of 1837, designed by Alexander Jackson Davis in New Haven. Typically, it is loosely Classical in design with applied Egyptian Style columns used as an exotic decorative element. The columns have a distinctive bulge, intended to resemble bundles of papyrus tied together below the capitals. Such columns are also the major distinguishing feature of later Egyptian Revival houses such as the house in Hancock Street, Boston, Massachusetts, of 1870. This tall townhouse represents the eclectic mixture typical of the style as the columns are combined with a Mansard roof, while the chimneys, so essential to such a house, are concealed as much as possible from the street. Other features of this rarest of historical revivals include the use of sloped walls and window frames that are narrower at the top than at the bottom.

Above: Henry Austin: gate of Grove Street Cemetery, New Haven, CT, 1845. The Egyptian Revival was more commonly used for memorials, cemeteries, and prisons than houses.

Right: Egyptian column; such elaborate decoration is usually not found in American revival examples until the twentieth century.

Right: Alexander Jackson Davis: Apthorpe House, Hillhouse Avenue, New Haven, 1837. Detail of doorway with Egyptian Revival columns.

Below: Alexander Jackson Davis: Apthorpe House. The Egyptian Revival is one of the rarest styles for houses in America. Typically, such houses are more generically Classical with distinctive Egyptian-style ornament, such as papyrus-shaped columns.

Swiss Chalet

Like other historical revival styles, the Swiss-chalet style was introduced into America by Andrew Jackson Downing through his house design pattern books. *The Architecture of Country Houses*, published in 1850, showed several model designs of the style, and Downing stressed the importance of an appropriately Romantic site which was to be bold, mountainous if possible, or in a wild picturesque valley.

The style had some following in those parts of America where snow fell and other criteria deemed appropriate by Downing could be met. The essential character of original Swiss chalets is retained although naturally there was no need for large stones on the roof or accommodation for cows at first-floor level. Rough-cut wood was used as the essential building material. In general the siding was made of rustically cut boards, most typically used in a one-inch module nailed to a balloon frame rather than the post and lintel construction of the original Swiss model. Galleries (which often projected widely), large windows (sometimes dormer windows were used for second-floor bedrooms), balconies, and steeply overhanging roofs of the Swiss models were characteristic features. Sometimes low-pitched hipped roofs gave an enhanced rusticity and picturesque quality to the form.

Many Swiss-chalet homes were built on stone foundations and had elaborately cut wooden decoration, particularly on the outside galleries which were so prevalent a feature of the style. Also characteristic was the use of cast-iron wood-burning stoves with a system of flues leading to high stone chimneys, as, typically, the houses were without fireplaces.

Several good examples of Swiss-style houses still survive in Hartford, Connecticut, built for German factory workers in 1858 by Samuel Colt, in an area known as "Little Potsdam."

Above: Swiss-style houses built by Samuel Colt, Hartford, CT, 1858.

Above: Swiss cottage, Tolland, CT. The Swiss cottage mode was characterized by wide overhanging eaves, ornate surface decoration, and frequently a large balcony on the second story.

Above: Swiss-style houses built by Samuel Colt, Hendricxsen Avenue, Hartford, CT, 1858. Colt built a street of these houses for German workers at his wicker factory; the neighborhood was known as "Little Potsdam," and is near the firearms factory.

Left: Swiss/French cottage, Cohasset, MA.

Octagon

In 1849, Orson Squire Fowler popularized the eight-sided residence in his pattern book *A Home for All, or the Gravel Wall and Octagon Mode of Building*. The octagonal house was presented as a convenient and inexpensive house, providing, it was argued, the maximum amount of practicable living space with no "dark and useless corners," a reduction of "heat loss through the walls," an increase "in sunlight and ventilation," and a low construction cost. The book was a great success, going into seven printings, and was followed by others in the mid century. It appears that many such houses were built across the country, most commonly in New York, New England, and the Midwest, though few survive. It would seem that the habit of living in square houses was difficult to break and that there were disadvantages such as the fact that although the exteriors of such houses were octagonal, the rooms were not, often resulting in awkward shapes with decreased rather than increased light and ventilation.

Fowler built his own octagonal house in Fishkill, New York, incorporating hot and cold running water, speaking tubes, indoor toilets, and other modern amenities, and advocated the octagon house as a means of promoting both mental and physical health. The octagon house in Portland, CT, of around 1854 is based on plans published by Fowler. The Philip Armour House, Irvington-on-Hudson, NY, built as a two-story octagon in 1860 with a central tower—an essential component of

Above: Octagonal houses were designed to offer the maximum of area covered with the minimum of materials, and were associated with health and social reforms.

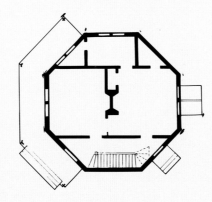

Above: Orson Squire Fowler: plan for octagon house, published in *A Home for All, or the Gravel Wall and Octagon Mode of Building*, 1853. Fowler was the chief promoter for octagon houses.

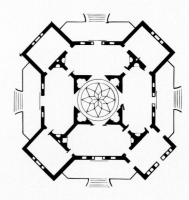

Above: Samuel Sloan, plan of Longwood, octagon house at Natchez, MS. Published in *The Model Architect*, 1852. Building of this elaborate house was interrupted by the Civil War, but finished later.

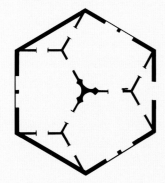

Above: Plan of hexagonal house, published in *The House, a Pocket Manual of Rural Architecture, New York*: Fowler and Wells, 1859. Another ideal centralized plan; this design may never have been used.

Above: Plan of first floor of the round house of Enoch Robinson, Somerville, MA, 1856. The difficult construction and challenges of interior planning ensured that few of these idealized houses were built.

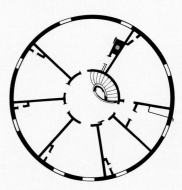

Above: Plan of second floor of the round house of Enoch Robinson. The central rotunda is thirteen feet in diameter.

the building type—was expanded twelve years later by its then owner, with the addition of a dome and veranda. There are occasional variants on the form, with even more sides, such as the sixteen-sided house from the 1850s in West Townsend, Massachusetts. This period also produced houses with curved walls and no corners, such as the Enoch Robinson House on Atherton Street, Somerville, Massachusetts, and the Jonathan Bowers House of 1872 in Lowell, MA.

Above: Enoch Robinson House, 36 Atherton Street, Somerville, MA, 1856. This unusual round house was praised by one of Fowler's associates.

Above: Decagon House, Newton, MA. Variants of the octagonal design are sometimes found, such as this ten-sided house in Massachusetts.

Above: Sixteen-sided house, West Townsend, MA, c. 1850s. Also in Massachusetts, this house has even more sides.

Above: Octagon house, Portland, CT, c. 1854. Based on plans published by the phrenologist Orson Squire Fowler, octagon houses were thought to promote mental and physical health.

Above: Octagon house, Richmond, RI, 1857.

Left: Philip Armour House, Irvington-on-Hudson, NY, 1860, with 1872 addition. Built as a two-story octagon in 1860, this house was expanded with a dome and veranda by the new owner, Joseph Stiner in 1872.

Utopian Dwellings and Worker Housing

Experiments in utopian or idealistic living form a constant thread in American culture whether in terms of individual people or groups seeking an alternative way of life. Utopian communities in America pre-date industrialization, but undoubtedly the most famous individual experiment in the construction of an alternative way of living was that undertaken in the middle of the nineteenth century by the noted philosopher and naturalist, Henry David Thoreau (1817–1862) between July 1845 and September 1847, on the shores of Walden Pond, Concord, Massachusetts. To set this dwelling (and Thoreau's precise account of his construction of it) in the context of the other nineteenth century domestic buildings detailed in these chapters is illuminating and instructive.

Thoreau constructed his own one-room cabin (now reconstructed at Walden Pond) from recycled timbers, with a cellar which, he writes, was dug in two hours, second-hand windows, and a chimney, all for twenty-eight dollars and twelve and a half cents. In his essay "Economy" he details the labor he undertook single-handedly and the exact cost of all the materials "excepting the timber, stones and sand, which I claimed by squatter's right…because very few are able to tell exactly what their houses cost, and fewer still, if any, the separate cost of the various materials which compose them." The result of his labors was "a tight shingled and plastered house, ten feet wide by fifteen long, and eight-feet posts, with a garret and a closet, a large window on each side, two trap doors, one door at the end, and a brick fireplace opposite."

Here Thoreau lived and worked in a state of self-sufficiency for two years. The continuing resonance of his work and of the site itself are linked, it would appear, to those rarest of circumstances achieved by Thoreau at Walden Pond, which were also recommended by the English Romantic poets as prerequisites for creativity: silence, stillness, and solitude.

Above: Worker housing at Lowell, MA, Boott Mill Complex, c. 1830s.

Whereas a reconstruction of Thoreau's cabin exists and is much visited, the dwelling places of utopian communities, perhaps by their very nature, are difficult if not impossible to trace. The architectural possibilities for housing such communities were many and various, although only religious groups such as the Shakers really developed them. The Cloisters (see page 45), on Main Street, in Ephrata, Pennsylvania, built between 1741 and 1743 is a rare eighteenth century example of residences for an idealistic religious community. A feature of the Cloisters are the segregated sleeping quarters with the men's dormitory in a separate building from the women's.

From the second decade of the nineteenth century, Robert Owen, the British philanthropist, reformer, and utopian socialist and his followers in America demanded a "new moral world," seeing the conventional private domestic dwelling as a major obstacle to the development of society, particularly as it concerned women. Following on from his pioneering work in Britain, Owen projected a self-contained community development at New Harmony, Indiana, in 1826 as well as some fifteen other experimental communities.

At New Harmony, Owen had Stedman Whitwell (d.1840) draw up designs for a communitarian structure, with individual living spaces grouped around communal centers. New Harmony proposed that its community be balanced in all its elements—spiritual, economic, social, and physical—and this proportionate concept resulted in an appropriately harmonious rectilinear plan for the utopian community. Individual living spaces were to be grouped around communal centers, but it was never built.

Charles Fourier, whose ideas inspired the building of about thirty associations or "Phalanxes" from the 1840s in America took the idea of female emancipation in the home still further, claiming that "the degree of emancipation of women is the natural measure of general emancipation."

The Fourierists, or Associationists in America, from the 1840s onward were to erect "phalansteries," such as the North American Phalanx in New Jersey in 1843, where over 125 people formed the community. Here the communal facilities included a kitchen, bakery, and laundry, with dormitories providing sleeping accommodation, though private apartments with or without kitchens were also built on the site.

The pragmatic counterpart of the utopian community may be said to be the low-cost housing built for workers after the Industrial Revolution in America. This ranged from boarding houses and corporate row houses such as those at Lowell, Massachusetts, to corporate worker houses like those built in smaller mill towns such as Harrisville, New Hampshire, where small cottages were built as two-family homes between 1820 and 1860.

In New England, the new textile factories introduced at Pawtucket, Rhode Island, created a need for housing large numbers of workers. The Pawtucket mills were founded in 1793 by a man called Slater who "borrowed" his ideas from the mills in England where he had been apprenticed.

The mills at Lowell, named after one of the founders, Francis Cabot Lowell, were also cotton and wool mills and eventually thousands of workers were employed there. The need for a larger workforce led the Lowell mill owners, and others, to encourage female workers, who, as in Europe during the Industrial Revolution, often found mill work more appealing than farm work, despite the difficult conditions. An innovation at Lowell was boarding houses for single women.

In New England, three-family homes, or triple deckers, were popular in the late nineteenth century. They often shared facilities such as common toilet and water supplies and were typically clustered together near the factories as in surviving examples at Hartford, Connecticut, and Jamaica Plain, Massachusetts. Each of these examples is built to generous proportions and is shingled with a spacious porch. The Hartford survivor has unusually elegant Ionic columns supporting the three-level front porch.

Industrial Worker Houses

Above: Worker housing at Lowell, MA, Boott Mill Complex, c. 1835. The new factories introduced at Pawtucket, RI, and Lowell, MA, created the need to house large numbers of workers. An innovation at Lowell was boarding houses for single women, who were entering the industrial workforce in large numbers for the first time.

Above: Worker houses, Harrisville, NH, 1820–1860. In smaller mill towns such as Harrisville, cottages were built as two-family homes.

Above left: Triple decker, Hartford, CT. In New England, three-family homes called triple deckers were popular in the late nineteenth century. This one has unusually elegant Classical columns supporting the three-level front porch.

Above: Triple decker, Jamaica Plain, MA, late nineteenth century.

Left: Luther S. Raymond House, Newton, MA, 1832. A small house for a mill worker.

Construction Elements—Tower Roofs

The late nineteenth and early twentieth centuries saw a great variety of roofs on towers, reflecting the different style currents. Late twentieth century houses introduced a new degree of expressive design; towers began to be treated as sculptures rather than as little houses. The evolution of style is clearly shown in these details.

Above: Conical roof on tower.

Above: Steeply pitched pyramidal tower roof.

Above: Steeply pitched flared four-sided tower roof.

Above: Curved mansard tower on Second Empire Baroque-style house.

Above: Octagonal dome tower roof.

Above: Bell-shaped tower roof.

Above: Crown-shaped tower roof.

Above: Onion dome tower on Queen Anne house.

Above: Minaret shaped tower on Queen Anne house.

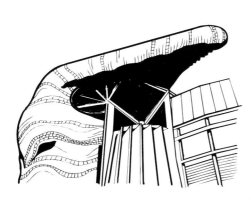

Above: Postmodern gable; organic shape. Bart Prince House in Corona del Mar.

Above: Abstract tower, with flat roof: Frank Gehry, Schnabel House.

Above: Postmodern tower on the Norton House, Santa Monica, by Frank Gehry.

Chapter 4

High Victorian

Doreen Ehrlich

I n Britain the reign of Queen Victoria spanned sixty-four years, from 1837 to 1901, and the term "Victorian" is commonly used on both sides of the Atlantic to define this period. Various architectural styles, including Gothic Revival, crossed the water early in the period, from the late 1830s on. The styles proved adaptable to use in the domestic architecture of the United States, from grand individual mansions to the housing needs of the new industrial towns. However, it is the architectural styles of the last forty years of Victoria's reign, from about 1860 to the turn of the century, that are normally perceived as being "Victorian." From mid-century onward, the High Victorian Gothic style took over from the Gothic Revival, which had been based in the main on forms derived from English medieval castle and cathedral architecture of the eleventh to fifteenth centuries. The High Victorian Gothic style was based on different architectural prototypes, drawn mainly from medieval examples from Northern Italy, and from Venice in particular.

Major advances in industrialization and in building technologies and the rapid expansion of the railroads were instrumental in the dramatic growth of the style, bringing about a radical change in domestic architecture throughout America. Balloon-framing had evolved by 1835 and such was the success of this easy, quickly erected, and inexpensive system of construction that whole cities were built with extraordinary speed using it. Balloon-frame construction was popularized by the many pattern books of the period, including A.J. Downing's *The Architecture of Country Houses*, and made possible

Right: Detail of arch patterns, Newton, MA. Alternating bands of color and irregular shapes offered vibrant design possibilities to the Victorians.

irregular forms of domestic dwelling rather than the traditional "box" form. Mass production made it possible for retailers to offer complex decorative components of house design, as well as key features such as roof treatments, doors, and windows to a much wider market rather than such luxuries being affordable to only wealthy households. The expansion of the railways also ensured that these components could be transported to sites across America at relatively low cost, resulting in the widespread use of the elaborate and complex detailing so characteristic of the High Victorian style in domestic buildings throughout the country.

High Victorian style in American domestic architecture was inspired, as it was in Europe, by the work of the uniquely influential English theorist and critic, John Ruskin. In his key work *The Seven Lamps of Architecture*, published in 1849 and a seminal influence throughout the later nineteenth century and beyond to the present day, Ruskin laid out certain principles, including those relating to the fabric of the building and the principle of color (known as

Above: House, Newton, MA. Ruskinian Gothic. This stone house features the polychromy and Venetian Gothic forms advocated by John Ruskin in his books *The Seven Lamps of Architecture* (1849) and *The Stones of Venice* (1851–1853).

Left: Calvert Vaux (1824–1895) and Frederick E. Church (1826–1900): "Olana," the Church Home, Route 9G, Olana, NY, 1870. The name "Olana" is derived from Arabic, and means "Our Place on High."

Right: Calvert Vaux and Frederick E. Church: "Olana." Detail of tower showing the intricate use of color.

polychromy) being integral to the building rather than being applied to it. This led to the distinctive forms of "constructional coloration" in bands of multicolored brick, slate, and other decoration so characteristic of the style, which is sometimes termed "Ruskinian Gothic."

Whereas the style was used throughout the United States for public buildings such as churches, municipal institutions, libraries, and banks, it was also felt to be appropriate for housing, and in urban areas this results in a homogeneity of public and private buildings that is characteristic of both America and Europe in the period.

Ruskinian Gothic can be seen in its most elaborate form in such key works as the Pennsylvania Academy of Fine Arts, Philadelphia, Pennsylvania, built in 1876 by the architect Frank Furness, where Venetian Gothic window forms are employed together with various textured and colored bricks and polychrome stone to give a richly decorative effect. Comparable effects may be seen in such examples of Ruskinian Gothic domestic architecture as the house in Newton, Massachusetts, which also features the use of polychromatic materials and motifs drawn from Venetian architecture advocated by Ruskin in such works as *The Stones of Venice*, published in 1851–1853.

Another very different form of the High Victorian style may be seen at "Olana," the extraordinary exotic mansion built for the painter Frederick Church (1826–1900) in 1870 and set in a 260-acre estate in the

Hudson Valley, New York. The house is symptomatic of the widespread Victorian interest in the Orient. This was seen in its most colorful form in the homes and studios of successful artists of the time such as Lord Leighton in England.

Olana (the term is derived from the Arabic and means "Our Place on High," was Church's home and workplace for some thirty years. The artist was famous for the grandeur of his landscape paintings, which take as their subjects spectacular sites worldwide, such as *The Heart of the Andes* (1859) and *The Parthenon* (1871), both in the Metropolitan Museum of Art, New York. Church suffered from arthritis which affected his painting, and after a trip to the Middle East in 1868 decided to create a Persian villa, to be conceptualized as a work of art on canvas but realized in actuality in the valley, woodlands, and meadows that formed his estate with its spectacular views of the Hudson.

In the realization of his ideas, Church enlisted the help of the leading landscape architect, Calvert Vaux (1824–1895), co-designer with Frederick Law Olmsted of Central Park, New York. Church produced over 300 plans for the villa and the estate and a whole series of watercolor drawings. Throughout the design and execution of the project Church had control of the smallest details, extending to the choice of individual trees and internal fittings. Practicalities were important—the lake, which was excavated by 1875, provided water for the farm and house as well as providing an essential component of the landscape, which Church conceived as a foreground for spectacular views of the Hudson and the Catskills. The house is arranged around a central courtyard and the windows are strategically placed to provide framed views of nature. Church's studio provides an invaluable insight into the working life of a successful painter of the period and the house as a whole is a treasure trove of exotica, from the oriental furnishings and richly decorated and stencilled rooms to the minutely realized exterior details.

The house remained in Church's family until 1964 and was purchased by the State of New York two years later. Church's working drawings ensure the precision of conservation work and the house is open to the public, providing a major resource for an understanding of its times.

Second Empire

Whereas both the major historical revival styles of the later nineteenth century, the Italianate and the Gothic Revival, took their inspiration from the romantic past, as did the High Victorian, buildings built in Second Empire style were rooted in the present and considered modern in their time. The style takes its name from France, from the Second Empire of Napoleon III (1852–1870). The period is famous for the rebuilding of Paris, with the wide boulevards and grand buildings that made the city the world capital of style and art that it was to remain until 1945. The international expositions of 1855 attracted thousands of visitors to Paris from all over the world and buildings imitative of the Second Empire style could subsequently be seen across Europe.

Above: John Graves House, 51 Hillhouse Avenue, New Haven, CT, 1862. An exceptionally ornate Second Empire house.

Above: George Lord Little House, Kennebunkport, ME, 1875. An unusually tall Second Empire house.

Above: Horatio Moody House, Kennebunkport, ME, 1866.

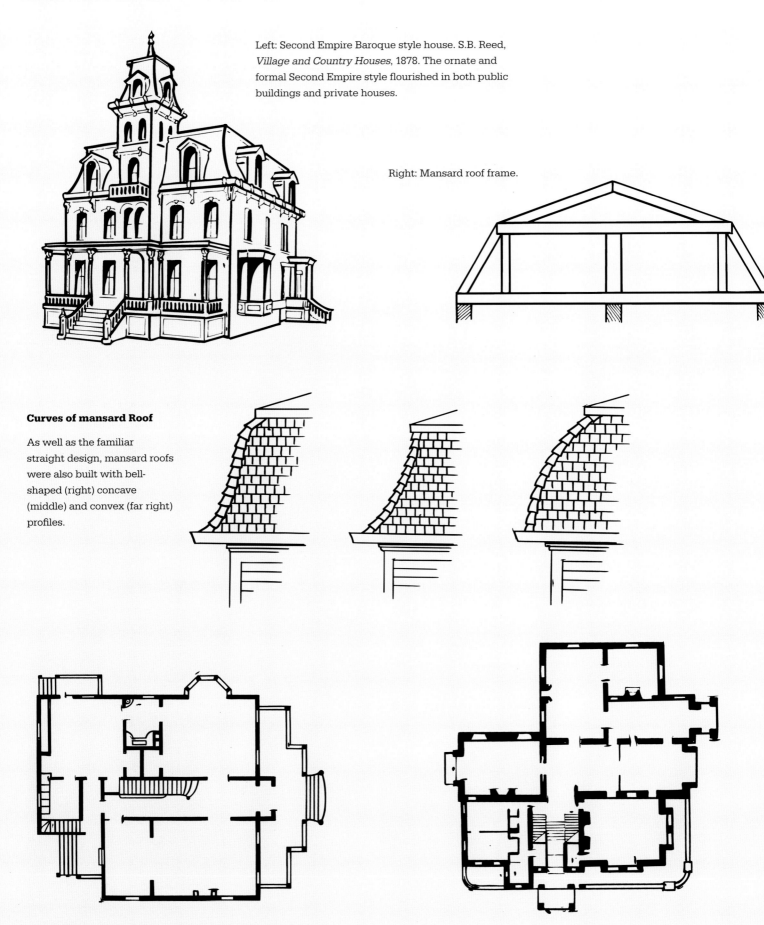

Left: Second Empire Baroque style house. S.B. Reed, *Village and Country Houses*, 1878. The ornate and formal Second Empire style flourished in both public buildings and private houses.

Right: Mansard roof frame.

Curves of mansard Roof

As well as the familiar straight design, mansard roofs were also built with bell-shaped (right) concave (middle) and convex (far right) profiles.

Above: Plan of mansard house. S.B. Reed, *Village and Country Houses*, 1878.

Above: Richard Morris Hunt: plan of Chateau-sur-Mer, Newport, RI, 1852.

The major impact of the style, however, was on architecture in America, where it became the dominant style from 1860 until the Second Empire in France was destroyed in the Franco-Prussian War of 1870–1871, though examples can be found dating to the 1880s. Second Empire houses can be found across Northeastern and Midwestern states during the period; they are less prevalent on the Pacific Coast and in the South. The style was particularly popular for both public and private building in America during the early years of the Grant administration (1869–1877), and it is sometimes nicknamed the "General Grant Style." Its extravagance was a decisive factor in its fall from fashion in the economic panic of 1873 and the depression that followed.

The Second Empire style is distinguished above all by the mansard roof. The mansard was named after its inventor, the seventeenth century French architect, Francois Mansart, and was considered to be both functional and aesthetically pleasing. The height of the roof and the fact that it was dual pitched and hipped allowed almost a full story of what would otherwise have been unusable attic space to be utilized. Indeed, the great popularity of the mansard roof might be explained by this fact, though it also provided a distinctive roofline for domestic dwellings. In cities such as London where strict planning laws prohibited buildings above a certain height, the restrictions could be circumvented by the use of a mansard and the characteristic dormer windows. The mansard could also be added relatively easily to existing buildings, giving them both valuable additional room-space and an air of fashionable modernity.

The house that introduced the Second Empire style and the mansard roof to the United States was built by the architect Richard Morris Hunt (1827–1895) at Newport, Rhode Island, between 1852 to 1872, and is known as Chateau-sur-Mer. Another, even more elaborate, house with two towers from the later years of the style is the Hubbell House in Des Moines, Iowa, 1869, built by William W. Boyington. Each demonstrates complex variations on the mansard roof and the fact that the main components of Second Empire houses are very similar to those used in the Italianate Style, as can be seen in the veranda and tower details

Above: Richard Morris Hunt (1827–1895): Chateau-sur-Mer, Bellevue Avenue, Newport, RI, 1852/1872. This house introduced the Second Empire style and the mansard roof to the United States. The style is named after the second empire of Napoleon III, who ruled France from 1851–1870. Renovations and expansion of the Louvre in this style added to its popularity.

of the Hubbell House, and in the window, door, and porch details of both houses. Chateau-sur-Mer has the loggia so typical of the Italianate Style in its Tuscan villa variation.

The elaborate detailing of both houses is typical of the style as are the decorative patterns of color and texture to be seen in the roof. Some houses have multi-colored and patterned slate tiles or even tin plates as roof covering, below which was a small bracketed cornice called a "French Curb," as on the Hubbell House. Some houses, again like the Hubbell House, added to the mansard roof a mansard tower, or rather, in this case, two towers with different profiles on front and rear elevations.

Chateau-sur-Mer, "Castle-by-the-Sea," has a very unusual convex-style mansard roof, which is exceptionally deep and is crowned by an elaborate tower with the iron cresting surmounting it that is another distinctive feature of the style. Chateau-sur-Mer, has a massive asymmetrical silhouette and is particularly eclectic in its mixture of motifs both externally and internally: its Turkish room mixes Oriental, American, and European styles in a manner distinctively of its time.

Arched windows on the main stories are another common feature of the style: often these are floor to ceiling and set in pairs. One- or two-story bay windows are also characteristic and appear wherever the houses were built.

The earliest uses of the Second Empire style wedded variations on the essential mansard roof to a form which is basically Italianate. However this relatively modest form was unable to accommodate more demanding lifestyles with a taste for the florid decoration that was a hallmark of design during this period of serial production and improved communication. An eclectic mixture of disparate elements can be seen to make up many of the more palatial mansions built in the Second Empire style, and can also be seen in the many more modest houses which added Second Empire elements to existing buildings.

Perhaps the most eclectic of all Second Empire mansions is that designed by Stephen Decatur Button (1813–1897) as a summer retreat for the Pennsylvanian coal baron, J. B. McCreary at Cape May, NJ, in 1869. The palatial mansion adds a sixty-foot tower with Gothic-style lancet windows to customary Second Empire elements such as a mansard roof. Stained glass abounds throughout the house which combines such medieval elements

Above: William W. Boyington (1818–1898): Terrace Hill, the Benjamin Franklin Allen House, now the Iowa Governor's Mansion, 2300 Grand Avenue, Des Moines, IA, 1866–1869. One of the most elaborate Second Empire homes.

with the latest technology in the form of gas lighting. Many of the original ornate gas lighting fixtures remain as well as much of the interior decoration. The Gothic elements of the imposing exterior elevation give the house its popular name, "The Abbey."

Left: Stephen Decatur Button (1813–1897): "The Abbey," J.B. McCreary House, Columbia and Gurney Streets, Cape May, NJ, 1869. This house adds Gothic lancet windows to the tower of the house, contributing to the name "The Abbey."

Right: Stephen Decatur Button: "The Abbey," J.B. McCreary House, Cape May, NJ, 1869.

Above: Second Empire house, Kennebunkport, ME, 1866.

Above: Second Empire house, Portsmouth, NH.

Above: Second Empire villa, Jamaica Plain, MA.

Above left: Garth Woodside Mansion, 11069 New London Road, Hannibal, MO, 1871. Second Empire style.

Above right: First Governor's Mansion, the Albert Gallatin House, 1526 H Street, Sacramento, CA, 1877.

Left: Mansard cottage, Kennebunkport, ME.

Left: Second Empire cottage, Hingham, MA.

Stick Style

The Stick Style grew from the "Picturesque Gothic" style first popularized by A.J. Davis and A.J. Downing in such publications as Davis' *Rural Residences* of 1837 and Downing's 1850 publication *The Architecture of Country Houses,* and was further developed in the pattern books of the 1860s and 1870s. The invention of the balloon-frame and the steam-powered scroll saw made wood the preferred material of construction, especially as lumber was in plentiful supply in many areas and was both cheaper and less difficult to work with than stone. As a style it is generally considered to be a linking development between the Gothic Revival and Queen Anne, while all three styles ultimately have their roots in medieval English domestic architecture with its emphasis on the vernacular.

The style can be found in the early 1860s in the work of Richard Morris Hunt (1827–1895), who espoused Downing's advocacy of the importance of "truthfulness" in wooden buildings. The result is the revealing of crucial components of the balloon-frame construction on the elevation of domestic buildings for the first time. It appears, however, that in contrast to the contemporary Italianate and Second Empire styles, relatively few Stick buildings were constructed. The style was quickly supplanted in the Northeast by the Queen Anne movement, which attained widespread popularity.

In San Francisco, however, a distinctive style of townhouse developed, in part due to the plentiful supplies of redwood. This made possible the rapid

Above: Stick Style house, Stony Creek, CT.

growth of the city from the Gold Rush period on, and here the style continued into the later 1880s and beyond. Many of the finest surviving examples of the style are carefully preserved, painted in the distinctive colors first remarked upon in the *San Francisco Chronicle* in the 1880s as a defining characteristic of the local style.

Downing's advocacy of truth to material in the use of wood as a building material was very quickly departed from, with the surface decoration becoming all-important and its relationship to the underlying structure of the balloon-frame becoming increasingly blurred. The wooden sticks, or strips, used to outline the windows and doors and framework of the house, are applied to the surface rather than being an integral part

Above: Stick Style, detail of porch framing, Villa Vista, 32 Prospect Hill Road, Stony Creek, CT, 1878.

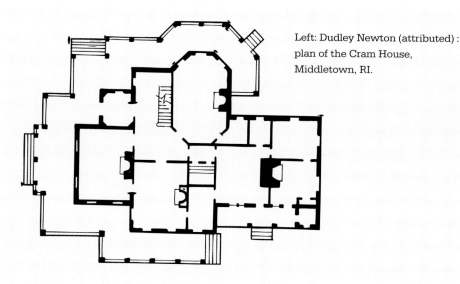

Left: Dudley Newton (attributed): plan of the Cram House, Middletown, RI.

Above: Henry Austin (1804–1891): Villa Vista, Stony Creek, CT, 1878.

the wooden framework that supports the house. Such thoroughgoing "truth to materials" was rare in other Stick Style houses. Other features of the Griswold House, such as the steeply-pitched gable roof and the "sticks" of the porch railings and the exposed porch rafters were to become characteristic features of the style. The irregularity of the form may also be seen in the asymmetry of the façade and its use of board-and-batten and vertical siding and bracketed purlins (horizontal roof beams used to support the roof rafters): all features which, as discussed, ultimately derive from English medieval architecture.

The eclectic mix of motifs that forms the Stick Style can be seen to draw not only on the early Gothic Revival as advocated by Downing and Davis in their influential pattern books but also the contemporary styles of Carpenter Gothic and Swiss Cottage styles. Such characteristic features of Carpenter Gothic as the fancy scroll-sawn bargeboards are mixed with typical Swiss Cottage devices such as long and narrow outside galleries with wooden railings in Stick Style. Many of these features can be seen in the Villa Vista, designed by Henry Austin (1804–1891) in Stony Creek, Connecticut. Villa Vista, constructed in 1878, is remarkable for its unusually elaborate porch, which is in two tiers, and the highly decorative stick roof trussing and cross gables. The porch supports are also unusually elaborate and curved in a

of the structure as they were in the half-timbered construction of earlier styles.

In many respects, the John N.A. Griswold House, Bellevue Avenue, Newport, RI, designed by Richard Morris Hunt in 1862–1863, is one of the finest examples of the Stick Style, as well as being one of the earliest. Here the diagonal "sticks" are exposed structural components of the balloon-frame—the vertical and horizontal members are, indeed, exposed elements of

Left: Richard Morris Hunt (1827–1895): John N.A. Griswold House, Bellevue Avenue, Newport, RI, 1862–1863. A pioneering example of the Stick Style.

Above: Edward Potter (1831–1904): Mark Twain House, 351 Farmington Avenue, Hartford, CT, 1874.

Above: Edward Potter (1831–1904): Mark Twain House, Hartford, CT, 1874.

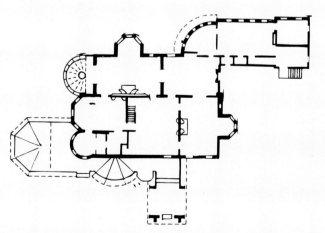

Above: Edward Potter: plan of the Mark Twain House. The Twain House reflected the writer's individualistic personality and prominent social position.

form reminiscent of medieval arches, while the main roof is steeply pitched. The roof of the tower has an exceptionally high pitch and tops the square tower so typical of Stick houses (in contrast to the round towers of the related Queen Anne style that succeeded it).

Surviving gable-roofed Stick houses are concentrated principally in the Northeastern states, and Hartford, Connecticut, has some particularly fine examples. Two of these belonged to famous writers of the day, in an area of woodland on the north branch of the Park River where a community of wordsmiths took up residence at Nook Farm. While Harriet Beecher Stowe's cottage is open to the public it is the home of one of America's foremost men of letters that is of particular interest. The elaborate dwelling occupied by Mark Twain has been carefully restored and is also open to the public. Mark Twain— the pen name of Samuel Clemens(1835–1910)— commissioned the house in 1874 and wrote seven of his most successful works there, including *The Adventures of Tom Sawyer* (1876) and *The Adventures of Huckleberry Finn* (1884).

The house is distinguished by its irregularity which gives it an individuality that is both characteristic of its owner and of the flexibility of the Stick Style. Its roofline is especially remarkable, with a profusion of steeply pitched gables, curiously shaped towers, and tall, medieval-style chimneys with elaborate detailing. The house has fine porches and galleries and was much used for entertaining (Twain was renowned for his hospitality). It contains such typical Victorian social spaces as a billiard room, which Twain also used to write in. The house was richly decorated in 1881 with fine wall coverings and a profusion of elaborately carved woodwork, while its famous owner's fascination with new technology is also in evidence in the form of the first private telephone in Hartford.

Stick Style is remarkable for both its picturesque qualities and the flexibility which made it possible for both architects and builders to adapt it to varying lifestyles, from that of a celebrity like Mark Twain to the new owners of townhouses in San Francisco.

Right: Frank Furness (1839–1912): Emlen Physick House, 1048 Washington Street, Cape May, NJ, 1878.

Below: Samuel and Joseph C. Newsom: William McKendrie Carson House, Second and M streets, Eureka, CA, 1884–1886.

Above: Henry Luce: house, Mt. Vernon Street, Boston, MA, 1840/1887. A rare example of the English Queen Anne style, this house was redesigned by Luce in 1887. Oscar Wilde is said to have stayed here on a visit to America.

Left: Sidney Richmond Burleigh (1853–1931): Fleur-de-Lys Studio, 7 Thomas Street, Providence, RI, 1885. Another English Queen Anne house, built by an artist and founder of the Providence Art Club.

Queen Anne

Queen Anne takes its name and popularity from England of the early 1870s, where a group of architects, the most notable of whom was Richard Norman Shaw (1831–1912), set about the reform of London's architecture in a search for a style that could be used not only for domestic architecture but also for schools and other public buildings. Indeed, in London the prototype London Board Schools were the first to use the style, with urban houses quickly following. The name given to the form was a popular one, if inaccurate and vague, as it had little to do with the style prevalent in the brief reign of Queen Anne (1702–1714), when the mode of building was essentially English Renaissance. Rather, "Queen Anne" as a style borrowed heavily from the preceding

Left: Queen Anne house, Hudson, MA. Detail of tower and gabled dormer with elaborate carvings.

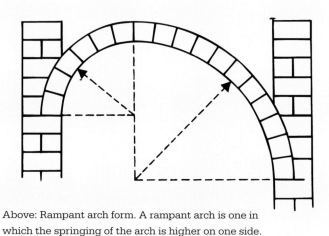

Above: Rampant arch form. A rampant arch is one in which the springing of the arch is higher on one side.

Above: Henry Hobson Richardson: Watts Sherman House, Salve Regina University, Newport, RI, 1874–1876. One of the first Queen Anne houses in America, it also marks the beginning of the Shingle Style.

Above: Henry Hobson Richardson: Watts Sherman House, Newport, RI, 1874–76. Detail.

Tudor and Stuart eras, using brick and stucco, elaborate gables, half timbering, and a variety of window forms, including the oriel window. The emphasis was on craftsmanship and the style rapidly became popular in England, spreading to the United States by at latest 1876, the year of the Philadelphia Centennial, where it received wide coverage, quickly supplanting the two most popular contemporary styles, Second Empire and Gothic. Its chief rival, the Romanesque style, was essentially stone-built, which put it beyond the reach of most Americans in terms of cost.

The Queen Anne style may be seen as the culmination of all the Victorian styles in its eclectic mixtures of elements. From the Italianate style, especially the Tuscan villa variant, came the essential asymmetry, and the richly patterned and textured surfaces are a marked feature of the High Victorian Gothic style. The organic appearance of buildings in this style owes much to the Gothic Revival

Above and above right: Queen Anne style decorated bargeboards.

as do the popular turrets, while the half-timbering and clapboards are reminiscent of Stick Style, as was the widespread use of gingerbread trim. Shingles were used as cladding and brick was a favored building material, as can be seen in the Watts Sherman House (see page 243). Wood was the most prevalent construction and detailing material, used for characteristic details such as spindlework and for the popular asymmetrical porches which help identify the style, from grand country houses to modest suburban dwellings.

Above all else the defining feature of Queen Anne was the decorative detailing which used an exuberant mix of color and wooden appliqué in sunflower or sunburst forms: a decorative motif which was used throughout the West in the latter part of the nineteenth century. Sunflowers and sunburst designs could be found in decorative schemes throughout America during the period. A symbol of life and creativity, the sunflower was used in many forms, including ceramic decoration, metalwork, and stucco. Queen Anne borrowed widely in its eclectic use of decorative forms—swags and Roman garland appliqué was common, as was the use of tinted and stained-glass windows.

Such detail was readily sourced from the widely circulated pattern books of the period, as were house plans, room schemes, and elevations. The widespread

Left: Villa Montezuma, the Jesse Shepard House, 1925 K Street, San Diego, CA, 1887. Built for the author, musician, and noted spiritualist Jesse Shepard.

Above: Brick house, Middletown, CT, 1880s.

Above: House, Wickford, RI, 1883.

use of such sources meant that there are very few regional differences between the houses in towns across the country during the latter years of the nineteenth century and well into the twentieth.

Ease of construction and economies of building meant that wooden Queen Anne houses could be erected by competent carpenters, although grander, architect-designed houses in the style also survive in quantity throughout the country.

One of the first Queen Anne houses in the United States is generally agreed to be the Watts Sherman House, at Newport, Rhode Island, built between 1874–1876 by Henry Hobson Richardson who designed buildings in a variety of styles including Romanesque. In silhouette, the Watts Sherman House has the proliferation of gables and tall, medieval-style chimneys so typical of the Queen Anne style and in the fact that it uses shingles it may be regarded as also marking the beginning of the Shingle Style. The Watts Sherman House was originally rectangular in plan, but the architect Stanford White, who had worked on the house when it was first built, extended the house to an L-shape between 1879 and 1881. He also redecorated three of its main rooms. The interior of the house is typically Queen Anne in its spaciousness, although alterations and later additions in the second decade of the twentieth century make it more difficult to appreciate the originality of the house in its time.

In California, the adaptability of such a style can

be seen at its most exotic in the Villa Montezuma, built for the local celebrity author, musician, and mystic, Jesse Shepherd, in San Diego in 1887. The brick-built house, which has Californian redwood shingles, is topped by an onion dome and the roof-lines feature ornate cresting. At the other end of the Queen Anne scale, it is useful to compare the Watts Sherman House with such suburban houses as those at Jamaica Plain, Massachusetts, and Oak Park, Illinois. Here in Boston and Chicago it was possible to construct houses in the fashionable style for families of relatively modest means and without the aid of an architect, using local builders.

Whether in the form of a home in a new suburb, or as one of several townhouses in a new urban area, the Queen Anne style was infinitely adaptable to needs across the United States. From the earliest adaptation of English examples, such as the Watts Sherman House, the form developed an inventive indigenous American spindlework style which became dominant during the 1880s. However, there were still adherents to Shaw's later form. These houses were masonry-built, though they were relatively rare due to their larger price tag. By the 1890s the style was remarkable for its use of an increasing number of Classical components, such as Palladian windows, a sub-style known as Free Classic. The Queen Anne style was long-lived: it may be said to have only finally died out by the end of the first decade of the twentieth century.

Above: Queen Anne house, Newton, MA, 1883.

Left: Queen Anne house, New Haven, CT, c. 1882.

Above: McConaghy Estate, Hayward, CA, 1886. A twelve-room Queen Anne farmhouse.

Above: George Barber: Pillow-Thompson House, 718 Perry Street, Helena, AK, 1896.

Right: George W. Patterson House, Fremont, CA, begun 1850s, enlarged in 1889 and 1913.

Above: F. W. Wetherbee House, Waltham, MA, 1892.

Above: John A. Walls: Heritage House, 8193 Magnolia Avenue, Riverside, CA, 1891.

Above: Queen Anne house, Jamaica Plain, MA.

Above: Robert Swain Peabody (1845–1917) and John Goddard Stearns (d. 1917): Hayes Q. Trowbridge House, New Haven, CT, 1907. This Shingle Style house displays elaborate patterning in the shingle covering.

Left: Queen Anne house, Oak Park, IL.

Above: Queen Anne house, Hudson, MA, 1893.

Shingle Style

Shingle Style takes its name from the building component that covers exterior surfaces and renders them smooth, however complex the shape of the building. Shingles may made of thin wood or other materials, laid in regular overlapping rows with the thicker ends on display. The shingles weather naturally whatever the material, ageing gracefully, although many shingled walls and roofs have now been replaced with composition shingles.

The shingle cladding of the exterior surfaces not only gives its name to the style, but serves as a typological term to distinguish what would otherwise be seemingly disparate styles or free interpretations by many of the leading architects of the day. Unlike popular

contemporary styles such as Queen Anne, the Shingle Style could be adapted easily to vernacular mass housing, and architectural magazines publicized the style in its heyday, which lasted the decades from 1880 to 1900.

The style originated when such well-known architects as Henry Hobson Richardson of Boston, and McKim, Mead and White of New York began to build summer houses for wealthy clients in seaside resorts in the Northeastern states, such as Cape Cod, Newport, and coastal Maine from the late 1870s. Many of these survive today, with scattered examples of the style being built well into the first decade of the twentieth century in other regions.

Like Queen Anne, which adapted English prototypes to become an unmistakably American style, Shingle borrowed from other traditions both old and new. Shingled

Above: Henry Hobson Richardson (1836–1886): Mrs. M.F. Stoughton House, Brattle Street, Cambridge, MA, 1882–1883.

Shingle Style

Above: Diamond cut.

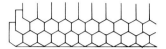

Above: Hexagonal cut.

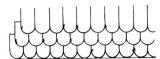

Above: Rounded cut.

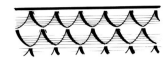

Above: Cut in scale pattern.

Below: Wavy cut.

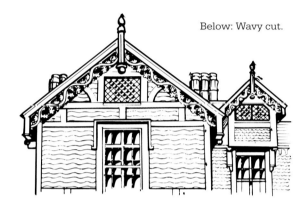

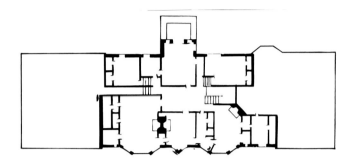

Above: McKim, Mead and White: plan of the first floor of William Low House, Bristol, RI, 1887. Demolished.

Above: Shingle Style house. The Shingle Style offered a more unified surface design than the Victorian Gothic or the Second Empire style. Houses were unified by broad forms and the use of a continuous skin of wooden shingles.

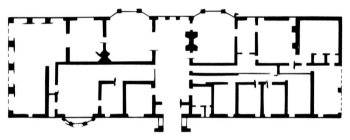

Above: McKim, Mead and White: plan of the second floor of William Low House, Bristol, RI, 1887. Demolished.

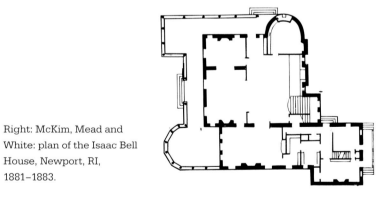

Right: McKim, Mead and White: plan of the Isaac Bell House, Newport, RI, 1881–1883.

Above: The surface texture of Shingle Style houses was enriched by patterns in the shingles created by skilled craftsmen.

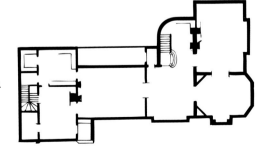

Right: Henry Hobson Richardson: plan for Mrs. M.F. Stoughton House, Cambridge, MA, 1882–1883.

surfaces were used on Queen Anne houses as well as homes with asymmetric plans and elevations, and wide porches. The porches, which were so marked and popular a feature of other contemporary styles, often surrounded coastal Shingle houses completely, to take advantage of the sea air. The so-called Richardsonian Romanesque used Romanesque arches and irregular sculptural shapes, often with massive stone first stories, though the last is comparatively rare in Shingle Style. The form also borrowed such features as Classical columns and gambrel roofs from the New England colonial designs of the seventeenth century—a particularly significant feature of even relatively modest buildings in Shingle Style in the coastal and island towns around Nantucket, Massachusetts.

A key building in the Shingle Style is Stonehurst, the Robert Treat Paine House of 1884–1886 at Waltham, Massachusetts, by Henry Hobson Richardson (1836–1886). Stonehurst occupies a spectacular scenic site commanding extraordinary views of the Charles River. Robert Treat Paine was advised on the choice of site by the famous landscape designer Frederick Law Olmsted, who went on to design the landscaping and terracing of the 134-acre site. The landscape was to become literally part of the building with Richardson's decision to use boulders drawn from the site as a dramatic feature of the design.

Richardson had already used glacial boulders in his design for the Gurney House in Beverly, Massachusetts, and they form an essential part of Olmsted's design of Central Park, New York. At

Above: Charles McKim, William Mead and Stanford White: Isaac Bell House, 70 Perry Street, Newport, RI, 1881–1883.

Stonehurst boulders clad the first floor and the towers to striking effect, while on the garden front, a shingled first-floor loggia above a porch constructed from bouldered piers opens onto the curved terrace designed by Olmsted, thus integrating the house and its landscape in an extraordinarily harmonious and organic manner. The recessed east porch is also constructed from boulders as are the low Norman towers. On one of these is mounted a huge sundial which charts the sun's progress throughout the day across the bolders and shingles of the exterior. The seamless qualities of the Shingle Style can be seen at their most dramatic here—the cladding is unbroken by decorative detail of any sort, so that the play of light over stone and shingle surfaces produces a unique effect.

Stonehurst is Richardson's most intact house and the interior is thus of particular interest. The main focus of the house is a large central stair-hall which extends from the entrance to the north in a huge expanse of uninterrupted space to the summer parlor in the east. The Japanese influence on such an open-plan design is enhanced by the detailing of such components as the open wooden screens of the staircase and great hall and by the stenciled designs on walls and ceilings and by the red coloration of the glazed walls. Stonehurst represents a synthesis of disparate elements by an exceptional architect, which survives almost as originally built.

In contrast, another remarkable Shingle Style house, the William G. Low House at Bristol, Rhode Island, built by the well-known architectural firm of McKim, Mead and White in 1887, has been demolished. The Low

Above: McKim, Mead and White: William G. Low House, Bristol, RI, 1887. Now demolished, this was one of the greatest Shingle Style houses.

Left: Henry Hobson Richardson (1836–1886): Stonehurst, the Robert Treat Paine House, 577 Beaver Street, Waltham, MA, 1884–1886. (See page 250.)

Below: Henry Hobson Richardson: Robert Treat Paine House, Waltham, MA, 1884–1886.

Above: Henry Hobson Richardson: Robert Treat Paine House, Waltham, MA, 1884–1886.

Above: Bruce Price: William Kent House, Tuxedo Park, NY, 1886. Bruce Price was a noted Shingle Style architect, and this house had a strong impact on Frank Lloyd Wright's design for his own first house.

House was notable for the geometry of its gable—a huge unbroken triangle on both the ocean and entrance sides—and for its singular plan which was two rooms deep, some forty feet long but nearly 140 feet in breadth. The entire exterior, both walls and roof, was covered with the same square-cut shingles which gave the whole house an extraordinary continuity of surface and enhanced the elemental geometry of the triangular form. The Low House appears astonishingly modern in the photographs which are all that is left of the building, but appears to have had little influence in its time. However, another McKim, Mead and White house on Rhode Island, the Isaac Bell House in Newport of 1882–1883, remains to give some idea of the high quality of the practice's work in the Shingle Style, along with many other more modest houses of the period along the Northeastern seaboard and elsewhere.

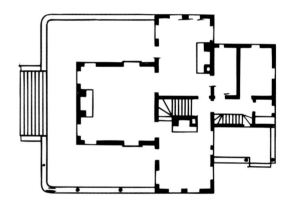

Above: Bruce Price: plan of the William Kent House, Tuxedo Park, NY, 1886.

Above: Bruce Price: Travis C. Van Buren House, Tuxedo Park, NY, 1886. This house featured a prominent variant of a Palladian window, and a smoothly sculpted doorway which resembled a cave entrance.

Left: "The Kedge," the Henry Miller House, Macculloch Avenue, Morristown, NJ, 1870–1880.

Below: Windward House, 24 Jackson Street, Cape May, NJ, 1905.

Above: Shingle Style house, Morristown, NJ, 1892.

Above: Longfellow, Alden, and Harlow: Shingle Style house, Cambridge, MA, 1894.

Above: Shingle Style house, Cohasset, MA.

Medieval Castles

The so-called "medieval castles" were built from the fourth decade of the nineteenth century well into the twentieth century across the United States and represent a final, extravagant flowering of the Gothic style. As with the earlier manifestations of the Gothic, their forms are ultimately derived from European examples of dwellings built during the middle ages. However, the characteristic details of the typical medieval castle or fortified dwelling were transmuted in Europe during the late eighteenth and early nineteenth centuries into a vocabulary of forms which had their inspiration in a romantic nostalgia for the middle ages, and also characterizes the literature and design of the period. This "architecture of Romanticism" came first to America in the form of engraved images of such eighteenth century English buildings as Strawberry Hill, home of the cultural critic and arbiter of taste, Horace Walpole. This was a "gothick" mansion, built between 1749 and 1776, in Twickenham, London, as was the medieval-style extravaganza of Fonthill Abbey (1796–1807) in Wiltshire, built for William Beckford who, like Walpole, wrote a celebrated Gothic novel.

These fantastical eclectic forms were taken up in America during the early nineteenth century and elaborated upon to provide impressive dwellings, often in spectacular locations. The harmony of structure and setting was essential to what came to be known as the Picturesque Gothic, indeed the leading English theorist of the style, Richard Payne Knight, designed his own home, Downtown Castle, as the first house in Europe to conform to his rule that "houses should be irregular where all the accompaniments are irregular." The proposition that an asymmetrical building should harmonize with the landscape, rather than imposing its symmetrical presence on it as in Classical-style dwellings, was extraordinarily influential in both Europe and America.

In the United States, several key buildings in the genre were designed by one of the most important architects of the Gothic style—Alexander Jackson Davis (1803–1892). Davis's first domestic building in Picturesque Gothic was Glen Ellen, designed in 1832 for a client, Robert Gilmor of Baltimore, who had recently returned from Scotland after visiting the home of Sir Walter Scott, whose novels helped promote a romantic image of the middle ages.

Above: Alexander Jackson Davis: Lyndhurst, 635 S. Broadway, Tarrytown, NY, 1838/1865.

The asymmetrical and "picturesque" qualities of this type of building were further elaborated by Davis in subsequent works, the finest of which is undoubtedly Lyndhurst (1865–1867), at Tarrytown, New York. The term "picturesque" derives from the Italian "pittoresque" or "as in a picture", and as it stands today Lyndhurst is truly termed "picturesque" from every angle. Davis's compositional abilities make it seem an inextricable part of its spectacular site. The architect's original house on the site was a more modest Gothic dwelling built some thirty years earlier for another owner, General William Paulding. The house was then called Knoll and marks a distinct development in style from Davis's first exercise in the genre, Glen Ellen. Lyndhurst represents a greater elaboration of more authentic medieval detail, derived from the contemporary work of the influential medievalist English designer and architect, Augustus Welby Pugin. Modest Knoll was virtually doubled in size for its second owner, George Merritt, while the building stone has the distinction of having been quarried by inmates at Ossining prison ("Sing Sing").

The fairy-tale roofline of Lyndhurst, with its pinnacles, turrets, and crenellations, forms a spectacular focal point of the extensive landscaping which covers some sixty-seven acres, while the interiors are equally distinguished. Various styles of medieval vaulting are used and there is a profusion of fine art glass and medieval-style furnishings throughout. Nineteenth century fashion is represented by various modish surface finishes, ranging from marbelization to the leather wall-coverings so popular in the lavish homes of the period.

Above: Thomas J. Smith: Edwin Forrest House, "Fonthill," W. 261st Street and Palisade Avenue (now part of the College of Mount Saint Vincent), Bronx, NY, 1848. This medieval castle was built by one of the most famous actors of the nineteenth century.

Unlike its English namesake, Fonthill Abbey, which drew on elements of English medieval religious architecture, including the central octagon of Ely Cathedral, for its forms, was designed to evoke a fortified medieval castle, complete with look-out tower. It was built in 1848 for the famous Shakespearian actor Edwin Forrest (1806–1872) and now forms part of the College of

Mount Saint Vincent. Forrest achieved considerable fame in both the United States and in England as well as notoriety off-stage—his feud with his English rival, William Macready, resulted in the catastrophe of the Astor Place riot in New York, in May 1849, during which a large number of Forrest and Macready's supporters were killed. Forrest's reputation was further damaged by an acrimonious divorce which dragged on for nearly two decades. The actor never recovered and from mid-century he was seen on stage only rarely and abandoned the newly built Fonthill for his native Philadelphia, where he lived reclusively for the rest of his life.

Later in the nineteenth century, the medieval castle-style building became even more extravagant, and was often used to reflect and enhance the owner's wealth and social standing. Perhaps the most famous example was the Potter Palmer Mansion, formerly at Lake Shore Drive, Chicago, built between 1882 and 1885 for Potter and Bertha Honore Palmer, Chicago's real-estate king and society queen, who had purchased most of the land on what was soon to be called Chicago's Gold Coast. As high society left the formerly fashionable Prairie Avenue and followed the Palmers to Lake Shore Drive, property values in the newly fashionable quarter quadrupled within a decade. The ostentatious house, with its distinctive silhouette, was demolished

Left: Henry Ives Cobb (1859–1931) and Charles Sumner Frost (1856–1931): Potter Palmer Mansion, formerly at 1350 N. Lake Shore Drive, Chicago, 1882–1885.

Above: Richard Morris Hunt: Biltmore, the Vanderbilt Estate, Asheville, NC, 1889–1895. A 250-room mansion built by George Washington Vanderbilt in the style of a French chateau; in particular, it is modeled on the chateaux of Blois, Chenonceau, and Chambord in the Loire Valley. The façade is 390 feet long.

of French Impressionist paintings, now part of the Art Institute of Chicago collection, in the seventy-five foot, three-story picture gallery which formed such a striking feature of the design.

However splendid its contemporaries, the grandest of all mansions in the elegant chateau style of French architecture is without doubt the 250-room mansion designed for Mrs. W.K. Vanderbilt on George Washington Vanderbilt's 130,000-acre estate in the Great Smoky Mountains, near Asheville, North Carolina. This grand house is also discussed in the Eclectic Revivals chapter later as it is something of a crossover, representing a late flowering of the Victorian taste for castles as well as being an early example of the Chateauesque form. The architect was Richard Morris Hunt (1827–1895) who had trained at the Ecole des Beaux Arts in Paris, traveled in Europe, and numbered among his clientele some of the wealthiest members of high society for whom he built palatial homes.

in 1950, but in its heyday became the center of Chicago society, as Bertha Palmer entertained famously and exhibited her renowned collection

Biltmore, which cost some four million dollars, introduced the chateau style to America, took six years to build from 1889, covered five acres, and employed hundreds of foreign artisans in its construction.

Left: Richard Morris Hunt: Biltmore, the Vanderbilt Estate, Asheville, NC, 1889–1895.

Richardson Romanesque

One of the most innovative of all later nineteenth century architects in America, Henry Hobson Richardson (1838–1886) designed many remarkable public buildings, including the monumental Trinity Church in Boston (1872–1877), a structure of such power and originality that it became the foremost church of its time in America, while at the same time inaugurating the Romanesque style for both public and private buildings. An equally radical and extraordinarily building, which was to have great influence on twentieth century architecture in America, is the Marshall Field warehouse, Chicago, of 1885–1887, completed after Richardson's premature death at the age of forty-eight.

Richardson's background, training, and knowledge of European architecture were unique in their time. Born in Louisiana, he attended Harvard and studied at the Ecole des Beaux Arts in Paris during a period when Napoleon III and his architect, Baron Haussmann, were transforming the city into the most splendid capital in Europe. Even as a student, Richardson had studied the architecture of the past, touring the Romanesque churches of France, particularly those in Normandy and, when the Civil War blocked his return to the United States, learning first hand about key English Romanesque (known as Norman) sites such as Durham Cathedral. While in England, Richardson also would have had the opportunity to have seen the work of such contemporaries as Richard Norman Shaw and William Burges as well as the earlier work of William Morris, a key influence on much later nineteenth century domestic architecture, particularly in terms of the vernacular.

During the 1860s and 1870s Richardson designed several houses in the styles fashionable at the time, which ranged from Queen Anne and Second Empire to Stick, while in the 1880s he designed remarkable Shingle Style houses such as Stonehurst. The first of his few Romanesque houses, as distinct from public buildings, was the rectory for Trinity Church in 1879–1880, and he was to complete but few houses in the style before his death in 1886. The style became popular for large public buildings as well as for a few houses and was utilized by other architects following Richardson's lead. Two years after his death, Richardson's life and work were to

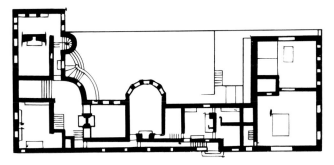

Above: Henry Hobson Richardson: plan for J.J. Glessner House, Chicago, 1885. This urban Romanesque house has a more open garden side, in contrast to the formal street façade.

become the subject of the first monograph ever to be written on an American architect and this prompted the building of more domestic buildings in the style during the 1890s. However, by its very nature Richardsonian Romanesque was an expensive style and never became widespread. It necessitated solid masonry construction and could not be copied inexpensively in wood like Stick and other late Victorian styles. Thus houses in the style are confined to very few examples by named architects in the main, and are mostly to be found in larger cities in Northeastern states. The finest examples are undoubtedly by the architect whose name is given to the style.

Above: Henry Hobson Richardson: J.J. Glessner House, 1800 South Prairie Avenue, Chicago, IL, 1885.

Above: Henry Hobson Richardson: J.J. Glessner House, 1800 South Prairie Avenue, Chicago, IL, 1885.

Above: Henry Hobson Richardson: J.J. Glessner House, Chicago, IL. Rear view.

The style incorporates such distinctive motifs as large, round arches, more truly Syrian than Romanesque, squat chimneys and columns, and deep-set doors. Windows emphasized the massiveness of the architectural forms. These ideas were assimilated into domestic architecture throughout the country, though the style was relatively shortlived.

Richardson's best-known house in the style is the John J. Glessner House of 1885, in Chicago, Illinois. Completed after Richardson's death, the street elevation bears striking similarities to Richardson's design for the Allegheny County Jail of 1883–1886 with its heavily rusticated ashlar walls, large round-headed arched entrances, and deep-set windows, while the courtyard elevation is similarly monumental. Squat chimneys and Romanesque columns accentuate the solidity and horizontal emphasis of the building as well as its sense of monumentality. However austere and defensive the qualities of the exterior, the emphasis of the interior was on comfort and fine design, and in this respect it has many similar design elements to Richardson's most famous country house, Stonehurst, built for Robert Treat Paine in 1883–1886. Like Stonehurst, the Glessner House is relatively open in plan, with fine timbered ceilings and paneling and a remarkable staircase. An unusual and significant survival is the spacious kitchen with a great iron range topped by an fine brass cooker hood. Fully restored and open to the public, the Glessner House provides impressive witness to Richardson's powers as a domestic architect.

Equally impressive if very different in concept and execution is the F.L. Ames Gate Lodge at North Easton, Massachusetts—part of a complex of buildings designed for the Ames family at North Easton, which included the Oakes Ames Memorial Hall and the Old Colony Railroad Station of 1881–1884. The landscaping of the buildings at North Easton was by Richardson's mentor and friend, Frederick Law Olmsted, the leading landscape designer of the day, who was working on his most famous urban landscape, Central Park in New York, at the same time. The Gate Lodge, which was designed to house guests in some style, is perhaps Richardson's most singular composition and one in which he was apparently allowed remarkable independence. The huge, piled-up bouldered walls and marked horizontality of the lodge are complemented by the finely tiled roof which is bright red and, like the entire structure, carries echoes of Japanese

Left: Eyebrow dormer; H.H. Richardson: F.L. Ames Gate Lodge, North Easton, MA. This heavy-lidded dormer barely breaks the continuous skin of shingles.

Above: Henry Hobson Richardson: F.L. Ames Gate Lodge, North Easton, MA, 1880–1881. Richardson's use of glacial boulders gives a primitive and solid appearance to the house; the dramatic arch creates a dynamic visual and spatial effect.

Left: Henry Hobson Richardson: F.L. Ames Gate Lodge, North Easton, MA, 1880–1881.

design. The rugged exterior gives no hint of the assembly of small rooms and large "Bachelor's Hall" which is the focus of the entire complex design.

If the exterior of the lodge speaks of shelter in a sophisticated and elegant rendering of one of the most ancient forms of domestic architecture, the central feature of the interior reinforces this. The central hearth takes the form of a large brownstone fireplace with remarkable carvings of the signs of the zodiac by the sculptor Augustus Saint Gaudens and Persian blue glass tiles by Tiffany. The sense of shelter offered by the fireplace is further enhanced by the elegant inglenook which is topped by a dark-green leather canopy supported on tall carved posts. Richardson's work of the last five years of his life reinforced his claim to be considered, with Louis Sullivan and Frank Lloyd Wright, as one of the greatest American architects.

Above: Thomas Annan (1837–1904): Samuel H. Cupples House, located on the John E. Connelly Mall, St. Louis, MO, 1888. A lavish forty-two room mansion, built of Colorado sandstone in the style of H.H. Richardson. It is now owned by St. Louis University.

Above: Wilson Eyre, Jr. (1858–1944): Dr. Joseph Leidy House, 1317–1319 Locust Street, Philadelphia, PA, 1893–1894. This eclectic house adds Gothic windows to an urban Romanesque mansion.

Above: Phelps House, 1146 Grand Avenue, Carthage, MO, 1895. This imposing stone house is built of local limestone; it was designed by the first owner, William Phelps.

Above: Henry Hobson Richardson: F.L. Ames Gardner's Cottage, North Easton, MA, 1884–1885. A very different design on the North Easton estate shows the architect's flexibility.

Folk Victorian

The term "Folk Victorian" is used to identify simple, often symmetrical, one- or two-story folk houses, either box-like or L-shaped, which incorporate spindlework and other decorative details in imitation of more elaborate and expensive Victorian styles. The decorative detailing was added to plain and practical vernacular forms countrywide in working-class urban districts and in farmhouses in the countryside. Wherever they are found, the houses are less elaborate and sophisticated than those they emulate. Five principal subtypes have been categorized, some like the side-gabled roof, one- and two-story forms are found across the country, while others, like the one- and two-story variants on the pyramidal folk form, are found only in the Southern states. Typically the practical form of the structure is retained without such additions as bays or elaborate moldings.

The houses are found across the United States and like other, contemporary Victorian styles, Folk Victorian enjoyed widespread popularity. Like other styles its very existence was made possible by the growth of the railroad system in the later nineteenth century. The trains made available heavy wood-working machinery, thus supplanting the skills of local carpenters and making economically possible detailing in a variety of styles and forms. Hitherto this was expensive to produce in locally available timber. Not only the machinery was now available though, Italianate or Queen Anne detailing, for example, could be bought at local lumber yards in pre-cut, jigsaw-fashioned lengths, ready for use at home. Thus the local vocabulary of forms of timber detailing, which was traditionally supplied by neighboring craftsmen for folk houses, could be supplemented by a series of fashionable and cheaply produced features that were standard countrywide.

These modish additions were normally grafted onto relatively unadorned, existing folk structures, most notably to that focal point of the façade of most houses of the time, the porch. The supports for the porch could be extensively styled—most popular were either Queen Anne-style turned spindles that offered the possibility of various forms of elaborate detail or Italianate Style square posts with chamfered corners.

The statement made by this newly fashionable addition to a simple folk house might be further embellished with elaborately cut lace-like spandrels above the posts, while the porch interior might be decorated with friezes suspended from its roof. Where the most popular form of applied decoration, Queen Anne spindlework, is used the underlying forms of the symmetrical façades can still be seen, serving to differentiate the designs from authentic Queen Anne buildings, which have varied wall and window treatments and an overall eclecticism of forms.

Queen Anne was only one of a number of fashionable styles which might be grafted on to an existing structure by means of the new ready-made detailing. The choice of detailing was wide, ranging from Greek Revival to Gothic and Italianate, and occasionally mixed elements from several different styles.

Above: House, High Street, Middletown, CT.

Above: House, Ludlow, VT. Greek Revival, but with a large arched balcony within the roof gable.

Folk Victorian houses may be seen in several regional variants across the United States. Local variants include, for example, the common, side-gabled, one-story type, which has received the addition of a second-story— popular in houses along the Gulf Coast. The essential symmetry of the house was retained and often embellished with Queen Anne spindlework. Other, front-gabled two-story forms with jigsaw-cut detailing are most often found in the Northeast, while narrow, one-room-wide, so-called "shotgun" types (so called because a gun could be shot straight through the house) were a characteristic form in towns and cities in the South.

Another common sub-typical form of Folk Victorian was the simple, symmetrical pyramidal-roofed type with characteristic porch running the entire length of the façade. In Southern states, the full-façade porch was often constructed in two tiers, while in Texas, porch friezes often feature jigsaw-cut stars, a motif used throughout the Lone Star state.

Historical styles could thus be adapted by Folk Victorian owners who were not employing architects to dictate a prevailing form. They therefore had the freedom to express their own preferences in building a distinctive dwelling that would reflect their personal tastes. Even such seemingly circumscribed styles as Greek Revival, which in standard designs used a set vocabulary of forms, could be adapted to individual preferences, as can be seen in a house at Ludlow, VT, which is Classical in style, but has a large arched balcony within the roof gable. Elements of the Greek Revival style are also used in the house with a tower at Haddam, Connecticut, which offers a striking mélange of styles, including a Greek Revival gable, Renaissance arches on the porch and windows, and a Second Empire lantern and tower. The fashion for Second Empire Baroque was featured in houses which combined elements drawn from the Italianate Style.

Above: House with Tower, Haddam, CT. A striking mélange of styles, including a Greek Revival gable, Renaissance arches on the porch and windows, and a Second Empire lantern and tower.

Above: Gothic Revival house, Haddam, CT. A simple frame house, with Gothic gingerbread and Renaissance arches on the porch.

Above: Luther Burbank House, Santa Rosa, CA; a simple Greek Revival house, modified in the 1870s.

Folk Victorian dwellings such as the Haddam house use a whole variety of fashionable current styles if not always in such profusion. Another simple frame house in Haddam is more restrained in its use of historic features. Here Gothic Revival elements predominate, with gothic gingerbread and Renaissance arches on the porch.

Folk Victorians, or Symmetrical Victorians, as they are sometimes known, survived as a separate form into the first decade of the twentieth century in all states until the form was supplanted by other modish eclectic styles, such as the Colonial Revival which persists into the twenty-first century.

Construction Elements—Windows

The evolution of style is revealed in the variety of windows used in American houses over the years. Glass was expensive at first, so the earliest colonial homes used small panes in leaded casement windows. In the eighteenth century, larger panes became available, and double hung sashes became more prevalent. Increasing Classicism is reflected in the Palladian window. More shapes became available, as builders sought to increase the light and ventilation of homes with increasingly sculptural shapes. Dormer windows increased the comfort level of upper floors, and expressed house styles in miniature.

Above: Diamond-paned casement, found in first period (seventeenth century) homes and Shingle Style and Colonial Revival houses.

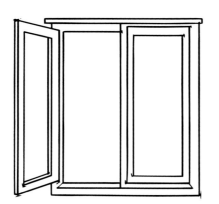

Above: Casement window; found in early colonial homes, Colonial Revival, and also some modernist houses.

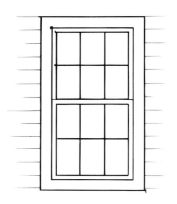

Above: Double-hung, six-over-six sash window, found on early Greek Revival houses.

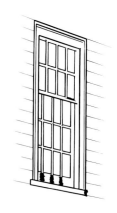

Above: Eight-over-twelve sash window. Twelve-over-twelve is also found; six-over-six and four-over-four are more common.

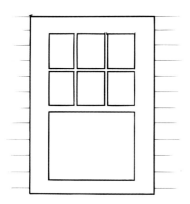

Above: Six-over-one sash window. Larger plate glass is a later development.

Above: Palladian window, a classical form common in Georgian and Colonial Revival houses.

Above: Gable window.

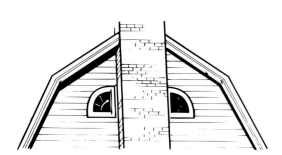

Above: Gable windows on a Dutch colonial house.

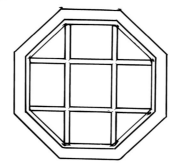

Above: Hexagonal window on modern Colonial Revival house; round and oval windows are also common in nineteenth and twentieth century architecture.

Above: Diamond-shaped window on modern Cape house.

Above: The large decorative diamond lattice set behind a plate-glass window on modern Colonial Revival houses imitates earlier leaded-glass colonial windows. The lattice pattern is larger, though, to avoid obstructing the view.

Above: Bay window on modern ranch house.

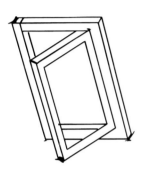

Above: Awning (swings from top, and opens outward or inward).

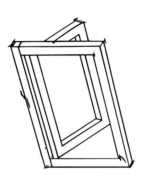

Above: Hopper (swings from bottom, and generally opens inward).

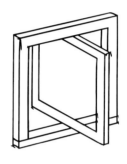

Above: Pivot; rotates from the middle.

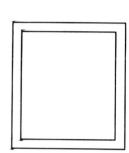

Above: Large plate-glass picture windows developed in the twentieth century and became a staple of suburban developments. The large expanse of glass reflected modern technology, and also offered the promise of contact with nature.

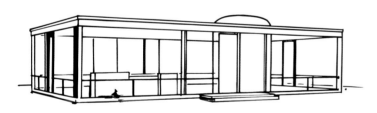

Left: Plate-glass curtain wall; Philip Johnson's Glass House, New Canaan, CT. Modern technology made it possible to create an entire wall of glass.

Above: Large round windows are found in Art Deco and Modernist homes. In the 1920s and 1930s, the windows frequently resemble portholes of ships; in the late twentieth century, they become much larger.

Above: Shaped windows are common on Postmodern houses; in this case, there is a symbolic connection to the seaside location.

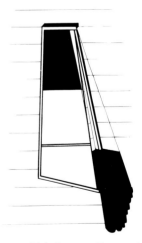

Above: Trapezoidal shape on Postmodern house. Contemporary architects sculpt with light and space in their designs.

Left: Dormer window with pedimented roof, found on mansard roof.

Above: Dormer window, with gable roof. Dormers take on a wide range of forms, reflecting the different stylistic periods.

Above: Dormer window, with semicircular roof.

Above: Dormer window with segmental roof, found on a French eclectic house.

Above: Dormer window with swan's neck gable roof (rare), found on a Colonial Revival house.

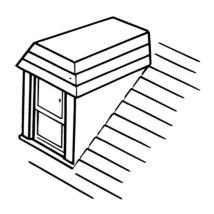

Above: Dormer window with shed roof.

Above: Dormer—jerkin-head, or clipped roof dormer. Frank Furness: Emlen Physick House, Cape May, NJ, 1878.

Above: Dormer—deck style, with hipped roof and flat top.

Chapter 5

Eclectic Revivals

Abby Moor

A number of factors shaped the stylistic eclecticism of late-nineteenth century American architecture. The English colonial style of the Eastern Seaboard and New England, and the Spanish colonial style of the West Coast and Southwestern states were seen as the formal types which best represented a genuine American heritage. Although the United States had no distant architectural past, the Spanish and English colonial designs were seen to embody the historical era of the founding of the republic, while simultaneously serving as a perceived "immediate" continuation of European high architectural traditions of the more distant, mythical past. However, one of the more interesting questions which arose as a broad spectrum of "revival" styles emerged—ranging from the Renaissance and Classical, to the Medieval and Colonial—was "whose origin is most appropriate?"

Above: Longfellow and Harlow: Colonial House, Brattle Street, Cambridge, MA, 1887. A very accurate version of the eighteenth century Georgian style.

Dutch Colonial Revival

Above: Dutch Colonial Revival style house. The intersecting gables are never found in original Dutch colonial houses.

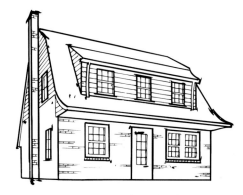

Above: Dutch Colonial Revival house, early twentieth century. This house features a pronounced Flemish "kick" in the upturn of the eaves.

Above: Western false-front buildings; the false gables of Dutch urban architecture may have inspired the false fronts which became familiar in Western architecture.

The trend toward architectural eclecticism, which began in America around 1880, reflected the need for appropriate and adaptable styles, which could serve for both new housing and private landmark buildings. To be successful, these stylistic renewals had to offer the possibility of both prestige and more common interpretation by designers and builders. The nineteenth century had been marked by a mass immigration of European settlers. By the end of the century large corporate and mercantile interests, whose owners and directors required their own suitable architecture, had come to dominate the realms of production, distribution, employment, and consumption. These factors also combined to create the widespread need for popular housing at the opposite end of the spectrum to the class of fabulously wealthy patrons seeking built symbols of wealth, power, and taste.

Certainly by the 1890s what we now refer to as the Eclectic movement in architecture was a full-blown "revival" movement. In part it was informed by current Arts and Crafts designers who advocated a return to the vernacular and a stylistic expression based upon regional building traditions. Recourse to a regional vernacular style was seen by some as a moral proposition. It had to do with how individuals and nations legitimately formed their identities.

But at the same time, most of the American architects who sought to be fashionable were not adverse to drawing upon the achievements of their predecessors, especially in designing elaborate townhouses and mansions for their wealthiest patrons. Stylistic eclecticism became a form of merchandising the architect's products. But unlike the efforts of preceding Victorian practitioners, whose work was at times characterized by an unfettered mix of past stylistic motifs, the Eclectic movement emphasized a new authenticity in the adaptation of period styles. In this approach it was directly influenced, initially by the 1876 American Centennial Exposition in Philadelphia, where the exhibition buildings drew directly upon architectural formulas imported from England, and subsequently by the 1893 World's Columbian Exposition in Chicago at which the exhibition facilities were constructed in a commanding Neoclassical form. This new direction toward the more correct reinterpretation of the past placed new value on the precise rendition of European-derived styles. The trend was also deeply influenced by the large number of architecture and design source books and magazines now available. Such sources provided a vast array of models from the colonial and more distant European past from which designers and architects could draw their inspiration, and from which potential patrons, no matter how modest, could chose.

During the final two decades of the nineteenth century, the Eclectic Revival was thus born discreetly, as a new generation of European-trained, American architects commenced the construction of a number of opulent homes for hugely affluent patrons. As their new architectural statements filtered down into the less ambitious housing market, a wide selection of styles came to compete with one another for popularity in the

Left: Neoclassical house, Evanston, IL.

fashionable marketplace where newly sharpened distinctions were increasingly made between each stylistic "period" type.

A further significant factor which stimulated the late-nineteenth century's move toward a national preference for eclecticism was the widespread appearance of the balloon-framed house. From its development in the 1830s, this construction method changed the course of housing in America and facilitated the unparalleled growth of new suburbs throughout the country. The majority of American houses had always been of wood, rather than masonry. The balloon-frame method effectively did away with traditional joinery by producing timber-milled materials to standard specifications, and required little more than partially-skilled labor and mass-manufactured hardware for the construction of a new home. Balloon-framed houses took the form of more or less standardized rectangular boxes, and could be constructed rapidly of inexpensive materials and person-alized by imaginative detailing. As discussed in the previous chapter some quite fantastic combinations of subsidiary spaces—such as bays, balconies, and cupolas—were introduced with all manner of stylistically mixed detailing in milled-wood pieces. Under these conditions, housing design became an exercise in the marketing of fashionable styles as potential occupants increasingly bought into the identities they aspired to and style itself became an American commodity.

Colonial Revival

Following the Centennial celebrations of 1876 in Philadelphia, and still aching from the strife of the Civil War, America was drawn to a romanticized recollection of the Enlightenment values and achievements of the era of the founding of the republic. A renewed taste arose for the stability and elegance of the architectural heritage of the colonial past, and the Colonial Revival style in contemporary architecture was born of this nostalgia.

Much like the subsequent impact of the 1893 World Columbian Exposition, the effects upon national taste of the year-long 1876 festivities were deeply felt. For celebratory and historic purposes, the exhibition buildings had been constructed in a carefully researched "colonial" style. What began as an historical acknowledgement, however, quickly became the height of fashionable taste as the American public came to embrace rather than deny its national past.

The Colonial Revival style thereafter enjoyed ongoing appeal, becoming a mainstay of housing design in America from its origin in about 1880 through the post-World War II era, and never really disappearing. Over that period the style developed a great deal of formal variety, depending on how much an architect or designer departed from or enhanced original historical prototypes. This is especially evident in alternative treatments

Colonial Revival

Above: Colonial Revival style small house. The Colonial Revival gained momentum after the 1876 Centennial exhibition in Philadelphia, which called attention to our national heritage.

Above: Simple Colonial Revival house, published in *The Books of a Thousand Homes, vol. I: 500 Small House Plans*, New York, 1923. The Colonial Revival was easily adapted for more modest homes, and became one of the most popular revival styles.

of details in and on doorways and windows. Non-historicised housing types also received a veneer of colonial-style ornamentation meant to mimic original colonial models and appeal to a pervading sense of national heritage.

Generally, identifying characteristics include a generic Classicism and a great attention to the detailing of doors and windows. Sashes were usually double-hung with multiple glazing. Windows are organized in pairs, or are triple-hung, often with false shutters. All façade features are typically symmetrically distributed, with the entrance door centered. The latter may be enclosed beneath a single porch or one running the full length of the façade and supported on a platform beneath a colonnaded hipped roof. The door is usually highlighted in the overall composition by a broken pediment or perhaps a simpler form of crown. In more historically accurate examples, as in the original models, there is an emphasis on the quality of craftsmanship. Floor plans tend to be acutely symmetrical, and ornamentation may include restrained and understated Classically-derived detailing. Most Colonial Revival houses are of two stories.

One subtype, often referred to as the "Georgian Revival" style, looked directly to original models in England as well as to colonial reinterpretations. Many surviving landmark buildings are of this popular category and display a restrained elegance even if they are

sometimes quite modest in scale. The best of these, however, do not borrow directly from their prototypes, but are based on study and research, laying the foundation for an informed reinterpretation of original models. This approach gained popularity between 1900 and 1910. The results were at once accurate and evocative of original colonial examples. Landmark examples include the Westbury House in Long Island designed by the British architect George Crawley and dating from c. 1906, and a great number of houses by the successful New York architectural firm of McKim, Mead and White, who also designed in the Shingle Style.

Above: Colonial Revival house, Brunswick, ME.

Above: Colonial Revival house, Newton, MA.

Above: Colonial Revival house, Waltham, MA.

Above: Colonial Revival house, Kennebunk, ME.

Above: McKim, Mead and White: John L. Andrew House, 32 Hereford Street, Boston, MA, 1884–1886. A blend of Georgian Revival and Italian Renaissance.

Left: Baxter House, Bowdoin College, Brunswick, ME. Colonial Revival house, early 1900s.

Above left: McKim, Mead and White: 199 Commonwealth Avenue, Boston, MA, 1890. An example of a Federal Revival house, blending well in the context of Boston architecture.

Above right: McKim, Mead and White: Pickman House, 303 Commonwealth Avenue, Boston, MA, 1895. Inspired by the local tradition of bow-front houses, this house echoes the early nineteenth century Greek Revival in Boston.

Left: John H. Pierce House, Pierce Park, Lincoln, MA, 1900. A very close copy of the Longfellow House, Cambridge, MA, (1759).

Neoclassical Revival

Controlled and unmannered in comparison to the contemporary Beaux-Arts style, the Neoclassical Revival style equally demonstrated the current fashion for a Classical vocabulary inspired by the 1893 Columbian Exposition in Chicago. It drew primarily from Greek and, less so, Roman prototypes, and was dominated by the Greek orders. Moldings are severe rather than ornamentally enriched, statuary never stands along the roofline or on the façade, and the round arch infrequently appears. The impression is one of grace combined with post-and-lintel construction, although modern, reinforced materials were used. The scale and proportions of the style are suitably massive, but it also became quite popular in middle-class housing where the scale was refined to reflect the more modest demeanor of the buildings, and orders could be of both single and double height. Surfaces were usually burnished or were treated to give a similar impression.

The frontage is dominated by a pedimented portico supported by free-standing columns, the whole composition characterized by a rational and symmetrical distribution of parts. The style typically has slim, simplified columns of the Ionic or Corinthian orders, and may well combine the two, whereas this type of formal amalgamation appeared infrequently in the original

Above: Thomas MacDonough Russell House, 343 High Street, Middletown, CT, 1901–1902.

Above: J. Eugene Freeman: Alexander Dunsmuir House, 2960 Peralta Oaks Ct., Oakland, CA, 1899.

American Classical Revival and Greek Revival models. Such admixture was facilitated by the debut of readily available, mass-manufactured architectural details produced of industrial composites. Colonnaded, sometimes semi-circular, porticos and gabled extensions appear with some frequency as lateral extensions. Varieties of windows include the horizontal transome set above the window pane, and arched, paired or even triple windows and bay windows—the last extending from the side of the main mass.

Curved porticos of the colossal order appeared rarely in original models, whereas in the nineteenth century the Neoclassical balustraded parapet along the roofline which echoed a raised porch on the ground story made its appearance, but was again atypical of original revival examples. Another telltale sign of the Neoclassical is the use of the more flamboyant broken pediment which is complex in outline and placed above the principal door or individual windows. As the Neoclassical style developed the original fluted column was sometimes transformed into a square,

free-standing pier of broad proportions, and typically lacking a capital.

Between six and eight subtypes of the style have been identified. The most common were either of double height with a principal full-height porch of about one-third the length of the façade, and colonnaded in the colossal order with pedimented and gabled roof above, or the same double-height porch motif occupying the full length of the façade and bearing a flat roof. The latter type was especially popular between 1925 and 1950. During the same period the one-story cottage type with a dominant centralized dormer, hipped roof, and colonnaded porch of either part or full width was also fashionable for smaller homes. Here the porch was covered by the overhang of the main hipped roof. There are also a number of other subtypes that appeared less frequently. The style was popular in the South, but continues even today in larger-scale urban houses where it serves partially as a sign of the owner's aspirations for status, and it stands as an architectural metaphor for both colonial American and European social distance.

Above: Neoclassical house, now Admissions Office, Bowdoin College, Brunswick, ME.

Right: Robert Swain Peabody (1845–1917) and John Goddard Stearns (d. 1917): Louis Stoddard House, Prospect Street, New Haven, CT, 1907.

Below: Stephen Bartlett: Connolly House, Boston College, Hammond Street, Chestnut Hill, MA, 1902.

Left: Neoclassical Revival. Connolly House, Boston College, Hammond Street, Newton, MA, 1902. The monumental Ionic portico sets the tone for this large suburban house.

Right: Sears "Magnolia" model house. The most upscale models of mail-order houses also offered Neoclassical designs.

Above: Brown and VonBeren: house, Prospect Street, New Haven, CT, 1905.

Above: Parker, Thomas and Rice: Frederick Lothrop Ames House, now Donahue Hall, Stonehill College, North Easton, MA, 1905.

Above: Governor's Mansion, 99 Cambridge Road, Maple Bluff (near Madison), WI, 1928.

Tudor Revival

Main characteristics of this well-known and popular style, which ran from about 1890 to 1940, include a dramatically and steeply high-pitched roof dominated by conspicuous cross gabling and often side gables with false rather than constitutional half-timbering, which is present on over fifty percent of examples. Immense multi-flued chimneys are typically crowned with ornamental chimney pots, and buildings in the style commonly have tall, slender windows, which appear in multiple groups and have multi-pane glazing. The principal entry door is generally inset into the façade beneath an arch (either rounded or Tudor arched). Although the Tudor style was usually executed in either stone or brick, other varieties of cladding include wood and stucco, some of these examples having simulated thatched roofs and parapeted gables. At least six distinct subtypes of the style have been identified in domestic housing.

The style is amongst the most highly romantic and picturesque of the so-called vernacular revival styles, and like other "revivals" of the late nineteenth century confirms a design trend striving for greater accuracy in its use of source material. The Tudor Revival was a development upon both the preceding Queen Anne and Stick Style types. It consistently incorporated the latest in modern materials, while both its distinctive form and general ethos were based upon new interpretations of late-medieval, English vernacular forms (though it also drew from the nineteenth century Gothic Revival style in England and is therefore something of a composite type). Prototypes included a wide variety of structures as diverse as the vernacular rural house and to the more manorial residence. Forms consistently emphasize this Anglo-medieval origin, while decorative ornamentation, especially around entry porches and even windows, may be more eclectic in nature and based upon a diversity of models, primarily from the Italian Renaissance, but even including the motifs of open eaves and exposed rafters preferred by practitioners of the contemporary American Arts and Crafts movement. The name of the style is somewhat misleading, as formally there is little

Above: Tudor Revival house, East Hampton, New York. The English Tudor style offered a structural clarity with its half-timbering and also the appeal of tradition.

Above: Tudor half-timbering. In later variants the half-timber pattern would be imitated with boards on the surface of the stucco.

Above: Tudor arch.

Above: English Cotswold style small house; the Sears "Willard" home, 1932. The steeply sweeping entrance gable and informal plan was associated with English country cottages.

Above: Tudor Revival house, from *Loizeaux's Plan Book No. 7*, Plainfield, NJ, 1927; a popular design.

Above: "Modern English Home," from *Loizeaux's Plan Book No. 7*, 1927.

Above: "False-thatch House" published in *Loizeaux's Plan Book No. 7*, Plainfield, NJ, 1927. The look of traditional thatch was imitated with shingles.

Above: Blithewold, 101 Ferry Road, Bristol, RI, 1908. Originally built as a Shingle Style house in 1896, Blithewold was rebuilt as an English country house after a fire in 1906.

Above: William H. Van Tine: Fair Lane, the Henry and Clara Bryant Ford House, Evergreen Road, Dearborn, MI, begun 1912. A blend of Prairie Style and English or Scottish baronial architecture resulted after the initial plans of Marion Mahoney Griffin, a former associate of Frank Lloyd Wright, were replaced by the eclectic architect Van Tine.

Above: George A. Crawley: Westbury House, 71 Old Westbury Road, Old Westbury, NY, 1906. An English style house of the period of Charles II.

Left: Casement window from Stan Hywet Hall.

representative of the original sixteenth century English Tudor period.

The earliest dwellings in the style were exclusive, architect-designed houses dependent upon English prototypes from the Elizabethan and Jacobean periods. Something of a pseudo-Tudor style emerged around 1900 in more modest housing in which steeply gabled forms and some characteristic detailing was superimposed upon wooden-framed houses with traditional spaces. However, this modest variant remained comparatively uncommon and only lasted until just after World War I.

Above: Charles Schneider: Stan Hywet Hall, the Frank A. Seiberling House, 714 N. Portage Path, Akron, OH, 1912–1915. The name "Stan Hywet" is old English for "Stone Quarry;" this sixty-five room Tudor Revival country house was built for the founder of the Goodyear company.

Although buildings in this style were known slightly earlier, during the 1920s and 1930s they became extremely fashionable for both large and small American homes. As the style increased in popularity it quickly incorporated a new technology of masonry veneering which closely imitated the play of rich materials on landmark examples such as the Stan Hywet Hall of 1912–1915 in Ohio with its strongly asymmetrical front façade and classic Tudor Revival features. The Tudor became a leading style in suburban housing, easily rivaling the Colonial Revival in the variety of its individual interpretations, and the Craftsman in its impact upon the American suburb. As taste in fashion began to change nearing World War II, the Tudor style faded in popularity, but reappeared again in the mid-1970s enjoying something of its own revival. It thereafter remained a popular, albeit much simplified suburban house style.

Above: Smith, Hinchman and Grylls: Meadow Brook Hall, Oakland University, Rochester, MI, 1926–1929.
A 110-room English Tudor castle, built for the Dodge family; now owned by Oakland University.

Right: Ralph Walker and Leon
Gillette: Coe Hall, Planting
Fields Road, Oyster Bay, NY,
1918–1921.

Below: Tudor house,
Easthampton, Long Island, NY,
c. 1920s.

Left: Ralph Adams Cram (1863–1942), Charles Francis Wentworth (1841–1897) and Bertram Grosvenor Goodhue (1869–1924): Tudor style house, Brattle Street, Cambridge, MA, 1892. Half-timbering became extremely popular for suburban homes.

Below: Tudor style house, Waltham, MA, 1920s.

Left: Tudor cottage, Mendon, VT. Smaller houses, influenced by Cotswold cottages, were very popular during the 1920s and 1930s. Sears and other mail-order house companies offered several models.

Below: Tudor style house, Newton, MA, 1920s.

Chateauesque

During the American Eclectic Revival period there was also a strong current of interest which looked not to English, but to French architectural tradition. It is generally thought to have originated with the architect Richard Morris Hunt. Hunt was not overly fond of English-derived design, and was among the first generation of American architects to finish architectural coursework at the famed Ecole des Beaux Arts in Paris. By the 1880s his French-derived style was well-suited to patrons such as the Vanderbilt family for whom Hunt executed a number of spectacular commissions. His formal Parisian education had made him partial to French design, and this Francophile taste was eagerly shared by many of his encouraging employers. A townhouse (now destroyed) designed by him in the early 1880s for William K. Vanderbilt in New York was the earliest example of the Chateauesque style in America. Its influence led to a new national taste for the style, which other well-to-do clients shortly imitated, aspiring to possess its massive and imposing forms of white limestone which Hunt had based directly upon French Renaissance models of the Loire Valley.

As the style developed in America, its drew upon a large spectrum of details gleaned from stately French originals, although Hunt's own work often betrays his

Above: Richard Morris Hunt: Ogden Goelet House, Ochre Court, Salve Regina University, Newport, RI, 1892. Built as a private house, this is now the administration building for Salve Regina University.

Above: Detlef Lienau: Lockwood-Mathews Mansion, 295 West Avenue, Norwalk, CT, 1864–1869. An eclectic sixty-two-room mansion with elements of the Gothic Revival, Second Empire, and Chateauesque styles.

Above: Chateauesque urban house. French chateaux provided a rich source of inspiration for urban upper classes.

Above: Nicholas J. Clayton: Walter Gresham House (the Bishop's Palace), 1402 Broadway, Galveston, TX, 1887–1893.

preference for specifically sixteenth century models. Chief characteristics of the style include a dramatic focus on sharply pitched and hipped roof structures adorned with a plethora of richly ornamented, vertical detailing such as spires, finials, pinnacles, turrets, and sculpturally-shaped chimneys, as well as roof cresting and numerous wall-dormers which break upward through the cornice.

Certainly, the style was uncommon due to its flamboyant character, the quality of masonry, and expensive craftsmanship required, but it is found in other examples across the country from between about 1880 and 1910. Although landmark buildings other than those by Hunt tended to be both smaller and less elaborate, these were usually aspirational in comparison to the high style of established taste evident in Hunt's most important surviving structure, the Biltmore. Completed in 1895, this was designed for George Washington Vanderbilt, and is now promoted as one of the the largest private homes ever constructed in the United States.

Designed as the centerpiece of a spacious rural site, the exterior of the house is a compilation of rich detailing borrowed from a collection of different buildings constructed in the same architectural style. The elaborate Biltmore compared favorably with sixteenth century French models in both its magnitude and opulence, and made an unmistakable statement about its patron's aspirations to mimic a European tradition of country life. For obvious reasons, the influence of the style on American architecture was not widespread. The style was virtually impossible to translate into a vernacular form. However, other examples of the style, dating as late as around 1910, are most frequent in the Northeast.

Right: Charles Brigham (1841–1925): Burrage House, 314 Commonwealth Avenue, Boston, MA, 1899. Inspired by the Vanderbilt House in New York, this is an impressive example of the French Renaissance style.

Below: C.P.H. Gilbert (1863–1952): Isaac D. Fletcher House, East 79th Street, New York, NY, 1897–1899.

Left: House, Walnut Street, Newton, MA, 1890s.

Below: Joseph W. Northrup: Chateauesque house, Whitney Avenue, New Haven, CT, 1896.

Right: William H. Allen
(1884–1935): house,
Whitney Avenue, New
Haven, CT, 1895.

Below: De La Salle,
Chateauesque house,
Bellevue Avenue,
Newport, RI.

Beaux Arts

Richard Morris Hunt's influence, however, was not limited to his relatively rare buildings in the Chateauesque style. At the height of his career he was selected as one of several American architects trained at the Ecole des Beaux Arts to design principal buildings in the Beaux Arts style at the enormous World's Columbian Exposition of 1893 in Chicago. Beaux Arts designs quickly became the prototypes for innumerable large-scale commercial and public buildings across the country. In the realm of private housing, the style was again largely excluded from a more vernacular translation because of the expense of its heavy masonry and lavish detailing.

With its formal vocabulary grounded in the Classical tradition—incorporating both Greek and Roman heritage—and equally drawn from the Renaissance reinterpretations of Italy, the Beaux Arts style espoused the architectural ethics of rationality and symmetry. With its arcuated façades and groups of paired or equidistant columns it also incorporated sumptuous ornamentation in the form of floral garlands and swags, shields, panels, and friezes. Columns were principally Ionic or perhaps Corinthian, offset by engaged pilasters. Windows were rhythmic and symmetrical, and central doorways were pronounced. In Renaissance fashion, the ground-story façade was typically rusticated. The type is distinguished by either the flat or low-pitched hipped roof, or the more majestic mansard roof which derives from seventeenth and eighteenth century Renaissance prototypes. As a primarily Classical style, the Beaux Arts shares some detailing with other, contemporary Classical Revival styles, but these rarely embody such vivacious decorative surfaces, sculpturally accentuated cornices, or window and door surrounds of such intricate detail. Other Classically derived styles employ quoins with altogether more restraint.

Richard Morris Hunt was not the only, or even the most influential practitioner of the style, but his strong Francophile sentiments popularized him as one of its leading exponents. Other fashionable practitioners who helped to spread the style between 1890 and the late 1920s included the New York firm of McKim, Mead, and White, whose outstanding houses are among the most renowned domestic expressions of the style.

Above: Richard Morris Hunt (1827–1895): Marble House, Bellevue Avenue, Newport, RI, 1888–1892. This house was inspired by the Petit Trianon at Versailles.

Left: Beaux-Arts classicism in a private house; Vanderbilt Estate, Hyde Park, NY. A perfect example of academic classicism, skillfully recreating the image of ancient classical culture.

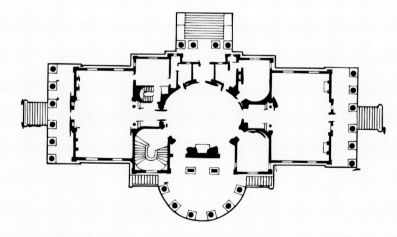

Above: Plan of the Vanderbilt Estate, Hyde Park, NY.

Right: Richard Morris Hunt (1827–1895): The Breakers, Ochre Point Avenue, Newport, RI, 1895. This enormous summer house, built for Cornelius Vanderbilt II, was inspired by northern Italian palazzi.

Below: Richard Morris Hunt: The Breakers, Newport, RI, 1895.

Left: John Merven Carrère (1858–1911) and Thomas Hastings (1860–1929): Nemours, the Alfred I. Dupont Estate, Wilmington, DE, 1909–1910.

Below: Horace Trumbauer (1868–1938): The Elms, Bellevue Avenue, Newport, RI, 1898. This house was modeled after the Chateau d'Asnieres near Paris.

The Breakers in Newport Rhode Island, designed by Hunt for Cornelius Vanderbilt around 1895, is one of the earliest and most important landmark examples of the style in domestic architecture. It is typical of domestic examples in that it was situated in a semi-urban environment in which the homes of the affluent clustered, and it was architect-designed specifically for the client. Similar landmark examples appear around the nation's capital, and major Victorian cities such as San Francisco. Most of these were constructed before the middle of the second decade of the new century, although the style continued to be used for similar homes, typically the property of industrial tycoons, until the collapse of the economic market in the late 1920s.

One side effect of the importation into America of the Ecole des Beaux Arts aesthetic was the impact it had on early twentieth century urban planning. One of the main principles of the style was a particular concern for formal relationships of space around and between structures. This principle stimulated America's "City Beautiful" campaign of around 1900. Hunt was among the first American architects to help plan an overall civic space based on such principles in the World's Columbian Exposition of 1893. A number of important urban centers shortly thereafter executed similar designs in their own communities, including Philadelphia and Cleveland. Carefully planned suburban communities of landmark Beaux Arts designed houses soon arose with tree-lined streets and open public parks also based upon the Beaux Arts ideal, suggesting how quickly the nation was able to adapt new strategies to its own needs.

Right: Stanford White (1853–1906): Rosecliff, Bellevue Avenue, Newport, RI, 1899–1901.

French Eclectic

The third of the French revival styles to gain popularity in the early twentieth century was the so-called "French Eclectic." As with the slightly earlier yet more formal and pretentious Chateauesque and Beaux Arts styles, the French Eclectic drew directly on French prototypes, but in this case expressed a specific taste for vernacular models from rural France, preferring to emulate farm buildings and manor houses of the Norman period. The style drew on a wide spectrum of sources from the French countryside, and was characterized by both asymmetrical farmhouse forms and symmetrical manor-house types; thus shapes, materials, and detailing are extremely rich and diverse. These many examples of the style, however, are allied in their dependence upon the sharply hipped roof, outward flaring eaves, and absence of a predominant cross gable above the front façade. Houses constructed in the style are typically of masonry—stone or brick—with stuccoed walls. They may have strictly decorative half-timbering recalling the vernacular origins of the contemporaneous Tudor Revival style and are equally medievalizing in their impact.

Of the three common subtypes, the symmetrical, asymmetrical, and towered or "Norman cottage" type, the latter is by far the most fantastic and boasts a dominating rounded tower with a conical roof. The tower acts as the principal entryway and stands at the inside junction of an L-shaped plan.

Above: Albert Kahn (1869–1942): Edsel Ford House, Grosse Pointe, MI, 1927.

There are few examples of this vernacular and picturesque style dating from before 1920, but the style did become somewhat popular for suburban housing during the 1920s and 1930s, though after that it fell from favor until the post-war period. Its popularity resulted from combined factors. Following WWI a number of photographic studies of French vernacular housing were published in America, including in 1921 *Small French Buildings*, which included drawings by the New York architects Henry M. Polhemus and Louis A. Coffin, both among early devotees of the type. Equally important, American servicemen had journeyed to France during WWI, where they saw for themselves the many personalized examples of vernacular country dwellings. Together these factors creat-

Above: French Eclectic house, twentieth century. The steep hipped roof is characteristic of French design.

Above: French Eclectic house with round tower, twentieth century. Echoing Norman chateaux, this house has an informal L-shape, round tower, massive chimney, and even an eyebrow dormer.

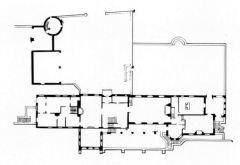

Above: Frederick J. Sterner, with Polhemus and Coffin: plan of "Falaise," Capt. Harry F. Guggenheim House, Long Island, NY, 1920s.

Above: Frederick J. Sterner, with Polhemus and Coffin: "Falaise," Capt. Harry F. Guggenheim
House, Long Island, NY, 1920s.

ed both a taste for the style and provided models from which architects and builders could work.

One of the most important surviving landmark examples of the style is "Falaise," the grand country house designed for Harry F. Guggenheim—a gentleman of Francophile tastes who had served in France during the war—by the architect Frederick J. Sterner in collaboration with Polhemus and Coffin, who had become authorities in America on the subject of French-style houses. This grand Norman-style home dates from the 1920s. It is situated along the "Gold Coast" of northwestern Long Island, which at the time boasted many expensive homes designed in the latest architectural fashions.

"Falaise" is based specifically upon Norman-style country dwellings, which were characterized by substantial enclosed entry courts. Viewed from the back, it has an unmistakable medieval flavor in the irregularity of windows and dormers, the steep roofs composed of tiling, and the tall fortress-like masonry walls. From the front, however, the building gives the impression of

being comparatively small and has an unexpected feeling of quiet intimacy in keeping with its vernacular ethos. Detailing throughout is inspired directly by medieval precedent, including the traditional, diamond-paned casement windows.

Above: William Adams Delano (1874–1960) and Chester Holmes Aldrich (1871–1940): Elizabeth Hooker House, New Haven, CT, 1914.

Above: House, Chestnut Hill, MA.

Italian Renaissance

The so-called "Italian Renaissance" revival style which ran from between approximately 1890 to 1935 was in part a Utopian metaphor in material form. It espoused grand architectural forms, sunlight, and formal gardens in place of steel and technology, and asserted itself as a vivid icon of "civilized" Mediterranean, rather than regional American, identity. With its evocation of luxuriously dry, habitable climates and resistance to the built traditions of North America and Northern Europe, it carried forward the passions of early twentieth century American "Mediterraneanizers" for Edith Wharton's popular *Italian Villas and Their Gardens* published in 1904 with illustrations by Maxfield Parrish.

In fact, this was not the first Italian Renaissance revival in American architecture, but the second, having been preceded in the mid-nineteenth century by the Italianate Style, which was only inexactly based upon Italian architectural models. The new, second revival was more faithful to its prototypes and, following the appearance of some rare but superb eclectic landmark examples, went on to influence design in American houses until about 1930.

Its main characteristics included a very low-pitched, hipped roof. Tiles were typically used for roofing material. The pitch extended into overhanging eaves carried on ornate corbels situated at rhythmic intervals and sometimes paired. The upper story followed Italian

Above: House, Morris Avenue, Morristown, NJ.

tradition in being shorter than the more symbolically predominant and taller ground-story façade, and may be found set back from the lower elevation, or divided from it by a running entablature sometimes broken or surmounted by a central triumphal arch motif. Windows were thus smaller in scale and proportion, and less ornate in treatment. The main ground-story façade carries the dominant decorative treatment, having round-arched windows or window surrounds with engaged columns or pilasters, or simple pediments alternating with architraves. Quoins may be used to imply or even mimic rustication on the ground story, and also served to dramatize receding and projecting masses. The whole of the building, usually in the form of a "mock"

Above: Italian Renaissance style urban house. The Renaissance villas of Rome and Florence provided excellent models of urban architecture.

Above: Italian Renaissance Revival house, Washington, D.C., 1907–1908. A formal house with a Palladian arch motif on the second-floor balcony.

Above: These houses were based on originals such as this, Filippo Brunelleschi's Pazzi Chapel, church of Santa Croce, Florence, 1440–1461.

Above: Italian style suburban house, from Loizeaux's *Plan Book No. 7*, 1927. Simpler Mediterranean-style houses were popular across the country.

Left: House,
Commonwealth Avenue,
Newton, MA, c. 1920s.

villa, was often raised upon a podium with full or partial balustrade and centralized steps. Designs were strictly symmetrical.

Light-hued stone or brick masonry was employed throughout the landmark examples. It is typically rendered with a smooth layer of pale stucco. As the style increased in popularity and found its place in more medium-sized homes in the growing suburban sprawl, technological advances of WWI facilitated the application of a single layer of brick or stone over an otherwise wood-framed structure. Especially favored for larger homes in the American South and parts of the Mid-West,

the style had decreased in popularity by the mid-1930s, and was never really appropriate for popular housing.

The John Deering house in Miami, called "Vizcaya," and dating from 1916, ranks alongside the Isabella Stewart Gardner House (now Museum) of 1899 in Boston by the architect William Sears, as certainly one of the very best and most authentic Italian Renaissance style landmark houses in America.

It was conceived as a country villa and winter residence in the outlying Florida countryside. The patron, James Deering, invited the New York designer Paul Chalfin, who had studied in Rome, to oversee the

Left: House, West
Hampton, Long Island, NY,
c. 1960s.

planning, and Chalfin appointed Francis Burrall Hoffman as the supervising architect, with the added attraction that Hoffman had studied at the Ecole des Beaux Arts in Paris. Chalfin envisaged Vizcaya as a literal recreation of an Italian rural estate in the same way that Isabella Steward Gardner set out to virtually reproduce a sixteenth century Venetian villa. The motivation of both was less to revive than to transplant. However, due to Chalfin's vision, Vizcaya is somewhat unique amongst early twentieth century grand American houses in its refined and authentic treatment of all architectural features, as well as furnishings which were gathered from throughout Europe, including original cornices and stone fireplaces, furniture, fixtures and fittings, and tapestries, and even walls and ceilings. The extraordinary craftsmanship and detail of the house are unsurpassed. Although flamboyant in its interiors, the house is nonetheless reticent in its architectural design. Concessions were made in part to modern technology in the concrete walls, which reproduce the stucco-rendered

Above: Vail Mansion, Morristown, NJ, 1916–1918.

masonry of the Italian prototypes, and are properly heightened by lighter-hued stone ornament and the tiled roof. Architectural stonework, water, and an extensive Italianate garden worked together to produce a remarkably convincing and organic design overall.

Above: Willard T. Sears (1837–1920): Isabella Stewart Gardner House, 280 Fenway, Boston, MA, 1902. Mrs. Gardner took an active role in the design of this mansion, planned to house her art collection.

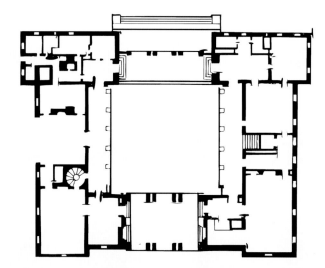

Right: Francis Burrall Hoffman: plan of "Vizcaya," the James Deering House, Miami, FL, 1916.

Below: Francis Burrall Hoffman (1882–1980): "Vizcaya," the James Deering House, Miami, FL, 1916.

Above: Villa Montalvo, the James Duval Phelan House, Saratoga, CA, 1912.

Above: Tournament House, the William Wrigley, Jr., House, 391 South Orange Grove Boulevard, Pasadena, CA, 1908–1914. This Mediterranean house is now the headquarters of the Tournament of Roses Association.

Above: J.W. Dolliver: Grand Island Mansion, 13415 Grand Island Road, Walnut Grove, CA, 1917. A large Italian Renaissance style villa, with fifty-eight rooms.

Left: Aldredge House, 5500 Swiss Ave, Dallas, TX, 1917.

Above: Dwight James Baum (1886–1939): Cà D'zan, John Ringling winter house, 5401 Bay Shore Road, Sarasota, FL, 1924–1926. The style of the house was inspired by the Doge's Palace in Venice and the old Madison Square Garden in New York.

The Mission Style

Architectural revival styles which developed out of the Spanish tradition emerged during the final quarter of the nineteenth century. They originated as part of the broad wave of cultural recollection of America's colonial past, which swept the country after the 1876 Centennial Exposition in Philadelphia. Their debut on the Pacific Coast followed closely upon and complemented the Georgian prototypes that had arisen along the Atlantic seaboard. The inception of Spanish revival styles occurred largely in California, but quickly spread to other areas with a Spanish colonial heritage, including New Mexico, Arizona, Texas, and Florida.

Most commonly referred to in its abbreviated form, the "Mission" revival style, dating from circa 1890 to 1920, at first centered in California where surviving examples are still concentrated. Several extant California missions, such as that in Santa Barbara completed as late as 1820, and those in San Louis Obispo, San Diego, and Santa Clara, remained as prominent links to the recent Hispanic past. Their restrained forms, adjacent gardens, and arcaded monastic complexes established landscaping and architectural models for construction and building design along the Pacific Coast.

Although a rebirth of the "Mission" aesthetic had been proposed in the late 1880s by a few individual Californian architects enthused by Arts and Crafts praise for regional vernacular tradition, the earliest Mission revival buildings did not appear until the mid-1890s when architectural details isolated from the original Mission Style were used on a modest scale in some commercial and public structures. A free transmission of elements derived from the type gained some momentum, for example, when the Southern Pacific and Santa Fe railroads approved the Mission Style for its stations throughout the Southwest. At first, however, elements from the style appeared only sporadically in domestic housing, mostly on a modest scale, and also in a few larger-scale landmark examples, but few of these have survived. The style was then more freely adopted in other areas, spreading to the East, where its popularity was stimulated by new trendsetting construction and architectural magazines. In suburban housing, the Mission Style was ultimately supplanted after World

Right: Spanish Mission Style bungalow, based on bungalow designed by J. T. Pomeroy, architect. Published in *The Books of a Thousand Homes, vol. I: 500 Small House Plans*, New York, 1923. The entrance of this small bungalow leads to a nearly enclosed patio.

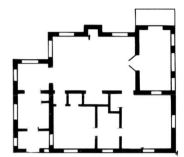

Right: Plan of a Spanish Mission bungalow, J.T. Pomeroy, architect. Published in *The Books of a Thousand Homes, vol. I: 500 Small House Plans*, New York, 1923.

Above: Spanish Mission Style house, from *Loizeaux's Plan Book No. 7*, 1927.

Right: Mail-order Spanish Eclectic: "The Alhambra" model, available in 1918–1929 Sears catalogs. Shaped parapets were a distinctive feature of many Mission revival houses.

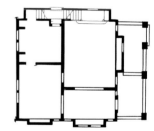

Right: Mail-order Spanish Eclectic: plan of "The Alhambra" model, available in 1918–1929 Sears catalogs.

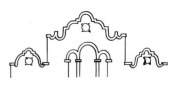

Above and above right: Mission Style parapets.

War I by the more romantic and less ascetically associative Spanish Eclectic style. The majority of surviving examples date from between 1905 and 1920.

Formally, the Mission vernacular was characterized not by archaeological or historical accuracy, but by a somewhat free adaptation of major features drawn from historic models. In domestic housing, these details were largely applied to a traditional "boxed" form. In the common symmetrical subtype, such as the Bianchi House in Dallas from 1912, a single-story porch was centralized against the main façade, supported by broad, square piers and topped with an ornamented, subsidiary roof parapet. In both symmetrical and asymmetrical subtypes, the principal façade was typically adorned with this type of decorative, most often scrolled or stepped, parapet wall at the roof line, mimicking those of the historic missions. Roof parapets might also serve as the frontage of a dormer, and could boast small quatrefoil, oval, or arcuated windows. The contour of the parapet was often adorned with red tiles and, as in fanciful examples such as the Holt House in Redlands, California, from 1903, the parapet overall was often far more elaborate than original mission prototypes. In the asymmetrical subtype, the porch was offset to one side, while the vertical thrust of the main façade continued upward to form the dominant parapet wall. However distributed, the porch was characteristically formed with long, low arches mimicking the cloister arcades of mission prototypes.

Characteristics of the style also include broad, overhanging eaves open to the rafters from below, serving to guard against the intensive heat of the sun by wrapping the exterior walls in a deep envelope of shade, helping to cool the whole of the building. Roofs were typically covered with red terracotta tiles recalling the style's Mediterranean and Hispanic origins, and providing significant color and texture. In more modest examples, wall surfaces were smooth stuccoed or plastered, usually painted white, light cream, or a gay climate-associated color. Exteriors are generally somewhat stern, while surface detailing only rarely interrupts the smooth planar walls, with the exception of an unadorned stringcourse tracing the contours of some arches and selective gables, impost moldings, and water canals which protrude from the façade in rhythmic sequence. Exceptions to this would be surviving landmark houses such as the Holt House mentioned above where, departing from conventions in which decorative detailing throughout remained minimal, the lower façade has highly exaggerated round-arched arcades and an extravagant wave-like parapet wall, the resulting effect being highly sculptural.

Although rare in domestic structures, the façade might terminate in twin towers at each end, either arcaded or domed. The superb Burrage House by the architect Charles Bingham in Redlands, California, of 1901, is an outstanding example of this unusual type, and includes attractive arcaded side wings.

Left: Spanish Eclectic house, Mission Style bungalow, VFW Parkway, West Roxbury, MA.

The Spanish Eclectic

Soon, a far more popular style for domestic houses than the slightly earlier Mission Style sprang up. The Spanish Eclectic, often called the later Spanish "Revival" style, also originated in California, but became equally popular throughout the Southwest, especially in Texas, and came to have a far greater variety of detail and more historical accuracy than its predecessor.

Throughout the 1920s, Los Angeles in particular industrialized on an unprecedented scale. This necessitated the opening of new avenues for both city planning and suburban expansion. Nothing symbolized the creation of a new urban Californian identity better than the Spanish Eclectic architectural form. Not only in housing, public, and commercial building and public squares, but even in new street names the ambience of the Spanish colonial era was evoked. The small affluent California community of Santa Barbara came to reorder its entire downtown in the new style during the 1920s, while with the endorsement of the powerful Allied Architects Association, the city of Los Angeles looked to the New York architect Bertram Grosvenor Goodhue to redesign significant public buildings in their downtown in an Hispanic revival style.

Goodhue had masterminded the formulation of the Spanish Eclectic style at the Panama-California exposition in San Diego in 1915, and had come to be regarded through his first-hand study of Spanish colonial and Andalusian sources, as the guru of the emerging style which he had done much to promote as the predominant architectural type in the public mind. He had written an in-depth work on Spanish colonial

Above: Spanish Eclectic house, VFW Parkway, West Roxbury, MA.

architecture, and expressed the prevailing need to embrace and reinterpret the wealth of Hispanic heritage to be found in the former colonies of the southwestern United States and Latin America. His rational ordering of large reinforced-concrete forms in the style in 1915 led to its earliest interpretation as a graceful and refined vernacular form appropriate to modern homes.

Encouraged by his vision, other architects who aspired to work in more fashionable styles turned toward America's rich Hispanic heritage, as well as to Spain itself, for prototypes. A good number of publications soon aided the growth of the style's popularity, including a series of articles, including drawings and photographs, published in *The Architectural Record* from 1923 by Arthur Byne and Mildred Stapley who had themselves journeyed to Spain on an architectural and antiques tour.

Above: Spanish Eclectic house. Stucco houses inspired by Spanish architecture were especially popular in California and the Southwest, but are found across the country.

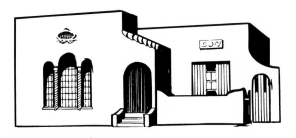

Above: Spanish Eclectic house. This type was based on Andalusian style of building, with expanses of plain wall broken by few windows, and centered around a courtyard.

In contrast to the more grandiose gestures of Los Angeles architects and planners, the small California city of Santa Barbara developed a distinctive revival style based upon Spanish colonial prototypes which came to be known as the Santa Barbara school of architecture. Stylistically and symbolically the city went some way toward repossessing its Hispanic past when it adopted the Spanish Eclectic as its semi-official civic style. Its local virtuoso was the former Harvard- and Beaux Arts-trained architect George Washington Smith who, beginning with his own house in adjacent Montecito in 1916, formulated a Spanish Eclectic architectural style grounded in a picturesque Andalusian idyll of massed white geometric planes and surfaces, austere façades, a very few shuttered windows along otherwise windowless walls, red-tiled roofs and understated parapets, and a cool and secluded courtyard garden. Smith completed numerous Spanish Eclectic style houses in both Santa Barbara and Montecito during the building boom of the early 1920s, including the Burke House of 1923, with his preferred

Above: George Washington Smith: Burke House, Santa Barbara, CA, 1923.

Below: Scotty's Castle, Death Valley, CA, 1922–1929.

Above: Spanish Eclectic house, Montgomery and Nibecker, architects. Published in *The Books of a Thousand Homes, vol. I: 500 Small House Plans*, New York, 1923.

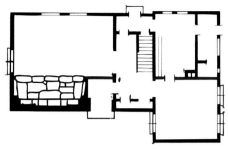

Above: Plan of ground floor of Spanish Eclectic house, Montgomery and Nibecker, architects. Published in *The Books of a Thousand Homes, vol. I: 500 Small House Plans*, New York, 1923.

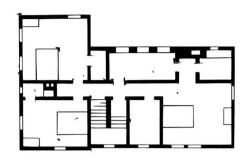

Above: Plan of second floor of Spanish Eclectic house, Montgomery and Nibecker, architects. Published in *The Books of a Thousand Homes, vol. I: 500 Small House Plans*, New York, 1923.

"birdhouse" chimney. His work established a new restrained architectural form, which was reproduced in houses throughout the Southwest, Texas, and Florida. The style peaked during the 1920s and 1930s, but began to decline in popularity nearing WWII. Landmark examples are unusual outside of these regions. One of the most flamboyant landmark buildings in the style is a house known as Scotty's Castle by Walter Scott, begun in 1924. Now a museum on the edge of California's Death Valley, it shows an elaborate expression of the style, including various forms of the tiled, ornamental chimney tops.

The style is extremely varied in form and detailing, but its subtypes seem to share a number of common features. Walls tend to reproduce a Mediterranean effect in light-colored brick or stucco with smooth surfaces. Roofs are typically finished off with red tiles, either in the half-cylinder Mission type or the S-curved Spanish type. Eaves usually end at or near the line of the wall, having little overhang. The roof is low-pitched. It can be flat, hipped, side-gabled, or cross-gabled, or sometimes both hipped and gabled, but the predominant type is cross-gabled with a single front-facing gable. The façade is consistently asymmetrical, with round arches set above

Left: William S. Hart House, Newhall, CA, 1927.

Above: Harold Saxelby: Epping Forest, the Dupont Estate, Jacksonville, FL, 1926–1927.

principal windows and doors and often ornamented with wrought-iron decorative grilles. It may also show decorative air vents with stucco or tile finishes. In some examples, the façade may extend to form a wing wall in the shape of a parabolic arch.

Both plan and façade usually have an attractive asymmetry, sometimes enhanced by towers, both round and octagonal, and typically with a combination of varying roof levels and forms on one house. This creates the impression of a rambling accrual of casual vernacular modifications to an original mass, as is particularly apparent in the Scotty's Castle arrangement of varied masses, porches, balconies, and arcaded porches. Houses are typically one or two stories, but often have a variety of different sub-levels. They may have projecting "shed" units, and inset entryways beneath a cantilevered tiled overhang or within an arcaded porch. Such covered porches, typically situated on the rear elevation, can be one- or two-story. Exterior stairs leading from upper floors into a partially enclosed patio are frequent in the more elaborate examples.

Exterior gardens, patios, and balconies are usually approached through paired doors, while doors in general are typically highlighted by decorative architectural detailing in the form of, for example, pilasters, polychromed tiles, or spiral columns. There is usually a single window positioned as a focal point of a portion of the main façade. It may be parabolic or even triple-arched. All details throughout the house tend to be patterned after authentic Spanish models, including fixtures and fittings, grilles, tiles, door knockers, wrought- or cast-iron balconies, fountains, and decorative gates.

Monterey Style

A truly eclectic architectural expression, the slightly later Monterey Style was in effect, another, albeit less rugged, adaptive readjustment of historical precedent. It flourished between approximately 1925 and 1955 in two identifiable phases. From circa 1925 to 1940 the style favored some of the finer detailing of Hispanic models, and was a mixture, on the one hand, of Hispanic structural traditions and Spanish colonial ornamentation with, on the other hand, features readily adopted from Anglo-American prototypes of New England. Of the latter, massed spaces with a pitched roof were favored. In subsequent examples, this fusion of types was more heavily weighted toward the expression of Anglo-American detailing.

The earliest buildings in the style appeared in California and, though never really a popular style as such, it was also known in examples of single-family suburban housing between 1925 and 1950. Examples are found throughout America, although the Monterey Style was never suitable for large tracts of popular housing.

Principal features of the style are seen in an elegant and restrained sub-type of two-story domestic houses which have an infrequently hipped, but low-pitched gabled roof at the junction of an L-shaped plan, and a second-floor balcony, with doors of full height, cantilevered over visibly heavy lintels drawn outward from the mass of the house. The balcony is typically integrated beneath the principal roof, and the roofline itself supported by posts which may be augmented in later examples with ornamental tracery or carved corbels.

Importantly, the style is marked by a juxtaposition of textures which are used to articulate, for example, the ground story—usually brick—from the upper elevation— frequently wood cladding in board-and-batten or possibly shingle. Roofing is most commonly shingle, but the tiled roof is also known. Detailing is usually of simple wood on doors and window surrounds, a feature drawn from Spanish colonial prototypes, and often includes the use of wood false shutters to create rhythm across the façade. Windows are typically symmetrical, disposed in three planes across the façade, with the windows situated toward the far ends of the façade and at the entryway in the center, but there are also asymmetrical examples.

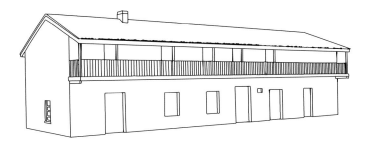

Above: Monterey Style house. The prominent balcony is typical of this type of dwelling.

Above: Drawing of a larger Monterey Style house.

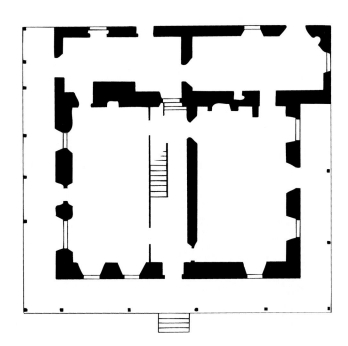

Above: Plan of Monterey house. Note that the balcony virtually surrounds the house.

One of the better-known subtypes takes its name—"Creole French"—from its slim columns, which articulate a balcony and combine with decorative iron balustrades. This type gained some popularity after WW2 and is often seen to be best represented by the landmark example of the Bywaters House of 1951 in Dallas, Texas.

The Pueblo Revival

While national magazines were showcasing the fashionable Spanish Eclectic trend in architecture during the 1920s, a more discreet and organic vernacular style had already found its way into the hearts of many regionalists in the Southwestern United States. The Pueblo Revival style perhaps dates as early as 1905. It enjoyed competitive success in some Southwestern areas until about 1940, and continues among some devotees to be used to the present day. As a vernacular "revival" style it is characterized by the simulation or reproduction of Native American prototypes. Its practitioners look specifically to local, indigenous inspiration and craftsmanship, espec-ially in the production of adobe-like surface texture. The style appeared initially in California early in the twentieth century. It then became very popular in housing, commercial, and public buildings in and

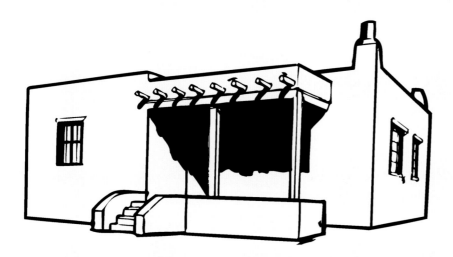

Left: Pueblo Revival house, Santa Fe, NM. c. 1925.

Left: Pueblo Revival house (Conkey House), Santa Fe, NM, c. 1934.

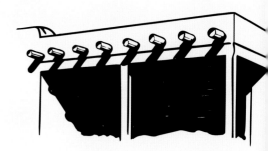

Right: Detail of Pueblo Revival house, showing exposed "vigas" (beams).

around Albuquerque and Santa Fe, New Mexico, as well as in Arizona, where local original prototypes of Native American "pueblo" dwellings of adobe construction survive. During the 1920s and 1930s there was some spread of the style through the Southwest, but its appeal was limited.

Early examples of the Pueblo Revival aesthetic show evidence of details derived, in part, from Spanish colonial precedent, most notably the flat roof. However, the style is generally considered an amalgamation of historical references. It is largely based upon very simple organic, earth-like forms, a simple stepped and or terraced profile, and the use of natural, locally available materials. A massing of earthen-like wall typically receives a stucco rendering, irregularly textured over adobe bricks. The final appearance suggests methods of hand-execution with a "time-battered" patina in homage to the weathered deterioration of surviving Pueblo settlement dwellings. Walls, characteristically, slope gently inward, suggesting a pyramidal massing of forms and volumes, and the walls show blunted and rounded corners and edges, again imitating hand construction techniques.

In profile and in roof line, the Pueblo Revival-style building is generally stepped upward with irregularly positioned terraces. The upper layers of these two- or even three-story houses often boast a variety of heights, staggered so that the building appears to have grown organically with increased usage and demand rather than being built to a preconceived "technical" or "architectural" plan. Upper volumes can be set asymmetrically above a low-lying ground-story volume, and may appear as a series of individual "pods" huddled together to cre-

ate the mass of the building. The exterior may also incorporate garden plots partitioned inside parapet walls extending outward from the house, personalizing the landscape in the immediate vicinity of the home and imparting to the overall composition the impression of agricultural occupation. This layout evokes myths of foundation, territorial identity, and indigenous origin.

The roofs of Pueblo Revival houses are characteristically flat, surrounded by a shallow parapet. The façades are typically punctuated from the inside out, with projecting undressed rafters known as "vigas" which suggest the myth of a pre-colonial post-and-lintel vernacular construction method. Similarly, parapet elevations tend to be punctuated just beneath the roof line in the local tradition of "canales" or rain-water spouts which, as in the Mission Style, combine with the projecting roof beams to give the stoic stucco wall surfaces a delightful sculptural quality brought on by the simple revelation of functional and structural components.

An apparent dependence upon locally available materials is unambiguous. Rough-surfaced wooden lintels above windows, and untreated porch and balcony posts—for which trim tree trunks of similar diameter are sometimes substituted—supporting arcaded verandas or "portales" speak of a pre-industrial age. Verandas may even harbor clay ovens and/or fireplaces, generally set into an interior corner of the large space in which distinctions between inside and outside are blurred. Some late examples include a rough-hewn wooden ladder set between roof layers, a device meant to symbolically recall the origins of the building type—a ladder would have provided the only means of access to the higher levels of original Pueblo dwellings.

Chapter 6

Pre-World War II—Modern Houses

Abby Moor

The Craftsman Style

As stylistic eclecticism reached particular intensity in American architecture during the initial decades of the twentieth century, Southern California was a center of economic prosperity. But beginning in the 1890s, as stylistic regionalism asserted itself in the rest of the country, in Southern California three predominant styles of housing emerged. The Italian Renaissance or Mediterranean and Spanish Revival styles, which were rapidly adopted by local contractors and land developers, have already been discussed. By the end of the first decade of the new century these forms were quickly competing for prominence with the new, uniquely Californian development of the Craftsman bungalow.

The bungalow-type of small-to-medium-sized suburban house had emerged by about 1903, dramatically departing from customary American architectural practice in not borrowing directly from recognized antecedents.

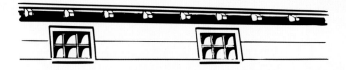

Above: Rafter tails, from a Craftsman bungalow in Cape May, New Jersey. Exposed rafter tails are one of the hallmarks of the style.

Above: Craftsman bungalow. Popularized in journals such as *The Craftsman*, bungalows such as this became one of the most widespread house types. Combining influences from the Arts and Crafts, Japanese design, and the Shingle Style, these small houses provided comfortable and flexible living space.

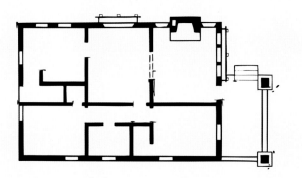

Left: Plan of "Argo" bungalow, Loizeaux home, 1920s.

Left: Street of bungalows, Pasadena, CA.

Below: Bungalow, Sewell Avenue, Cape May, NJ, 1920s.

Left: Otis Townsend House, Cape May, NJ, 1915. Most bungalows are one or two stories in height. This is a large bungalow with clipped (or jerkinhead) gable roof, brackets, and exposed rafter tails.

Above: Log hut design from Herbert Chivers's *Artistic Homes*, 1912. A fusion of the desire for rustic authenticity and the Arts and Crafts movement can be seen in this deliberately primitive porch.

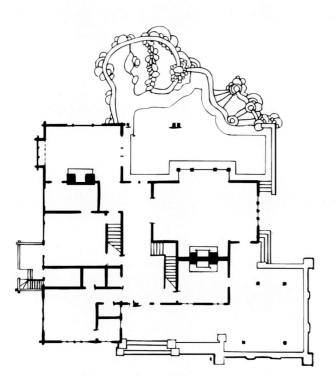

Above: Charles Sumner Greene and Henry Mather Greene: plan of the Gamble House, Pasadena, CA, 1908.

The bungalow takes it name from a remote predecessor, a vernacular cottage prototype found in Bengal, with which it shared vague formal similarities. By the early 1900s the type was flourishing in Southern California. It had been recognized as an especially suitable solution to the needs of the current housing boom which required unlimited individual variety in a basic prototype for reasonably priced domestic architecture appropriate to the climate. With the design insight of a few California architects such as the Greene brothers—Charles Sumner and Henry Mather Greene—in Pasadena and Bernard Maybeck in Berkeley, the Craftsman bungalow grew into a significant statement of Arts and Crafts values skillfully adapted to a California lifestyle.

As a regional response to conditions of climate and population growth, the bungalow type could not have been better. Typically of one-story, the standard form featured both a covered porch and a patio, and good-sized rooms configured in an open floor-plan which eliminated poorly lit entry halls. The plan was altogether functional and also comparatively inexpensive in its wood, local stone, and often shingle construction. It stood as a superb achievement in affordable, single-family housing.

The popular version was innovative in its basic design features. It was usually situated above ground level, resting on a partially revealed basement story and characterized by a low-pitched, gabled roof which might also be hipped. Overhanging eaves were wide and of open construction, revealing rafters, braces, and joists below. Covered porches often ran the full length of the façade, their roofs carried upon sloping and decorative wood or often stone or cobblestone pillars which swelled up from ground level to well above the floor level of the porch itself.

As a result of the bungalow's popularity in California, an abundance of pattern books were published with plans and building specifications for the bungalow type. As the style spread, builders and developers throughout the country constructed whole neighborhoods with streets lined with this new single-family house. Further, "kit" houses were manufactured and sold complete with precut timber, plans, fixtures, and fittings. These pattern-book-prompted kits were relatively simple to construct on site, and with them the story of American architecture can begin to be told in

Above: Otis Townsend House, Cape May, NJ, 1915. This is an unusual three-story bungalow.

terms of an early, prototype version of flat-pack design. As a result of these various factors, a large portion of American towns came to include bungalow suburbs before the end of the 1920s. The Craftsman bungalow was a dominant form of smaller-scale vernacular housing in America from about 1905 through the mid-1920s when it began to diminish in popularity.

There were also more elaborate and costly hand-crafted examples of the Craftsman bungalow, the most important landmark example being the Gamble House in Pasadena by Greene and Greene. Although such finely wrought, detailed expressions of the type passed from fashion by about 1915, they left a lasting legacy to the history of American architecture. The Greene brothers practiced together in the leafy Los Angeles suburb of Pasadena from 1893 to 1914, though they continued to collaborate until about 1923. Up until about 1909 they specialized in the design and execution of what we would today refer to as landmark examples of the bungalow type. It has been said that the Greene brothers produced the "ultimate" bungalows in works such as the Robert R.

Above: Charles Sumner Greene and Henry Mather Greene: David B. Gamble House, Westmoreland Place, Pasadena, CA, 1907–1908. A masterpiece of Arts and Crafts architecture by the leading California exponents of the bungalow.

Left: Gustav Stickley (1858–1942): Craftsman Farms, 2352 Route 10, Parsippany, NJ, 1911. Log home.

Below: Gustav Stickley: Craftsman Farms. Detail.

Blacker House of 1907, the David B. Gamble House of 1907–1908, and the Charles M. Pratt House of the same period. Their work shows influences from the English Arts and Crafts movement and its American counterpart (the designs and aesthetic predilections of Gustav Stickley), an interest in Japanese-inspired wood construction, and their own training in the manual arts. Their landmark examples of the type are intricately detailed, expensive, and handcrafted both inside and out. These houses received considerable press coverage in contemporary design and architectural journals, such as *House Beautiful*, *The Craftsman*, *Architectural Record*, and the *Ladies' Home Journal* where Frank Lloyd Wright also published his innovative designs. This scale of coverage helped to familiarize the rest of the nation with the bungalow style, and undoubtedly helped to create the market for its unique interpretation of housing design.

The Gamble House is a large, asymmetrical and shingle-clad wooden structure with multiple layers, porches, and verandas, positioned in extensive Japanese-style gardens. The emphasis throughout is on the relationship of the horizontal line of the house to the surrounding landscape. The house boasts many of the exquisite features that the more humble, but optimistic bungalow dwellers were able to incorporate only in moderation, if at all. As in many of the landmark examples, the entrance figures as one of the dominant features of the house. A central door is flanked by one each of a pair of somewhat narrower screened doors, the whole set beneath a crowning row of transom windows. The composition in each panel is of iridescent

Above: Craftsman house, Newton, MA, 1909. Constructed by E. C. Hammond, using plans from Gustav Stickley's *Craftsman* magazine, published in October 1905.

and translucent art glass with broad, stained wooden surrounds. In details such as this the Greenes explored the incorporation of Japanese-inspired patterned detailing into the very fabric of the house. The extensive use of fine timber, especially in all framing details and as the predominant material of the interior design, awakens cultural memories of indigenous crafts traditions, and shows the certain inspiration of a Japanese architectural aesthetic. It lends a pseudo-primitive and unblemished design ideal to a house which cultivates an personality of comparative, but deceptive, casualness in its detailed handwork, undisguised joinery, and all-pervading naturalness.

Like other examples of the bungalow type, the Gamble House represents lifestyle aspirations. In materials and form it is designed to lay easily within its natural surroundings, and appeals not only for its evocation of an effortless lifestyle, but for its apparent informality and semi-exotic picturesque qualities. The cantilevered sleeping porches and sheltered terraces extend living space beyond the walls of the house and out into the gardens. The house represents a strategy for California living. The design acts as a metaphor for the healing and restorative forces of the landscape and nature; a metaphor which will be encountered again in the nascent Modernist works of Rudolph Schindler and Richard Neutra.

Above: Charles Sumner Greene and Henry Mather Greene: Duncan-Irwin House, Pasadena, CA, 1906. A bungalow on a very large scale.

Right: Bungalow,
Waltham, MA.

Below: Bungalow,
Rockland, MA. This
bungalow shows a strong
Japanese influence.

Above: Bungalow, Coxsackie, NY.

Above: Bungalow, Belvidere, NJ.

Above: Bell Bungalow, Cape May, NJ, 1920s.

Prairie Style

It has often been said that the origins of modern American domestic architecture lay in the vision of Frank Lloyd Wright, and in his struggle to synthesize currents already present as early as the Shingle Style and as late as the contemporary work of his mentor, Louis Sullivan. Drenched as turn-of-the-century America was in styles of the European past, Wright's endeavors to discard all borrowings and to replace them with an utterly new form of modern design in the form of the so-called Prairie Style seem almost Herculean.

Wright's Prairie Style developed in the 1890s, and flourished between 1901 and his departure for Europe in 1909. It continued to serve as a model for smaller-scale buildings until about 1920. However, he was not the only practitioner of the new style, but was part of the emerging Chicago School which also included Sullivan, as well as George Grant Elmslie and George Washington Maher who had also been present with Wright in Sullivan's Chicago studio. What all shared by the time they left Sullivan's tutelage was a belief in the value of regionalism in architecture.

Above: Walter Burley Griffin (1876–1937): Carter House, Evanston, IL, 1910. The Prairie Style is a modernist mode which avoids traditional ornament.

In his earliest designs, Wright continued to express the authority of contemporary and historical types. In the Charnley House of 1892, designed while he was still employed in Sullivan's office and possibly in conjunction with the older master, there are both Italianate and exotic orientalizing influences derived directly from Sullivan's practice. His own house in the Chicago suburb

Above: The Prairie Style home (William Martin House, Oak Park, IL, 1903). Echoing the horizontal lines of the Illinois prairie, Frank Lloyd Wright's architecture offered innovative concepts of space and a Modernist style not based on European revivals.

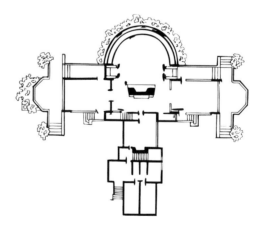

Left: William Gray Purcell and George Grant Elmslie: plan of the Bradley, or "Airplane" House, Woods Hole, MA, 1911–1912. This house dramatically "breaks the box" of traditional design.

Above: Mail-order Prairie School: "The Aurora" model, available in 1918 Sears catalog. The Prairie Style was widely copied in the Midwest.

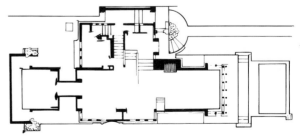

Above: William Gray Purcell and George Grant Elmslie: plan of the Purcell-Cutts House, Minneapolis, MN, 1913.

of Oak Park, constructed in phases between 1889 and 1909, shows the acute influence of H.H. Richardson's conventional and historicist Neo-Romanesque manner in its pyramidal profile and its T-shaped plan. There is also a marked recollection of Sullivan himself in the attempt to replace Western decorative motifs with more exotic ones devised from the study of the British designer Owen Jones's *Grammar of Ornament*, published in 1856, and containing an encyclopedic collection of source patterns from all over the world. What is already apparent in this house is Wright's accentuation of the masonry core—one of the most important leitmotifs of his career—and an emerging relationship between the domestic residence and nature. In the second-floor, barred-vaulted play-

Above: William Gray Purcell (1880-1965) and George Grant Elmslie (1871–1952): Bradley ("Airplane") House, Woods Hole, MA, 1911–1912. Dramatically sited at the end of a promontory, this shingle-covered house is a fine example of the Prairie Style.

Left: William Gray Purcell and George Grant Elmslie: Purcell-Cutts House, Minneapolis, MN, 1913.

room, Wright placed built-in window seats, which doubled as storage areas for toys, so that they were on the precise level of tree foliage immediately outside. The playroom was thus elevated into an idyllic, secret space which was at once therapeutic, safe, and unspoilt, where child and nature shared a primitive spirit. Wright's two-story studio was added to the building between 1897 and 1899. It is attached to the house by a separate corridor, and is formed by a large square space below with an octagonal balcony suspended above. The space is dramatically lit by skylights and art-glass windows, and already shows throughout the design of both interior and exterior the muted color harmonies of amber, brown, and earthen green which would remain at the core of Wright's palette for the remainder of his career. Significantly, Wright had already begun to experiment with the possibilities of machine-cut glass in contrast to the hand-cutting techniques favored by the contemporary Arts and Crafts movement. For Wright, art-glass stained with color brought both light and color into an interior without interrupting perception of the fabric of a building. Machine-cut glass produced straight-edged, geometric designs, which for Wright were distinctly modern and thus clearly sympathetic with architectural form.

The Winslow House at River Forest, built in 1893, was the first house in which Wright's representative low-hipped Prairie-style roof made its appearance. In other ways, however, the house remained transitional—its

Above: Frank Lloyd Wright (1867–1959): Wright House, 951 Chicago Avenue, Oak Park, IL, 1889. Wright's first house was for himself, and was a Shingle Style house with a dominant triangular gable. The porch eases the transition between exterior and interior, and the materials exhibit natural colors and textures.

Above: Frank Lloyd Wright: William H. Winslow House, River Forest, IL, 1893–1894. Detail of entrance.

Left: Frank Lloyd Wright: William H. Winslow House, River Forest, IL, 1893–1894. His first house after leaving Sullivan's office introduced the new Prairie Style.

Left: Frank Lloyd Wright: Charnley House, 1365 North Astor Street, Chicago, IL, 1892. The Charnley House was a commission for Sullivan and Adler, Wright's employers, but is thought to have been largely designed by Wright.

windows being both casement and sash for example. Wright subsequently used the former type exclusively, and the combination of running windows with isolated or "spot" fenestration. The mature Prairie Style was shortly to be dominated by Wright's preference for windows in running strips. This house, however, also solved one of the most significant planning problems for any urban domestic dwelling: how to present a formal bearing and yet respond to requirements for informality and family life? In the Winslow House Wright suggested a solution by designing dual façades, that is both an "urban" aspect toward the street side, and a "rural" aspect facing onto the garden. The former was distinguished by formal symmetry, while the latter was

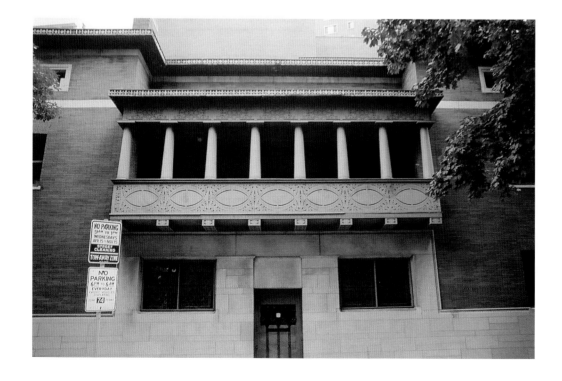

Left: Frank Lloyd Wright: Charnley House, Chicago, IL, 1892.

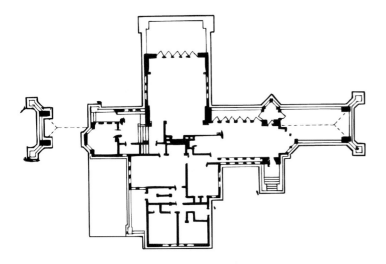

Above: Frank Lloyd Wright: plan of the Ward Willits House, Highland Park, IL, 1902–1903.

enclosed along the lower elevation, representing one of Wright's Prairie sub-types. Proportions are measured, and the forward elevation is enlivened with the heavy, rounded entry arch derived from Sullivan, but here positioned asymmetrically and imbedded within low-lying parapet walls which make accessibility an intentionally processional affair. The façade displays the signature ribbon windows on the upper floor of this characteristically two-story house, and the luminosity of the glass is offset by the impregnable impression given by the massed masonry. The house is raised on a concrete podium, and distinguished by the low-hipped roof with broad sheltering eaves splaying outward over the second-floor windows. From the exterior, the low-hung

asymmetrical, accommodating irregular functional spaces of the interior at the same time as it anticipated a unique, private relationship with nature which would become a hallmark of the mature Prairie type.

Wright's Prairie Style emerged fully in about 1901. It corresponded with his three public announcements of his ideas. In 1901 he gave a lecture entitled "The Art and Craft of the Machine" at the Hull House Settlement in Chicago, arguing machine technology was appropriate to architecture, if guided by the artist. In the same year he published two articles, both containing plans for domestic dwellings, in the influential periodical the *Ladies' Home Journal.* Here he showed that in his mind the Prairie aesthetic was firmly formulated. His layouts showed open ground plans, low-pitched roofs and low-lying parapet walls, all elements accommodated within a strongly horizontal format and integrated with care into the site. These dominant features were contrasted with spacious, double-height interior spaces and a strong vertical accent in the hearth-chimney area.

Both the Heurtley House and the Ward Willits House of 1902 express this mature formulation, and show the main characteristics of the style. The masonry mass of the Heurtley House is marked by a strong horizontal stress. The plan is delineated in a horizontal sweep across the site. The mass is formidable, isolated, and primarily

Above: Frank Lloyd Wright: William Martin House, Oak Park, IL, 1903.

Above: Frank Lloyd Wright: Arthur Heurtley House, Oak Park, IL, 1902.

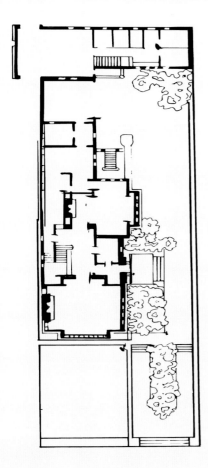

Above: Frank Lloyd Wright: plan of the Isidore Heller House, Chicago, IL, 1897.

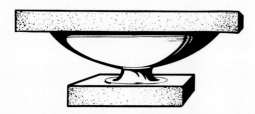

Above: Frank Lloyd Wright: urn, Robie House, Chicago, IL. Integrating the house with nature was one of Wright's chief tenets, and these signature urns symbolically define that goal.

Above: Roman bricks used by Frank Lloyd Wright at the Robie House and other Prairie houses; note the raked horizontal mortar joints which emphasize the horizontal lines.

Above: Frank Lloyd Wright: Isidore Heller House, Chicago, IL, 1897. An urban house, the Heller House features decorative Art Nouveau-like sculptures in the frieze.

mass of the immense masonry chimney is a subtle reminder of the centrally positioned "sunburst"-patterned hearth inside the house. One of the signature features of the Heurtley House is the alternating brickwork courses. The pattern of projecting bricks against smooth ones also signals alternating sequences of rose-hued and deeper red bricks. Although Wright never replicated this unique patterning, the care with which he designed texture and color into the very fabric of the Prairie structure is typical of his mature style. In Wright's philosophy, the true nature of construction materials was never to be disguised, but celebrated for its individual distinguishing qualities. In the Frederick Robie House of slightly later, 1906, Wright again designed a patterned sequence produced by the combination of brick and mortar on the façades. The Robie House bricks are narrower and longer than normal, and set between courses of cream-colored mortar, serving to emphasize the dramatically long and low horizontal disposition of the house. In some Prairie examples, Wright even had the horizontal joints of mortar deeply recessed in contrast to

Right: Frank Lloyd Wright:
Ward Willits House,
Highland Park, IL,
1902–1903.

vertical joints which remained entirely flush with the brick surfaces, again producing subtle but very effective detailing as ribbons of horizontal shadow were intensified along the surface of a house.

The Ward W. Willits House in Highland Park exemplifies the other primary sub-type of Wright's Prairie houses. Many its features remain the same, but are vastly different in execution. The Willits House, like the later Robie House in Chicago, is dramatically low-lying, but rambling in format, startling in its asymmetry, and picturesque in its appeal in contrast to the symmetrical mass and structural qualities of the Heurtley House. Wright's prominent use of uncolored and unornamented cement stucco on the exterior of a domestic dwelling was most unusual at this time. Stucco was considerably less expensive than any form of masonry, and a large number of Wright's Prairie houses were built with this as the primary material. The smooth texture helps to create vivid, abstract rhythms of solid and void across the elevations, and is in stark contrast with the darker

Right: Frank Lloyd Wright:
P.A. Beachy House, Oak
Park, IL, 1906.

Left: Frank Lloyd Wright:
Darwin D. Martin House,
Buffalo, NY, 1903.

wood trim which emphasizes the horizontality of the plan and profile.

The interior of the Willits House is also typical of Wright's mature Prairie style in the use of screens and grilles to separate main spaces, facilitating his destruction of the confined "box-like" spaces of Victorian homes which he so loudly criticized. In design the screens and grilles are entirely modern. They are staunchly rectilinear in format, typically fabricated after machine cutting, and designed as integral to the interior and to the fabric of the house itself. Their use facilitated the opening up of internal spaces with a new spatial simplicity that Wright argued belonged to modern architecture.

Scholars have often suggested that Wright's feeling for open-planned interior design, which employed such methods of screening and emphasized the placement of the hearth at the center of the plan, was critically influenced by the architect's fondness for Japanese

building tradition. Although he had looked to Japanese design as early as 1890, the role played in the development of Wright's architectural aesthetic by the Japanese Government's reconstruction of the Ho-o-den Temple at their national exhibit in the Columbian World Exposition in Chicago in 1893 has consistently been recognized as decisive. There Wright studied the positioning of the Japanese "tokonama" (the small shrine central to Japanese home life) as the immovable feature at the center of the interior where it became the focus of familial and domestic ceremony. His subsequent focus on the masonry mass of the hearth in the Prairie house is highly suggestive of that prototype. In Japanese culture it embodied notions of spiritual shelter within opened and screened spaces of remarkable fluidity, much as the hearth for Wright was the single solid mass in interiors that he increasingly opened up to accommodate the fluctuating requirements of the private family home. He

Above: Frank Lloyd Wright: Frederick G. Robie House, 5757 Woodlawn Avenue, Chicago, IL, 1908–1909.

Above: Frank Lloyd Wright: Isobel Roberts House, River Forest, IL, 1908.

may also have assimilated the Japanese taste for flat-planed, unpainted wood from the same exhibition.

Other characteristic features of Wrightian Prairie houses can be found in many examples of his built work, ranging from the Darwin D. Martin House of 1903 and the Avery Coonley House of 1907–1908, to the late examples of the Thomas Gale and Robie houses, both finished in 1909. The latter include entrances increasingly set asymmetrically, concealed behind entry porches or mazes of low-lying parapet walls, which established both real and symbolic boundaries between the private spaces of the home and the public spaces outside. The off-setting of the entry door also freed the front elevation of conventional symmetry, and allowed Wright to build the street façade either as an intricate, geometric pattern of lights against darks, glass against stone or stucco, the smooth against the textured, or to translate it in a thoroughly three-dimensional fashion as a collection of cantilevered, concrete and brick parapets moving forward into space and obscuring the mass of the house behind. The latter treatment is best exemplified by the landmark Robie House, the most widely and immediately publicized of all Wright's Prairie houses. It was perhaps the one domestic structure of the period which irrevocably ushered in a new modern era of residential architecture in America.

The majority of Wright's Prairie houses had been constructed of wood and cement stucco. But the Robie House presented a fluid amalgamation of brick, concrete, and steel. Its profile was mysteriously

Above: Frank Lloyd Wright: Mrs. Thomas Gale House, Oak Park, IL, 1909.

streamlined and its low-lying mass seemed at once to hover and then rise up from the ground. To date in Wright's career, it was the most machine-age of all his domestic designs and it heralded a new type of untried, ultimately innovative residential dwelling which immediately provoked comparison with other fledgling twentieth century trends. In Germany, the Robie House became known as the "Dampfer"—the ocean-liner—the association being one of progress, internationalism, and modernity. It was truly a landmark achievement.

Above: Frank Lloyd Wright: Mrs. Thomas Gale House, Oak Park, IL. A precociously Modernist house, with cantilevered balconies.

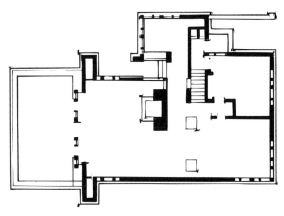

Above; Frank Lloyd Wright: plan of Mrs. Thomas Gale House, Oak Park, IL.

Organic

In its application to architecture, the term "organic" is, again, perhaps best-known in relation to the work of Frank Lloyd Wright. But neither did it originate with him, nor is it unambiguous when used in describing his work. The notion of the "organic" in architecture has a pedigree which predates Wright as well as his "lieber meister" Louis Sullivan who described ideal relationships between architectural structure and ornamentation with organic metaphors drawn from botany, arguing that nature revealed itself in art.

The very notion of an organic architecture is closely related to the Western supposition that a building is an ally against the strange, irrational, and wild desolation of the wilderness that nature seems to represent. The landscape offers an undisciplined, primitive counterpart to the rational order of human civilization and thus needs to be tamed. In response to this presumed hostility, the integration of people into the world takes the form of dwellings and their immediate surroundings—such as gardens—symbolizing humankind's ability to first subdue and then reorder nature by rational and forceful means.

By the early nineteenth century a more sympathetic approach was apparent in the Romantic movement, which saw nature as imbued with divinity. That divinity was expressed in the visible irregularity of the

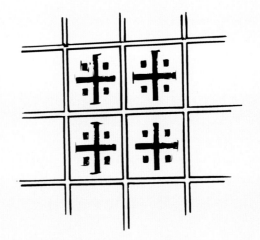

Left: Concrete blocks used by Frank Lloyd Wright for his "textile" houses; Millard House, Pasadena, CA, 1923. In the 1920s, Wright experimented with a new technique of building houses of concrete blocks, "woven" together on steel rods.

natural world. For architects, this meant the individual peculiarities of each site, area, and region. From this a new emphasis on the picturesque quality of architecture arose, placing special emphasis on the idea of the "genius loci"—the individual character of each specific site. Good design emerged from man's inherent empathy with the site. It was the architect's responsibility to draw upon the whole history of architecture in finding the most effective forms for responding to each site in the case of domestic buildings. Intertwined with this concept of the genius loci was the Romantic notion that nature itself was the primary vehicle for restoring the spirit of God to industrialized, alienated modern society. The unspoilt landscape was a rejuvenating force. It could shape the human soul.

Long before Frank Lloyd Wright, the American writer Andrew Jackson Downing argued against fashionable architectural stylism, maintaining that true architecture took its forms directly from the land and plants of its own region. For Downing, each house was intrinsically tied to its genius loci by its shapes, colors, and textures. He admonished builders to curtail any pronounced contrasts between a structure and its site. Architecture should harmonize with its surroundings in every way and should be received by the landscape as if it were an integral part of it.

The earliest seminal example of modern "organic" architecture in America was Wright's "Fallingwater," built in 1935–1936 in Bear Run, Pennsylvania, as a holiday home for the Kaufmann family. The house is still

Above: Frank Lloyd Wright: Bogk House, Milwaukee, WI, 1916.

Above: Frank Lloyd Wright: Barnsdall House, 4808 Hollywood Boulevard, Los Angeles, CA, 1920. Built for Aline Barnsdall, this house was Wright's first in California. It is inspired by Spanish colonial styles, with the interior courtyard and Aztec designs in the powerful form of the façade. The hollyhock pattern was based on Barnsdall's favorite flower.

Above: Frank Lloyd Wright: "La Miniatura," the Millard House, Pasadena, CA, 1923–1924.

Above: Frank Lloyd Wright: Barnsdall House, Los Angeles, CA, 1920.

337

Above: Frank Lloyd Wright: Taliesin East, Spring Green, WI, 1911.

Above: Frank Lloyd Wright: Richards Duplex apartments, Milwaukee, WI, 1916. The Richards Duplexes were one of Wright's experiments with lower-cost housing.

regarded as Wright's most visionary response to a residential project, and has become an icon of organic architecture. In the design of Fallingwater, Wright addressed the principle of the organic in a number of different senses simultaneously. By doing so he rejuvenated the term for an entirely new, twentieth century context.

Architectural historians have suggested a variety of ways in which Wright interpreted the organic in the design of Fallingwater. In its most basic sense, the term can be used as a growth metaphor, to allude to the process or appearance of a thing growing naturally. Fallingwater is set in a woodland haven immediately above a cascading waterfall where the Kaufmann family had enjoyed sunbathing. Rather than position the house alongside the cliffs, Wright daringly anchored the back of the structure into the hillside with four concrete piers which suspended it directly above the water. A stone tower containing the main fireplace rises through the center of the house, forming the axis about which the plan revolves. Remarkably, the house seems to thwart a standard orientation, appearing to change its direction depending on the point of view. Its three stories are

articulated by a series of outside stairways and deep concrete parapets and terraces revolving outward from the core. The whole is a bold composition of animated lines and planes in which sheltering bays and alcoves recede into cave-like shadow while the dramatically cantilevered terraces reach outward into the unchecked growth of the surrounding woodland. Upper stories face directly into the forest's foliage. The two predominant natural features of the site, however, which both helped to determine the plan of the house and subsequently became an integral part of it, are the cascading waterfall below and the jagged stone cliffs from which the structure seems to swell.

Fallingwater is equally organic in the sense that it tangibly incorporates features of the landscape into its design, both inside and out. Wright imbedded boulders and rocks which had fallen away from the cliffs into the fabric of the house, predominantly in and around the fireplace as hearthstones. Throughout, stonework has been laid as layers of stratification with roughly receding and projecting surfaces, simulating the patterns found on the broken ledges of the cliff. The main floor area of the plan is equally jagged on the side where the house

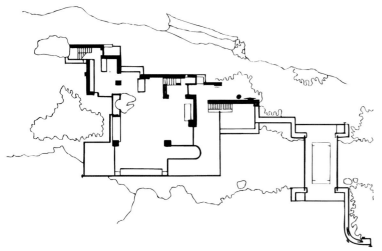

Above: Frank Lloyd Wright: plan of Fallingwater, Bear Run, PA, 1935–1936.

Left: Cantilever;
Frank Lloyd Wright,
Fallingwater.

Above: Frank Lloyd Wright: Edgar Kaufmann House, "Fallingwater," Mill Run, PA, 1935–1936. Built as a weekend house for the Kaufmann family, Fallingwater rejuvenated Wright's career, which had faltered during the depression and under competition from International Style architects.

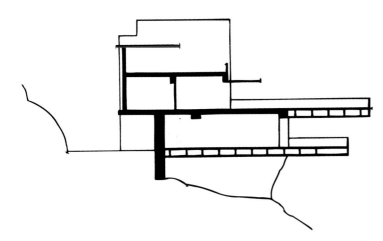

Above: Frank Lloyd Wright: section through Fallingwater showing support trusses for cantilevered balconies. The house was anchored into the hillside, with the mass of the building counterbalancing the dramatically free balconies.

is implanted into the cliff side. Descending from the center of the living area, a stair enclosed by stone walls leads nowhere but directly into the water's edge beneath the house. The house at once contains and reproduces the site's prominent characteristics, realizing Wright's sought after union between a building and its landscape.

Fallingwater also embodies the Romantic dichotomy between the natural and the artificial or mechanical, between nature and man. But it achieves the solution so aspired to in Romantic theory in the startling success of Wright's synthetic approach. Wright's real accomplishment at Fallingwater is the way in which by apparently unforced and intuitive means the building places man fittingly in nature. The house seems to perfectly accommodate man and nature together. All of the ingredients of the structure blend quietly and comfortably, without internal opposition. Wright's radical use of new engineering allowed the reinforced-concrete trays which form the terraces to be supported by the piers in a fashion entirely unprecedented in residential, and most commercial architecture. Yet the picturesque grace with which he formulated such an engineering feat engendered no jolting opposition with the beauty of the natural site. The streamlined shapes of the concrete cantilevers can be seen to be working in alliance with natural forms. The problematic relationship between man and nature could be resolved by architecture. In Fallingwater, Wright showed the way for the next generation of American architects and, if anything, set a new standard by outperforming nature in the design of a house which appears to hover weightlessly, scorning gravity.

The commission for Fallingwater restarted his career and gave him renewed energy for other projects, including the Broadacre City scheme and the development of his ideas for the Usonian house. After the stock market crash of 1929, the economic depression which engulfed the country forced a re-evaluation of national architectural priorities. Wright, like other American architects, looked to the design of programs which would bring affordable housing to middle-income families of professional groups such as educators, broadcasters, and writers, while relieving the congestion and

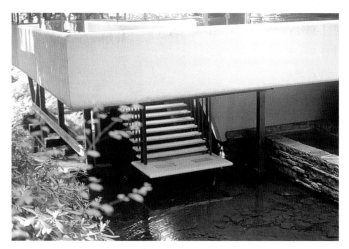

Above: Frank Lloyd Wright: Edgar Kaufmann House, Fallingwater. Detail.

hardships of city life.

The Broadacre City project was initially realized in a model constructed by Wright's students at the Taliesin Fellowship in 1934, but the scheme itself was never built. In it Wright proposed the transference of much of the inner-city infrastructure to the healthier conditions of the countryside, greatly improving the quality of life for residents, while integrating this unique suburb into the natural topography of the countryside.

Wright's ideas in part heralded emerging Utopian

Left: Frank Lloyd Wright: Edgar Kaufmann House, Fallingwater. Wright's distinctive dynamic space and open composition is carried to new levels here.

notions of population dispersal into anti-urban settlements. He forecast this would occur through the agency of the telephone and telegraph, radio, and the automobile, and be facilitated by standardized production of housing stock. In form, the Broadacre City plan was shockingly futuristic. In some respects it is reminiscent of the near contemporary work of Buckminster Fuller. But in the proposed organization of the city's infrastructure Wright's betrayed his democratic and egalitarian idealism. For example, an acre of land for the individual cultivation of food was to be afforded each person of a given age. Here Wright revived the social proposition of a cottage-industry economy, but his Utopian quasi-agrarian town—as often noted—provided only certain, limited benefits for the individual in terms of architecture and city planning, while side-stepping the realities of labor and resource requirements of a nation based on automated mass-production.

However, the principles of the Broadacre City project were closely allied with Wright's conception of the Usonian House. The term "Usonia" had appeared in Wright's writings as early as 1925 and was an acronym which he credited to Samuel Butler for the "United States of America." Wright proposed this type of dwelling as the most suitable to the changing and future conditions of the American continent, suggesting the formation of Usonian communities along the lines of Broadacre City. The Usonian system was an integrated approach to design and building. The residential plan changed, and so did its method of construction.

The Herbert Jacobs House of 1936 in Madison, Wisconsin, was Wright's first completely Usonian residence to be built, and is clearly designed for convenience, comfort, and economy. Its elements would characterize this radically new housing type. The building was set directly upon a cement base at ground level, therefore rising from the earth without the intervention of the podium Wright had so preferred in his Prairie houses. Lapped board replaced clapboard, and the walls were sandwiched with a plywood core encased in insulating and waterproofing paper, and then screened in board-and-batten. Supporting elements are usually masonry piers of brick, stone, or concrete block, and thus the sandwich walls are protective rather than load bearing. Long, floor-to-ceiling sequences of running windows could be inserted as screens, both unifying

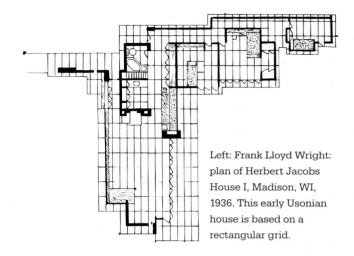

Left: Frank Lloyd Wright: plan of Herbert Jacobs House I, Madison, WI, 1936. This early Usonian house is based on a rectangular grid.

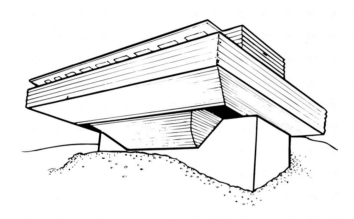

Above: Frank Lloyd Wright: Sturges House, Brentwood, CA, 1939. Another dramatic cantilever that almost gives the illusion of flight.

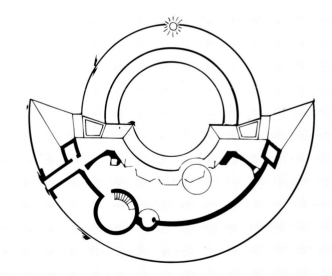

Above: Frank Lloyd Wright: plan of Herbert Jacobs House II, Madison, WI. The second house built for Herbert Jacobs is a "solar hemicycle," a curving house partially set into the ground and oriented to maximize the use of solar energy.

341

Left: Frank Lloyd Wright: Herbert Jacobs House I, Madison, WI, 1936. An early example of the low-cost Usonian house.

the interior of the house with the landscape outside, and segregating the ordered world of man from the tumult of the natural elements.

Inside, the kitchen—or "Laboratory" as Wright called it—and living areas were integrated into a single flowing space with the kitchen separated only by built-in shelving systems. The dining area was typically situated in an alcove or window bay directly adjacent to the kitchen, often with no intervening partition wall between the two. Angled walls functioned as stiffening elements in the structure and also created intimate

alcoves for private use. Furniture, bookcases, and cabinets were built into the fabric of the house, opening floor space and facilitating freer movement throughout. Usonian houses are typically of an L-shaped plan, the front often marked by a ribbon of high clerestory windows giving privacy and seclusion, while the sides and whole of the back are consistently designed with floor-to-ceiling windows running the length of the façades. Roof levels were varied to accommodate interior lighting from the clerestory or from fixtures set directly into the facing boards of

Above: Frank Lloyd Wright: George Sturges House, Brentwood, CA, 1939.

Above: Frank Lloyd Wright: Wingspread, the Herbert Johnson House, Wind Point, WI, 1937.

the ceiling.

The Usonian was not built to a predetermined plan, but easily modified by Wright to each client's requirements. The main objective was to simplify all factors of construction and to eliminate anything that was unnecessary to the fluid use and affordability of the house. In each case, the plan and building materials were dictated by use and site. Constricted client budgets were accommodated by the architect addressing the economic realities of the era. The simplest construction methods and materials were always used. In some instances clients bought the materials pre-cut to Wright's specifications and constructed the house themselves. Interior features including furniture and shelving were made of cut plywood, and could be designed to be either or both free-standing or built-in, although Wright himself preferred to make ample use of the latter type. Heating systems were sandwiched between the cement plinth and the characteristically Cherokee-red tile flooring. The mass of the masonry hearth remained at the center of the plan, often accompanied by built-in brick or plywood settles of reduced geometric design.

Wright's Usonian designs are often eclipsed in historical importance by his more famous Prairie houses, but in the long run have had a far greater and long-lasting effect on the history of American housing.

Among Wright's most important contributions to the realm of American architecture resulted from his foundation of the Taliesin Fellowship, an architectural training program, in 1932. The history of the Fellowship is well-known. From 1932 to 1959 its apprentices and members combined to form his professional architectural practice. The early years were spent at Taliesin in Wisconsin, but by 1934 the group had begun to winter with Wright outside of Scottsdale, Arizona, where Wright decided to build his new home and headquarters at Taliesin West, constructed between 1937 and 1959. The complex of buildings comprising the site were endlessly modified by Wright and almost entirely built by members of the Fellowship. The structures respond to what Wright called the "stark geometry" of the surrounding mountains in color, form, and texture. The massive walls throughout are composed of the ample natural stone

Above: Frank Lloyd Wright: Wingspread, the Herbert Johnson House, Wind Point, WI, 1937.

and boulders found along the desert floor, then bound together with cement. But interiors are opened up by translucent glass roofing and window-walls, and the whole marked by an angular complexity of slanting planes with which Wright mimicked the natural terrain. The Taliesin apprentices soon became a vital source of new energy in the further development of architecture in America. Wright's associates at Taliesin included Richard Neutra, and John Lautner whose work carried forward the organic aesthetic formulated by Wright.

Construction Elements—Roofing Materials

A vast array of building materials became available in the modern era for roofing, from traditional thatch to synthetic materials.

Above: Organic materials: thatch.

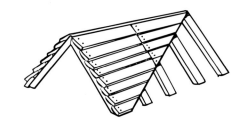

Above: Organic materials: boards.

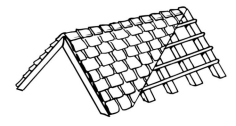

Above: Organic materials: wood shingles.

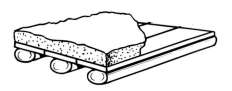

Above: Mineral: adobe (earth).

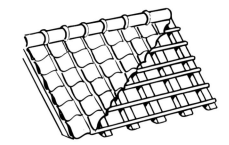

Above: Mineral: slate.

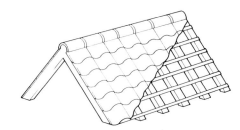

Above: Mineral: ceramic tile.

Above: Asphalt and composites: tar.

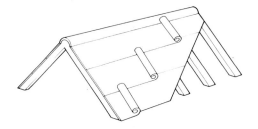

Above: Asphalt and composites: composition rolls.

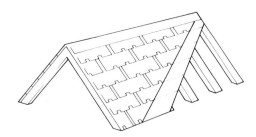

Above: Asphalt and composites: composition shingles.

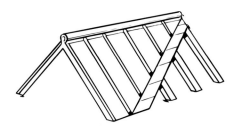

Above: Metal: sheets.

Above: Metal: panels.

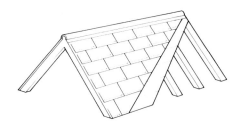

Above: Metal: shingles or tiles.

Modernist

During the early decades of the twentieth century, Americans became increasingly familiar with architectural expressions of the European avant-garde through publications such as the English periodical *The Studio*, republished as *International Studio* in the United States. This was only a single example from the vast array of available sources by which the burgeoning "Modernist" forms of European architecture came to influence the architecture of America, and all were widely read. Modernism soon took on a uniquely American inflection in the work of architects such as Irving Gill, Charles Eames, and Buckminster Fuller, as well as in that of the

many émigré architects such as Eero Saarinen from Finland, and the Austrians Rudolf Schindler and Richard Neutra.

The Modern style of the 1920s and 1930s, particularly in California, was primarily developed in landmark houses designed by a progressive generation of younger architects influenced simultaneously by Frank Lloyd Wright and the European avant-garde. Their work tended to be characterized by the prominence of a flat roof expanse beneath which sleek, glass-enclosed volumes were arranged asymmetrically and held in place not by load-bearing walls, but by a superstructure assembled of narrow, machine-manufactured steel beams set in a grid pattern. This method relieved the walls of

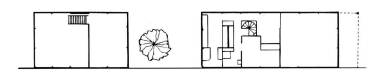

Above: Charles and Ray Eames: plan of the Eames House, first floor, Pacific Palisades, CA, 1948–1949.

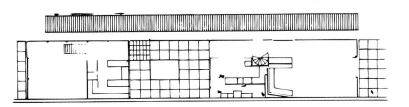

Above: Charles and Ray Eames: plan of the Eames House, second floor, Pacific Palisades, CA, 1948–1949.

Left: George Fred Keck: the Duncan House, Flossmore, IL, 1941. One of the earliest solar houses.

Right: Streamline Moderne house, Michigan Avenue, Miami Beach, FL. The new abstract designs appeared in Art Deco-influenced houses across the country.

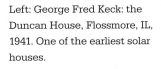

Left: George Fred Keck: plan of the Duncan House, Flossmore, IL, 1941. The house faces south, with a large expanse of glass to collect solar energy.

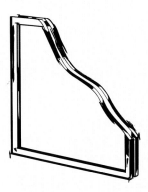

Left: Thermopane window, double panes of glass with an air space in between for greater insulation value, introduced by Libby-Owens-Ford in 1935.

Above: William Hebbard and Irving Gill (1870–1936): Marston House, Balboa Park, San Diego, CA, 1905.

Above: Eliel Saarinen: Saarinen House, Cranbrook, 39221 Woodward Avenue, Bloomfield Hills, MI, 1930.

encumbrance, allowing the house to be sheathed in a gridded glass framework in which a window itself turned the corner of the building, being the single, but transparent, boundary around interior space. Many such buildings were raised above ground level on concrete piers or stilts, while others rose directly from a cement foundation. Seminal examples tend to be multi-layered if more than a single floor, or strictly one-story at ground level. In many cases, interior volumes move outward in many directions from one or more imaginary axes. Characteristically, glass-enclosed rooms open via large sliding glass doors directly into the landscape, and window and doors frames are reduced to metallic strips and fascias of sheet metal. Many examples supplement living

Left: Charles Eames (1907–1978) and Ray Eames (1912–1988): Eames House, 203 Chataqua, Pacific Palisades, CA, 1948–1949.

Above: George Fred Keck (1895–1980) and William Keck (1908–1995): The House of Tomorrow, 1933. This house was built for the 1933 Century of Progress Exposition in Chicago.

Above: Richard Neutra (1892–1970): Kaufmann Desert House, 470 Vista Chino Drive, Palm Springs, CA, 1946–1947.

space with the addition of large roof terraces. Exterior surfaces are typically white or light cream-colored and, although usually hand-troweled, are smooth rendered. Despite their often streamlined and technological imagery, many landmark examples were designed as pavilions for enjoying nature, and are surrounded by carefully controlled man-made landscapes, which are intended to function as an extension of the architectural composition. This series of generalizations, however, is subject to a number of sub-types developed by individual practitioners.

Irving Gill had worked for Louis Sullivan in Chicago together with Frank Lloyd Wright. During the 1890s he set up his own practice in San Diego where his early work showed the influence not only of the Chicago School, but also of the stuccoed Southern California Spanish vernacular. As his mature style developed, forceful, abstracted cubic forms came to predominate. Gill's interpretation of the modern included an ongoing involvement with concrete construction methods, and the fabrication of broad, flat surfaces relieved by irregular windows and rounded Spanish-derived arches. Residential design was formulated by Gill in smooth flat and white or cream-colored walls, deprived of ornamentation. His roof line was typically a flat plane set above irregularly grouped and layered masses. His houses give an overall impression of being plain and hygienic, but are relieved of any aggressive quality by their gentle equilibrium of masses, the sophisticated asymmetry of

spaces, and the quiet simplicity of doors and windows. As door and window surrounds had traditionally been the site of decorative detailing, Gill along with other Modernists reduced as many framing components as possible in a general trend toward the simplification and standardization of construction. The architect had even experimented with frameless doors by 1902.

In his work Gill created a dialogue between the past, the regional, and the progressive. His particular form of regionalism sustained authentic culture while incorporating vital new elements such as standardized concrete construction. At one point he investigated the use of wall segments prefabricated in standard molds, which could be assembled after hardening. The style of housing he developed, however, was not necessarily of such universal appeal and his intent was not to further global architectural modernization. For forward-looking architects such as Gill, Modernism was a flexible rather than a universal idea. His buildings such as the villa for Walter L. Dodge in Los Angeles of 1914–1916, and the Horatio West Court terraced housing project in Santa Monica of 1919–1921, reflected the climate conditions, middle-income housing needs, and urban lifestyle of Southern California at the time. To some degree Gill's work set the pattern for a basic style of California housing through the 1930s, but was largely overshadowed in other parts of the country by simplified versions of the more streamlined and modish "Art Moderne" flat roof and asymmetrical spaces. The latter employed curved

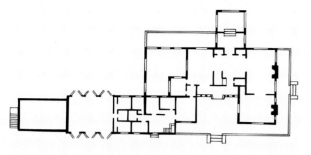

Above: Irving Gill: plan of the Dodge House, Los Angeles, CA, 1916.

Above: Elevation of the Schindler House by Rudolph Schindler, Los Angeles, CA, 1922. Schindler's own house had no historical ornament and was frankly functional in design.

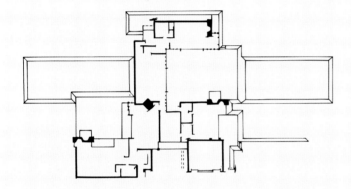

Above: Plan of the Schindler House by Rudolph Schindler, Los Angeles, CA, 1922.

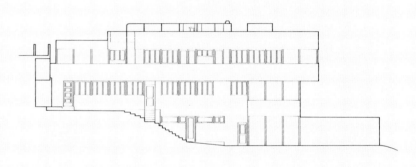

Above: Elevation of the Lovell Health House by Richard Neutra, Los Angeles, CA, 1928.

Above; Angled elevation of the Lovell Health House: Richard Neutra, Los Angeles, CA, 1928. The wide expanses of glass were meant to maximize the healthful effects of sunshine. The house uses modern technology to create a curtain wall, in the manner of skyscrapers.

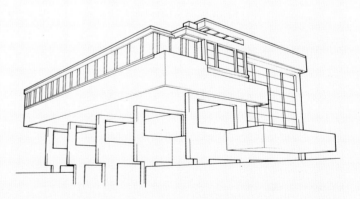

Above: The dramatic cantilever of the Lovell Beach House, Los Angeles, CA, 1927–1929.

Left: Irving Gill
(1870–1936): Dodge House,
Los Angeles, CA,
1914–1916. Demolished.

surfaces, a dominant coping along the roof line and sequences of highly ornamental horizontal banding and grooving across the façade, in addition to linear-patterned balustrades.

Among the first generation of Modernist architectural practitioners in America was Rudolph Schindler, who had trained in his native Austria, but after arriving in the United States had worked with Wright from 1918. After forming his own practice in Los Angeles in 1921 he went on also to work in collaboration with Richard Neutra after 1925. Like Neutra, Schindler spent his American apprenticeship with Wright, but was also strongly influenced, perhaps more directly, by European Modernism and especially Cubist affirmations of pure

Above: Rudolph M. Schindler (1887–1953): Schindler House, 835 North King's Road, West Hollywood, CA, 1921–1922. Schindler designed an innovative house and studio for himself and another couple, who lived here in an unusual cooperative arrangement.

Above: Rudolph M. Schindler: Lovell Beach House, Newport Beach, CA, 1922–1926. An early example of the International Style in the United States, the second story of this beach house is dramatically cantilevered.

Left: Richard Neutra (1892–1970): Philip Lovell House, Los Angeles, CA, 1927–1929. Born in Vienna, Neutra worked with leading architects there before coming to the United States in 1923. He worked briefly with Frank Lloyd Wright before establishing his own practice.

form. Unlike Gill, Schindler focused on the design of costly private villas, and among these produced some of the most influential designs of early twentieth century American architecture in a "Modernist" style.

Both the Schindler House in West Hollywood of 1922 and the more famous Lovell Beach House in Newport Beach, California, of 1925–1926, are further examples of a personalized and eclectic interpretation of the modern form, but in this case are in some ways more directly related to Le Corbusier's maxim that houses should be "machines for living in," therefore importing a strong contemporary European inflection into the American scene. Schindler was less taken by the purity of abstract form than concerned with the manipulation of structure and light. Both the Schindler House and the Lovell Beach House originally incorporated open-roofed sleeping porches and interior walls of unmasked cement, evidence of how thoroughly still-radical construction materials were being embraced for the purposes of domestic architecture.

In the Lovell Beach House, Schindler lifted the whole of the house up off the narrow ocean-side site on five massive concrete piers. These frames intersect with the horizontal trays forming the two floors to define interior spaces. The partially cantilevered sleeping porch (originally unroofed) of the second story reaches out-

ward toward the ocean, while the main rectangle of the house sits behind. Although in the design of Schindler's own house the influence of Wright was predominant, here he has drawn upon the visual language of the European avant-garde and treated the house as a refined, geometric entity whose apparent monumentality overpowers the small patch of open ground directly beneath the house. Schindler's statement has no American precedent. It is individualized through the configuration of the piers and the anonymous intersections of verticals and horizontals which frame the glass walls of the three visible sides of the main block. The whole of the composition seems to be controlled by an invisible gridded network. The relationship between the house and nature is apparently ambivalent. Primary components of beach living—sun, water, and air—are reinterpreted not as elemental forces, but as catalysts or technologies for the benefit of the individual. Architecture come to express a regional utopian lifestyle.

If Schindler embodied the abstract modernity of the domestic home, Neutra did the same for a new futuristic society. The house he designed for the same patron—the California fitness authority Philip Lovell—is a metaphor in built form for the optimistic and mechanistic modernity of twentieth century life. The Lovell "Health" House, dating from 1927 to 1929, shares much of the visual

Right: Richard Neutra
(1892–1970): Philip Lovell
House, Los Angeles, CA,
1927–1929.

impact of Schindler's work and speaks of a new style in American architecture. It is a modular structure built to a strict grid. Its components are treated as individual fragments of an all-embracing gridded space which extends not only inside, but outside the house and beyond. It is constructed of a steel framed skeleton fabricated in sections, and then welded together on site upon a concrete foundation; the whole process taking just forty hours. The steel sash windows, part of the integral structure, are distributed in running bands over much of the building. The skeleton was covered with sprayed-on concrete known as "gunite," and gives the appearance of having been completed throughout with mass-manufactured components. Its spaces are staggered and the house is flat-roofed, in part raised above ground on slender piers, diminishing the preponderance of traditional mass while emphasizing the comparative lightness of volume. White stuccoed terraces appear to float in tandem with the contours of the craggy hillside. In this house Neutra commandeered technological imagery in order to reflect a society governed by industrial processes and regulation, and to equate the health of individuals with an essentially technocratic vision of the future.

Schindler and Neutra, as well as their contemporary Pierre Koenig and the later architect Craig Ellwood, measured the future of architecture in terms of industrial technology. To greater or lesser degrees all shared an ambition to relieve architecture of its dependence upon traditions of hand craftsmanship, and therefore promoted the use of industrially produced components for domestic housing. Ellwood produced three designs for the Case Study House program between 1945 and 1962. A scheme comprising twenty such houses by progressive Modernist architects including Charles Eames was originally commissioned for the magazine *Arts + Architecture*. Within the context of post-World War II American architecture, this was something of a militant gesture which in part defied traditions of the building trade by favoring a housing strategy which promoted the notion of "good" contemporary design for its incorporation of mass-manufactured building products and, by the end of the scheme, the endorsement of industrial steel framing for standard use in housing. Mundane industrial products came to be promoted in architecture not only for their reduced cost and functional value, but equally for the raw simplicity of their aesthetic form.

Above: Eduardo Catalano: Catalano House, Raleigh, NC, 1954–1955. The roof is the primary element of this house.

Right: Bruce Goff (1904–1982): Gene Bavinger House, Norman, OK, 1950–1955.

Below: Eduardo Catalano (b. 1917): Catalano House, Catalano Street, Raleigh, NC, 1954–1955.

International Style

The term "International Style" originated with the American architect Philip Johnson. It was the title of an exhibition of modern architecture and design he organized at the Museum of Modern Art in New York in 1932 and had been derived from the book *Internationale Architektur* of 1925, written by the first director of the Bauhaus design school in Germany, Walter Gropius. The earliest European architects to practice in this style did not themselves use the term, but following the MOMA exhibition the name gained common currency. It is now used to denote an avant-garde swing in architectural design which, although often dated from c.1925 to c.1945, can more accurately be seen to have its inception around the time of World War I in the European architecture of, for example, Josef Hoffmann, Adolf Loos,

and Walter Gropius. The style was more fully developed in Gropius' designs for the Dessau Bauhaus buildings of 1925–1926 in Germany. In design for residential structures the early landmark example is the Villa Savoye near Paris of 1929–1931 by the Swiss architect Charles-Édouard Jeanneret, known as Le Corbusier. That house remains one of the most famous monuments of the style.

During the inter-war years European architects and designers had intentionally sought a new stylistic agenda which, they argued, repudiated all visual and structural suggestions of the architectural past. But in America, with the exception of Frank Lloyd Wright, design for domestic architecture remained dependent upon revivalist styles and ideas derived from the national past. Perhaps the most important single factor which breached this conservatism was the immigration of the Bauhaus masters Walter Gropius and Ludwig Mies van der Rohe to the United States from Germany during the 1930s. Both were fleeing the tyranny of Nazi Germany.

The new so-called International Style they introduced into the American scene was characterized by a robust asymmetry, assertively cubic shapes, a great confidence in the use of glass and metal—usually steel—for the framework, proportionally large windows disposed in running horizontal bands, the absence of any moldings and the placement of windows flush with the wall

Above: Ludwig Mies van der Rohe (1886–1969): 860–880 Lake Shore Drive, Chicago, IL, 1948–1951. The individual units of this high-rise are more adapted to traditional living styles than the Farnsworth House, and have been continuously successful.

Above: Ludwig Mies van der Rohe: 860–880 Lake Shore Drive, Chicago, IL, 1948–1951. The entrance level is deliberately very minimalist in these buildings.

Above: Pierre Koenig, Case Study Home, California. International Style houses feature stark rectilinear patterning, open plans, and transparent walls.

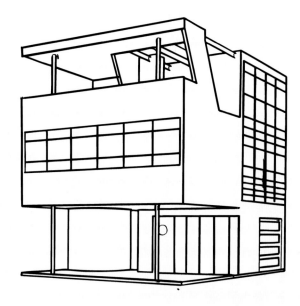

Above: Albert Frey and A. Lawrence Kocher: the Aluminaire, now at New York Institute of Technology, Central Islip, Long Island, NY, 1931. Another experiment in technology, the Aluminaire has recently been restored.

Above: International Style house—Gropius House, Lincoln, MA, 1938.

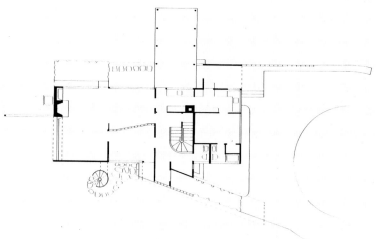

Above: Walter Gropius: plan of the Gropius House, Lincoln, MA, 1938.

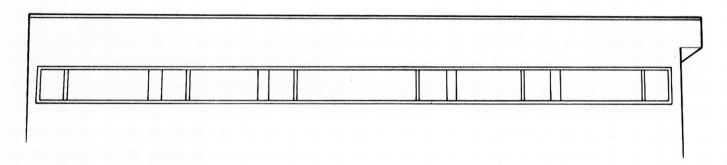

Above: Drawing of ribbon window, Gropius House, Lincoln, MA.

Above: Albert Frey (1903–1998): Frey House II, 686 Palisades Drive, Palm Springs, CA, 1964. Frey worked with Le Corbusier in Paris in the 1920s before coming to America in 1930.

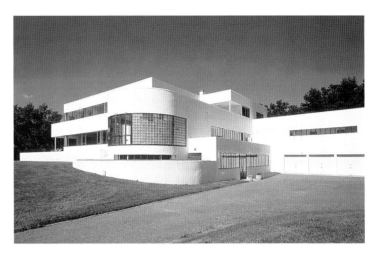

Above: Edward Durrell Stone (1902–1978): Mandel House, Bedford Hills, NY, 1933–1934. The entire vocabulary of the International Style is here—ribbon windows, flat roofs, sleek white walls with no ornament or traditional forms.

Above: Pierre Koenig (b. 1925): Case Study House #22, Los Angeles, CA, 1959. A classic Modernist house overlooking Los Angeles. The curtain wall of glass and open plan are used to dramatic effect.

Above: Walter Gropius (1883–1969): Gropius House, Baker Bridge Road, Lincoln, MA, 1938. Signature elements of the International Style include the ribbon window, the white color, the abstract geometry and lack of ornament.

surface. The ground plan was completely open, versatile and spacious, and the exterior was almost always white rendered, often of cement with stucco above.

After arriving in America, Gropius was appointed head of the Architecture Department at Harvard in 1938, and Mies took up an equivalent post at the Illinois Institute of Technology in Chicago. Their pioneering Modernism, especially in its application to domestic structures, was received in America with cautious skepticism by some and distress by others. Before the post-war era, relatively few International Style residences were either commissioned or constructed in the United States, although there was a marginally more receptive response to the style in the design of public and some commercial buildings.

One of the most important new residences in the style was the house Gropius built for himself outside of Boston in 1938. In its emphasis on geometric form and pure surfaces, the house clearly incorporated the advanced design principles of, at this time, European pedigree.

The shape of the flat roof is tied into the workings of the drainage system, and obviated the need for unsightly guttering and downpipes. Some portions of the asymmetrical façade appear cut-out, allowing for more than one discreet entrance and the addition of an industrial spiral staircase to the side elevation. The house also has an exterior aluminum blind which is operated from inside, and by deflecting heat helps to control the temperature within. There are multiple horizontally disposed windows, but also anti-heat mechanisms within the house to control warmth and cross-ventilation. The cubic porch is composed of a platform structure with vertical screens.

Inside the house, living spaces are multi-purpose with only necessary divisions, and the central space opens outward to combine with all subsidiary areas. There is only one hallway in the building. One of the most progressive features of the house resulted from Gropius' belief that in domestic architecture high-grade

Left: Walter Gropius: Gropius House, Baker Bridge Road, Lincoln, MA, 1938. The vertical wooden siding is one acknowledgment of the New England building tradition.

Above: Mail-order Modernism: "The Bryant" model, available in 1938 and 1939 Sears catalogs. The new Modernist styles even made inroads in the traditionally oriented mail-order catalogs of Sears and other building companies.

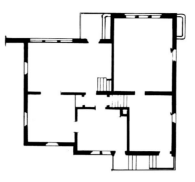

Above: Plan of "The Bryant" model, available in 1938 and 1939 Sears catalogs. The plan is still somewhat conventional.

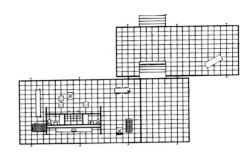

Above: Ludwig Mies van der Rohe: plan of the Dr. Edith Farnsworth House, Plano, Illinois, 1945–1951. The Farnsworth House approaches Mies' ideal of an uninterrupted "universal space."

materials used in readily available, mass-produced, and simply-designed industrial and commercial components—often available from stock catalogs—were most appropriate for fixtures and fittings. For Modernist designers like Gropius, mass-produced components took on an almost sacred quality and stood as metaphors for democratic principles and economic prosperity. The only custom-made feature of the house is the curvilinear banister of the interior stairway.

Gropius also insisted upon a reduced color palette for the house. The exterior is white and gray, and the interior a combination of gray, brown, and white. Walls throughout the building are strictly white. In large part, Gropius saw this revolutionary house as proof that industrial products of American mass-manufacture were natural parts of highly sophisticated contemporary design.

The Farnsworth House, designed by Ludwig Mies van der Rohe for his enlightened patron Edith Farnsworth in Plano, Illinois, and dating from 1945 to 1951, is another milestone of the International Style in American residential architecture. It is perhaps the strongest statement yet

Above: Ludwig Mies Van der Rohe (1886–1969): Dr. Edith Farnsworth House, 14520 River Road, Plano, IL, 1945–1951. Distant view. This weekend house for Dr. Farnsworth was one of the purest examples of Miesian International Style architecture. Although the client was not completely satisfied, it is a modern classic.

Above: Ludwig Mies Van der Rohe: Dr. Edith Farnsworth House, Plano, IL, 1945–1951. Near view. This kind of Modernist architecture requires that the owner adapt to its constraints.

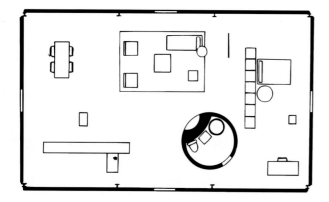

Above: Philip Johnson: plan of Glass House, New Canaan, CT, 1946–1949. Johnson's house is a model of elegant simplicity.

in America of the application of thoroughly modern technology to a domestic residence. The house is constructed of steel-section and glass sheet. Its volumes are aggressively cubic and its forms undiluted by historical referencing or decorative detailing. The asymmetrical plan is arranged in two contiguous but staggered rectangles, one the raised house and the second the stepped platform. Floor and roof slabs are together supported on eight, white-painted vertical steel beams, raising the house above the ground and opening up the walls to accommodate the running panes of sheet glass. The entry platform is offset to the "front" of the house and first connected to the ground and then to the building

Above: Philip Johnson (b. 1906): Johnson House, New Canaan, CT, 1946–1949. Distant view. Built during a period when Johnson was very close to Mies, this house exemplifies the new Modernist style.

Left: Philip Johnson: Johnson House, New Canaan, CT, 1946–1949. Close view. The transparency which characterizes modern architecture is clearly shown here. Unlike earlier centuries, it is not mass, but space which is the dominant element.

Left: Philip Johnson: House, New York, NY, 1950. The International Style adapted to an urban townhouse.

Above: Bertram Goldberg: Marina City, Chicago, IL, 1964, 1967. Goldberg sought to create an alternative to the glass box of the International Style with these circular towers. A parking ramp is included on the lower levels.

by short series of wide steps at two levels. The interior is sandwiched between the flat platform of the roof and that of the base. It is relatively small, and approximately one-quarter the length of the supporting platform is given over to a patio open on three sides but sheltered beneath the flat roof. Glazed from floor to ceiling, the interior is a single open space but for the understated articulation of kitchen and bathroom by wood partitions. In order to accommodate storage, Mies used a freestanding wardrobe which rises to just above half the height of the interior and divides the sleeping and living domains. Due to the transparent walls, the house lays comfortably within its site rather than intruding upon it, and offers uninterrupted views over the valleys beyond. The Farnsworth House was a perfection of Mies' experimentations with the basic form of the open pavilion which he envisaged as an open interior "floating" space without visible means of support. He had sought a free-floating volume outlined by two plates which would comprise the skeletal construction, and a perfect façade which was not façade but rather a transparent curtain wall.

The Farnsworth House provided the immediate model for the summer house Philip Johnson designed for himself in 1949 in New Canaan, Connecticut. Johnson had studied under Gropius at Harvard and then gone on to be Director of the Architecture and Design department at the Museum of Modern Art in New York, and had also worked with Mies on the Seagram Building as a project architect. One of the primary differences between the Farnsworth House and Johnson's House in New Canaan, however, is that where Mies tended toward the use of standardized steel sections to make a strong statement about structural finish on a façade—essentially a decorative statement—Johnson was determined to

obscure structure through the manipulation of surface. His "Glass House," as the summer residence came to be called, is even more transparent than the Farnsworth and departed radically from Mies's concentration on structural logic as the basis of contemporary architecture.

Despite their differences, however, the two houses seem to share a common aesthetic. The Johnson House has the same flat roof, the same rectangular "box" form, the same radical dependence on function, the same constructional use of stock structural members, and the same banishment of architectural "waste" that is prominent in the Farnsworth House. It could be said that Johnson's design is even more reductive that Mies's. Living is no longer a matter of Victorian privacy. The private house has become a showcase for a marriage between a culture of affluence and progressive design. In the Johnson House, only the bathroom space is private, walled with a huge brick cylinder which punctuates the open flow of the interior and sympathetically marries organic materials (the shallow plinth upon which the house rests is also brick-faced) with anonymous, industrial ones. Johnson admitted that in the house he adapted many details from Mies's work, including the treatment of the corners of the rectangle and the varied relation of the structural columns to the window frames. Both architects relied upon standard industrial sections of steel for the framework, although in its proportions the Johnson House, despite its very small size, has a feeling of monumentality which takes the place of the lyricism injected into the asymmetry of the Farnsworth design. In the end, both houses remain picturesque "villas," and their elegant use of industrial metalwork signaled modernity and the validation of industrial forces in residential architectural design.

The Modern Age

Abby Moor

The single most crucial design problem any architect can address is the house; it is the one building type that responds to all of the basic human requirements, and which stimulates in the creative mind the largest variety of personal interpretation. The house shapes how the human being lives on a daily basis, and through the history of architecture it has been the single most important storehouse of our traditional cultural values, while at the same time the site of our most progressive thinking. Never has this been more evident than in the decades since World War II.

Lifestyle, aspiration, security, and privacy are implicit in a house, as are achievement and permanence. When we study types of houses, we study other people's ways of living. Every celebrated architect of the twentieth century has designed at least one celebrated house. Through the house, both the patron and the architect become known to us. Moreover, the most consistent commission for the majority of American architects is the design, restoration, renovation, or amplification of the single-family home. For all of these reasons, the house continues to hold a very special position in our imaginations, as well as in architectural culture.

Since the late 1940s, new and different types of vernacular and architect-designed houses have arisen in America alongside the more traditional types

Right: Charles Gwathmey (b. 1938): Gwathmey House and Studio, Amagansett, NY, 1965.

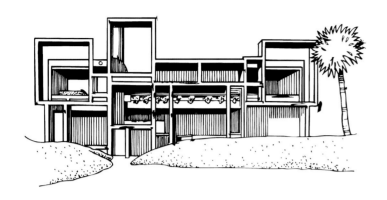

Above: Paul Rudolph: Arthur W. Milam House, St. John's County, FL, 1962. The Milam House is an abstract sculpture of rectangular forms which incorporates a machine-like efficiency of space and function in the manner of Le Corbusier.

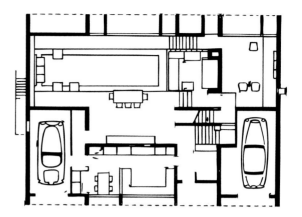

Above: Paul Rudolph: plan of Arthur W. Milam House, lower level, St. John's County, FL, 1962.

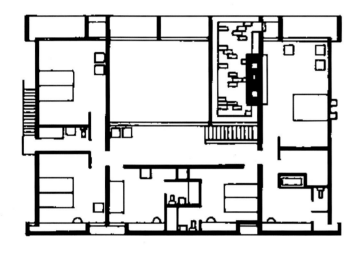

Above: Paul Rudolph: plan of Arthur W. Milam House, upper level, St. John's County, FL, 1962.

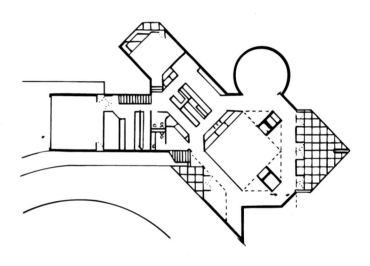

Above: Romaldo Giurgola: plan of Dayton House, Wayzata, MN, 1970.

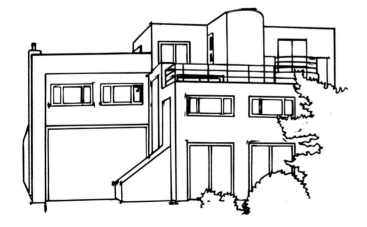

Above: Modernistic seaside house. Seaside houses invited informality and experimental designs in the 1960s and 1970s.

Above: Shed style modernistic house. East Hampton, NY.

which continue to carry symbolic value to those who live in them. There was a massive growth of housing in the decades of prosperity which followed the war. Mass housing dominated the market in the era of the baby boom in terms of numbers, although a smaller number of very experimental houses has dominated the field of architectural criticism. The tensions between high culture and mass culture have never been more intense, or led to more interesting results.

When house construction started-up again in earnest following the end of World War II, the many new styles of the vernacular modern American home sprang up in a wide variety of fairly adaptable sub-types. These often renewed or developed pre-war styles found in the expanding suburbs of the 1930s. The most fundamental type of post-war suburban house was the single-family dwelling which accommodated returning G.I.s and their burgeoning families.

Above: Gwathmey Siegel: Taft Residence, Cincinnati, OH, 1979.

Above: Gwathmey Siegel: Spielberg Residence, East Hampton, NY, 1988.

Above: American Foursquare house, from *The Books of a Thousand Homes, vol. 1: 500 Small House Plans*, 1923. The boxy square house was easy to build, and was widespread in urban and suburban communities. It was related to some of Wright's Prairie School designs.

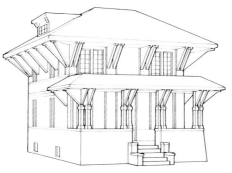

Above: Thomas Alva Edison: Foursquare home made of poured concrete, 1907. Edison patented techniques for constructing houses almost entirely of concrete. These met with only limited success, however.

Above: American Foursquare house, derived from Frank Lloyd Wright's Prairie School designs, published in a pattern book in 1928.

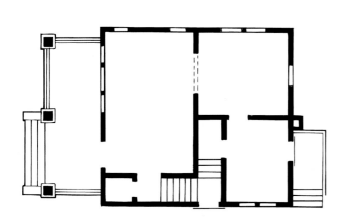

Above: Plan of typical American Foursquare house, Loizeaux home.

Above: Square Prairie Style house, published in *The Books of a Thousand Homes, vol. I: 500 Small House Plans*, New York, 1923.

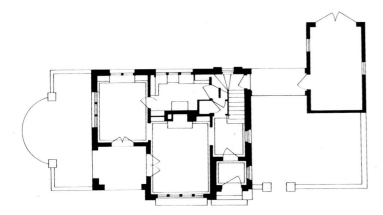

Above: Plan of square Prairie Style house, published in *The Books of a Thousand Homes, vol. I: 500 Small House Plans*, New York, 1923.

Above: One-story Foursquare house; the Wards "Gary" model, 1927.

Vernacular Houses—the American Foursquare

In the first decades of the century, the Prairie house pioneered by Frank Lloyd Wright had been transformed into the popular American Foursquare type. These were typically rather large, cubic, or simple rectangular two-story structures with a low-pitched hipped roof, and usually asymmetrical entrance. The typical vernacular interpretation of the type may have had the addition of a single-story wing or carport, and many examples were further adapted with a front entry porch reminiscent of the piered, low-pitched frontages of the earlier Craftsman or Bungalow style. Foursquare houses were available through pattern books and builder's catalogs, and were built across America. Bill Clinton's birthplace in Arkansas was such a house. Thomas Alva Edison even patented a nearly all-concrete house for mass production; the concrete model remained a curiosity, however.

Above: American Foursquare house, near Belvidere, NJ, c. 1920. This house clearly shows the resemblances to Frank Lloyd Wright's simpler Prairie School houses.

Above: Foursquare house, Brunswick, ME,

The Challenge of Providing Housing for the Masses

Suburban planning became a crucial issue after the war. It drew directly upon the strategies of the military during the war years for the efficient erection of new housing for military staff and their families, but also looked to the planned housing formulated to accommodate the large numbers of people working in the defense industries. The model for many post-war schemes was the utopian project initiated in the Oak Ridge community of Tennessee, drawn-up during the war by the New York and Chicago based firm of Skidmore, Owings & Merrill—best known by their initials S.O.M.—who also achieved a distinguished international reputation in the field of modern corporate architecture.

But the most famous, as well as controversial early post-war pre-planned suburban housing scheme was that at Levittown, Long Island, built by William and Alfred Levitt during the late 1940s, using the most innovative construction methods and modeled immediately upon building practices developed to facilitate the war effort. The Levitts adopted swift construction processes that relied upon standardized dimensions and components. An assembly-line method was introduced in the work-force facilitating the completion of singular, specialized tasks at each site by individuals who moved from house

Above: William Levitt (1907–1994) and Alfred Levitt (1894–1991): Levittown, Long Island, NY, 1946–1951. View of a typical street; rows of standardized Cape Cod and Ranch houses dominated the settlement of Levittown.

Above: Bill Clinton birthplace, Hope, AK, 1917. An American Foursquare house.

Right: William and Alfred Levitt: house, Levittown, Long Island, NY, 1946–1951. Although the original design options were limited, Levittown owners have frequently altered their houses to create individualized residences.

Right: William and Alfred
Levitt: house, Levittown,
Long Island, NY,
1946–1951.

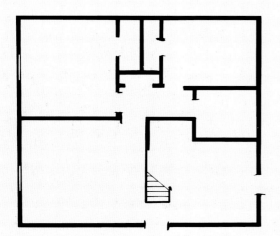

Above: Plan of standard Cape house, Levittown, Long Island,
NY, 1947. Practical and efficient, plans and exterior designs
were standardized for mass production.

to house in sequence. By utilizing what were essentially industrial production methods, the Levitts were able to produce new homes quickly and efficiently, keeping costs low and production high. For example, once the concrete foundation slab was poured, the exterior and interior wall frames were fabricated rapidly from standardized joists, then raised into place, wall boarded, roofed, and shingled. Levitt's methods were not far removed from those developed for wartime pre-fabricated housing, and in the end produced similar results.

Levittown is rather less important historically for its two earliest styles of small houses, than for being a ready-made housing community which embodied a notion at the heart of the American Dream: individual home ownership and occupation. The first stages of the new community were spread out over former farming land. Long axial boulevards accommodating through traffic separated smaller "villages" of long curving streets lined with single-family dwellings. The focus of the scheme was to provide affordable housing—both rental and subsequently owned—in the form of small, compact detached units with front gardens and driveways, all "villages" having unfenced common ground behind the rows of identical houses, each of which had its own backyard.

These instantaneous "villages" were initially composed of Levitt's Cape Cod style house, developed from 1947, and after 1949 also of the Levitt Ranch House. Both were essentially boxlike structures of remarkably simple plan raised above a poured concrete slab into which standardized plumbing and under-floor heating elements were set. Each of the Cape houses followed the same internal plan. Two bedrooms were aligned across the back of the house, separated by the back door, while the kitchen and living room were aligned across the front of the building. The bathroom was situated immediately behind the kitchen, allowing all the plumbing to be concentrated along both sides of a single internal wall, thus reducing costs and facilitating quick and efficient installation. Living spaces were small and opened onto one another, but could be extended into the unfinished attic space at the occupier's own expense.

The Cape House had its stylistic precursors in historic New England housing types with steeply pitched roofs, simple side gables, false shutters, and wood cladding. The slightly later Levitt Ranch style drew on Californian prototypes and offered a split-level roof and a reversal of the interior organization of rooms, having the living area facing onto the garden and thus reflecting concepts of relaxed suburban living with family and neighborhood leisure

Above: Cape style house, Kennebunk, ME. Mid-twentieth century.

activities outdoors, concentrated in the backyard and the common.

Despite its forceful homogeneity as a pre-planned lifestyle community, Levittown was a thoroughly innovative concept which had serious repercussions in the planning and growth of the American suburb.

Left: Cape style house, Kennebunk, ME. Mid-twentieth century.

Right: Ranch house, Waltham, MA. One of the most popular mid-century designs, the Ranch house was adapted from California ranches and Prairie School houses. The low-pitched roof and the horizontal windows distinguish it from the Cape style houses.

Developer Houses

Outside of complete planned communities such as Levittown, other new stylistic sub-types in post-war suburban housing came to be preferred by property developers, and are therefore referred to as "Developer Houses." These were the Minimal type with front and side gables, the Ranch, Split-Level, and Contemporary box-style, and the Shed type. Of these, the Ranch-style home was by far the most popular throughout the country. Because of its sprawling aspect, the Ranch-style home has come to signify the prosperity associated with private land ownership, although they can also be quite modest in size. Originating in California in the 1930s, the style predominated in domestic house design through the end of the 1960s, and remains a very popular and adaptable type today. It is typically a single-story structure with a staggered frontage and low-pitched roofs. It gives the impression of the building stretching laterally across the surface of the landscape, and may incorporate large open-planned living areas, floor-to-ceiling windows and double glass doors along stretches of the rear façade, in addition to substantial hearths. Windows along the front elevation are generally smaller, and often horizontal in format. The type usually boasts built-in one-, two-, or even three-car garages as an integral part of the structure, with access directly off the kitchen or utility room. Eaves are usually deep and the plan typically includes front and side gables in an asymmetrical "L"-shaped format. The length of the house along the prospect of approach emphasizes its sprawling form, suggesting the comparative availability of land and the luxury of outdoor living. The Ranch-style house may have exposed rafters, and any variety of traditional detailing drawn from earlier historic styles, but false shutters are somewhat common, and either wooden and brick cladding or a combination of both may be used.

Above: Ranch house, early 1950s. Derived from California ranches and Prairie School houses, the Ranch house became ubiquitous in the mid-twentieth century.

Above: Ranch house, Cape May, NJ.

Above: Garrison colonial house, Newton, MA, 1936.

Above: Split-Level house, Waltham, MA, c. 1960s.

Above: Windmill House, Arlington, MA, 1930s. An offbeat Dutch colonial house with a built-in windmill.

Above: Drawing of Split-Level house, c. 1960. The Split-Level house offered more space and privacy for larger families.

The Minimal Traditional House

In comparison, the so-called "Minimal traditional" postwar type is essentially a composite style, expressing traditional plans and the massing of volumes, but without the decorative exuberance of pre-war Eclectic models. This type of house tended to be small and compact, rather than expansive, with eaves confined to the plane of the elevation, a single front-facing gable, and the pitch at an intermediate level. The overall impression is of an updated cottage-type dwelling, and this style is usually of a single story. The garage is usually sited separately behind the house, but may be attached via a passageway leading out from the side of the main structure. The type became common in suburbs during the 1940s and generally represents modest single-family homes on smaller individual plots. Exterior cladding may be stone or brick on the first-story with wood above if the house is of two floors, or two materials may be combined within a single-story façade, the second surface treatment comprising the inside of the front-facing gable. The latter elevation usually carries a larger-than-average picture window.

Above: Split-Level house c. 1960s.

Above: Bay and oriel window on Split-Level house.

Above: MLTW (Charles Moore, Donlyn Lyndon, William Turnbull, and Richard Whitaker): Condominium 1, Sea Ranch, Gualala, CA, 1965.

Split-Level Homes

As new theories of domestic American family life blossomed during the prosperity of the 1950s, the Ranch style home was modified, one lateral wing being compacted into a double elevation, usually with an integral garage and family activity rooms on the lower-ground level and bedrooms above. The formal reception or living area, as well as the kitchen, entryway, and utility rooms remained on the main or "mid" level, which accommodated the quiet interior areas as opposed to the "noisy" rooms for family games and the new technology of the television. This Split-Level style became very popular on the Eastern Seaboard and in the Midwest, where the basement was already a traditional part of the family home, but was less common in the damp conditions of the South, as well as in the Western states where the more arid climate encouraged larger, more open ground-hugging designs.

Above: Richard Meier (b. 1934): Grotta House, Harding Township, NJ.

Above: Romaldo Giurgola (b. 1920): Dayton House, Wayzata, MN, 1970.

Above: Arquitectonica: Spear House, Miami, FL, 1978.

Above: Krueck and Olson: Steel and Glass House, Chicago, IL, 1980.

Contemporary and Shed Style Homes

The remaining two most popular types of post-war house were the so-called Contemporary home, and the more architecturally dynamic Shed style. The earliest of these was the Contemporary style which originated as an architect-designed type during the mid-to-late 1950s. It quickly adapted the flat roof of the more European International Style, from which it also derived the use of exterior roof supports, large asymmetrical expanses of windows, and mock cantilevered verandas. The type tends to juxtapose faceted geometric planes and masses, and relies on textures and materials to give detail to the façades, incorporating little if any decorative detailing. Within this type there is a sub-type which emphasizes the front-facing gable.

One of the most interesting developments in post-war American housing design was the "Shed" style which emerged during the early 1960s. Its characteristic feature is the massing of multi-directional roof forms, often combining the traditional vernacular shed-roof type with its distinctive downward pitch with one or more gables. Each of the roof structures denotes a separate internal volume of varying height and shape. The whole appears to be an amalgam of separate parts, arbitrarily joined together to form a single dwelling. The inspiration for this development was the emerging Postmodern aesthetic of young progressive architects such as Robert Venturi, whose interest in formalizing the vernacular in contemporary architectural expression gave rise to this style's characteristic collusion of

Above: Steven Holl (b. 1947): Berkowitz Ogdis House, Martha's Vineyard, MA, 1984.

expanding and receding geometric masses. The best and most well-crafted examples of this well-to-do suburban style have board siding affixed diagonally, but in the original models by Venturi and Charles Moore wood-shingle, and vertical or horizontal siding were also used. Windows tend to be small and asymmetrically distributed, and no details are allowed to interrupt the dramatic effects of convergence and contrast between the separate masses.

Above: Modernist house, Moon Hill, Lexington, MA.

Above: Round house, Edelweis Road, Ludlow, VT.

Right: Modernist beach house, shed roof, Dune Road, West Hampton, Long Island, NY.

Neo-Eclectic

During the post-war period, a great assortment of domestic architectural styles has seemed to gain and lose popularity almost arbitrarily, offering a very wide selection of types and design schemes to the more recent buyer. This may have made the process of selecting design types difficult for builders, developers, and consumers, but has demonstrated the natural eclecticism of American taste. Housing types have embraced a remarkably wide range of responses to innovation, building techniques, the use of materials, as well as ecological solutions. Such imaginaton and practicality can be seen in houses across the economic board.

Right: Modernist house, Dune Road, West Hampton, Long Island, NY.

Left: Late-Modern beach houses, Dune Road, Hamptons, Long Island, NY.

Within a wide range of Eclectic-inspired housing styles, however, a number of specific sub-types have been identified. Most can be found in select suburbs throughout the country in greater or lesser states of elaboration, while on the whole landmark examples of these "Neo-Eclectic" styles remain unusual.

In the first decade after World War II, the Eclectic styles popularized during the 1920s and 1930s continued in post-war construction, until superseded by a vernacular translation of the Modern Style, which remained dominant from the late 1950s through to about 1970. Trends in architectural taste, however, began to turn

Left: Late-modern beach house, Dune Road, Hamptons, Long Island, NY.

Above left: House, Waltham, MA, c. 1960s. A cross-gable, minimal traditionalist house.

Above: Developer house, Waltham, MA, c. 1990s.

Left: Neoclassical Revival house, Andover, MA. Central portico.

Below: House, Hammersmith Village, Saugus, MA. Central portico.

Above: House, Hammersmith Village, Saugus, MA. Full-height colonnade.

Above: Neoclassical Revival house, Coxsackie, NY. Full-height colonnade.

Above: Colonial Re-revival house, Danvers, MA.

Above: Colonial Re-revival house, Kennebunkport, ME, 1990s.

Above: Colonial Re-revival house, Kennebunkport, ME, 1990s. The Palladian window on the third floor is a tip-off that this is a contemporary house.

Above: Tudor Re-revival house, Andover, MA.

Above: Colonial Re-revival house, Kennebunkport, ME, 1990s. A Garrison colonial, accurately copied from earlier examples.

Above: Colonial Re-revival house, Kennebunkport, ME, 1990s. Garrison colonial with dormers, which are purely decorative, and not historically accurate.

Above: Victorian Re-revival cottage, Cape May, NJ, 1986. This house blends perfectly with the Victorian architecture which characterizes Cape May, and is nearly indistinguishable from original Victorian homes.

toward more conservative models during the late 1960s when traditional forms were resurrected and restyled into what is now called the "Neo-eclectic" phase of American housing.

Initially the new "mansard" roofing style emerged in both domestic housing and small-to-medium-scale commercial building. It was especially suitable as a means of dressing up block-shaped apartment complexes, adding a pseudo-monumentality to their elevation and profile. The slightly sloping elevation of the high raised roof, flat on top, proved a comparatively inexpensive means of infusing a European-derived urbanity into otherwise conventional structures, and was also a compelling surface for embellishment with ornamental roof detailing, the most popular being shingling. In later, more modish, examples arched pillars of windows rise through the line of the cornice. Other Neo-eclectic styles which appeared toward the end of the 1960s and continue into the present day include the Neo-French, Neo-Colonial, Neo-Tudor, Neo-Mediterranean, Neoclassical Revival, and Neo-Victorian. The majority of these trends were not originally architect-designed, but rather introduced into the market by property developers and builders seeking variations on established themes and employing only a modicum of historically derived detailing. Most of these styles are found in both suburban housing and apartment complexes where their free adaptation has gained them a stable degree of popularity nationwide.

Above: Quonset Hut frame, Quonset, RI. The Nissen Hut was said to have been modeled on Iroquois lodges, and the Quonset Hut frames clearly resemble eastern Native American shelters.

Above: Quonset Hut, Quonset, RI, 1940s. Quonset Huts were an improved version of prefabricated housing known as Nissen Huts produced in Britain during WWII. They answered a need for inexpensive mass housing during the conflict.

Pre-Fabricated Housing—Folk Architecture for the Machine Age

A further significant trend in the history of American post-war housing whose historical importance should not be undervalued is a renewed interest in "Folk" houses. Since the 1940s some of these have been in common use, whereas others began and remain associated with a more scientific stream of architectural thought, while another group is dependent upon the pre-fabricated industrial construction schemes used so effectively during the war. The Quonset Hut is one of the most fascinating of these types. Originating in 1941 as an all-purpose, pre-fabricated unit composed of pressed-wood linings, and pre-manufactured wood ribbing covered by a sheathing of corrugated sheet steel, the Quonset Hut was developed for use by the U.S. Navy. It was produced during the war with standardized components and in pre-specified sizes. For a structure of its size, the Quonset Hut was abnormally light, straightforward to assemble and disassemble, made of relatively inexpensive materials, and easily transportable for military use throughout the world. During the war, nearly 200,000 were constructed. After the war a good number were returned to the States where they often acquired the status of military surplus. As such, they remained an inexpensive but

Left: Quonset Hut, Abingdon, MA, c. 1940s. Originally built in great numbers as prefabricated housing during WWII, only a few Quonset Huts still remain as houses.

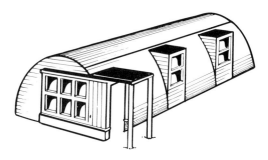

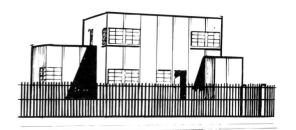

Above: Customized Quonset Hut home, with dormers and portico, from 1947 brochure.

Left: Motohome, prefabricated steel house. Garden City, Long Island, NY. An experimental house built of steel.

Right: Diagram of double-wide mobile home, showing how two ten-foot-wide units are joined to make a twenty-foot-wide home (double-wide). The ten foot width allows them to be transported on highways.

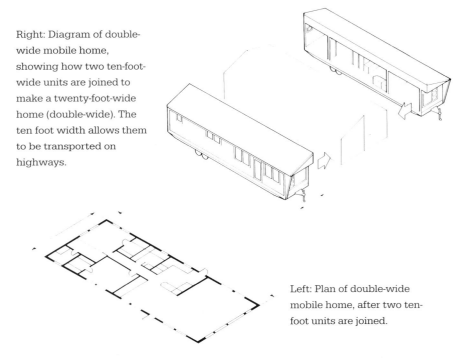

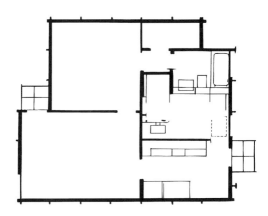

Above: Plan of Motohome, prefabricated steel house. Garden City, Long Island, NY.

Left: Plan of double-wide mobile home, after two ten-foot units are joined.

Above: Lustron all-metal house, model # 02, West Roxbury, MA, c. 1949–1950. These early metal houses included many modern conveniences. The exterior was designed to require no maintenance. Pictures were hung on walls using special brackets. Several thousands of these houses were sold before the company went out of business.

Above: Lustron all-metal house, model # 02, Brookline, MA, 1949–1950.

Above: Frank Lloyd Wright: Walter Rudin House, Madison, WI, 1957. Another example of Wright's experimentation with designs for pre-fabricated houses.

sound investment, and were quickly transformed into low-priced housing, as well as agricultural and industrial work and storage space. Their spacious interiors and all-weather, all-terrain capacity meant that they were at once attractive for rural or low-income domestic use, and were soon easily remodeled into permanent dwellings using residential-style windows, doorways, porches, and heating systems. Unfortunately, few examples of such homes survive and the Quonset Hut is now found primarily in agricultural settings.

The concept of prefabrication in housing, however, originally dated back to the mid-nineteenth century when both European and East Coast American manufacturers devised basic prefabricated units which were easily transported by train to the mining communities proliferating in the American North West during the Gold Rush. Pre-fab houses and agricultural buildings were available through American mail-order firms by the turn of the century, and at the root of American architectural practice there has consistently existed an underlying ambition to formulate a successful scheme for making readily affordable mass housing through industrial production. The Quonset Hut has been only one manifestation of this dream.

Other factory-built, ready-made inexpensive housing types which invite the nuanced manipulations of individual-owner taste include the mobile home. Again, this is a pre-manufactured unit which is relatively easily transportable to any desired site. The linear plan of the interior, composed of a line of rooms opening off a long hallway, allows their positioning on small, narrow plots of land. But as two units may be placed together side-by-side, the basic unit also functions as a module which can be multiplied to accommodate a somewhat larger site. The mobile home developed during the post-war era out of the house trailer so popular during the 1950s and 1960s, but differs from its precursor in that today once positioned it remains permanently stationed, having foregone its original mobility as it grew in size and the complexity of its made-to-order interior furnishings and appliances. The mobile home is popular throughout the country and remains both an affordable and economical housing solution.

Above: Mobile home, Brunswick, ME. Mobile homes are among the most common pre-fabricated homes in America today.

Above: Mobile home, Brunswick, ME.

Left: RV (recreational vehicle) parked on mounting blocks; Brownsville, VT. Reviving the tradition of nomadic housing, some Americans live in recreational vehicles (RVs) which they drive from one location to another, frequently migrating between North and South with the seasons.

Below: Mobile home, Dutch Village Trailer Park, Hudson, NY. Although based on standardized units, many mobile home parks see considerable customization.

Ecologically Conscious and Handmade Houses

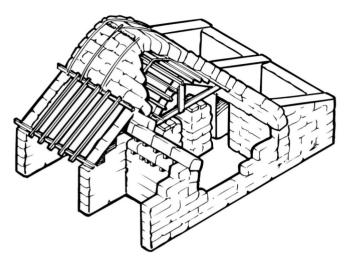

Above: Straw bale construction diagram; walls and roof made of straw. Bales of straw are stacked up over steel anchoring rods, and covered with stucco. The technique was developed in plains communities over 100 years ago, and is being revived.

Above: Earthship—walls made of recycled automobile tires; windows and passive solar heating. Ecologically conscious builders have made inventive houses from recycled materials which use almost no commercial power.

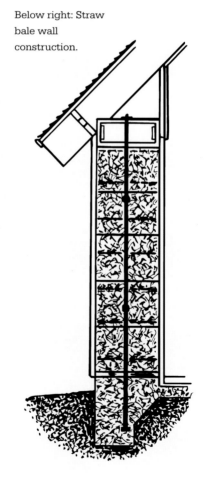

Below right: Straw bale wall construction.

Right: Rammed earth construction; dirt tamped down inside form frame. One of the oldest building techniques in the world has found new uses.

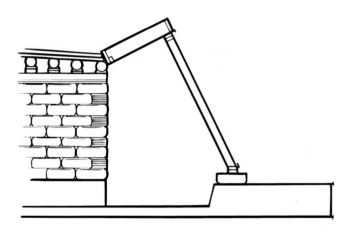

Above: Earthship—wall made of recycled automobile tires; solar heating space.

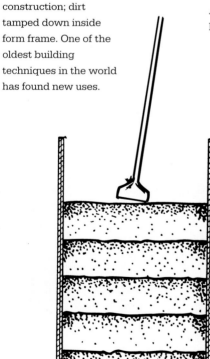

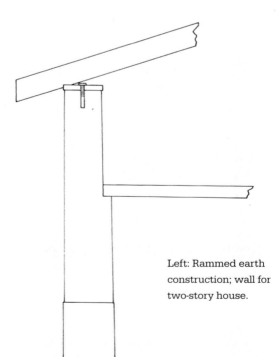

Left: Rammed earth construction; wall for two-story house.

Above: A-Frame house, Woodstock, VT.

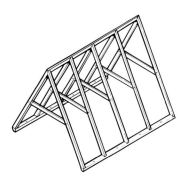

Above: A-frame house—diagram of the simple-to-construct frame structure.

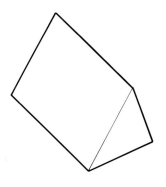

Above: A-frame house—basic gable shape; other shape variants can be found.

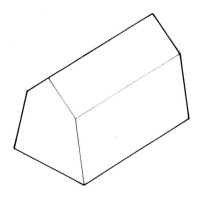

Above: A-frame house—gambrel type gable.

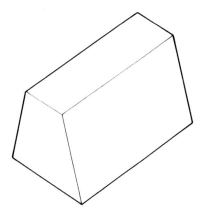

Above: A-frame house—truncated top variant.

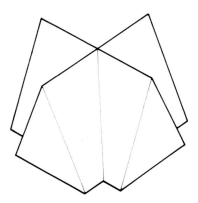

Above: A-frame house—intersecting gables.

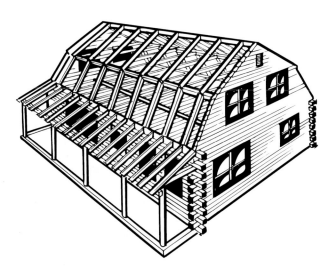

Above: Diagram of modern log cabin kit frame. The modern log cabin updates the traditional form.

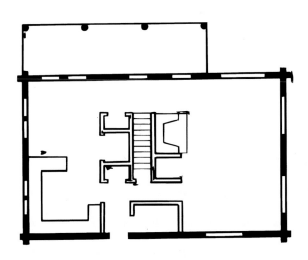

Above: Plan of modern log cabin kit frame.

Above: Log home, Haddam, CT. Log cabins have never been more popular, and many companies provide either post-and-beam kit houses or custom-designed houses.

Above: Log home, Brownsville, VT.

Handmade Houses

Other, perhaps less nationally popular types of houses which nonetheless warrant mention and effortlessly fall within the broad category of Contemporary Folk include the many American handmade houses of unique quality and character. These clearly reflect the continuation of early crafts building traditions, as well as the enduring need for shelter. But they replace a taste for common comfort with a highly expressive desire for thoroughly personalized environments. Examples include the extraordinary work of the California artist James Hubbell, such as his Boys House of 1984 in San Diego and his Rainbow House in Julian which was built over a period of ten years in the 1980s by himself, his family and apprentices. Both structures are highly sculptural in their spaces and surfaces, reflecting their inception in clay models. Their extreme organic fluidity is in part

Left: Log house/chalet, near Pico, VT.

Above: Swiss Chalet, Pico, VT. Swiss chalets have become very popular in mountain resort regions.

Above: Swiss Chalet, Pico, VT.

dependent upon their method of construction—sprayed concrete over large-scale fabricated steel armatures. All the detailing, including windows, fixtures and fittings, are handmade, giving the whole of the composition a remarkable aesthetic harmony. Most of the materials were recycled by Hubbell from orthodox construction sources, having been cast aside as unsuitable for the precision of modern practices. In design and construction, such examples express the improvisation and individuali-ty of a continuing American folk tradition and, in Hubbell's case, both houses remain carefully tied to their natural surroundings by their often local materials and the cascading elevations and layering of their organic forms.

Handmade houses, the rural and beguiling log cabin house, and even the widespread A-frame vacation home all express a quintessential desire to look to the primitive and to notions of the simple life in the configuration of

Left: Swiss Alpine Chalet, Sherburne, VT.

Left: A-frame home, Woodstock, VT. The A-frame design was first created by Rudolf Schindler in 1934, who had been asked to create a "Tudor" style house for a rural retreat. It became very popular in the 1960s and 1970s. Many are now disappearing, to make way for larger houses.

Above: A-frame home, Ludlow, VT.

domestic dwellings. The log cabin is a popular model for picturesque homes built from commercially available kits or by custom builders. It remains a potent signifier, carrying symbolic power in its allusions to the fictional primitive wholesomeness of early American life. The Log Cabin recalls American cultural values of pioneering self-sufficiency and closeness to nature. There is a revival of the type by each new generation which looks in part to folk tradition to establish its own bearings on the relationship between architecture and nature.

The modern A-frame house is also connected to folk traditions of the country's past, but the A-frame design was first created by Rudolf Schindler in 1934, who had been asked to create a "Tudor" style house for a rural retreat. Its construction has been greatly simplified by the omission of a conventionally horizontal roof. Instead, the side walls are angled together to create a monumen-

tal gable rising from the base forming each side of the building. Despite the potential awkwardness of the lack of vertical walls, this type of house can be unusually spacious in its open plan and its provision for loft platforms. The type is popular and works with a large selection of materials. Although it is not commonly used for permanent residences outside of the Northwest, it is a frequent model for vacation and beach homes throughout the country and became especially popular from the late 1960s onward. Many are now disappearing, however, being demolished to make way for larger houses.

In comparison, the Geodesic dome also satisfies the basic requirements for shelter and is a simplified, prefabricated housing type. But in the end it was far too radical in form, volume and materials to ever gain popularity in the American housing market. During the 1960s the type drew popular interest with the increasing celebrity of one

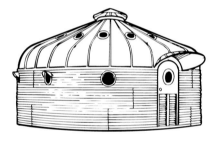

Above: Drawing of a Geodesic dome house. The geodesic dome was an invention of Buckminster Fuller. The central plan and geometric construction lent simplicity to the construction.

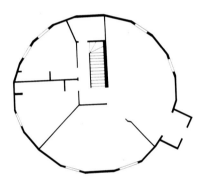

Above: Plan of a Geodesic dome house. Odd shaped rooms are inevitable with round buildings.

Above: Drawing of a Dymaxion prefabricated house. Invented by Buckminster Fuller, Dymaxion houses built from the base of farm silos with a yurt-like roof were offered as inexpensive housing during WWII.

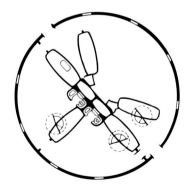

Above: Plan of a Dymaxion prefabricated house. The futuristic aspect of this house is reflected in the flexible partitions.

Above: Wallace Neff: concrete balloon house at Falls Church, VA. This domed house was formed by pouring concrete over an inflated balloon; when the concrete had set, the balloon was deflated.

Above: Drawing of a traditional yurt. Independent builders have revived the ancient Mongolian yurt as an alternative to traditional framed buildings.

Right: Mill, Lowell, MA.
This former textile mill has
been converted to
condominiums.

of its chief proponents, Richard Buckminster Fuller, in America's alternative press. When a Geodesic dome was selected for the United States Pavilion at the World's Fair of 1967 a degree of notoriety resulted, but the futuristic geometric structure along with the dome's strictly non-organic materials failed to endear the model to the American public. The rigid frame of the generic Geodesic dome type could be made from pre-formed metal or even plastic. This was then wrapped in a flexible plastic skin or rigid panels of manmade materials.

Buckminster Fuller had originally designed his "4-D Utility Unit" housing—or "Dymaxion House" in the mid-1920s in an endeavor to produce mass-manufactured inexpensive housing of futuristic form. In that early model the living quarters were encased within a fabric of glass and casein, the whole suspended from a utility "mast" and was self-sustaining with integral generator, disposal facilities, and air compressor. Buckminster Fuller's conceptions were more dependent upon engineering than architectural precedent, and even the subsequent Geodesic dome type continued to betray an overtly technocratic idealism combined with ecological notions about sustainability in the hope that such ideas would infiltrate popular culture. Other futuristic dwelling types have been developed over the years, and while demonstrating the assumption that modern technology offers the best solutions for social housing, all have remained too unconventional to satisfy America's taste for middle-class comfort.

In the last few decades, ecological concerns have motivated homeowners to return to some of the oldest building technologies in the world, creating houses from adobe, "cob" houses made of mud and straw, mounds of earth, or bales of straw. (Straw bale houses were built on the western prairies in the late nineteenth century.) Often created from inexpensive or recycled materials, these houses can be very energy efficient, and have a minimal impact on the environment. Solar energy is exploited through large areas of glass, facing southern exposures, and heat trapped in walls made of earth or even recycled automobile tires. The term "earthship" has been coined to describe such houses. Some individuals interested in tribal designs have also built yurts, conical tents originating in Mongolia.

Recycled Housing

Not just materials, but whole buildings have been recycled to provide housing. Nearly any type of building can be and has been converted for residential use, including old factories, churches, schools, barns and even railroad cars.

The origin of the loft conversion in America lay in the SoHo district of New York City during the 1950s. Yet the model for the American loft is found in the attics and often purpose-built artists' "ateliers" clustered in the Montmartre area of Paris in the late nineteenth and early twentieth centuries. Those precedents were not necessarily large, but usually designed for individual occupancy. Most importantly, they offered a cheaper alternative to conventional inner-city dwelling and became some of the earliest live/work spaces. Their interiors were generally undivided and typically high-ceilinged in nineteenth century fashion, with a raised platform accessed by a ladder accommodating a sleeping area. They merged minimal domestic requirements with open, unencumbered studio space, and became both the architectural and symbolic model for an alternative bohemian way of urban living for artists, designers, writers, dancers, students, and academics in post-war America. They spawned a somewhat romanticized live/work culture which had at its base the credo that "art is a way of life," with no conceptual separation between private domestic living, on the one hand, and professional creative pursuits, on the other.

Loft living for residential use is primarily an American phenomenon, but has been exported worldwide, spreading rapidly to major European cities such as Berlin and London, where its bohemian lure coupled with the offer of spacious and cheap urban living has increasingly attracted media attention. Representations of loft living in newspapers, interior, architectural, and lifestyle magazines and on television have further disseminated the idea over the past thirty years. In part as a consequence of this attention, loft living is no longer simply a sub-cultural domestic alternative harnessing the potential of disused industrial space, but has become a mainstream international architectural movement. In the United States, it remains strictly urban and, although still tied to its origins in the cheap and cheerful, is now also signified by new high-style, expensive, architect-designed buildings containing loft-style residential properties available on each floor. As a consequence, the early downmarket loft has now been redefined by the prosperous urban-property market.

Loft living in New York began as a quest for inner-city spaces inexpensive to let and large enough to accommodate artists' working requirements. The live-in studio with few if any facilities offered both economy and the sought-after internal wasteland that could be reshaped

Above: Converted fire station, Hose 8, Prospect Hill, Newport, RI, 1887. Many find the use of historical structures which were created for other purposes as houses to provide an intriguing contact with history.

Above: A former barn converted to a residence. Concord, MA.

Above: Graham Gund: Church Court condominiums, 492 Beacon Street, Boston, MA, 1983. The bell tower was converted to one seven-floor condominium.

level, with production and storage areas in the floors above.

One of the main attractions of these typically three- or four-story buildings was their cast-iron framing. This construction technique originated around the 1850s and produced large, open-plan floor spaces dotted throughout with vertical cast-iron columns. Large tiered windows often occupied the whole of the front elevation. The cast-iron columns of the frame and the interior structure relieved the façade of its load-bearing function so that much larger than normal expanses of glass, sometimes of floor-to-ceiling height, formed the façade. The amount and quality of illumination was ideal for artists. 1950s occupation often began illegally as a result of zoning restrictions, but local law has been changing since then to facilitate residential occupation in many American cities.

when and where appropriate. During the 1950s, artists in New York City began to occupy the expansive spaces available in buildings originally constructed in the nineteenth century for small-scale, light industry and manufacturing—such as print works and publishing, garment and apparel workshops, typewriter and glove makers, polishing, laundry, and furniture makers—as well as small warehouses for imported goods. A retail space given over to selling was often situated on street

During the 1950s and 1960s architects and architectural practices also began to recognize the spatial and residential advantages of lofts. The loft quickly became theoretically associated with fundamental principles of the Modern Movement and in particular the spatial and structural approaches of Mies van der Rohe. The origins of a Modernist architectural aesthetic were even seen in the large, free-plan spaces and structural systems of industrial cast-iron building. Occupation of these often

Left: Graham Gund: Church Court condominiums, 492 Beacon Street, Boston, MA, 1983. After a fire in 1978 destroyed the Mount Vernon Church, it was converted to condominiums.

abandoned historic inner-city structures since the 1950s has, however, brought to light their architectural and technical design achievements, ultimately leading to calls for their restoration and conservation.

Many loft interiors now intentionally juxtapose the actual shell, including roof joists, with more personal material symbols such as contemporary furniture in order to make a clear statement about the revitalization of the industrial past by the architecturally sympathetic and informed present, thus remaining objectively clear on what is being conserved and why. This approach avoids bringing heightened and obsessive attention to America's romance with its industrial past, a marketing device current amongst fashionable developers who have commodified the industrial relic. nineteenth century buildings are increasingly being carved up by developers who provide a somewhat raw loft "shell" which can be architecturally personalized by each individual purchaser and metamorphosed into another chic apartment. Only in extreme cases are loft spaces divided up to resemble box-room apartments.

Although it began in the individual and personal sphere, the question of loft conversion and preservation has moved into the realm of the public and perhaps even national good. As the loft aesthetic came increasingly to celebrate the restoration of a building's original, typically

Above: St. Mark's Church condominiums, 90 Park Street, Brookline, MA.

nineteenth century, structure, spaces and fittings, entire inner-city districts comprising derelict and decaying factories and warehouses have been reconsidered for their potential value as urban housing. The loft is now more and more seen as a regenerative force by urban theorists, some of whom look to the lessons of post-war reconstruction in European cities. Advantages have been recognized in looking to remnants of a past industrial age in relation to contemporary urban housing needs, and the reclamation of existing buildings judged in

Left: Ralph Adams Cram, Charles Francis Wentworth and Bertram Grosvenor Goodhue: Newton Corner Methodist Church, 515 Centre Street, Newton, MA, 1895; now converted to condominiums. This ornate church, not one of Cram's favorites, was inspired by Mexican baroque.

Adaptive Reuse—Recycled Architecture

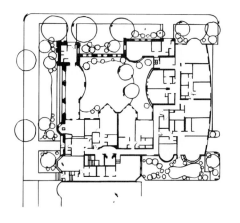

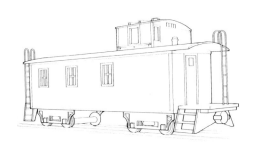

Above: Moore, Grove, Harper, architects: Converted barn on the Choptank Eastern Shore, MD, 1978. As appreciation grew for old buildings during the 1970s, many old structures were creatively adapted for use as houses.

Above: Graham Gund: plan of Church Court condominiums, Beacon St., Boston, MA, 1985.

Above: Railroad caboose converted to a house, West Coast.

opposition to clusters of new high-rise blocks. Since the mid-1980s it has been increasingly argued that the historic architectural "shell" of a city should remain primary, and that reclamation maintains the natural diversity of inner city architecture and the multiplicity of urban life. The success of the old is being judged by its application to the present.

Indeed many of the concerns which surround loft conversion equally apply to the conversion into living or live-work spaces of barns, windmills and mills which have become the historic rural equivalents of the inner-city loft. Such structures are increasingly being restored and converted, being prized for their idyllic, pastoral values and extensive, picturesque interior spaces.

Postmodern

Applied to architecture as early as the 1940s, the term "Postmodern"—literally meaning "after the Modern"—took on new value during the 1960s and 1970s as it became broadly associated with the emerging stylistic pluralism of pop culture in the United States. In many respects "Postmodern" was a timely reaction against the dominant purist ideology of the Modernism of Mies van der Rohe. Struggling to free itself from the earlier 20th century transition to a modern idiom which took on board seminal ethical and technological issues of the

industrial machine age, the new Postmodern approach was less optimistic overall and began to question universal confidence in the benefits of machine technology. Stylistically the term is more closely associated with developments in architecture of the 1970s and 1980s. Its emergence at that time was part of a more general cultural development in design which endeavored to revive a whole series of ideas, materials and "quotable" imagery from the past which had been adamantly rejected by the Modernist creed as too banal, too populist, too colorful, too common.

The style received its theoretical underpinning in three influential arguments. The first of these was published by the architect Robert Venturi in 1966 in *Complexity and Contradiction in Architecture*, where he proposed paradox, opposition, enigma, intricacy, and vagueness as fitting replacements for the simple clarity and technological emphasis of International Modernism. In response to Mies van der Rohe's dictum "Less is More," Venturi argued "Less is a Bore." The historicist refinement and stylistic sophistication of his own work and that designed in collaboration with Denise Scott-Brown, however, prove his approach to be anything but an idiomatic re-assembling of cliché prototypes. With Scott-Brown and Steven Izenour he subsequently published *Learning from Las Vegas* in 1972. Despite the sound arguments of its authors, the book quickly became

Left: Michael Graves
(b. 1934): Schulman House,
Princeton, NJ, 1976–1978.

something of a populist manifesto. Venturi and Scott-Brown proposed adopting a wide perspective, embracing the visual language of America's rich consumer cultural and encouraging architecture to reflect the materials, imagery and aesthetic principles of even popular advertising. The architectural historian Charles Jencks then published *The Language of Postmodern Architecture* in 1977, using the terminology of his argument to distinguish his own critical stance against Modernist principles.

As Postmodernism in American architecture developed, it came to combine stylistic eclecticism with historicist quotation, looking to a pluralism of sources and inviting the infusion of humor, irony, paradox and wit into the design of a building. The door was thus opened for architecture to become a carrier of popular visual imagery, and in this the Postmodern aesthetic departed radically from the mainstream emphasis on technology and structure.

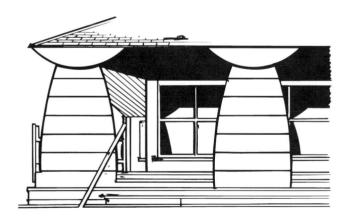

Above: Postmodern Classical columns. The shapes of these columns are reminiscent of Classical shapes, but are flattened and appear more like sign boards than load-bearing structural elements.

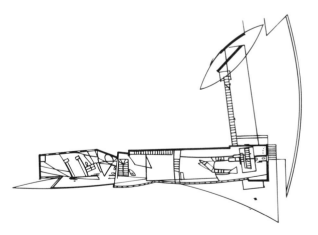

Above: Scogin Elam and Bray: plan of Chmar House, first floor, Atlanta, GA, 1991.

Above: Steven Izenour (1946–2001): George and Hildegard
Izenour House, Stony Creek, CT, 1985–1986.
Postmodernism explored traditional materials and
historical forms, but approached them with a new freedom
and love of complexity.

Internationally the Postmodern style in architecture
has had its greatest achievements in public and commercial buildings, where revivalist historical detailing, often
profuse superficial ornament and brightly articulated
surface colour and pattern have been combined for dramatic impact. In domestic American architecture the
style has been perhaps less theatrical, but no less sophisticated in its condensed architectural statements. There
are a number of landmark examples scattered throughout the country, but the earliest of these were privately
commissioned buildings, and the style has taken some
time to filter down into suburban housing where it has
become little more than yet another "type" of domestic
imagery to be selected by a potential home owner.

One of Venturi's earliest contributions to American
housing came with the commission to his Philadelphia
firm—an architectural partnership with William Short
and John Rauch—for a federally subsidized apartment
block named Guild House, for the Friends
Neighborhood Guild, also in Philadelphia, designed

Left: Franklin D. Israel
(1945–1996): Drager House,
Oakland, CA, 1995.

Above: Allan Greenberg (b. 1938): Farmhouse in CT, 1986.

Above: Frank Gehry (b. 1929): Sirmai-Peterson Residence, Thousand Oaks, CA, 1983–1988.

between 1961 and 1963 and constructed during 1965–1966. In the end the project was severely criticized, in part because the commissioning body understood the symbolic content of the finished building in a way unintended by the architects. In the final design as built, some symbolic features were adopted from popular culture and applied to the context of social housing for the aged. The façade was given a public character by the large signage derived from trends in contemporary retail marketing which was at the time increasingly shaping the visual culture of modern American society. Mock-Classical divisions of the façade were interposed in the glazed brick surrounding the central entrance and as a stringcourse placed at the fifth floor, but these elements were ridiculed as a tawdry and tasteless comment on the economic position of tenants in federally subsidized housing. Finally a fabricated, gold-anodized aluminum sculpture in the form of a television antenna was installed centrally on the roof. The architects argued the symbol represented an occupation of the elderly and therefore social reality, but the commissioning body saw the sculpture as disparaging.

This unusual iconographic component, however, did not in the end diminish the value of the otherwise sensitive design approach Venturi and his associates took towards the residents' real needs. Rather than adopting the newly popular open-planned interiors, the design incorporated traditional "box" rooms with sufficient

light, a Roman thermal window on the upper front façade, a stepped-back south façade, agreeable interior passageways and details, and an overall homely, conventional atmosphere. The exterior of the building itself was designed to symbolize these qualities. Although the subsidized scheme necessitated ordinary building methods and materials, these requirements were celebrated in the design of the facades where the conventional brickwork, double-hung sashes and the surrounding chain-link fence came to represent the mundane, often difficult reality of the social context. Whether or not one condones the design as befitting social housing, in the end the Guild House building was an undisguised symbolic statement of its own humble purpose.

The Vanna Venturi House of 1961–1964 in Chestnut Hill, Pennsylvania, was Robert Venturi's first significant single-occupant domestic undertaking. Designed and built for his mother, the house is comparatively small with Classically symmetrical elevations back and front. The front elevation is an abstracted and greatly simplified quotation of the temple-fronted central block of Palladio's Villa Maser of the 1550s. Symbolic allusions such as this throughout the house are clear and multi-layered. Evoking Frank Lloyd Wright's principle that the hearth is the conceptual as well as structural core of the home, Venturi situated the flat rendered façade of the chimney at the focal center of the house, unveiling it through the split gable of the front elevation and

Left: Robert Venturi (b. 1925): Vanna Venturi's House, Chestnut Hill, PA, 1963. Front view. This is the first Postmodern house, created by Venturi for his mother in a suburb of Philadelphia.

Above: Frank Gehry (b. 1929): Norton House, Venice, CA, 1983. This house, located on the boardwalk, features a fanciful version of a life-guard tower at the front.

emphasizing its compositional impact by placing it off center within the vertical rise of the chimney block. This motif of a central rift or cut through the fabric of the building has appeared again in Venturi's work, and has become a much copied hallmark motif of the Postmodern idiom. Classical allusions are also typical of the style. In this design, they are triggered by the mock lintel above the central opening, as well as by the narrow molding of the false arch superimposed above it. The monumental scale of the historical motifs is disproportionate to the small scale of the house, creating an architectural tension within the composition, while contradicting historically "correct" application. The distribution of space within the house is no less complex, but like the exterior the interior remains surprisingly simple in its overall effect. In the end, the house is remarkably basic, comprising of fundamental planes and volumes, its detailing reduced to little more than doors, windows, chimney and gabled roof. It is a statement about the domestic architectural genre, the constituents of a house and the nature of shelter. The design was something of a final assault on the principles of Modernism, and provided both a model and a theoretical justification for the re-incorporation of earlier taboos such as architectural narrative and applied decoration which have become hallmarks of the style.

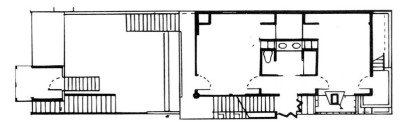

Above: Frank Gehry: Plan of Norton House, third floor, Venice, CA, 1983.

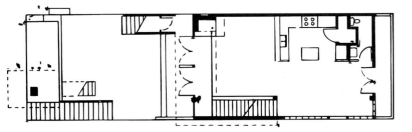

Above: Frank Gehry: Plan of Norton House, second floor, Venice, CA, 1983.

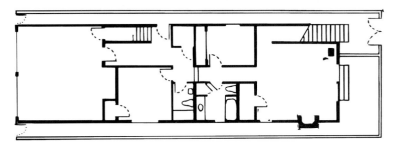

Above: Frank Gehry: Plan of Norton House, first floor, Venice, CA, 1983.

Frank Gehry, Antoine Predock and Bart Prince are also considered major proponents of Postmodernism, although their individual approaches differ dramatically. Gehry has broken free of the traditional constraints of residential architecture by embarking on each new project for a domestic dwelling as if it were a controlled experiment. In every case the design of a house is an independent investigation into architectural traditions and ideals. For this reason Gehry's residential designs often seem disassociated from one another and from his famous cultural commissions. Gehry's work, however, touches upon many of the concepts proposed by Frank Lloyd Wright, as does that of many practitioners of the Postmodern genre. One of these principles is that a building should be viewed as a sculptural object contextualized within its landscape.

Gehry's first house, his own residence in Santa Monica of 1978, was a reworking of a traditional California-style cottage, disordering the original plan and interposing atypically harsh industrial materials representative of vernacular urbanism into the domestic site. In doing so, Gehry transferred the architectural rules of one building genre to another, creating a private home which was robust in its critique on domestic tradition. Gehry also continued Wrightian considerations in breaking out of the box-like floor plan, substituting an apparently disordered organization in the interior and creating a sculptural composition made

Right: Frank Gehry: Gehry House, 1002 22nd Street at Washington Avenue, Santa Monica, CA, 1978. Frank Gehry's houses use common materials in unusual ways, making them both blend in and stand out from their surroundings.

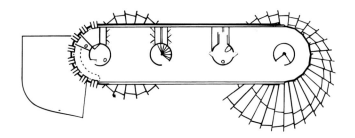

Above: Bart Prince: plan of Prince House, third floor, Albuquerque, NM, 1985.

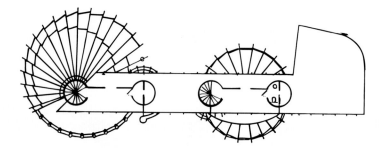

Above: Bart Prince: plan of Prince House, second floor, Albuquerque, NM, 1985.

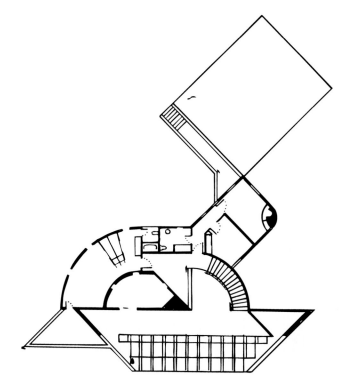

Above: Antoine Predock: plan of house in the Sandia Mountains, second floor, Albuquerque, NM, 1977.

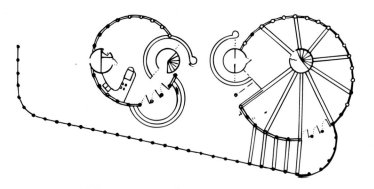

Above: Bart Prince: plan of Prince House, ground floor, Albuquerque, NM, 1985. Experimental architects explore new geometric compositions and plans which combine openness with drama.

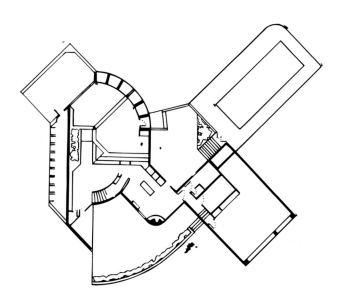

Above: Antoine Predock: plan of house in the Sandia Mountains, first floor, Albuquerque, NM, 1977.

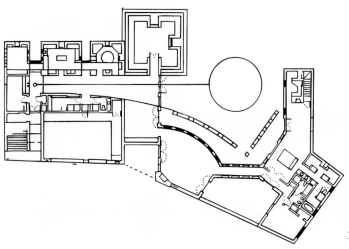

Left: Antoine Predock: plan of Fuller House, Phoenix, AZ, 1986–1987.

up of various single-room spaces of different sizes and dimensions, inside and outside. In a sense, Gehry approaches architecture as pure shape, combining separate forms together into a whole which reappraises the aesthetic role of the house in the urban landscape.

Antoine Predock's domestic design equally shows the continuing inspiration of Frank Lloyd Wright on late-twentieth century American architecture. Practicing in the Southwest, he is an heir to Wright's principles of regionalism. Although Predock typically employs concrete and blocks as his primary materials, he adamantly retains the notion of local context in the design of a domestic dwelling. Replacing an idealistic dependence on local materials with a Postmodern use of mass industrial ones, Predock nonetheless formulates his houses with a sensitivity to ethnic forms, colours and textures. His shapes are staggered, broken and irregular. The

Above: Antoine Predock (b. 1936): Fuller House, Phoenix, AZ, 1986–1987.

Right: Bart Prince (b. 1942): Bradford Prince Residence, Albuquerque, NM, 1987–1988. This house was built for the architect's father.

house becomes a meeting of diverse independent parts. But the rhythmic patterns of form and light also betray Predock's enthusiasm for ancient Southwestern mysticism, and his buildings are instilled with historic allusions and a narrative quite alien to the Modernist creed.

In contrast, the late Modernism of Bart Prince is expressed in a thoroughly organic idiom in which all parts and features of a building flow together. Prince neither uses traditional materials, nor typical materials in a traditional way. He combines wood with glass and man-made compounds in a fashion which allows all the surfaces of a house to flow naturally into one another as a complete organic whole. One effect of this is that separate distinctions between rooms are imprecise. His houses typically have a richness of surface texture which

Above: Bart Prince: Bart Prince Residence, Albuquerque, NM, 1983–1984. The architect's own house and studio.

creates an architectural vocabulary all his own; one which is almost mystical in its folklore-like narrative. Prince's highly expressive interpretation of form and structure add to the impact of his houses which have been criticized as more stage-set than home.

New Urbanism

A recent development is the creation of entire planned communities, such as Seaside, FL (1984–1991) and Celebration, near Orlando, FL (1996), which seek to restore not only pre-modern architectural forms, but

also pre-modern community structures to create an idealized vision of small-town life. Seaside, near Panama City, Florida, built by Andres Duany (b. 1949) and Elizabeth Plater-Zyberk (b. 1950), was the first example of the New Urbanism, a return to small-scale urban development and vernacular architecture. Celebration, near Orlando, Florida, 1996, is another example of the New Urbanism, built by a subsidiary of the Walt Disney Corporation. The public has responded positively to these centrally planned developments, which provide a complete living environment.

Above: Bart Prince: Joe Price House, Corona del Mar, CA, 1984–1989, 1994–1996 (addition).

Above: Neo-Shingle Style house, Dune Road, West Hampton, Long Island, NY. The return to historical precedent is clear in this house.

Above: Neo–Shingle Style house, Dune Road, West Hampton, Long Island, NY. The sweeping central arch identifies this as a contemporary house.

Left: Neo-Stick Style house, Stony Creek, CT. The domed framework of boards shelters a modern solar energy panel.

Below: Eclectic House, Cape May, NJ, c. 2000. This large house utilizes Classical and Victorian forms, but is on a much larger scale than the original models, and the somewhat chaotic combination of forms cannot be found in the nineteenth century.

The Architects

The following is an A-Z listing of a number of the most influential architects who have had impact on American domestic and public architecture. Not all of them visited the United States—Palladio and Vitruvius being the most obvious examples—but all of them have left their mark. Each entry contains a thumbnail biography, and describes the type of architecture they practiced. Some of these people had only a short architectural career, indeed many of the earliest American architects were amateur designers who earned their living in other spheres, Thomas Jefferson being, of course, the chief exemplar of this. Furthermore it is sometimes difficult to provide more than the sketchiest details of eighteenth and nineteenth century architects as early records have not always survived. These men, however, still worked under European and Classical influence, albeit putting a distinctively American slant on their work.

During the eighteenth century public buildings started to be erected, as civic dignitaries wanted to emphasize the importance of their town. City halls, state capitols, and large churches began to appear, each building giving a local architect the opportunity to stamp his mark on history.

The United States started to lead the architectural world after the great Chicago fire of 1871; the ensuing building boom instigated the greatest rethink of city architecture in history. New building techniques and technologies allowed forward-thinking architects such as the firm of Adler and Sullivan to devise the skyscraper and a new, uniquely American style evolved that in turn influenced the rest of the world. From the late nineteenth century buildings went up and up in ever more extravagant and daring designs, occasionally harking back to historical precedent but increasingly exploring original directions. Some architectural styles of necessity went up a blind alley by being so individualistic and idiosyncratic that they attracted few if any followers, but the mainstream gathered momentum and progress continued. Twentieth century architects took architecture ever further by exploiting every new advance in technology and design, and contemporary architects are carrying on their tradition.

Adam, Robert (1728–1792)

Adam was a leader of the Classical Revival movement and both his architectural work and exuberantly colorful interior styling were widely imitated. Born in Scotland, in Kirkcaldy, Fife, he studied at Edinburgh University before joining his father's architectural practice in 1746. It was the start of a brilliant career that would see him appointed architect to King George III and the Board of Works in 1762. A partner in the family company from his father's death in 1748, Adam's main formative influence was the Classical architecture of Venice and Rome, seen when he studied in Italy in the 1750s. In 1768 he resigned from the Board of Works and entered Parliament as the Member for the County of Kinross. His greatest work dates from this period—the Adelphi terrace (from the Greek "adelfoi," meaning brothers) that he and his brothers built on the banks of the Thames, Kenwood House (1768), the interior of Syon House (1769), and Osterley Park (1775–1776). In his final years he worked in Edinburgh where he produced some fine work—the Old College of Edinburgh University (1778) and Culzeen Castle (1777–1792). He died in 1792 and was buried in Westminster Cathedral.

Adler, Dankmar (1844–1900)

Born in Stadtlengsfeld, Prussia, Adler emigrated to the United States with his father in 1854 and subsequently studied architecture in Detroit and Chicago. He designed the Central Music Hall in Chicago and in 1881 entered into partnership with Louis Sullivan—their firm of Adler and Sullivan would become one of the most influential practices of the late nineteenth century. Adler provided the engineering skills and Sullivan the aesthetics. Their work served as a bridge between the Classical Revival of the nineteenth century and the simple functionality of modern architecture and was profoundly influential to twentieth century architecture. Among their buildings were the Wainwright Building in St. Louis (1890) admired and revered by many as the perfect expression of the first skyscraper style. Another important building—the apogee of their success—was the Transportation Building for the World's Columbian Exposition in Chicago in 1893. Their partnership dissolved in 1895.

Austin, Henry (1804–1891)

Best known for his work in New Haven, Connecticut, where he lived and practiced for over fifty years, this innovative architect started his career working for Ithiel Town as a builder. He went on to produce numerous public, private and commercial buildings and works such as New Haven's City Hall and Railroad Station, the John Pitkin Norton House, and the monumental Egyptian Revival gateway at the Grove Street Cemetery in 1845. Austin's abilities also took him further afield: away from New Haven he worked in other parts of New England and the mid-Atlantic states. His forte was the Italian villa style for which he was much in demand. The most notable example of this is Victoria Mansion (built as the Morse-Libby House) in Portland, ME.

Below: Henry Austin: Morse-Libby House (also known as the Victoria Mansion), 109 Danforth Street, Portland, ME, 1859.

Breuer, Marcel Lajos (1902–1981)

A leading member of the Modern Movement, Breuer was born in Pécs, Hungary, where he started his studies. In 1920 he went to the Bauhaus in Weimar and was attracted by Walter Gropius's approach to art and architecture. Graduating in 1924, he was given charge of the furniture workshop where he designed the first tubular steel chair, the Wassily (1925). He taught at the Bauhaus in Dessau until 1928, when he moved into private practice in Berlin. After an unsuccessful period during which he built only one private house (in Wiesbaden, 1932), he worked for a short time in Switzerland and London before emigrating to the United States in 1937 following an invitation from his old mentor, Walter Gropius. He joined Gropius as Associate Professor of Architecture at Harvard University, a position he held until 1946. Together they designed several outstanding houses and Breuer developed a bold sculptural use of poured concrete. From 1946 until retirement in 1976, he ran a New York practice whose early work was largely for domestic buildings. In 1952 he worked as part of a team on the UNESCO headquarters in Paris (completed 1958), and his later work included major public designs such as St. John's Abbey, Collegeville, Minnesota (1953–1961); the U.S. embassy at The Hague (1958); the Whitney Museum of American Art, New York City (1966); and the New York University Technology I and II buildings (1969).

Below: Charles Brigham: Burrage House, 314 Commonwealth Avenue, Boston, MA, 1899.

Brigham, Charles (c. 1840–1925)

Born in Watertown to an old local family, Brigham attended the local school, Watertown High. He enlisted in the army in September 1862 and after hostilities ceased started practicing. At the end of the decade he joined John Hubbard Sturgis to form the firm Sturgis and Brigham. Until the untimely death of his partner some twenty years later, the firm proved very successful, designing the Boston Museum of Fine Arts (1870–1876), the Church of the Advent and many fine private mansions. After Sturgis died, Brigham continued alone and was responsible for a wide variety of building types across America—from Redlands, California, to the First Church of Christ, Scientist, Boston (1906), a major additional wing to the Massachusetts State House, the Maine State House, St. Mark's Catholic Church, Dorchester, and Foxboro State Hospital, plus many other churches and libraries. Eventually Brigham moved to Shelter Island, New York, to live out his last years with his sister, dying there in 1925.

Brown, Joseph (b. eighteenth century, d. unknown)

Brown was the architect of the oldest Baptist church in America—the First Baptist Church, Providence, Rhode Island (1774–1775). In style the meetinghouse is a combination of classic English Georgian and New England meetinghouse. It was built to Brown's design by unemployed ships' carpenters and shipwrights at a time when there was little or no other work.

Buckland, William (1734–1774)

Born in England in 1734, Buckland trained as a joiner in London before emigrating to the United States. He was working in Virginia by 1755 as a joiner, designer, and architect, though he seems to have worked mostly on interiors. He is credited with the fine interiors of Gunston Hall (1755–1759) and Mt. Airy (1761–1763), both in Virginia, and the Chase-Lloyd House in Annapolis, Maryland. His last commission was also in Maryland—to build the Hammond-Harwood House which was begun in 1774, the year of his death at age forty.

Above: William Buckland: Hammond-Harwood House, 19 Maryland Avenue, Annapolis, MD, 1773–1774.

Bulfinch, Charles (1763–1844)

Above: Charles Bulfinch: Second Harrison Gray Otis House, Mount Vernon Street, Boston, MA, 1800–1802.

Born into a wealthy Boston family in 1763, Bulfinch studied at Harvard before traveling in Europe between 1785 and 1787. While in Paris he met Thomas Jefferson, who suggested that he concentrated his studies on Classical architecture. Enthused with what he saw, he returned to Boston heavily influenced by the churches of Sir Christopher Wren in London and determined to improve his home city's architecture. He was responsible for many fine Neoclassical buildings, such as the Massachusetts State House (1798), New South Church (1814), and Massachusetts General Hospital (1820). He also successfully worked in other states, most notably with the Connecticut State House (1796) and the Maine State Capitol (1831). With such experience behind him he was chosen to succeed Benjamin Latrobe as the architect of the U.S. Capitol in Washington, D.C. He held the position from 1817 to 1830.

Burnham, Daniel Hudson (1846–1912)

Leader of the Chicago School of Architecture, Burnham was born in Henderson, New York. His pioneering studies into urban planning had great influence over the development of cities across America. His early work was in the established Romanesque Revival style, but he progressed to develop what was to become known as the Richardsonian style. With his partner, John Wellborn Root, Burnham's great work in Chicago included the design of the Women's Temple and the Masonic Building (1890–1892), the Reliance Building (1890–1895), and the Monadnock Building (1890–1891). Burnham had the honor of being appointed chief of construction for the prestigious World's Columbian Exposition of 1893, in commemoration of the 400th anniversary of the discovery of America by Christopher Columbus. This huge project involved the creation of the "White City"—150 buildings over 600 acres that drew over twenty-seven million visitors. His later notable works include the Rookery Building, New York (1901), the Selfridge Building, London (1908), and the Union Railroad Station, Washington, D.C. (1909).

Davis, Alexander Jackson, (1803–1892)

Above; Alexander Jackson Davis: Lyndhurst, 635 South Broadway, Tarrytown, NY, 1838/1865.

One of the nineteenth century's most prominent architects, Davis was born in New York City, and spent most of his childhood in New Jersey. He began working as a typesetter in Virginia in 1818 but returned to New York to take up drawing and architecture, later forming a partnership with prominent architect Ithiel Town, designing largely in the Greek Revival style. In 1835, he struck out on his own, drawing upon a number of styles—but particularly Gothic Revival. A proponent of the Picturesque movement, integrating rural homes into the landscape, Davis created unusual and asymmetric villas, such as his masterpiece, Lyndhurst (1838/1865), in Tarrytown, New York. He also collaborated with horticulturist Andrew Jackson Downing (1815–1852) in popularizing the Picturesque and became its most prominent proponent. Davis designed not only buildings but furniture and interiors as well. He remained active until the 1870s, though his influence waned as a younger generation of architects emerged.

Duany, Andres (1949–)
Plater-Zyberk, Elizabeth (1950–)

The pioneers of New Urbanism, Duany and Plater-Zyberk are one of the rarest of successful architectural teams—a married couple. Duany was born in New York City in September 1949 but spent his early years in Cuba, moving back to the United States in 1960. Plater-Zyberk was born in Bryn Mawr, Pennsylvania, to a Polish immigrant family. Both studied architecture at Princeton University and acquired their graduate degrees from the Yale School of Architecture. In 1974 they founded Arquitectonica in Miami. The practice lasted four years during which time they became the first architects to build in the Constructivist Revival style. In 1980 they set up Duany, Plater-Zyberk and Company specializing in drawing up plans for private developers and urban municipalities. One of the company's earliest projects was the regulating plan and building codes for the new town of Seaside. Other plans include those for Providence, Trenton, St. Louis, Fort Lauderdale, and Los Angeles. Since 1979 Duany and Plater-Zyberk have taught Traditional Town Planning at the University of Miami. They are authors of the influential *Suburban Nation* (2000) that discusses the problems and solutions to American urban problems and suburban sprawl.

Eames, Charles (1907–1978)
Eames, Ray (c. 1916–1988)

Charles Eames was born in 1907 in St Louis, Missouri. Interested in architecture, he dropped out of college before qualifying but, nevertheless, set himself up in business as an architect and industrial designer in 1930. From 1936 he taught at Cranbrook Academy of Art where he collaborated with his colleagues Eero Saarinen and Ray Kaiser to enter a competition run by the Museum of Modern Art in New York for original furniture design. Their designs certainly were original—their entry made use of new materials such as molded plywood and steel rod frames supporting foam upholstery. In 1941 Eames married Ray Kaiser and together they set up a diverse design partnership in California. Their principal achievement architecturally was the seminal Santa Monica House (1949), constructed from standard building components but also incorporating industrial components. However, they are best known for their 1949 range of furniture, in particular the Lounge Chair which went into commercial production with the manufacturer Herman Miller ten years later. As a climax to their international achievements, the Royal Institute of British Architects awarded the couple the Gold Medal for their innovation and excellence in the fields of architecture, furniture design, film, graphics, and exhibition design.

Above: Charles Eames and Ray Eames: Eames House, 203 Chataqua, Pacific Palisades, CA, 1948–1949.

Eastlake, Charles Lock (1836–1906)

Born in Plymouth, England, in 1836, Eastlake studied under the prominent painter Sir Charles Lock Eastlake, his namesake and uncle. He continued his art studies at the Royal Academy in London before studying in Europe. On his return he wrote *Hints on Household Taste in Furniture, Upholstery and other Details* (published 1868), using aesthetic reasoning to decry the excesses of nineteenth century taste in favor of a more robust, straightforward style. The book was particularly welcomed in the United States where his aesthetic direction was popularly labeled the Eastlake Style. Eastlake followed his first success with another notable book—*A History of the Gothic Revival* published in 1872. He served as assistant secretary of the Royal Institute of British Architects in 1866, secretary from 1871 to 1877, and finally as a keeper at the National Gallery in London from 1878 until 1898.

Elmslie, George Grant (1871–1952)

A member of the Prairie (or Chicago) School, Elmslie worked his apprenticeship at the offices of Adler and Sullivan in Chicago. After the firm split he stayed with Louis Sullivan helping him on his banks in Midwestern cities. Elmslie was responsible for much of the detail work on the buildings until 1909 when he left to work in and around Chicago and became known as a member of the Prairie School of architects. He struck up a partnership with William Gray Purcell that lasted from 1913 to 1922 when Purcell's ill-health led to his semi-retirement.

Above: William Gray Purcell and George Grant Elmslie: Bradley ("Airplane") House, Woods Hole, MA, 1912.

Fowler, Orson Squire (1809–1887)

Fowler was a professional phrenologist and amateur architect born in Cohocton, Steuben County, New York. He graduated from Amherst in 1834 in phrenology and, together with his brother, opened a phrenology office in New York, publishing and lecturing prolifically on his subject. He came to architecture through his interest in marital happiness and

harmonious living. To this end he wrote an influential book entitled *A Home for All, The Gravel Wall and Octagon Mode of Building*. Known as the Octagon Style, it was based on a bee's honeycomb structure and was very popular between 1850 and 1860. Fowler promoted the style at every opportunity, truly believing octagons to be the answer to most problems of living—providing more floor space, better ventilation, allowing in more light, preventing heat loss, and being cheaper to build. Furthermore, the triangular spaces left in the angles from the octagon were made into cupboards and storage areas. A few thousand octagonal homes were built during the 1850s and 1860s, mostly in the Northeast and Midwest. In 1863 he moved to Boston, and in 1875 to Manchester, Massachusetts. He died at Sharon Station, Connecticut, August 1887.

Above: Orson Squire Fowler: octagon house, illustration from *A Home for All, The Gravel Wall and the Octagon Mode of Building*, 1853.

Fuller, (Richard) Buckminster (1895–1983)

Born in Milton, Massachusetts, Fuller studied first at Harvard and then at the U.S. Naval Academy, Annapolis, Maryland. In 1917 he developed energetic/synergetic geometry which some years later led him to devise a structural system which he termed "Tensegrity Structures." He experimented with structural design following the machine aesthetic with the intention of devising an efficient, practical, economic, and trouble-free mass production building system. For this he looked at the way aircraft chassis were produced and put together. His ideas culminated in the design for Dymaxion House in 1927, but it would be in the post-World War II years that he would gain renown, and his Geodesic domes would win international acclaim. Huge polyhedral frame enclosures, the largest of these domes were built for the Union Tank Car Repair Shop, Louisiana (1958), but it was as part of the U.S. Pavilion at Expo '67—Montreal World's Fair —that the Geodesic dome was brought to public attention. In 1970 he was awarded the Gold Medal of the American Institute of Architects.

Gehry, Frank (1929–)

Born in Toronto, Canada, Gehry moved with his family to Los Angeles in 1947, and has become a naturalized citizen. He studied architecture at the University of Southern California (1954), and, after a year in the army, urban planning at the Harvard Graduate School of Design. He then spent 1961 in Paris working for André Rémondet. He returned to Los Angeles in 1962 and established his own firm, Frank O. Gehry and Associates, where he quickly established a reputation as an architect who believed that "architecture is art" and imaginatively used inexpensive materials such as chain-link fencing, plywood, and raw concrete to create light-hearted, sculptural architecture. One of his earliest works was the Merriweather Post Pavilion of Music in Columbia, Maryland; another the Cabrillo Marine Museum (1979). He was awarded the highest honor in architecture, the prestigious Pritzker Architecture Prize in 1989 for his contributions to the field and his substantial practice—now of over 140 employees—is responsible for many important buildings such as the Walt Disney Concert Hall in Los Angeles, the Concord Amphitheatre in northern California, the Law School at Loyola University in Los Angeles, and the remodeling of an old ice warehouse in Santa Monica into an art museum and office complex.

Above: Frank Gehry: Gehry House, 1002 22nd Street at Washington Avenue, Santa Monica, CA, 1978.

Gill, Irving (1870–1936)

Above: Irving Gill: Dodge House, Los Angeles, CA, 1914–1916.

Gill was born in Syracuse, NY, the son of a New York contractor. Although he had no formal architectural training he traveled to Chicago in 1890 to seek a job with his hero, Louis Sullivan, the most influential architect of the period. Gill convinced Sullivan he was worthy of a position and worked in his office for two years before moving to San Diego. There he worked hard but unexceptionally for ten years with an ever-increasing awareness of local building styles, materials, and above all, landscape and flora. Working from a Classically proportioned framework, Gill used rectangles, cubes, and semicircles to assemble the shapes of his houses whose clean, symmetrical lines featured plain, unadorned, surfaces. Among his best-known projects were Bella Vista Terrace—low-cost homes in Sierra Madre, California (1910)—and a private commission, the Walter Luther Dodge House in Los Angeles (1914–1916).

Above: Bertram Goldberg: Marina
City, Chicago, IL, 1967.

Goldberg, Bertrand (1913–1997)

Goldberg will be remembered for his circular, ergonomic buildings and theories of kinetic living space. Born in Chicago, he
studied at Harvard University, the Bauhaus, and the Armour
Institute of Technology (now the Illinois Institute of Technology).
From 1937 he was the acting principal of Bertrand Goldberg
Associates. His early work was very Bauhaus-influenced and he
worked with Mies van der Rohe, but he became disenchanted with
Modernism and moved instead toward nuclear forms. He particularly espoused ergonomic circular buildings, which he considered
helped create a community feeling. To this end he experimented
with curvilinear concrete shell structures and developed this into a
theory of kinetic space based on non-parallel walls that set a space
in motion. His best known design is the Marina City complex in
Chicago with its twin "corncob" towers (1967). Other work in
Chicago includes the Astor Tower (1962), House of Blues Hotel
(1963), Hilliard Homes and Senior Homes (1966).

Graves, Michael (1934–)

One of the leading proponents of Postmodernism, Graves was born in Indianapolis,
Indiana. He studied architecture at college in Cincinnati and then Harvard University
before moving to Rome for two years, taking up a position as a Fellow at the American
Academy there. He returned to the United States in 1962 to take up a teaching post at
Princeton University. Greatly influenced by Le Corbusier, Graves's designs epitomized
clean and functional Modernism. However, as time went on he started to incorporate
architectural "quotations"—historical references to earlier styles. These included vaults,
Classical pilasters and columns, and even Egyptian pyramids. In tandem with such features,
by the 1980s his buildings became ever more colorful and ornamental. Some notable
works include the Hanselmann House, at Fort Wayne, Indiana, (1967), Alexander House,
at Princeton, New Jersey (1971–1973), Crooks House, at Fort Wayne, Indiana (1976), the
Portland Building, Portland, Oregon (1980), and the Humana Building at Louisville,
Kentucky (1982–1983). He also designs furniture and housewares. In 2001 Michael Graves
became the fifty-eighth architect to be awarded the American Institute of Architects Gold
Medal, recognizing that his "significant body of work has had a lasting influence on the
theory and practice of architecture."

Greene, Charles Sumner (1868–1957)
Greene, Henry Mather (1870–1954)

Brothers who worked together as Greene and Greene, their signature was a fusion of vernacular and Classical styles. Both attended the Manual Training High School, St. Louis, Missouri, where they learned metal- and woodworking skills, and then trained in the 1870s at the Massachusetts Institute of Technology's School of Architecture. In the early 1890s they moved together to California and for ten years produced good but unexceptional buildings. However, both brothers were interested in foreign cultural architectural styles, in particular those from Japan and Scandinavia with their combinations of craft and form. The Greenes took these precepts and fused them into their own work. Their most notable house is the David B. Gamble House, Pasadena (1907–1908), a very Japanese-influenced bungalow and a recognized masterpiece of Arts and Crafts design.

Above: Charles Sumner Greene and Henry Mather Greene: David B. Gamble House, Westmoreland Place, Pasadena, CA, 1907–1908.

Griffin, Walter Burley (1876–1937)

Born in Maywood, Illinois, Griffin went on to his local Illinois State University after which he worked for some years for the master of American architecture, Frank Lloyd Wright. In 1905 he set up in private practice himself, and five years later he married his colleague Marion Mahony, who had also worked with Wright. In 1912 Griffin won an international competition to design the new Federal capital of Australia—Canberra—on a greenfield site in southern New South Wales. These plans were soon abandoned but Griffin was invited to Melbourne anyway in 1913, and he became Director of Design and Construction for the new city, a post he retained for over ten years. Afterward he remained in Australia, setting up a successful private practice which he continued until 1935 when he went to India following an invitation to design a library for Lucknow University. He worked there until his death two years later.

Above: Walter Burley Griffin (1876–1937): Carter House, Evanston, IL, 1910.

Between 1901 and 1913, Walter Burley Griffin had designed some 130 houses, landscapes, and buildings, the majority built in the Midwest. Among these were W. H. Emery House, Chicago, Illinois (1903), Ralph Griffin House, Edwardsville, Illinois (1909), Adolph Mueller House, Decatur, Illinois (1906), Joshua Melson House, Anna, Illinois (1912), and the Stinson Memorial Library Anna, Illinois (1913).

Gropius, Walter Adolph (1883–1969)

Above: Walter Gropius: Gropius House, 68 Baker Ridge Road, Lincoln, MA, 1938.

One of the colossi of the period, Gropius was the founder of the Bauhaus, probably the most influential design and architectural schools of the twentieth century. Born in Berlin, Germany, he studied in Munich and then worked for Peter Behrens in Berlin. His first major commission was the design of the Fagus shoe factory at Alfeld in 1911. In 1918 he was appointed director of the Grand Ducal group of schools of art in Weimar: he amalgamated them and formed them into the Bauhaus. A revolutionary concept, the Bauhaus art schools aimed at a new functional interpretation of the applied arts, utilizing glass, metals, and textiles. But the bold use of unusual building materials was condemned as "architectural socialism" in Weimar, and, as a consequence, in 1925 the Bauhaus was transferred to Dessau into Gropius's purpose-designed building. His reputation grew to such an extent that he was even asked to design car bodies (by Adler 1929–1933). When the Nazis came to power the Bauhaus was closed, and in 1934 Gropius felt it expedient to escape to London. There he worked on factory designs and housing, including a revolutionary adjunct to Christ Church, Oxford, which was never built. In 1937 he emigrated to the United States where he became Professor of Architecture at Harvard (1938–1952). While there he designed the Harvard Graduate Center (1949). Later work included the American Embassy in Athens (1960).

Harrison, Peter (1716–1775)

One of the most accomplished gentlemen-architects of eighteenth century America, Harrison was born in England, and worked at first as a sea captain until he emigrated permanently to the New World in 1740. He married an American heiress and they settled in Newport, Rhode Island, where he worked in shipping. Like many wealthy gentlemen with leisure time, he took to architecture and studied books to learn the necessary skills. From 1748 until 1764 he designed a number of austerely Classical buildings based on his book learning, the most notable being Redwood Library, Newport (1748–1750). The success of this got him his next commission, the King's Chapel in Boston (1749–1754), and other work followed, including Christ Church, Cambridge, Massachusetts (1759–1761), a synagogue for Sephardic Jews in Newport (1759–1763), and the Brick Market, Newport (1761–1762). A number of these commissions were never quite finished to his satisfaction, as the money always seemed to run out—not the last architect to have this problem!

Holl, Steven (1947–)

Holl was born in Bremerton, Washington, and then graduated from the University of Washington architecture school. He spent a year in Rome and then did postgraduate work at the Architectural Association, London. In 1976 he established Steven Holl Architects in New York. His first professional commission was a sculpture studio and pool house in New York in 1980. Holl has developed a signature style based on his use of space and light. Among his important works are the Kiasma Museum of Contemporary Art (1998) in Helsinki, Finland; the Bellevue Art Museum, Washington State (2000); and the Chapel of St. Ignatius, Seattle (dedicated 1997). In 1989 he became a tenured professor at Columbia University and has also taught at other higher education institutions. He has won many awards for his architectural achievement, including the Arnold W. Brunner Prize for Achievement in Architecture as an Art (1990), New York A.I.A. Medal of Honor (1997), National A.I.A. Design Award (for Chapel of Ignatius, 1998), Alvar Aalto Medal (1998), Chrysler Award for Innovation in Design (1998), and the National A.I.A. Design Award (for Kiasma, 1998).

Hood, Raymond Mathewson (1881–1934)

Responsible for some of the great signature buildings of New York, Hood was born in Pawtucket, Rhode Island, and educated at Brown University and the Massachusetts Institute of Technology. In 1905 he crossed the Atlantic to attend the Ecole des Beaux Arts in Paris where he got his diploma in 1911. In 1922, with John Mead Howells, he won the competition for the Chicago Tribune Tower. This, his first major commission, was rich with Gothic detailing. He became the preeminent designer of skyscrapers in the United States during the 1930s. He was very keen on historicist styles—as demonstrated with his earlier American Radiator Building (1924), his first Art Deco building in New York City. Later works in New York were designed in a modern Rationalist style. One of his major achievements was the Daily News Building (1929–1930), designed through his firm of Hood and Fouilhoux, which also collaborated for the Rockefeller Center (1930–1940) and the McGraw-Hill Building (1930–1931). Hood was greatly influential in the Commission of Architects for the Century of Progress Exhibition in Chicago, and among other important positions and honors, he was President of the Architectural League of New York from 1929 to 1931. He died in Stamford, Connecticut.

Howells, John Mead (1868–1959)

Born in Cambridge, Massachusetts, the son of novelist William Dean Howells, John Mead Howells studied at Harvard and the Ecole des Beaux Arts, Paris, where he first met Raymond Hood. It was in partnership with Hood that he won the most prestigious competition of the period—the Chicago Tribune Tower Competition in 1922, beating among others both Eliel Saarinen and Walter Gropius with a Gothic-inspired design, which was built 1923–1925. He also collaborated on the Panhellenic Tower (now the Beekman Tower Hotel), which was constructed 1927–1928, and the Daily News Building. Howells also formed a partnership with another student at the Ecole des Beaux Arts, I. N. Phelps Stokes, with whom he worked on St. Paul's Chapel (1904–1907) at Columbia University, New York; a design (1908) for the New York Municipal Building; and the Paine Hall music building at Harvard University (1913).

Hunt, Richard Morris (1827–1895)

Above: Richard Morris Hunt: Chateau-sur-Mer, Bellevue Avenue, Newport, RI, 1852/1872.

Hunt was born in Brattleboro, Vermont to a wealthy colonial family that moved to Paris in 1843. The young Hunt went to the Ecole des Beaux Arts where he studied painting, sculpture, and architecture. After successful studies he was given the job of supervising the construction of additions to the Louvre and the Tuileries. He returned to the United States in 1855 where he worked on an extension to the U.S. Capitol in Washington, D.C. demonstrating his skills in the French Renaissance Revival style. From 1858 he ran a studio in New York but still traveled extensively in Europe. His eclectic designs include the Lenox Library—an early skyscraper—the Tribune Building (1873), and the Fifth Avenue façade of the Metropolitan Museum of Art, all in New York, the National Observatory in Washington, and the Yale Divinity School. He also designed many opulent private homes for wealthy clients such as J. J. Astor, but most notably the Vanderbilt estate known as The Breakers (1892–1895). Hunt was one of the founders of the American Institute of Architects.

Jefferson, Thomas (1743–1826)

The third President of the United States was born on his father's plantation, Shadwell in Albemarle County, Virginia. In common with other sons of gentlemen he was well educated in the classics so by the time he went to college he could read Greek, Latin, French, Italian, and Spanish. He attended the College of William and Mary where he first learned to love architecture. He was admitted to the Bar in 1767 and practiced until 1774 when the courts were closed by the Revolutionary War. He was

Above; Thomas Jefferson: Monticello, near Charlottesville, VA, 1769–1782; 1796–1809.

particularly attracted by the works of Palladio, whose drawings he closely adapted for the design of his own house, Monticello. He made precise scale drawings for his workmen to follow and was a particularly skilled draftsman. In 1769 he was elected to the Virginia House of Burgesses were he joined the Revolutionary Party. He was sent as a delegate to the first Continental Congress in 1774 were he played an important part, culminating in drafting the

Declaration of Independence. He was Governor of Virginia (1779–1781) and Minister to France (1784–1789) which gave him five years' opportunity to study the magnificent architecture all around him. As a Republican he realized that all great empires carry their legacy in their architecture and he sought to define a new architecture for a new independent American republic. In 1789 George Washington appointed him Secretary of State. Vice-President to John Adams in 1797–1801, he became President in 1801, and was subsequently re-elected with an increased majority. He died on July 4, 1826, on the fiftieth anniversary of the Declaration of Independence.

Kahn, Louis Isadore (1901–1974)

Born in Ösel (now Saaremaa), Estonia, Kahn and his family emigrated to the United States in 1905 and Kahn became a naturalized citizen in 1917. He graduated from the University of Pennsylvania and then taught at Yale from 1947 until 1957 and at Pennsylvania from 1957 until 1974. He was a pioneer of the functionalist architecture labeled as "New Brutalist," as exemplified by the Richards Medical Research Building, Pennsylvania (1957–1961). Much influenced by Buckminster Fuller's Geodesic designs, he designed the City Tower Municipal Building (1952–1957) with Anne Tyng. Further works include the Yale University Art Gallery (with Douglas Orr, 1953), the Salk Institute in La Jolla, California (1959–1965), the Indian Institute of Management, Ahmedabad (with Balkrishna Doshi, 1962–1974), and the Paul Mellon Center, Yale (1969–1972).

Keck, George Fred (1895–1980)
Keck, William, (1908–1995)

Interested in streamlined buildings and the latest use of technology, George Keck studied engineering and architecture before settling in Chicago in 1921, where he worked as a draftsman. Setting out by himself, his most important early commission was the Miralago Ballroom (1929), but it was the two houses for Chicago's Century of Progress World's Fair—the House of Tomorrow (1933) and the Crystal House (1934)—that made Keck's name. Both of the latter had plate-glass frontages and were built on an exterior featured a supporting steel frame and a steel flooring system, tubular pipes, steel and metal panels, and Venetian blinds. They obviously appealed to the wealthy Chicagoans because, following the fair, clients from Chicago's suburbs sought Keck out to design homes. Indeed, many of Chicago's rich North Shore properties were designed by Keck, whose best-known works include the Bruning House, Wilmette, and the Sloan House, Glenview, Illinois (1940). In 1946 Fred Keck's brother William, who had studied at the Chicago Bauhaus, joined his brother's practice as a partner. The commissions during this period came faster than ever before, with post-war affluence and greater market demand for modern design.

Below: George Fred Keck and William Keck: The House of Tomorrow, 1933.

Levitt, William (1907–1994)

Above: William and Alfred Levitt: House, Levittown, Long Island, NY, 1946–1951.

The quintessential architect of American suburbia was born in Brooklyn, New York. He attended New York University but did not stay to finish his course. Instead, in 1927 he took a job in his father's law firm. Two years later he set up Levitt and Sons and the firm started to work on its first houses, building on land his father owned in Manhasset. In 1941 the firm won a government contract to provide 2,350 housing units for defense workers in Norfolk, Virginia. Post-war America was suffering a simultaneous housing shortage and baby boom; the need was for huge numbers of affordable homes. Levitt knew just what to do. In 1947 he started Levittown on potato farmland on Long Island, New York. Applying assembly-line techniques to mass housing he built cheap houses quickly—his target was thirty to forty identical houses a day and in Levittown a staggering 17,000 homes were built. From then on he built more than 140,000 houses around the world. In 1968 Levitt sold his company to ITT Corp for $92 million in stock. The deal barred him from building in America for ten years so he used his money as collateral behind enterprises elsewhere around the world and when ITT crashed, Levitt was left in debt. He died in January 1994 in Manhasset, New York.

McKim, Charles Follen (1847–1909)

Born in Chester County, Pennsylvania, McKim studied architecture at the Ecole des Beaux Arts in Paris. He returned to the United States in 1872, and worked in the office of H. H. Richardson in New York. In 1877 he joined up with William Rutherford Mead, then two years later with Stanford White to found the architectural firm of McKim, Mead and White. They became the leading architectural practice in the United States, a position they held for many decades. The principals worked together to design Classical and Renaissance-influenced buildings and were instrumental in the Neoclassical Revival in the U.S. at the time. The firm designed a number of notable buildings, including the Boston Public Library (1887–1895), the Rhode Island State House in Providence, Madison Square Garden (1891), the Morgan Library (1903), Pennsylvania Station (1904–1910), and the Agricultural Building at the World's Columbian Exposition, Chicago (1893). McKim also took on special projects

Above: Charles McKim, William Mead and Stanford White: Isaac Bell House, 70 Perry Street, Newport, RI, 1881–1883.

such as the restoration of the White House and the revival in 1901 of Pierre l'Enfant's 1791 grand plan for Washington, D.C. involving boulevards, formal parks, and monumental public buildings. Personally convinced that aspiring young American architects needed foundation training in the European tradition, he was instrumental in founding the American Academy in Rome that he supervised from 1894. The American Institute of Architects awarded him its gold medal in 1909. He was elected an Associate of the American Institute of Architects in 1875, a Fellow in 1877, and its president 1902–1903. He died in September 1909 at his summer home in St. James, Long Island, New York.

McIntire, Samuel (1757–1811)

Leading Federal architect Samuel McIntire was born and died in Salem, Massachusetts. Known as the "Architect of Salem," he was a versatile craftsman who designed and produced furniture in the Sheraton style and interior woodwork in addition to his domestic architecture. Heavily influenced by Bulfinch. McIntire is credited with the design of one of the finest post-Revolutionary buildings in New England for his work on Jerathmell Pierce's house. Other works include the Salem courthouse (1785), finishing the work begun by Bulfinch on the extravagant Derby mansion (1794), and the Gardner-Pingree House (1804) both in Salem. While much of his architectural work no longer exists, over a hundred items of furniture survive.

Maybeck, Bernard (1862–1957)

Son of a wood carver, Maybeck loved elaborate decoration and idiosyncratic architectural details. His father sent him to Paris to learn to become a wood carver too, but Maybeck enrolled in the Ecole des Beaux Arts instead. After graduating he returned home to the United States and worked with Carrère and Hastings. Maybeck revered Greek and Romanesque buildings and based his own work on their principles while extravagantly covering them with embellishments, as well as building with a wide variety of apparently disparate materials. He settled in Berkeley, California where he remained for most of his life, designing private homes and larger public commissions—such as the First Church of Christ Scientist, Berkeley (1909–1911), and the Palace of Fine Arts at the Panama-Pacific Exposition, San Francisco (1915).

Mead, William Rutherford (1846–1928)

Above: McKim, Mead and White: John L. Andrew House, 32 Hereford Street, Boston, MA, 1884–1886.

Born in Brattleboro, Vermont in August 1846, Mead went to Norwich University and graduated from Amherst College in 1867. He began studying architecture in New York and then spent some time in Florence, Italy. On returning to New York, he struck up a professional partnership with Charles F. McKim. Two years later, in 1879, they were joined by Stanford White and named the firm McKim, Mead and White. Together they comprised the leading architectural practice in the United States. Even after the death of the other two principals, Mead continued to head the firm which worked on many prestigious projects. In 1913 Mead became the first architect to be awarded the gold medal from the Academy of Arts and Letters. Among many other honors, he became a Fellow of the American Institute of Architects, and president of the New York Chapter 1907–1908. King Victor Emmanuel made him a Knight Commander of the Crown of Italy in 1922 for his contribution to the introduction of Roman and Italian Renaissance architectural styles to America. He died in Paris in June 1928.

Mies van der Rohe, Ludwig (1886–1969)

The founder of the Modern style was born in Aachen, Germany, the son of a mason. He studied design under Peter Behrens and became a pioneer of glass skyscrapers. In Berlin he designed high-rise flats for the Weissenhof Exhibition (1927) and the German Pavilion for the Barcelona International Exposition (1929). He also designed tubular steel furniture, most notably the Barcelona chair. He became director of the Bauhaus in Dessau between 1930–1933 and emigrated to the United States in 1937. He became Professor of Architecture at the Armour (now Illinois) Institute of Technology in Chicago. Among his works in the United States are two glass apartment towers on Lake Shore Drive in Chicago. He also collaborated with Philip Johnson on the Seagram Building in New York (1956–1958). Other works include the Public Library in Washington, DC (1967) and two art galleries in Berlin.

Above: Ludwig Mies van der Rohe: Dr. Edith Farnsworth House, Plano, IL, 1945, 1950–1951.

Charles W. Moore (1925–1993)

Charles Willard Moore was born in Benton Harbor, Michigan in 1925. He earned a degree in architecture from the University of Michigan in 1947. He served in the army during the Korean War, and then worked in San Francisco. He earned an M.A. and Ph.D. in architecture from Princeton University. Moore taught at Princeton, and was assistant to Louis Kahn in the Master's Studio in 1958–1959. An inspiring teacher, Moore also taught at the University of California at Berkeley, Yale, the University of California at Los Angeles, and the University of Texas at Austin. Always a practicing architect, much of his professional work was with the firm "MLTW"—Moore, Lyndon, Turnbull, Whitaker. Their work at Sea Ranch, north of San Francisco, began in 1964. Moore co-authored twelve books, including *The Place of Houses* (1974) and *Body, Memory, and Architecture* (1977). He was awarded the gold medal by the American Institute of Architects in 1991.

Morgan, Julia (1872–1957)

Born in San Francisco, California and trained in engineering at the University of California, Morgan moved to Paris to study architecture at the Ecole des Beaux Arts and became the first woman to graduate from the course at age thirty. She registered as the first woman architect in California in 1904 and opened her office there two years later. Although she personally kept a low public profile, she estimated that she had designed and completed 800 buildings during her career. One of her most famous commissions was from William Randolph Hearst for his sprawling residences at San Simeon. The project lasted from 1919 until 1937 and demonstrates her mastery of light, space, and scale. Morgan also did much work for women's organizations including the Berkeley Women's City Club (1930).

Neutra, Richard Josef (1892–1970)

A leader of the International Style and one of the most influential modern architects, Neutra was born in Vienna, Austria. Between 1912–1914 he studied under Adolf Loos in Vienna and then moved to Berlin to collaborate with the Modernist architect Eric Mendelsohn in 1921–1923. He emigrated to the United States in 1923, arriving in New York, then moving to Chicago, where he worked for a short time with his architectural hero, Frank Lloyd Wright. In 1926 he moved to California where he is considered to have achieved his best work. He was particularly careful with the siting of his buildings and their innovative and imaginative use of

Below: Richard Neutra: Philip Lovell House, Los Angeles, CA, 1927–1929.

building technology. His first Californian commission, the Lovell Health House (1929) in Los Angeles, became his masterpiece. In 1932 Neutra designed his own home with office beneath in the Silverlake hills. Other important private works include the Kaufmann House near Palm Springs (1946) and the Moore House in Ojai (1952). His public works include the Channel Heights housing project in San Pedro (1932), the LA Hall of Records (1961–1962) and schools including Emerson Junior High School, Los Angeles (1938), and Palos Verdes High School (1961). He was determined to design inexpensive houses and continuously explored new techniques and materials, incorporating the latest ideas into his designs. Neutra put his thoughts onto paper in a number of works including *Life and Shape* (1962), *Projects and Buildings* (1961), and *Survival through Design* (1969).

Palladio, Andrea (1508–1580)

Andrea di Pietro della Gondola, one of the most important architects of all time, was born in Vicenza and initially trained as a stonemason. He developed a modern Italian architectural style based on Classical Roman principles away from the prevalent heavily ornamented and embellished Renaissance style. The Palladian style was widely followed all over Europe, most notably by Christopher Wren and Inigo Jones. Palladio remodelled the basilica in his home town of Vicenza and then extended his style to villas, palaces, and churches. One outstanding work was San Giorgio Maggiore, in Venice. His *Quattro Libri dell'Architetura* (1570) greatly influenced his successors, including many American architects of the eighteenth century.

Parris, Alexander (1780–1852)

Above: Alexander Parris: David Sears House, 42-43 Beacon Street, Boston, MA, 1818/1832.

A leading figure in the Greek Revival which dominated American architecture in the 1830s and 1840s, Parris was born in Halifax, Nova Scotia. He moved with his family to Maine while a child, then to North Pembroke. In the 1790s he worked as a carpenter in North Pembroke, Massachusetts, but was already fascinated with building design. By the time he was twenty he had already designed and built houses locally. He soon married and moved to Portland, Maine, a lively port in the midst of a building boom. One of his first jobs was to design and build a Navy commodore's house. So successful was this that the Navy engaged him to redesign and rebuild the harbor forts. When work dried up he moved to Boston, and during the War of 1812 served as a captain in the Army Corps of Engineers. Post-war he became apprenticed to Charles Bulfinch and was given full responsibility for the design of Quincy Market (1825) in Boston. Together they worked on Massachusetts General Hospital, Charlestown Navy Yard, the Watertown Arsenal, Massachusetts, as well as many other important buildings in Boston. As an architect he designed and built grand houses across New England and buildings such as the Pilgrim Hall Museum in Plymouth. His work with the Greek Revival style won him national and international acclaim. He died in his house on Washington Street, North Pembroke, in 1852.

Peabody, Robert S. (1845–1917)

Born in New Bedford, Massachusetts, Robert Swain Peabody was educated at Harvard and the Ecole des Beaux Arts in Paris, from which he graduated in 1868. He started practicing in Boston in the architectural firm Peabody and Stearns, a firm that won a silver medal at the Paris Exposition of 1900. He received many awards and honors during his life time and was president of the American Institute of Architects 1900–1901. He died at his summer home in Marblehead, Massachusetts.

Above: Robert Swain Peabody and John Goddard Stearns: Hayes Q. Trowbridge House, New Haven, CT, 1907.

Price, Bruce F. (1845–1903)

Born in Cumberland, Maryland in December 1845, Price decided early on in life to become an architect and was placed as a very young man in the Baltimore office of Alrensee and Neilson. After four years there, he went to Europe to study. Returning to the United States he set up in Baltimore practice with George Baldwin in 1873. Four years later Price moved to New York where he was commissioned to design prestigious office buildings, such as the American Surety Building (1894), St James Building (1897–1898), and the International Bank. He made his reputation, however, with the laying out the house of George Gould at Georgian Court in Lakewood, New Jersey (1896). Other notable buildings include the village of Tuxedo Park (1885–1886) and Tuxedo Park Library (1901) in New York, the Chateau Frontenac in Quebec (opened in 1892), several buildings at Yale University, Windsor Station, Montreal (1888) and the Hunt Memorial in New York City.

Purcell, William Gray (1880–1965)

A Prairie School architect, Purcell was born in Wilmette, Illinois and raised by his grandfather in Oak Park on the same street on which Frank Lloyd Wright would build his first home. Purcell graduated from Cornell University in 1903 and set up in partnership in Minneapolis, Minnesota with George Feick Jr. in 1907. George Grant Elmslie joined the company in 1909 and over the next decade Purcell and Elmslie (Feick left in 1913) became increasingly productive. Purcell was interested, in particular, in open-plan living and flexible space. His work included his own house, the William G. Purcell House (1913), Lake Place, Minneapolis, a true example of open-plan living. Other work included the Purcell-Cutts House (1913), Minneapolis, Minnesota. In 1920 Purcell went into semi-retirement because of failing health and moved to Portland, Oregon, where he began writing; from there he moved to Pasadena where he died.

Renwick, James (1818–1895)

Born in New York city into a wealthy and well-educated family, Renwick initially studied engineering—the family profession, following his father and two brothers—at Columbia University. He graduated in 1836 at which time he was already interested in architecture but had no formal training. His first major commission came in 1843—to design Grace Church in New York City. Three years later he was working on Romanesque designs for Robert Dale Owen, director of the Smithsonian Institution in Washington, DC. Renwick designed a Norman castle that was built 1846–1849 of red sandstone—a welcome distinction in Washington's otherwise Classical appearance. Other work was for Vassar College's main hall (1860) in Poughkeepsie, several churches, banks, hospitals, and asylums. He also designed a number of private houses for wealthy New Yorkers. Already known as a designer of churches, Renwick was asked in 1853 by Archbishop Hughes to design St. Patrick's Cathedral in New York, a job that turned out to be a long and much-delayed project. In 1855 Renwick journeyed to Europe where he particularly studied the great French Gothic cathedrals. His original design for St Patrick's was a grandiose Gothic scheme, which was not fully realized. He and fellow architect William Rodrique were given the contract in March 1859. It guaranteed $2,500 a year for the next eight years. The church was dedicated in 1879, and completed in 1888.

Richardson, Henry Hobson (1838–1886)

Above: Henry Hobson Richardson: J.J. Glessner House, 1800 South Prairie Avenue, Chicago, IL, 1885.

Born in Priestley Plantation, Louisiana, Richardson was educated at Harvard and then studied architecture in Paris at the Ecole des Beaux Arts (1859–1862). While in Europe he worked under Henri Labrouste and Jakob Ignaz Hittorf. He initiated the Romanesque Revival in the United States which led to a distinctively home-grown style of architecture called Richardsonian Romanesque which can be dated 1870–1895. The style recalls Spanish and French eleventh century Romanesque with massive stone walls, big interior spaces, and semicircular arches interacting together in a continuous architectural flow. He specialized in churches, the most famous of which is Trinity Church, Boston (1872–1877), but also designed other well-known buildings such as the Allegheny County Buildings in Pittsburgh and halls of residence at Harvard. He designed a number of private houses, railroad stations, and wholesale stores.

Root, John Wellborn (1850–1891)

Born in Georgia, at fourteen Root was sent to England to study. He returned to the United States in 1866 and enrolled at New York University where he got a degree in science and civil engineering in 1869. After working in New York he moved to Chicago in 1872, the year after the great fire. There he set up a practice with Daniel Burnham but the city was in recession in the aftermath of the fire and the firm did not initially prosper. It took almost a decade for steady work to appear. In the 1880s tall office buildings were in demand in Chicago and Root was at the forefront of architects working to produce flexible designs that responded to the demands of ever more complex modern living and business needs. The Rookery, Chicago (1885–1888) was an early example. His best work is considered to be the Reliance Building (1890–1895) and the Monadnock Building, Chicago (1889–1891), which relied on simple brick detailing for its decoration rather than the elaborate embellishments favored by his contemporaries. Sadly he died too young to explore his ideas further, although he left a prolific legacy of essays on the architecture of Chicago.

Saarinen, Eero (1910–1961)

Born in Kikknonummi, Finland, when Saarinen was thirteen he emigrated to the United States with his father Eliel, the leading Finnish architect (he designed the Helsinki railroad station). Eero came back to Europe to study sculpture in Paris (1929–1930) but then returned to America to study architecture at Yale University (1931–1934). After a time spent in Finland he went into partnership with his father and Charles Eames. Their intention was to pioneer a new approach to architecture and furniture design—examples of their work include the Christ Lutheran Church, Minneapolis, Minnesota (1948) and the General Motors Technical Institute, Warren, Michigan (1955) completed five years after Eliel died. Saarinen designed many public buildings in both the United States and Europe including the chapel at MIT (1954–1955), the Ezra Stiles and Samuel F. B. Morse College, New Haven, Connecticut (1960–1962), the US embassies in London and Oslo, the TWA terminal at John F. Kennedy Airport New York (1956–1962), and Washington's Dulles International Airport (1958–1963).

Schindler, Rudolf (1887–1953)

Schindler graduated from the Vienna Academy of Fine Arts. He was an admirer of Frank Lloyd Wright's work and in 1914, when invited to go to work for a Chicago architectural firm, he accepted with the thought that he could move on to work with Wright. He did exactly that in 1917, settling in California in the 1920s and doing much of the finishing work on Frank Lloyd Wright's Californian projects while Wright was away traveling. Concurrently, Schindler started up his own practice in which he intended to merge the latest European architectural ideas with the technological advances made by American architects. His masterpiece is the Lovell Beach House, Los Angeles (1922–1926). Using reinforced concrete, the house featured strong verticals and horizontals and floor-to-ceiling glass walls with the beach itself disappearing underneath the house to provide a home that was both beside and of the beach. Schindler favored sloping sites which allowed him full rein with his strong architectural lines. Also by the mid-1930s he was cladding his houses with wood. Like Frank Lloyd Wright, he liked to incorporate furniture into his buildings.

Above: Rudolph M. Schindler: Schindler House, 835 North King's Road, West Hollywood, CA, 1921–1922.

Sloan, Samuel (1815–1884)

Born in Chester County, Pennsylvania, Sloan became
a leading Philadelphia-based architect. He trained as
a carpenter and moved to Philadelphia in the mid-
1830s, probably working on the Eastern State
Penitentiary and the Pennsylvania Hospital for
Mental and Nervous Diseases. He only termed himself an architect after 1851 when he won a
commission for the Delaware County PA courthouse
and jail (1849), and an Italianate villa for Andrew M.
Eastwick (1850–1851). His practice thrived in the
1850s but the war and political scandal involving the
building of Philadelphia City Hall saw work dry up.
Indeed, his best-known work—Longwood, Natchez,
Mississippi—was begun in 1858 for Dr Haller Nutt
but left unfinished after the war broke out.
Nevertheless this Indian-style building with an onion-
dome cupola had a great effect on architectural
styles of the day and contributed to the verandah
becoming an important part of U.S. domestic architecture. After briefly working in New York, Sloan
returned to Philadelphia to rebuild his career. In
fact, however, most of his later work came from

Above: Samuel Sloan: Oriental Villa, Design I from
Sloan's Homestead Architecture, 1861.

North Carolina, so much so that he opened an office there, in Raleigh, where he died. Sloan
was an active architect who produced many good buildings, but he was also an author on
architecture. He published *The Model Architect* (started 1851), *City and Suburban Architecture*
(1859) among many other books. In July 1868 he started *The Architectural Review and American
Builders' Journal*, the first architectural periodical to be published in the United States.

Stern, Robert A. M. (1939–)

Born in New York City, Stern was educated at Columbia University and then Yale. He was a
well-known author and teacher before starting his own practice. He believes in design as a
process of cultural assimilation and that architecture is a communicative art. Most of his
designs have been for private houses and apartments such as Chilmark, Martha's Vineyard,
Massachusetts (1979–1983). Other famous commissions include the Norman Rockwell
Museum, Stockbridge, Massachusetts (1987–1992) and hotels for Euro-Disney in Marne-la-
Vallée, France. He became a Fellow of the American Institute of Architects in 1984. His
publications include *The Anglo-American Suburb* (1981).

Strickland, William (1788–1854)

An influential architect of the American Classical Revival, Strickland was born in Navesink,
New Jersey and studied architecture under B. H. Latrobe. He did most of his work in
Philadelphia and continually attempted to reconcile the proportions of Classical architecture

with the demands of modern living and work. In 1818 he won the Philadelphia competition to design the Second Bank of the United States, Philadelphia, Pennsylvania (1818–1824). It became his masterpiece, with Doric porticoes and elegant rooms. Other major Strickland buildings in Philadelphia are St. Stephen's Episcopal Church (1822–1823) with twin octagonal towers; Temple Mikvah Israel (1818); and the Philadelphia Merchant's Exchange (1832–1834) on a tricky triangular site which would have presented problems to a lesser architect—the nicest touch on this building is Strickland's magnificent rounded portico.

Sturgis, John Hubbard (b. nineteenth century–1888)

Aristocratic sophisticate who won well-paying commissions from wealthy clients, Sturgis traveled extensively in England picking up the latest architectural ideas. He had a twenty-year partnership with Charles Brigham as the firm Sturgis and Brigham. The firm concentrated on fine domestic architecture, most of the houses being around the Back Bay quarter of Boston and in Newport. However, they did produce fine public commissions such as the Boston Museum of Fine Arts (1872) and Boston Young Men's Christian Association Building.

Sullivan, Louis Henri (1856–1924)

Born in Boston, Sullivan studied for a short time at the Massachusetts Institute of Technology and at the influential Paris atelier of Joseph Auguste-Emile Vaudremer. On his return to the United States he worked for Frank Furness in Philadelphia and then in 1873 moved to Chicago (being rebuilt after the great fire of 1871) to work in the studio of William Lebaron Jenney. He then returned to Paris to the Ecole des Beaux Arts to finish his training. He joined the office of a German engineer, Dankmar Adler, and in 1881 they established what was to become one of the most influential of U.S. architectural practices—Adler and Sullivan. Together they were leaders of the Chicago School of architecture and were responsible for a string of successful designs, their hallmark being the rich detailing and ornamentation seen in projects such as the Auditorium Building (1887–1889). Sullivan became a prolific architect designing, among many others, the Transportation Building for the Chicago World's Fair (1893), the Bayard-Condict Building in New York, and the Guaranty Building in Buffalo. He is widely credited as the designer of the first true skyscraper, the Wainwright Building in St. Louis (1890–1891). His experimental skeletal constructions of skyscrapers and office blocks, particularly the Stock Exchange (1893–1894), the Gage Building (1898–1899), and the Carson, Pirie, Scott Department Store (1899–1901) in Chicago earned him the title "Father of Modernism." The author of many architectural articles for technical journals, he is credited with coining the adage "Form follows function." Sullivan's style remained in the nineteenth century and after 1900 he and the Chicago School lost out to the resurgence of Neoclassicism. The partnership with Adler ended in 1895 and Sullivan turned to designing much smaller-scale buildings, such as the Merchants' National Bank in Grinnell, Iowa (1914) and the National Farmer's Bank (1907–1908) in Owatanna, Minnesota. Sullivan died in poverty in a Chicago hotel room in April 1924.

Taliaferro, Richard (1705–1779)

Not a great deal is known about this popular colonial "gentleman architect" who worked extensively in and around Virginia, especially in the Tidewater region. His name rhymes with "oliver." The details of much of his work were destroyed along with many other Virginia county records during the Civil War. It is known that Taliaferro did a lot of work for James City County and is believed to have been responsible for the design of many of the grander houses in Virginia, possibly including Westover. He probably also had long discussions—and so influenced—Thomas Jefferson, a Virginia contemporary. His best-documented improvements are for public buildings, including the Governor's Palace, the Capitol, and the President's House at William and Mary College.

Thornton, William (1759–1828)

Born on the island of Tortola in the West Indies (now part of the British Virgin Islands) he studied medicine at Edinburgh, Scotland, then emigrated to the United States in 1787, becoming a citizen the next year. Although he was untrained in architecture, he still won the 1792 competition to design the U.S. Capitol in Washington, D.C. In 1794 Thornton was appointed a commissioner of the District of Columbia, and supervised the project until 1802. His original plans were later altered—mainly by Latrobe and Bullfinch—but the façade and central areas are much as he intended. He designed houses in Washington, including the Tayloe House, known as the Octagon, that would later become the headquarters of the American Institute of Architects.

Above: William Thornton: The Octagon, the Col. John Tayloe House, 1799 New York Avenue NW, Washington, DC, 1797–1800.

Town, Ithiel (1784–1844)

Born in Thompson, Connecticut, Ithiel Town was an important local architect who wrote and practiced mainly on the East Coast. He started working with Alexander J. Davis in 1829, and together they opened an office in New York. Their contracts included important commissions for the North Carolina State Capitol, at Raleigh, North Carolina (1833–1840) and the U.S. Custom House, in New York (1833–42). One of his best individual works is the Bowers House (1825–26) in Northampton, Massachusetts. Town was also a bridge builder and gave his name to the Town lattice truss

Above: Ithiel Town and Alexander Jackson Davis: Russell House, Wesleyan University, High Street, Middletown, CT, 1828–1830.

design of bridge construction (patented in 1820). It is said that 140 of the original covered bridges in existence in the United States use Town's lattice construction, which he reportedly licensed at a dollar per foot. Town was also an significant author, and among his writings are *Description of his Improvements in the Construction of Bridges* (1821) and *School-House Architecture*.

Upjohn, Richard (1802–1878)

Renowned for church architecture, Upjohn was influential in the spread of Gothic Revival in America. Born in Shaftesbury, in Dorset, England, he initially trained as a cabinet-maker. In 1829 he made the long Atlantic crossing to the New World and settled in Boston where he started to work as an architect under Alexander Parris. By 1834 he was able to start his own firm, making his name by designing Gothic churches, the most notable of which is the brownstone Gothic Revival Trinity Church in New York (completed 1846). In 1852, he published a book of his designs, *Upjohn's Rural Architecture*. Other works include the Isaac Farrar House and St. John's Church in Bangor, Maine (1837–39), City Hall, Utica, New York (1852–53), St Luke's Episcopal Church, Ascension, Brooklyn (1867–71), St. Mary's, Burlington, New Jersey (1846–54), Bowdoin College Chapel, Brunswick, Maine (1844–55), and Trinity Chapel, New York (1853). He was instrumental in setting up the American Institute of Architects and was its first president.

Above: Richard Upjohn: Edward King House, 35 King Street, Newport, RI, 1847.

Van Brunt, Henry (1832–1903)

In the 1880s van Brunt was one of the very few professionally trained architects working west of the Mississippi. Born in Boston and educated at Harvard, he practiced architecture in his home town with William Ware for twenty years before moving to Kansas City in 1887 to join his partner Frank M. Howe. They had opened their office in 1885, their main client the Union Pacific Railroad. Van Brunt, now aged fifty, moved to Kansas City to take personal advantage of the building boom the frontier town was enjoying. Together, he and Howe built many of the most important buildings in Kansas City using their progressive East Coast ideas combined with detailing from various historic styles. Their buildings include the Emery, Bird, Thayer Department Store, the George Blossom Residence, the Coates House Hotel, and the August Meyer Residence. Van Brunt also worked on railroad stations. The firm designed the Electricity Building for the Chicago World's Columbia Exposition of 1893. He retired to Massachusetts in 1899 and died there four years later.

Vaux, Calvert (1824–1895)

Above: Calvert Vaux and Frederick E. Church: "Olana," the Church home, Route 9G, Olana, NY, 1870.

The designer of Central Park, New York, Vaux was born in London and emigrated to the United States in 1850 to join his first associate, A. J. Downing. Later, with Frederick Law Olmsted, his considerable experience in landscape design helped them win the competition to design Central Park, New York, a precept of which was to sink all the roads into the landscaping so as to present rolling vistas of unblemished greenery. Together they turned a miscellaneous collection of squatters' camps and pig farms into the landscaped Central Park, a massive endeavor that included planting five million trees. The partners also planned the state reservation at Niagara Falls, and Prospect Park in Brooklyn as well as other parks across America. Vaux also drew up the plans for the Metropolitan Museum and the American Museum of Natural History. He published many works including *Villas and Cottages* (1857).

Venturi, Robert (1925–)

A foe of banal modern architecture, Venturi was born in Philadelphia and studied architecture at Princeton University. In the 1950s he worked for Modernist architects Eero Saarinen and Louis Kahn. By the 1960s he was rejecting the blandness of the International Style in favor of eclectic and playful designs that incorporated ornament and historical references for their own sake. Venturi helped to establish the tenets of Postmodernism with his 1966 book *Complexity and Contradiction in Architecture*. With collaborators Stephen Izenour and his wife Denise Scott Brown he wrote the influential *Learning from Las Vegas* (1972) which praised the vitality of neon-lit roadside Las Vegas architecture. His designs include the Vanna Venturi House in Philadelphia (1962), a house for his mother in Chestnut Hill, Pennsylvania (1962–1964), the Brant-Johnson House in Vail, Colorado (1976), and the Sainsbury Wing of the National Gallery in London (1991).

Vitruvius Pollio, Marcus (First century BC)

Vitruvius was a northern Italian in the service of Emperor Augustus for whom he worked as an architect, engineer, and writer. He wrote the only surviving Roman treatise on architecture, *De Architectura* (c.27 BC); his other works have not survived. A manuscript copy of *De Architectura* was discovered by the humanist Poggio Bracciolini in the monastery of St. Gall early in the fifteenth century. It was eagerly studied by Renaissance artists and architects. Vitruvius defined architecture as consisting of, "order . . . and of arrangement . . . and of proportion and symmetry and décor and distribution."

Walter, Thomas Ustick (1804–1887)

Thomas Walter's main claim to fame is that he designed and built the wings and enormous cast-iron dome of the US Capitol in Washington, DC adding them to the original building of Bulfinch's design. Work on the wings started in 1851 and the dome was constructed between 1855 and 1865, work continuing through the war years at President Lincoln's behest. Walter was assisted from 1855 by the French-trained Richard M. Hunt. The family architectural tradition was continued by Walter's grandson who studied architecture at his grandfather's office and went on to practice extensively throughout the South.

Ware, William (1832–1915)

Born in Cambridge Massachusetts in May 1832, Ware graduated from Harvard University in 1852. He studied at the Lawrence Scientific School before moving to New York to become a draftsman in the architectural offices of Richard Morris Hunt. Eight years later he moved to Boston to start his own firm in partnership with Henry van Brunt. However, Ware's architectural reputation rests not so much on his designs as on his gifts as an educator. In 1866 he was responsible for organizing the first school of architecture in the United States at MIT in Boston. Then, in 1881 he set up the School of Architecture at Columbia University in New York. He remained head of the school until 1903 when he was made Professor Emeritus. In 1901 Ware belonged to the commission that designed the buildings for the Pan-American Exposition in Buffalo, New York. He was awarded many architectural honors and plaudits and was the author of many technical books, including the definitive *Modern Perspective*. He died at his home in Milton, Massachusetts in June 1915.

White, Stanford (1853–1906)

Born in New York City, White learned architecture under H. H. Richardson, later moving to Paris where he lived with the family of the sculptor Augustus Sant-Gaudens. In 1872 he joined the office of Gambrill and Richardson in Boston and worked on the design for Trinity Church, Boston. In 1879, along with two old architecture friends, he formed the influential practice of McKim, Mead and White. He was usually responsible for the interiors of their designs with the ornamentation and decoration. He was a man of enormous creative energy with truly eclectic tastes. In New York his two surviving works—the Washington Square Arch and the Century Club—both display marvellous Renaissance ornamentation. He designed the old Madison Square Garden in 1889 for which he commissioned a statue of a nude Diana for the cupola that scandalized New York. In the tower itself he built an opulent private apartment and roof garden that became notorious for his extra-curricular goings-on. He was finally shot and killed there by the jealous husband of his lover, Evelyn Nesbit Thaw.

Above: McKim, Mead and White: 199 Commonwealth Avenue, Boston, MA, 1890.

Wright, Frank Lloyd (1867–1959)

The doyen of American architects was born in Richland Center, Wisconsin. He studied engineering at Wisconsin University but resolved to become an architect and set up in practice in Chicago after working for a period for Adler and Sullivan, during which time he designed private homes for the firm and his "Bootleg" houses for private clients. He developed his own unique style with his Prairie houses, long low buildings that merged with the landscape, such as the Robie House, Chicago (1908–1910). Always interested in the latest technology, he explored more daring and controversial designs that exploited modern technology and Cubist spatial concepts, developing this into his Usonian houses, such as the Herbert Jacobs House, Wisconsin (1936). He experimented continuously on his own homes—the first at Oak Park, Chicago, then Taliesin, at Spring Green, Wisconsin (1911) and a third home in 1938 with connecting studio and school, named Taliesin West, near Phoenix, Arizona. His buildings are largely confined to the Midwest, especially the Chicago area, and California where he constructed a series of textile-block houses such as the "Hollyhock" House in Los Angeles (1920) and the Mrs. G. M. Millard House in Pasadena (1923). One of his few foreign commissions was the earthquake-proof Imperial Hotel in Tokyo (1916–1920). Public commissions include the Johnson Wax office block in Racine, Wisconsin (1936), the Florida Southern College (1940), and the spiral Guggenheim Museum of Art in New York (1959). But his masterpiece, and the identification of much of his theories of architecture comes with the Kaufmann House, "Fallingwater," in Connellsville, Pennsylvania (1934–1937). His architectural ideas were internationally influential, especially his explorations of open-plan living. Wright also designed glass, furniture, and textiles for his buildings. He was a prolific writer of his thoughts and ideas on architecture and design. He died in New York after a long and successful career and is widely acclaimed as the greatest American architect of the twentieth century.

Above: Frank Lloyd Wright: "La Miniatura," the Millard House, Pasadena, CA, 1923.

A

A-frame   An inexpensive design for vacation homes, with the entire house contained within a steep gable, first designed by Rudolph Schindler in the 1930s.

abacus   On a Classical column, the flat section at the top of the capital, a square block which divides the column from its entablature.

adobe   Architecture built of sun-dried bricks found in the American Southwest in both Spanish colonial and Native American traditions. The word "adobe" is Spanish, and refers both to the mud bricks and, by extension, to the buildings made of them.

arcade   A line of repeated arches supported by columns; they may be freestanding, or attached to a building. The term also applies to a commercial gallery of shops, which may be fronted by an arcade, or have an interior atrium lined with arches.

architrave   The lowest portion of a Classical entablature, the architrave is the horizontal beam or lintel which spans the distance between columns. It is located directly below the frieze.

Arts and Crafts movement   A late-nineteenth century design movement of English origin which sought to counter the trend toward mechanically reproduced ornament and furniture with hand-made, artistically designed products. Objects and designs were influenced by the middle ages and the art of Japan. This movement had a strong influence on the early work of Frank Lloyd Wright; the Craftsman bungalows of Gustav Stickley and the California bungalows of Greene and Greene are other fine examples.

ashlar masonry   Masonry of regularly cut stones laid in horizontal courses with vertical joints.

B

balloon-frame   The balloon-frame was a lightweight framing technique based on the use of standardized lumber and wire-cut nails. Invented in Chicago in the early 1830s, this technique replaced the heavier post-and-beam construction of houses because it was cheaper, faster to construct, and did not require the same degree of skilled carpentry. The outer walls are sheathed with clapboards or board-and-batten siding. The term was said to reflect the fact that the houses went up as fast as inflatable balloons, or because the walls were so thin.

bargeboard   Bargeboards, or vergeboards, are decorative boards on the edge of gables in Gothic Revival houses; these are often elaborately carved.

battlement   A parapet with alternating cut-out and raised portions; this is derived from medieval fortifications; also called crenellation or castellation.

belt course   A horizontal course of masonry which marks the division between floors; the raised profile of the course also helps divert rain water. Also called a string course.

belvedere   A separate building or rooftop pavilion for enjoying a landscape view. When separate, such structures are generally called gazebos; those built on rooftops are called belvederes.

board-and-batten   A form of vertical siding comprised of boards laid side by side, with the joints covered with narrow battens for weather proofing. Most commonly found in Gothic Revival architecture.

bracket   A projecting support found under eaves, windows, or cornices. These may be used for structural purposes, but are often merely decorative. They are especially prominent in the Italianate Style of the mid-nineteenth century.

bungalow   A one-story house with longitudinal plan. The word derives from a Hindustani term for a small house with veranda built for British administrators in India in the nineteenth century.

A-frame

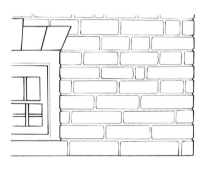

ashlar masonry

balloon-frame

C

cantilever   A beam or truss which is supported at one end only; the free-hanging portion may carry a balcony or part of a building.

capital   The top element of a column.

casement window   A hinged window which opens outward from the side, rather than having a movable sash; in proportion, it is usually taller than it is wide. These were used in the seventeenth century, and revived in the nineteenth century.

castellated   A parapet decorated with battlements or crenellations.

catslide   The long, steeply sloping roof formed by the addition of a lean-to on a seventeenth century house. In New England, the form is called a "saltbox house;" the term catslide is more frequently found in the mid-Atlantic and Southern regions.

chinking   Clay or mud used to seal up the gaps between the horizontal logs in early houses or frontier dwellings.

clapboard   Thin horizontal boards of tapering section used to seal houses against the wind and cold. Such boards covering the clay or plaster surfaces between the half-timbering of the post-and-beam structures of seventeenth century colonial houses were also called clayboards. The harsh American climate made this additional covering more necessary than in England. Clapboards became one of the most common wall coverings in wood-frame houses.

column   A vertical, round, structural post. In Classical architecture, the column usually consists of a base, shaft, and capital.

corbel   A projecting stone which carries a weight above it. These may be decorated. A series of progressively projecting stones may form a corbelled arch, or even a corbelled dome, as is found in Navaho hogans.

Corinthian order   The most slender and most ornate of the Classical orders; Corinthian columns have an elaborate base and a tall capital which resembles a basket with acanthus leaves growing through it. The height to width ratio of the column is about 10:1, and the entablature is about ⅕th the height of the column.

cornice   A projecting molding along the top of a building, wall, or arch which caps it off. In Classical architecture, the crowning feature of the entablature.

crenellation   See battlement.

crocket   An ornamental feature of Gothic architecture, crockets are small leaf-shaped projections found at regular intervals on the angled sides of spires, pinnacles, and gables.

crowstep   A stepped gable built in front of a pitched roof. Originating in northern Europe, this is commonly called a Dutch (or Flemish) gable or stepped gable.

cupola   A miniature domed shape which rises from a roof like a small tower, usually containing windows to let in light or for ventilation.

curtain wall   In modern architecture, a curtain wall is one which is suspended from the frame of the building, and does not carry any weight, but serves only to shield against weather. The term derives from medieval fortifications.

D

dentil   A small square block used in groups (like rows of teeth) for decoration in Classical architecture, typically under a cornice.

dependency   A smaller outbuilding that serves as an adjunct to a central building; also called flankers in the eighteenth century.

Doric order   The oldest and heaviest of the Classical orders. Doric columns have no base, and the capital is composed of a simple abacus and echinus. The height to width ratio of the column is about four or six to one, and the entablature is about the height of the column.

dormer   A window set vertically into a sloping roof, with its own separate roof and walls. The name is due to the fact that these were often set in bedrooms.

double-hung window   A window with two vertically sliding sashes, or glazed frames, set in grooves and capable of being raised or lowered independently of each other. These windows are of Dutch origin. Frank Lloyd Wright, who preferred casement windows, referred to these as "guillotine windows."

cantilever

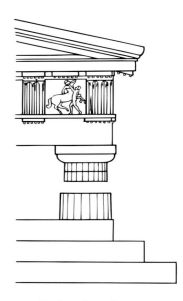

Doric order column

dormer window

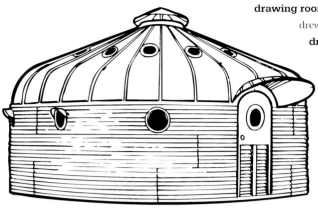

dymaxion house

drawing room The term is actually a shortened form of "withdrawing room," where people withdrew after dinner. Found in larger houses of the eighteenth and nineteenth centuries.

drip molding A molded shape designed to keep rain water from running down wall surfaces; the projecting form breaks the flow of water, so that drips fall away from the wall.

dymaxion house A round Modernist house designed by Buckminster Fuller in 1927, and revised in 1941, to highlight the use of technology and new materials.

E

eave The projecting end of a roof which overhangs a wall.

echinus The cushion-like molding under the abacus of a capital of the Doric order.

egg and dart An ornamental pattern found in Classical architecture, comprised of alternating ovoid (egg) and arrow (darts) shapes.

elevation A two-dimensional drawing made to show one face (or elevation) of a building.

engaged column A half-column which is set against or into the wall surface.

entablature The upper part of a Classical order, consisting of the architrave, frieze and cornice.

eyebrow dormer A low dormer of elliptical or segmental arch shape, with a continuous skin of roof shingles covering it, so that it looks as if the roof were raising an eyebrow. Most commonly found in Shingle Style houses of the late nineteenth century.

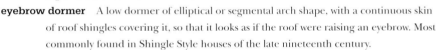

egg and dart

F

fan light A semicircular or elliptical window over a door; frequently found in eighteenth and early nineteenth century houses.

fascia A flat horizontal band or surface; in Classical architecture, these are found in the architrave.

fenestration From the Latin word for window, the term generally refers to the use of windows in a wall.

finial An ornamental form found on the top of gables, pinnacles and canopies in Gothic architecture. The most common shape is a fleur-de-lis formed of leaves.

flanker See dependency.

flute The vertical, grooved channel found on Classical columns. The concave grooves are separated by an arris.

frieze The middle division of a Classical entablature, a horizontal band between the architrave and the cornice. This may be decorated with sculpture.

G

gable The triangular end of a wall below a pitched roof and above the level of the eaves.

gambrel A gable roof with two angles of pitch on each side.

geodesic dome An innovative geometric design for domed houses patented by Buckminster Fuller in 1954.

gingerbread A term for the ornate scroll-sawn wooden ornaments on Gothic Revival houses, for instance the decorated bargeboards.

girt A heavy horizontal beam located above the posts in a seventeenth century timber-frame house. Girts are the major beams which surround (girdle) the exterior between floors and support the floor joists.

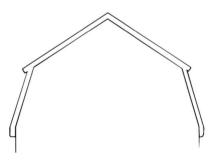

gambrel

guilloche   An ornamental pattern of two or more interlacing bands used on moldings in Classical architecture.

H

hacienda   A Spanish word for a large estate or ranch; also used to refer to the main house on such an estate.

half-timbering   A construction technique where the house is built with a timber frame (post-and-beam construction), with the spaces between the timbers filled in with plaster or brickwork.

hipped roof   A hipped roof is one which slopes upward from all four sides of the house, rather than ending in a gable.

I

inglenook   A recess for a bench or seat beside a fireplace; popular in Shingle Style houses.

Ionic order   A more slender and ornate order, Ionic columns have a base and a capital composed of scroll volutes emerging from a cushion. The height to width ratio of the column is about 9:1, and the entablature is about ⅕th the height of the column.

Ionic order

J

jerkinhead   A clipped (or hipped) gable form based on medieval shapes, and revived in some American houses of the later nineteenth and early twentieth centuries. It was used for dormers and roofs. The front portion of the gable is clipped, and bisected by an angled plane, giving a hooded look to the gable.

jetty (overhang)   The projection of an upper story over a lower story, typically found in seventeenth century New England homes such as the Parson Capen House. These overhangs may be decorated with pendills.

K

keystone   The central stone of an arch or vault; see also voussoir.

L

lancet   A narrow window with a sharp pointed arch found in Gothic Revival architecture.

lantern   A small round or polygonal turret crowning a roof or dome, with many windows for ventilation and to bring light into the building.

lean-to   A small structure added to the rear or side of a house to provide more space for a kitchen or additional bedrooms. Frequently found in early colonial homes; see also saltbox.

lintel   The horizontal beam which spans the distance between two columns or posts, or the opening of a window or doorway.

louver   In American architecture, a louver is one of a series of overlapping boards or narrow panes of glass used to fill a window opening, keeping out rain while allowing ventilation.

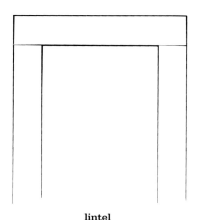

lintel

mansard roof

M

mansard roof   A characteristic roof form invented by François Mansart in France in the seventeenth century.

metope   The square space between two triglyphs in the frieze of a Doric order. Usually left blank in houses, it may contain sculpture.

molding   A carved or shaped band projecting from a wall or attached to it.

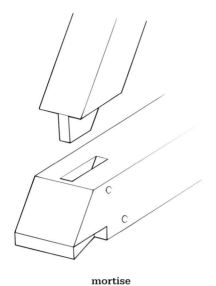

mortise   The carved slot in an element of a timber frame, shaped to receive the tenon at the end of another beam or post to make a secure frame.

mullion   A vertical element which divides a window into separate lights, or panes of glass.

N

nogging   The infilling between the wooden members of a half-timbered house of the seventeenth century; generally of brick, though wattle-and-daub was also used.

O

octagon   A geometric shape composed of eight sides of identical length. Octagon houses were popularized in the mid-nineteenth century by Orson Squire Fowler, a leading advocate of phrenology (the pseudo-science of reading character from the "bumps" on one's head). Thousands of octagon houses were built across the United States.

mortise

order   The term "order" refers to the various types of Classical columns when combined with their respective pedestal bases and entablatures. These include Doric, Ionic, and Corinthian; the combination of elements and proportions within these orders was governed by strict rules.

oriel   A bay window on an upper floor, when the bay does not continue to the ground.

P

Palladian window   A three-part window construction associated with the 16th century Italian Renaissance architect Andrea Palladio; a taller central window with arched top is flanked by smaller rectangular windows. The vertical elements are frequently treated like Classical columns or pilasters.

parapet   A low wall placed at the edge of a sudden drop, for instance at the edge of a roof.

pattern book   A book containing sample plans, ornamental details, and construction diagrams, popular in the eighteenth and nineteenth centuries.

pavilion   One meaning denotes a lightly constructed pleasure building in a garden; this term is also used to refer to a projecting portion or subdivision of a larger building, usually intersecting the main façade, or terminating the ends.

pediment

pediment   In Classical architecture, the triangular termination at the ends of buildings or over porticos, corresponding to a gable in medieval architecture, but framed with an enclosing cornice. In later usage, the term is used for any similar feature found above doors or windows; these may be round, segmental, or broken (open at the top).

pendill (or pendant)   A hanging decorative ornament found on the underside of the overhang, or jetty, of seventeenth century houses in New England, such as the Parson Capen House or the Stanley-Whitman House.

piazza   In the late eighteenth century, the term piazza was used for a porch.

pier   A free-standing solid masonry support, usually thicker than a column.

pilaster   A flat column, projecting slightly, attached to a wall. This can be of any Classical order.

pinnacle   A small turret or tall ornament which crowns spires, the peaks of gables, or the corners of parapets.

plate   A term for horizontal timbers laid upon walls to terminate or carry other timber

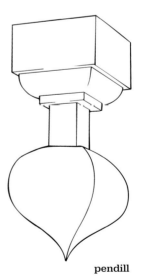

pendill

elements. When located at the top of a wall just below the roof, it is called a wall plate. The plate at the bottom of a timber frame is called a sill.

plinth   A square or rectangular base for a column or pilaster.

porte cochère   A French term for covered entrance areas designed to shield people and coaches from the rain.

portico   A porch with a roof supported by columns attached to the main entrance of a house.

prefabrication   The use of standardized components, manufactured at a central plant away from the building site, and shipped there for rapid assembly. This allowed the creation of "mail-order" and modular houses in the twentieth century.

purlin   In a roof, a purlin is a horizontal timber laid parallel with the wall plate and the ridge beam, providing additional support for the common rafters.

Q

quatrefoil   Literally, "four leaves;" an ornamental pattern comprised of four circular or pointed lobes. Frequently found in medieval revival styles. See also trefoil.

quoins   The larger dressed stones found at the corners of stone or brick buildings, typically laid in an alternating pattern. Originally used as structural reinforcements, quoins were also used as decorative elements; some American houses used wide cut boards over siding to imitate stone quoins in the eighteenth century.

Quonset Hut   Inexpensive prefabricated houses with semicircular vaulted interiors, first built at the Quonset, RI, naval base during WWII.

R

rafter   A roof timber which slopes upward from the wall plate to the ridge beam.

rafter tails   The ends of rafters which project out beyond the walls and are left visible under the eaves of Craftsman style bungalows.

ribbon window   A continuous band of windows, made possible by modern framing techniques, which emphasizes the transparency and open plans of Modernist architecture. A hallmark of the International Style.

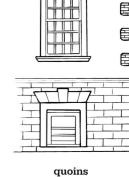

quoins

S

saltbox   A characteristic seventeenth century English colonial house form, comprised of a two-story gabled house with a lean-to addition, which is covered by an extension of the roof which maintains the same steep angle. The term was inspired by the resemblance of the resulting shape to seventeenth century salt boxes; in the south, the term "catslide roof" is also used.

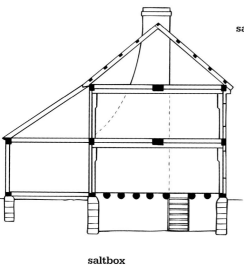

saltbox

segmental arch   A shallow arch based on a segment of a circle smaller than a semi-circle.

segmental arch

shotgun house

shotgun house   A long, narrow wooden house, usually one-story high and one room wide, with a hall running the length of one side. The name is derived from the assertion that one could fire a shotgun through the door and down the hall without harming the interior of the house (it is also called a "gunshot house"). The form may stem from African precedents, after being carried to the West Indies, the Caribbean, and ultimately America, by slaves.

sill   The principal wooden timber, or plate, at the bottom of a timber frame, to which the posts are attached.

soffit   The exposed flat surface on the underside of any overhead building component such as an eave, cornice, arch, or balcony.

string course   See belt course.

stucco   An exterior plaster finish made of portland cement, lime and sand mixed with water, and usually given a texture. Frequently used to cover adobe or to give a Mediterranean look over brick, stone or wood.

summer beam   In seventeenth century timber-framed houses, the summer beam was the largest beam spanning from wall to wall, and carrying the smaller floor joists for the second-story rooms. The term derives from an archaic term for a mule or pack horse which carries the heaviest load.

swag   A carved ornament which imitates a piece of cloth draped between two supports, or a garland of fruit and flowers.

T

tenon   The projecting tab at the end of a wooden beam or post, cut to fit into the mortise of another element to make a secure joint.

tipi   A lightweight, portable shelter used by native American plains tribes. It is comprised of poles arranged in a conical shape, and covered with bark or animal hides.

transom   A horizontal bar of stone or wood which separates a door from a window above. The term is also used to refer to the cross-bar within a window.

treenail   Oak pegs used instead of nails to fasten the mortise-and-tenon joints of post-and-beam structures.

trefoil   Literally, "three leaves;" an ornamental pattern comprised of three circular or pointed lobes. Frequently found in medieval revival styles. See also quatrefoil.

triglyph   Blocks separating the metopes in a frieze of the Doric order. These blocks usually have three grooves.

truss   A framing element composed of several members joined together to make a rigid structure.

U

Usonian houses   A term used by Frank Lloyd Wright to designate his later houses. Usonian is derived from "U.S.," and may also be based on Samuel Butler's Utopian novel *Erewhon*. The Herbert Jacobs House in Madison, WI, of 1936 is considered to be the first of the Usonian houses.

V

veranda   A roofed porch or balcony, open at the side, with thin supporting columns.

vergeboard   See bargeboard.

vernacular   The word for common speech, the term vernacular is used to denote folk-style architecture, based on the common practices of building at the time.

viga   The stout horizontal beams used for support in the roofs of adobe structures; the projecting ends are frequently left exposed.

volute   The spiral scroll in a capital of the Corinthian order.

voussoir   The wedge-shaped blocks used to form an arch; the central, uppermost one is called the keystone.

W

water table   A molded course of masonry which bridges the transition between the foundation wall and the thinner wall above it. The sloping form is sometimes enhanced with a drip mold at the lower edge to divert water from running down the foundation.

wattle and daub   A structure of woven sticks (wattle) smeared with clay (daub) used to fill in the spaces between the posts and beams of half-timbered houses. This infilling is also called nogging.

wickiup   A temporary dwelling built of arched poles covered by brush, bark, or mats. Wickiups were used by Native Americans in the American Southwest and California. Also spelled wikiup.

widow's walk   A small observation platform with a decorative railing around it, frequently found on the roofs of eighteenth and nineteenth century houses in New England and the Atlantic seaboard. These are popularly associated with seaman's families, but were also used to enjoy the view, even if not near the coast. See also belvedere.

wigwam   A building type used by Algonquians of the Eastern woodlands area of North America. The wigwam is built on a framework of lashed poles anchored in the ground, and bent into an arched or domed shape; the exteriors were covered with bark, reed mats, or thatch. These could be small single-family dwellings, or communal structures for several families.

wattle and daub

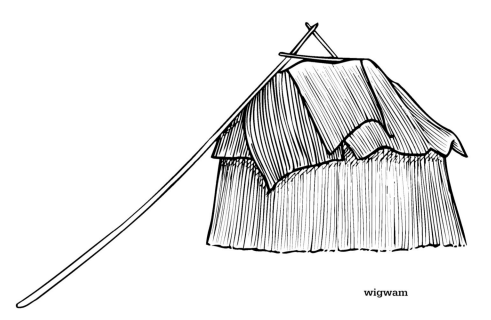

wigwam

The publisher wishes to thank all of the photographers and libraries that kindly supplied images for this book. Thanks to Jeffery Howe for supplying all of the photographs including the photographs on the front and back cover, with the following exceptions :

Chrysalis Images : 2 and 226, 6, 16, 21(top, bottom left and bottom right),53, 54 (top left), 67 (bottom), 97 (bottom), 106 (bottom), 102, 103 (top and bottom), 134 (top right), 138, 139 (left and right), 140 (top left and top right and bottom), 159, 160,161 (top and bottom), 165 (top and bottom), 166, 168 (top left and top right and bottom), 178 (top left and top right and bottom), 179 (top left and top right and bottom), 189 (bottom), 191, 192 (top and bottom), 193 (top and bottom), 194 (top and bottom), 195 (top and bottom), 197 (bottom left and bottom right), 205 (bottom left, middle right and bottom right), 209 (top and bottom), 213 (top, bottom left and bottom right), 231, 232 (top), 235 (top left and top right), 242, 245 (top left, top right and bottom), 246 (top right), 258 (top and bottom), 260 (bottom), 262(bottom), 263, 267, 279, 283, (bottom), 285 (top left, top right and bottom), 286, 287, 288 (top), 291 (middle and bottom), 292, 296, 297(bottom), 298 (top and bottom), 299, 300, 301, 307 (top left, top right and bottom), 308 (top and bottom), 312 (bottom), 313, 314, 321 (bottom), 367 (middle),

411 (top), 417 (top), 432 (top) ;

Paul Rocheleau : 2, 346 (top left), 357 (bottom right), 358, 359 (top), 362, 373 (top), 374 (top left and top right), 424 (bottom)

©Robert Holmes/Corbis : 22, 101 (left and right)

©Lee Snider/Corbis : 45 (top and middle)

©Joseph Sohm : Chromo Sohm Inc./Corbis : 59 (bottom)

Alan Weintraub/Arcaid : 62, 357 (bottom and left), 403 (top and bottom), 404

Julius Shulman : 64, 346 (top right and bottom), 349 (top and bottom left), 351, 352 (top right), 355 (top left and bottom), 413, 415 (bottom)

Richard Bryant/Arcaid : 71, 364 (top and bottom), 400 (top)

Edward S Curtis, supplied courtesy of Manuscripts, Special Collections, University Archives, University of Washington Libraries (Negative number: NA437): 76 (left)

John N Cobb, supplied courtesy of Manuscripts, Special Collections, University Archives, University of Washington Libraries (Negative number: NA2743) : 76 (right)

Hulton|Archive : 75 (bottom),78, 84, 85 (bottom)

Smithsonian Institution : 75 (top)

©Charles & Josette Lenars/Corbis : 80

©George H.H Huey/Corbis : 81(top left)

©Michael Freeman/Corbis : 81 (top right)

©Corbis : 81(bottom)

Solomon D Butcher, from Nebraska State Historical Society (Digital ID: nbhips 11101) : 90

Russell Lee, from Library of Congress, Prints & Photographs Division, FSA-OWI Collection (Call number: LC-USF342-T-031035-A DLC): 91 (top)

Library of Congress, Prints and Photographs Division : 91 (bottom left)

©Minnesota Historical Society/ Corbis : 93 (top)

Library of Congress, Prints and Photographs Division, Historic American Buildings Survey, Reproduction number "HABS, KY, 76-WHAL,1A-1": 94

©James P Blair/Corbis : 96 (bottom)

Library of Congress, Prints and Photographs Division, Historic American Buildings Survey, Reproduction number "HABS, VA,77-LYNHA.V,1-3": 125

Library of Congress, Prints and Photographs Division, Historic American Buildings Survey, Reproduction number "HABS, VA,91-____,1-4" : 126 (top left)

Library of Congress, Prints and Photographs Division, Historic American Buildings Survey, Reproduction number

"HABS, VA,91-____,1-7" : 126 (top right)

Library of Congress, Prints and Photographs Division, Historic American Buildings Survey, Reproduction number "HABS, NY,24-BROK,18-4" : 131 (top)

Library of Congress, Prints and Photographs Division, Historic American Buildings Survey, Reproduction number "HABS, MO,103-BETH,1D-1" : Page 135 (top)

©G E Kidder Smith/Corbis : 137 (top and bottom)

Library of Congress, Prints and Photographs Division, Historic American Buildings Survey, Reproduction number "HABS, TEX,253-SANYG,1-3 Nitrate": 142 (top right)

Library of Congress, Prints and Photographs Division, Historic American Buildings Survey, Reproduction number "HABS, PA,46-HORM,1-1" : 162

Library of Congress, Prints and Photographs Division, Historic American Buildings Survey, Reproduction number "HABS, SC,10-CHAR,5-; DLC/PP-01:SC-44" : 164

©Michael T Sedam/Corbis : 239 (bottom)

Library of Congress, Prints and Photographs Division, Historic American Buildings Survey, Reproduction number "HABS, RI,1-BRIST,18-4" : 251

©Buddy Mays/Corbis : 306 ;

Mark Fiennes : 312 (top), 397

Library of Congress, Prints and Photographs Division, Historic American Buildings Survey. Photographer H.R. Fitch (1905). Reproduction Number HABS, CAL,37-SANDI,10-8. From the Collection of the San Diego Historical Society : 347 (right)

M.Patrick/Architectural Association : 352 (bottom)

©Rodger Straus III/Esto All rights reserved : 355 (top right)

©Scott Frances/ Esto All rights reserved : 373 (bottom), 405

© Hendrich-Blessing : 374 (bottom)

©Paul Warchol Photography, Inc : 375 (top)

©Mark Darley/Esto All rights reserved : 398 (bottom)

©Peter Mauss/Esto All rights reserved : 399 (top left)

Natalie Tepper/Arcaid : 399 (top right)